THE BIOLOGY
of Mind

THE BIOLOGY
of Mind

ORIGINS AND STRUCTURES OF MIND, BRAIN, AND CONSCIOUSNESS

M. Deric Bownds
University of Wisconsin, Madison

JOHN WILEY & SONS, INC.

Cover Image   *Mark Thiessen/National Geographic Image Collection*

To order books or for customer service please, call 1(800)-CALL-WILEY (225-5945).

Library of Congress Cataloging in Publication Data:
Bownds, M. Deric.
   The biology of mind: origins and structures of mind, brain, and
   consciousness / M. Deric Bownds.
       p. cm.
   Includes bibliographical references and index.
   ISBN 0-891786-07-5 (alk. paper)
   1. Intellect. 2. Brain - Evolution   3. Genetic psychology.
I. Title.
QP398.B69   1999
612.8'.2—dc21   99-26155
                                            CIP

Printed and bound in the United States of America of America
10 9 8 7 6 5 4 3 2

Contents

Preface

Until recently, the study of mind, consciousness, and feelings was a subject for philosophy and religion, outside the province of hard science. This has changed in just the past few years, as advances in anthropology, animal behavior, evolutionary theory, linguistics, molecular neurobiology, psychology, and cognitive neuroscience have brought us to the threshold of resolving questions that have occupied philosophers for millennia:

- How does the human brain generate a "self"?
- What is the nature of the narrative "I" that we experience in our heads?
- What is the relationship between reason and emotion?
- How do genetic and environmental factors interact to determine the structure of our brains?

Interdisciplinary approaches to these questions are making it possible to construct models of mind and emotion that are amenable to experimental tests. The message of this book is that each of us is a society of minds that emerge from our evolutionary history and from the way our brains form as we grow up in a particular natural ecology and cultural setting. Each chapter contributes a few perspectives on the society of mind that forms, describing a subset of its elements. From our evolutionary history we derive the genetic instructions with which we begin life, and the particular mind and brain that each of us then grows is shaped and patterned by our surroundings. There are many roads to understanding our minds, many different windows through which we must peer. We approach the target from different directions when we take up the perspectives provided by neurobiology, cognitive psychology, animal behavior, linguistics, and evolutionary biology. We need to consider successive glimpses of different aspects of "mind." There are many ways to model ourselves, multiple versions of "this is I." We can utilize information on how our nervous systems evolved over millions of years, as well as high-technology gadgets designed to peer inside our brains as they work. This book tries to mix these two approaches—to assemble a description of our minds as a vast collective of agents that interact to construct an unconscious background out of which a narrative "I" emerges. You may well discover that the new ideas we suggest change your everyday perceptions and actions.

This writing began for the purpose of supporting a course for both science and non-science majors at the University of Wisconsin in Madison. It has proved useful in offering a continuous background, overview, and storyline that supports presentation of current work in each of the areas covered. Each chapter provides the core material for 1 to 3 of the approximately 45 lectures in a standard semester. This present book is an effort to share with a wider audience some of the fascination and excitement that have permeated both public and university lectures on the subjects it addresses. It falls somewhere in between a traditional academic text and a popular account. You will have an easier time with the book if you have had an introductory high school or college biology course. Sidebars are used at intervals to emphasize main points or self-experiments. At the end of each chapter is a summary, followed by thought questions and suggestions for further reading. Key words are italicized and defined in a glossary at the end of the book. If you would like more information on a particular subject that interests you, the references provided for each chapter should enable you to pursue the matter further. Detailed citations that support many of the factual statements made in the text can be found in a draft of this book on the World Wide Web at

http://mind.bocklabs.wisc.edu

In parts of this book, topics have been grouped in a way that corresponds to our subjective living experience, things we do every day—hence the chapters on perceiving mind, acting mind, emotional mind, and linguistic mind. The ideas can become more real and interesting if we use our subjective experience to engage them, and occasionally simple exercises are suggested to illustrate some of the mechanisms we consider. Such exercises can be instructive and fun if we don't lose sight of two points. First, what we think and feel is just the tip of the iceberg, compared with what is really going on in our brains. What we are aware of is something like the display on a computer screen as distinguished from the inner working of the computer. Second, our subjective experience can be very biased and distorted by factors of which we are unaware. Numerous psychological experiments have documented that our perceptions are not necessarily naive, reporting actual events outside or inside our bodies. Rather, they can be influenced by what we or someone else expects us to perceive. This is why traditional scientific inquiry insists on eventually putting our subjective insights into a form that can be tested impersonally by independent observers. Each of us can imagine that a particular process is going on inside our head, but it will remain thoroughly hidden there until its presence can be inferred from a third-person experimental demonstration.

This book encourages you to weave, through its ideas about how our minds work, a fabric of your own personal experience, feeling the richness that can come as these ideas inform your introspection about the mechanisms of your thinking, feeling, and acting. Our brains can rearrange space, time, thoughts, and emotions. Some of these processes can be made accessible to our awareness through simple mental exercises. It is not too difficult to sense motor programs of which we are usually unaware, to separate thoughts from emotions, and to note some of the ways in which we generate selves. Being aware of the mind's activities in the fractions of a second after new situations arise can have the practical consequence of offering some new options for our behavior. Questioning our common-sense perceptions of reality can also create a feeling of strangeness. Brain mechanisms are not guaranteed to feel familiar, warm, and cuddly. The objective reality we assume to be outside ourselves depends on our particular processes of perceiving it.

We begin with some background information in Chapter 1, *Thinking About Thinking,* which defines some terms and considers how a biological explanation of mind and consciousness might be approached. This is a necessary background for the four main parts of the book. Part I, *Evolving Mind,* is a description of our evolutionary history, starting with the Big Bang that created the universe and culminated in minds that can write and read a page like this one. Chapter 2, *Origins of Mind,* is an overview of the path from the appearance of the first simple behaviors of bacteria to the complex routines of our own brains, discussing the possible origins of such phenomena as sensations, perceptions, and emotions. It also offers a simple description of some of the basic processes that underlie organic evolution. Chapter 3, *Structures of*

Mind, describes how our modern human minds encapsulate a series of more primitive minds and brains that arose during vertebrate evolution. It provides an introduction to brain structures and some modern techniques used to study the brain. Chapter 4, *Primate Mind,* begins with a brief general discussion of the minds of animals and then focuses on the primate line from which we are derived, examining similarities and differences between our minds and those of monkeys and apes. Chapter 5, *Hominid Mind,* discusses stages in the evolution of intelligence in early hominids, the origins of language, and the emergence of modern humans. We consider some of the arguments for a universal evolved human psychology: that in many of our reproductive and social behaviors, we appear to express unconscious psychological mechanisms that evolved to meet conditions of a vanished time hundreds of thousands of years ago, long before the invention of agriculture and cities, when humans existed as bands of hunter-gatherers.

Part II, *Developing Mind,* describes how the templates set by our evolutionary history engage an ongoing interaction with the actual physical and cultural environment we face to generate the structures and modules of our modern minds and selves. Chapter 6, *Plastic Mind,* gives a brief outline of the development of our brains and discusses the plasticity in this process that evolved to permit us to adapt to novel or unpredictable environments. This plasticity is maintained to some extent in our adult brains, and it underlies both the learning of new skills and facts and the ability to recover from brain injuries. Our brains can actually rewire themselves when we learn new manual skills or learn to discriminate some sensory input in a more detailed way. Far from being locked in, as was thought until only a few years ago, many nerve connections in our brains are constantly shuffling about, testing what works best. Chapter 7, *Minds and Selves,* discusses the development and construction of our human selves. This process requires elaborate feats of learning and memory and draws on mechanisms that are a continuation of those that were active during the early development of the brain. We look at stages in human development and then consider interesting clues to the nature of a self that are obtained from studies on genetics, abnormal development, and patients with brain lesions. Nothing escapes the nudging of our genes. They set the limits on our repertoires of development and behavior. This is not to say we are their prisoners, but rather that we should appreciate how our options have been shaped by them.

Part III of the book, *Society of Mind,* takes a plunge into thinking about the many mind, brain, and body modules that underlie our perceptions and actions in the world—modules that form as a consequence of our evolutionary and individual developmental histories. Chapter 8, *Perceiving Mind,* offers a brief description of how our brains automatically filter and select (through processes of which we are largely unconscious) what fraction of the mass of incoming sensory information impinging on us is relevant for awareness. We frequently see in the external world what our previous experience leads us to expect to see, not what is really there. This is contrary to our common-sense notion that we see a world out there as it is, objectively. After a brief review of some characteristics of our sensing and perceiving, we shift our focus to visual competence. Studies on the visual brains of cats, monkeys, and humans have yielded fascinating insights into what visual consciousness is and where it resides. Chapter 9, *Acting Mind,* emphasizes the perspective that the most fundamental role of a biological mind is to move a biological body, and to do so quickly if danger is nearby. Mind and brain need to be defined in a way that considers the whole body and its ongoing reciprocal interactions with its world. This chapter offers a brief description of some of the brain structures involved in movement control and also considers models for this process.

In Chapter 10 of Part III, *Emotional Mind,* we continue a discussion, begun in Chapter 2, of emotions as evolutionary adaptations, and then we review modern experiments that suggest that our emotional minds are the foundation of our rational minds. The cathedrals of our intellect are infused by the inborn emotional wiring of our reptilian brainstem. It is much better to be informed of the ways in which our reason can be distorted as well as enhanced by our emotions than to imagine that we can always face the problems of the world in an objective way. Brain pathways that process emotional responses are more rapid than those that underlie reasoned ones, and some simple exercises will permit you to experience this distinction for yourself. The chapter ends with a topic of contemporary significance for most of us: how emotions that evolved as adaptations to our ancestral conditions can easily be misapplied to our modern circumstances, leading to debilitating stress and disease. Chapter 11, *Linguistic Mind,* continues discussions begun in Chapter 5, on the evolutionary origins of language, and in Chapter 7, on the development of language, to review evidence that underlying brain mechanisms support the language competence that we have evolved. This leads to the formation of localized modules in the brain that specialize in different aspects of language comprehension and generation. The location of some of these modules is revealed by brain lesions and also by imaging the activity of the brain during language performance.

Part IV of the book, *Modern Mind,* draws together a number of threads that run through the book to summarize our current understanding of the selves generated by our brains—selves generated just as automatically as a bird builds a nest or a beaver builds a dam. Chapter 12, *Conscious Mind*, looks from several different angles at the consciousness we construct. Ingenious experiments of cognitive psychology reveal agents of our minds that reorder time and space, and suggest that our perceptions and actions can be modeled as the result of an ongoing competition between alternative outcomes. This chapter makes the point that there is no central place in the brain where "it all comes together" and mentions some classical debates on whether the problem of consciousness can be solved. There isn't any "I" inside our heads, at least in the way we commonly suppose. Societies of neuronal agents carry out chores in a way that is more analogous to the performance of a chamber music group than to an orchestra with a central conductor. Further insight into the nature of our consciousness comes from studies on its altered states, as during sleep. We are left with the clear message that our conscious awareness is a very, very small fraction of what is going on in our brains—that most of the activity in our heads is being carried out by another "creature" largely inaccessible to our introspection, as alien to us as occupation by an extraterrestrial interloper.

Chapter 13, *Theoretic Mind*, brings the evolutionary story to the present by considering the emergence of the modern human mind, which is the basis of the explosion of human activity and culture in the past 4000 years. This is the mind that has generated external forms of symbol storage, such paraphernalia of our modern lives as the books and electronic media that account for much of what is in our heads. We all have modern minds coexisting with emotional and psychological machinery that evolved to meet the conditions of the Paleolithic era; and such machinery frequently is poorly suited to the conditions of modern industrial societies. The modern rational and individualistic self that many of us take for granted is a relatively recent phenomenon. Over most of human history, a more collective identity prevailed. But now, more than ever before, we are not just an unconscious part of organic evolution, we consciously and actively direct it. Does our knowledge of the mind and the past give us a crystal ball for predicting the future evolution of mind? The answer is no, but what we have learned does suggest some appropriate mental tools and attitudes for approaching an understanding of the evolution of evolution, or how change changes itself.

There is, in our efforts to understand how our human minds work, an urgency that derives from more than just our natural curiosity, for on its present course the human mind may be driving itself to extinction. In the last 50 years, the human population has increased more rapidly, and we have learned more about biology, than in all of previous human history. The rate of extinction inflicted on animal and plant species by humans is so great that our grandchildren may know only half the plant and animal species we see today. It is as though we all shared a secret, unspoken plan to go on consuming the world until there is no more planet left. If more people took to heart the material we will be considering—which illustrates the relativity of our mental processes and cultural styles, how intimately we are bound to our environment, and how many of our behaviors are adaptations to a long vanished past—perhaps we might be less intrusive on each other and on the environment. If we hope to shape our future in an intelligent way, we must understand both the evolutionary past that shaped our current behavioral repertoire and the details of how that repertoire is played out in the present.

Acknowledgments

I would like to acknowledge the early encouragement given to this book project by Owen Flanagan, Daniel Dennett, and Stephen Kosslyn. Marlin, Helen, Jonathan, and Sarah Bownds, and my partner Len Walker, have provided crucial family support. Several reviewers have provided invaluable comments, and I am indebted in particular to my colleague A.O.W Stretton for his close and critical reading of the manuscript. Several students, Cosma Shalizi, Deana Sasaki, and Jean Hetzel, have ably assisted with glossary and manuscript preparation as well as editorial tasks. Finally, I have thoroughly enjoyed interactions with publisher Patrick Fitzgerald, developmental editor Amy Marks, and production editor Susan Graham.

Chapter 1

Thinking about Thinking

This is a book about the biology of mind, and it is very tempting just to get on with the evolutionary story outlined in the first section of the book. However, before we can do this, it is necessary both to discuss some definitions of mind and consciousness and to ask how we might approach a scientific understanding of them. Before we can study whether or how the operations going on in our brain might explain consciousness, we have to begin to attempt a description of what it is that we are trying to explain. We must do some "thinking about thinking."

How do we define mind and consciousness?

One of the problems we face is that sometimes there seem to be as many definitions of words such as "mind" and "consciousness" as there are people using them. Each of these words refers not to a single entity, but rather to an array of phenomena. Webster's dictionary gives more than five definitions of the word "mind." These definitions are offered mainly with reference to humans. We need to consider also that other animal species besides ourselves have their own distinctive versions of mind.

Let's begin by thinking about experiences that we all share. You probably can remember moments of daydreaming or being lost in thought while driving a car and then noting with a start that you have been completely unaware of traveling the past several blocks. During all of this time, your brain was still processing all the relevant information, directing the steering, watching the road. An unexpected occurrence, like a child running into the road, would have immediately snapped your attention back to your driving. As another example, you can probably recall an occasion when you have focused on the verbal content of a discussion with someone and have realized only after some time that you have become annoyed, an emotional reaction that grew out of your awareness as your body reacted to signals sent by the other person's posture and tone of voice. Such simple experiences tell us that much more is usually going on than we choose to be aware of.

Our consciousness can include much more than we are aware of at a given moment.

Awareness

What we are aware of does not necessarily depend on its importance to us. We can be aware of trivial things and unaware of very important things. Reading these words might be most important to you right now, but you might also be partially aware of many things not relevant to this task—perhaps the sound of machinery in the next room, or your leg rubbing against the side of your chair. By the same token, you might be able to remember an occasion when you were walking down the street taking in random sights and smells and were unaware, until after the fact, of something very important: that you quickly dodged to the side after a shadow suddenly appeared in your path that might have been caused by a falling object.

In such cases we can, if we choose, switch the focus of our attention to what we have not been aware of. Underlying what we can be aware of, however, are many unconscious or implicit operations that may not be accessible to our introspection. These can occur, for example, in the fraction of a second just after we encounter new sensory stimuli. Current inputs are matched with past experiences of similar events to generate our perceptions. These unconscious processes can sometimes make mistakes that fool us. This happens in a well known experiment in which subjects are shown a brief view of an impossible playing card such as a red ace of spades. Many report seeing what their experience leads them to expect, either a black ace of spades or a red ace of hearts. The brain has edited the actual stimulus and reported something

We can be oblivious to unconscious or implicit mechanisms that bias our conscious awareness.

else. You may also have experienced another kind of biasing when, on meeting someone, you immediately liked or disliked that person, for no obvious reason. Perhaps the individual resembled someone from your past who was loved or feared? Emotional memories can act as filters to give a slight positive or negative "spin" to encounters in the present.

Thus our current focus of awareness is just a part of our consciousness, which in turn is a small fraction of the vast number of implicit or unconscious operations going on in our brains. Our minds are something larger than our consciousness, and they involve operations that extend beyond our brains. These brains are constantly involved in an array of interactions with other parts of our nervous systems: the spinal cord and autonomic nervous system, as well as muscular, endocrine, and immune systems. This whole ensemble is what carries out actions upon and within the physical and social environment to which we humans have adapted. We can change this environment, and this environment can change our minds. The fact that our minds exist in the context of such complex interactions makes it difficult to offer a precise definition of their boundaries. Probing these relationships is one of the goals of this book.

The nature and the bounds of our minds are quite fuzzy. A neat boundary between the thinker and the thinker's world doesn't exist.

Think of your stream of conscious awareness from moment to moment. Does it always feel the same? Although our awareness seems smooth and continuous, you will probably agree that it can be of several different kinds, and also built in stages of increasing complexity. To start at the more basic end of things, you probably have experienced some quiet moments during which your mind felt quite empty, or blank. The simplest notion of awareness is one that is devoid of the content of specific sensing and acting—the state of "just being" that is described by mystical traditions and meditators. At the next level, we all are familiar with various phenomenal states of awareness, such as what it is like to taste an orange or what it is like to feel pain when your forearm is pinched. This is what we mean by having sensations: a simple, direct, and unreflective experience. Behavior experiments raise the possibility that animals and human babies might have such phenomenally conscious states without any concept of a self.

Introspection and reflection

A next stage is being "conscious of" our feelings and thoughts, having introspective or reflective access to them. At this point we become selves, the "I" observing ourselves, and can do things like think about how it feels to taste an orange. A further twist is that our conscious awareness can be intentional: related to an object, action, or goal in the outside world. These latter forms of consciousness are clearly observed in higher primates as well as humans. However, talking to ourselves in our heads and talking to others—the narrative self consciousness based on grammatical language—seems to be unique to our human species.

The stages listed here are crudely drawn, and professional philosophers and psychologists would wish to make further functional distinctions. Their efforts to define the functional correlates of these and other phenomenal states of consciousness are very important, because we can't hope to address effectively the nerve activities in the brain that correlate with consciousness unless we have described what they are supposed to be doing.

How does consciousness emerge from a brain/body?

How do we set about explaining our conscious experience? How do we connect our two different worlds, the inner one of our subjective experience—how we feel, our emotions, what it is like to be somebody—and the objective world "out there" of objects that obey lawful relationships? The book you are holding is "out there"; your experience of it is "what is happening to me." Any complete description of mind or consciousness has to unify these into one whole and describe how they depend on one another. We don't yet know how to relate our subjective experiences to what our brains and bodies are doing, even though most practicing neuroscientists take it as an article of faith that we someday will. This current lack of understanding is generally called the explanatory gap, and it is the subject of intense debate and speculation among philosophers and scientists.

Defining the problem

Some in the field of consciousness studies insist on making a distinction between the "easy" problem and the "hard" problem of consciousness. The easy problem is said to be explaining the neural basis of things like attention, memory, and sensory motor coordination. These people say that no matter how much neuroscientists discover about these things, it won't crack the hard problem: They still won't be able to tell us why we experience the color and smell of a rose as we do. Third-person science will never get us to first-person experiences. There has to be something else, some really radical solution beyond the province of conventional psychology and neuroscience.

One response to this position, however, is to argue that the objective and the subjective refer to different ways of knowing rather than different bodies of knowledge. Why should translating between them be required for theories of consciousness? If we are materialists who take mind to be based on matter, any theories of consciousness must blend with neurobiological and psychological theories and descriptions. The hard problem, then, is being addressed by current experiments that are revealing neural correlates of conscious subjective experiences such as vision, attention, and memory. The challenge is to find a unified or integrated description of all of these experiences. (Approaches

A debate over the "easy" versus the "hard" problems of consciousness remains to be resolved.

to this problem are the subject of Chapter 12.) Once we have assembled enough of the pieces, the supposedly hard problem of consciousness may evaporate—just as the concept of phlogiston disappeared when the true nature of fire was illuminated, the mystery of light yielded to the discovery of electromagnetic waves, and the mystery of life (how each organism replicates itself) was clarified by the discovery of DNA.

This argument takes the view that there are no questions concerning the physical basis of consciousness that differ in principle from other ordinary problems about the physical and functional basis of genes, inheritance, or solidity and liquidity. However, it is also possible that at this point, we could be in the position of a person ignorant of relativity theory who is informed that matter is a form of energy but does not understand the physical concepts that link quantum phenomena to matter and energy alike. Future theory might provide the scientific concepts we need to close the explanatory gap.

Assembling an explanation

How, then, do we set about assembling an explanation for anything as complicated as our consciousness? We might start with some design principles that we know something about. We know that our bodies are hierarchical systems built up from smaller subunits and components, as shown in Figure 1–1. The ultimate particles of atomic physics make up our atoms and molecules. Our molecules then organize themselves into cells. Systems of nerve cells form our nervous systems and brains. The entities at each level are building blocks of those at the next level. The description can be expanded beyond our individual selves, as our minds become components of the larger entities of societies and cultures. Each level of this hierarchy has its own laws and theories, which armies of academic specialists study.

This book takes the tack of sidestepping, or bypassing, the issue of relating our brain operations to our subjective feelings (bridging the explanatory gap mentioned above), and suggests instead, as indicated by the solid arrows to the left of the dashed ones in Figure 1–1, that mind is what brain/body does—in the same sense that digesting our food is what the gut does. We can trace up through the lower levels in the hierarchy to observe that in practice, each level of organization, built up of simpler ones, has its own laws and that its members in turn serve as the building blocks for the next level of organization. We then ask what rules are working at this next level, and what new operating environment we are in.

We tend to visualize the assembly of our component molecules into cells, of our cells into tissues, and so on as being like working with

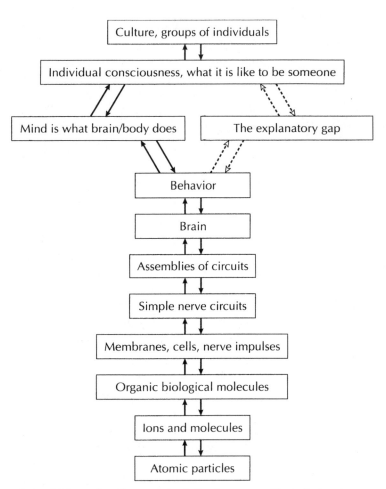

Figure 1–1   A hierarchy diagram depicting how complicated structures are built up from simpler ones.

building blocks or a simple erector set where things come together in an intuitive, linear fashion. This can be a misleading vision, for in fact, all complex entities, whether organisms or thunderstorms, are nonlinear systems. They emerge from their simpler components in a way that cannot be predicted by merely summing their components. Examples of nonlinear processes include schools of fish and flocks of birds (whose grouping is aided by attractive energies arising because the surrounding fluid moves with them), and groups of *lipid molecules* that organize themselves into a biological membrane by minimizing the repulsive forces between lipid chains and water molecules.

We might view consciousness as a higher-level or emergent property of the brain in the simple sense that solidity is an emergent property of water molecules when they are in a lattice at low temperatures. In this view, consciousness might be taken as a physical property of the processes of the brain in the same sense that solidity is a property of the molecules in an oak table or an icicle. The perspective that brain processes cause consciousness, but also that consciousness is a feature of the brain, avoids both the extreme of making mind separate from body and the excessively reductive materialistic view that mind is "nothing but" a group of molecules organized into nerve cells. In our present state of knowledge we can observe neuronal activity in the brain that correlates with, but does not explain, consciousness. We eventually hope to have a causal theory that explains why consciousness and neuronal activities are correlated, just as we now have causal theories that explain why the solidity of a substance correlates with its molecular structure, or why thunder and lightning are correlated during a storm.

We can think of our "mindstuff" as different from our "nervestuff" without edging back toward a dualism that separates body and mind, because we are talking about the same kind of distinction we make when we say that DNA is different from the elementary particles of atomic physics of which it is ultimately composed, even though its special properties are completely explicable from the properties of its constituent atoms.

It is important to avoid some potential confusion about explanations. We appreciate that more complex entities can be explained in terms of simpler components. Knowing what we do about nerve cells, we can see how the laws governing a nerve signal follow from the laws of chemistry and electricity, and in this sense we can "reduce" it to them. But this is a very peculiar relationship. Under other conditions, the same laws of chemistry and physics explain liquid crystal displays of wrist watches, clouds forming over the ocean, thunder and lightning, and sugar dissolving in our coffee. Those laws of chemistry and physics in turn follow from the laws of quantum mechanics, which the physicists call fundamental, but only under the conditions where we normally find matter. Quantum mechanics has very different consequences in particle accelerators ("atom smashers") and at the edges of black holes than it does in your kitchen. To propose a genuine explanation, we must be armed with knowledge of both the lower-level laws and the conditions under which they act. Those conditions are so variable that we could never hope to have the higher-level laws just "fall out" (as the physicists say) of the quantum equations. If we were to restart the universe, would everything happen in just the same way? Perhaps there would eventually be clouds and quartz crystals, but what about mushrooms and animals with nerve cells and action potentials— and, in particular, us, puzzling over consciousness? These are not all entities whose appearance anyone could have predicted just from the equations of quantum mechanics: There are simply too many different ways in which things could have been fit together by evolution.

Figure 1–1 shows arrows pointing in both the upward and downward directions. The up arrows indicate simpler things coming together to make more complicated things, such as lipid molecules making cell membranes, or the organ systems of our bodies constructing a skin or epidermis that encloses us. The downward arrows show that emergent entities can constrain and direct the components that built them up. A cell membrane is a physical compartment, or bag, that contains and exerts some control over all of its smaller components, just as on a larger scale our skins establish the context for what our muscles and other tissues can do. By the same token, if a whole organism constrains and regulates its component tissues, it should not surprise us that an emergent property like our subjective consciousness can organize, monitor, or direct the nerve assemblies of which it is constructed. And as we will see in later chapters, there is good evidence that this really happens. There doesn't have to be anything mystical about it. Our self-conscious behavior can affect and shape the nerve and muscle physiology in our bodies. Finally, the consciousness or mind that each of us experiences is not the final step in the causal chain, for it is strongly influenced and organized by the particular human culture in which we grew up.

Organism and environment

The hierarchy drawing in the previous section looks tidy, but it can give the false impression that complicated things build themselves in isolation. The building is instead a historical process that depends strongly on the environment in which it occurs. In the hubris that accompanied the early days of molecular biology, one could hear scientists say, in effect, "Give me the structure of human DNA and I will compute you a human." Today this is recognized as nonsense, and few now take that extreme sort of reductionism very seriously. DNA is expressed only in a complex environment, first in the egg and then in different tissues as they form. As the fertilized eggs that generated you and me started dividing to generate the trillions of cells in our bodies, they were partners in an exquisite series of interactions with other cells. Each of these cells contained all of our genes, yet only particular subsets of their progeny turned on the genes that were needed to specify a liver cell, kidney cell, or nerve cell. Their fate was instructed by their particular surroundings in the embryo, surroundings that contained a rich broth of growth factor molecules. If taken away from this broth and placed in a minimal solution of nutrients just sufficient to sustain life, these cells might live, but they would probably return to an undifferentiated state. Not only do cells within a developing embryo regulate each other, but the hormones in the embryo's intrauterine environment influence its sexual development and behavior. Embryos exposed to higher levels of testosterone, for example, emerge as more aggressive individuals.

The wiring connections in our brains—the specific circuits formed during development—depend on features of the sensory and motor environment in which we grow up after birth. If those environments are absent or abnormal, the brain develops differently. Just as the differentiated state of every cell in our body is maintained by constant flux and interaction with its environment (including other cells), so the differentiated state of our brains is maintained by unique details of our own environment. The brain we grow, the self we generate, the language we speak—all are functions of our unique history and culture. Language, thought, and ways of experiencing the world can be culturally relative and very different for those living in Western industrial cultures and those belonging to isolated Stone Age tribes in Borneo. None of us can claim to have a "God's eye" view of an objective external reality.

> *Our development is shaped by the very environment we try to describe scientifically. Thus there is an inevitable circularity to our knowing.*

This can lead us to an uncomfortable confrontation with our common sense belief that the way things seem to us is the way things really are. Of course, we all know that we make mistakes, and sometimes we are fooled by tricks and illusions, but the problem goes deeper than that. Each of us develops in a tight interaction with a particular part of the external world, in a particular human culture and language, and all our beliefs and ways of describing things are shaped by that interaction. We are one part of an interacting whole trying to understand other parts. The distinction between subjects and objects is not so simple as we commonly think. It is with a slightly dizzy sensation that we realize we are using our instrument of analysis (the brain) to analyze that very instrument of analysis (the brain), like asking an eye to see itself or a mirror to reflect its own image. Figure 1–2, a reproduction of the famous illustration by the Dutch artist M.C. Escher showing two hands shaping each other, illustrates the quandary. Which is the "real" hand? It sometimes can be useful for us to put aside our tendency to stamp a

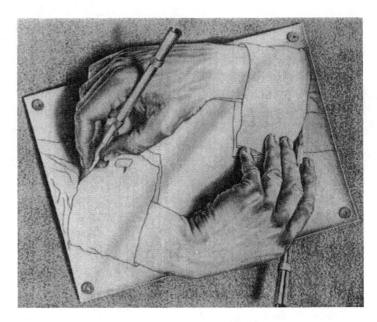

Figure 1–2   Which is the real hand? Both. We shape our environment, and our environment shapes us. M.C. Escher's "Drawing Hands" © 1999 Cordon Art B.V., Baarn Holland. All rights reserved.

seal of certainty on our experience, as though it perfectly reflected the world. The experience of anything "out there" is validated by the human structure, which makes possible "the thing" that arises in the description. This is not to deny that there is an objective world but only to say that our ability to describe it is shaped by our history of interactions with it. (We will consider the issue of the relativity of our knowledge a bit further in Chapter 7.)

Where is the "I"?

We still haven't faced head-on the question of where the "I" is in the space between our ears. Who is watching inside when you recall how the Mona Lisa looks? What is this consciousness or mindstuff? Perhaps you can imagine the "I" in your head as shown in Figure 1–3, corresponding to an array of purposeful little agents scrambling around inside, some watching the movie screen of what is going on in the outside world, others operating the levers on the control panels that direct our movements. But this just takes the problem back another step, like opening the Russian wooden doll toy that has another doll nested inside. Opening that doll, you find the next. The hunt for purposeful agents somewhere down in there becomes fruitless. As we look further inside the brain, we become increasingly convinced that there doesn't appear to be anyone at home. We don't find a specific place where there is a thinker or a feeler or an actor. Rather, there are billions and billions of nerve cells wired together in complex arrays. We search in

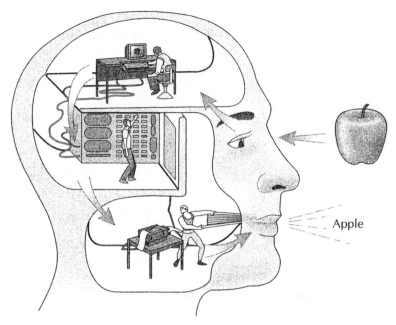

Figure 1–3   Where is the I? It can't reside in other little humans inside our heads, as suggested here, even though such a picture perhaps corresponds most closely to our subjective experience.

vain among all the specialized areas of our brain to find one that is the president. Is it in the frontal lobes? (We will take up this question in more detail in Chapter 12.)

It might be helpful at this point to peek at the sort of answer that is outlined in subsequent chapters. The best idea seems to be that the brain isn't like a classical top-down corporation or a computer run by a master central processor. Our consciousness is mechanically implemented by a process more analogous to an economy or an ecosystem—a distributed system without any central authority. There is no central place from which a puppeteer pulls all the strings. Our brains are a collection of semi-independent subsystems designed to perform specific jobs. They are not general-purpose problem solvers that invoke the same distributed, common processes for all tasks. They are more like a Swiss Army knife that has special gadgets for different tasks. Large computational problems (such as vision, audition, movement, and language generation) are split into a collection of parts processed by specific brain regions. These parts can be revealed when they are damaged by brain lesions or genetic mutations. And they can sometimes be directly visualized in living brains via imaging techniques or electrical recordings. The specialized modules are not isolated but interact extensively with each other. In Chapter 8 we consider one of the best-known examples of this, the different areas of the brain that process different aspects of a visual image, such as form, motion, distance, and color.

We seem to be a society of mind, built up of a hierarchy of agents referred to by different authors as simpletons, stable subassemblies, multiple drafts, component selves, and so on (the words vary more than the ideas). The modules are not what an engineer starting from scratch would have designed (supposing there were an engineer who could design a brain) but rather a hodgepodge of evolutionary adaptations and accidents piled one on top of the other, with some components possibly duplicated and adopted for uses and tricks quite different from their original "purpose." Consciousness, at least in part, was natural selection's way of endowing us with thoughts that helped us survive in the world of our ancestors, not necessarily thoughts that are consistent or true. These last points bring us to the subject of the first main section of this book, how biological evolution has shaped the minds we use today.

Just as we are stuck with the QWERTY keyboard—an awkward design that slows typing speed, devised in 1872 to avoid jamming of type bars that vanished long ago—so the modern brain makes do with modules designed to solve ancient problems.

SUMMARY

This chapter has spelled out a number of positions and attitudes adopted by most of those who study the scientific basis of mind. A working assumption is that mind has its origin in physical stuff, just like the rest of the universe that we know about. Mind is what our brain/body does. Consciousness arises from the activity of neurons. What it is for—its function—needs to be described, as well as the hardware that carries out its activities. For the purposes of this book, *mind* is very broadly defined as the sum of the vast number of operations that proceed as our nervous system interacts with other body systems and with the world to generate cognitions, only a fraction of which are accessible to our awareness. This book takes the optimistic view that we are not blocked, in principle, from understanding how our conscious awareness works. The "hard problem" of explaining what it is like to be someone may be resolved as we learn more from descriptions of what humans do and from experiments in cognitive psychology and neuroscience.

We can use what we already know about how our complex bodies are built up hierarchically, from simpler components, as a model for thinking about how consciousness might arise from groups of nerve cells. We have to admit that our processes of knowing are somewhat circular, because they are shaped and formed by the very environments they are trying to describe. But we are certain that the "I" of our subjective awareness is not like a little human, the 16th century's homunculus, residing somewhere inside our heads as a master puppeteer pulling all the strings. Rather, our consciousness is a distributed process that involves many semi-independent assemblies and agents whose activities are coordinated. One of the goals of this book is to sketch out the many components of our perceiving, acting, emotional, and linguistic minds that make us a society of mind. It is the origins of these components that we now want to consider by going back to the beginning and starting to tell the story of how our minds evolved over millions of years. ∎

Questions for Thought

1. Several levels of conscious awareness were discussed at the beginning of this chapter, levels that culminate in the internal narrative made possible by human language. Some psychologists have argued that without language there can be no conscious awareness. Do you agree or disagree with this? Why?

2. Given what you have read here about definitions of consciousness, awareness, and mind, how would you respond if someone asked you, "How do you define mind?"

3. René Descartes' famous formulation, "I think, therefore I am" posited a clear dividing line between the mind and the brain, assigning the former to a nonphysical or spiritual realm and the latter to the physical world. Perhaps the central point of this chapter is the contrary assertion that mind has a physical basis, just like the rest of the world we know about. What is your opinion on this question? (This is an issue we discuss further in Chapter 12.)

Suggestions for further general reading

Churchland, P.M. 1995. *The Engine of Reason, the Seat of the Soul: A Philosophical Journey into the Brain.* Cambridge, MA: M.I.T. Press. (A discussion of computational models of the brain based on modern findings in neuroscience and psychology.)

Clark, A. 1997. *Being There.* Cambridge, MA: M.I.T. Press. (This book emphasizes how mind and body are defined by their participation in an extended physical and social environment.)

Dennett, D.C. 1991. *Consciousness Explained.* Boston: Little, Brown. (A controversial and engaging introduction to philosophical and technical issues involved in explaining consciousness.)

Scott, A. 1995. *Stairway to the Mind.* New York: Springer-Verlag. (A discussion of how mind might emerge from assemblies of simpler components.)

Reading on more advanced or specialized topics

Flanagan, O. 1992. *Consciousness Reconsidered.* Cambridge, MA: M.I.T. Press. (A more advanced discussion of issues in the philosophy of mind, including naturalistic explanations of consciousness.)

Hardcastle, V.G. 1996. Ways of knowing. *Consciousness and Cognition* 5:359–367. (A discussion of how mind and consciousness are defined that suggests how the "explanatory gap" might be closed.)

Part I
Evolving Mind

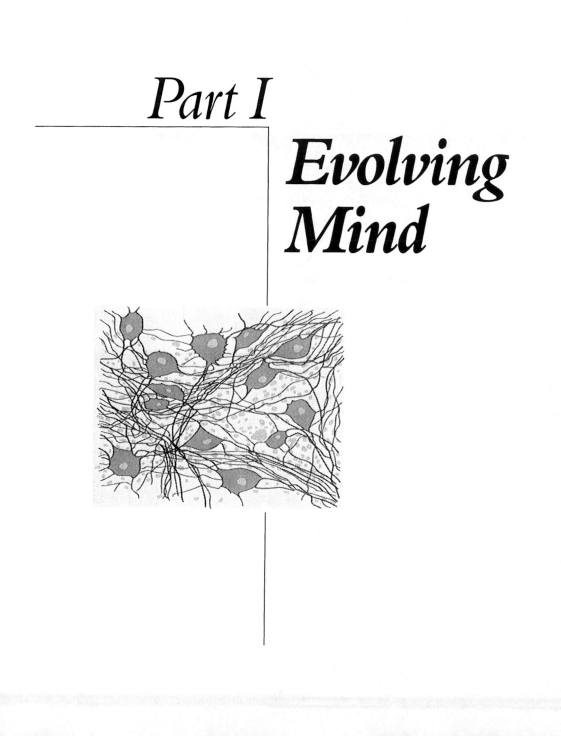

Chapter 2

Origins of Mind

Most of the issues raised in Chapter 1 are unique to human minds. We don't imagine that chimpanzees spend much of their time thinking about thinking. To start considering the processes that ultimately generated our self conscious thinking minds, we have to go back to a beginning when everyone agrees there could have been no minds as we know them. Before biological evolution generated bacteria and eventually chimps and humans, there was the earth. Before the earth there was the universe, which cosmologists tell us started with the Big Bang. This is thought to have occurred about 8–20 billion years ago, depending on which cosmologist you listen to. Our solar system arrived about 4.5 billion years ago, and life appeared on earth about 3.5 billion years ago. Descriptions of our universe are usually offered with an authoritative ring, but arguments over some minor details can have the feel of medieval theological debates. One of the problems to explain is how our galaxy, the Milky Way, can spin so fast without flying apart, for Newton's laws say there is not enough mass present to provide the gravity to hold it together. One solution is to postulate the existence of "dark matter," a mysterious substance that actually accounts for 90% of the mass of the universe. These issues of physics and cosmology are an interesting backdrop to the question of whether organic evolution might have occurred in other solar systems similar to our own, but we will stick to this planet. We have our hands more than full trying to figure out what happened here.

A tiny fraction of the earth's history is occupied by humans like ourselves. If we chart the total span on a single year's calendar, then each day represents 12 million years. In January the world was presumably unknown and inexperienced. The first forms of bacterial life arose sometime in March, about 3.5 billion years ago. During a very narrow window of time in early November, about 570–550 million years ago, virtually every phylum of marine invertebrate animal appeared. The first fish appeared around the end of November. The dinosaurs came around December 10 and departed on Christmas Day. Modern mammals began appearing over the last 4–6 days. Social primates, most of whom are tree-living herbivores and insectivores, appeared December 30–31. The first of our ancestors recognizable as humans didn't show up until the afternoon of December 31, 3–4 million years ago. Our species, *Homo sapiens*, appeared about 11:45 P.M. All of recorded human history unfolded in the final minute of the year. All of the hard-wired mental machinery that is specified by our genes was in place long before that final minute. Our nerve cells and nerve signals are fundamentally similar to those of invertebrates such as lobsters and beetles. We share with lower mammals brain circuits for eating, sleeping, sex, fighting, and fleeing. We have a social organization (hierarchy and division of labor) in common with langurs, baboons, and chimpanzees. We socially transmit learned behaviors like monkeys. The past is very much present in us.

The theory of biological evolution, essentially as outlined by Charles Darwin, is the cornerstone of our current understanding of how we came to be the way we are. Its description of how humans evolved from apes over the past several million years reflects the best efforts of modern science. It is a story, supported by a vast amount of evidence, that is universal among scientists across cultures. As sure as we are about its correctness, it still is not appropriate to adopt a "This is it!" attitude. Surely there are things we are still missing; whole new areas of knowledge may remain to be discovered. Also, we don't look to our current scientific world view to tell us about the purpose of existence or any possible realms of the supernatural.

We carry in our bloodstream the ionic composition of a primordial sea, and we share fundamentally similar nervous control mechanisms with the simplest of the invertebrate animals.

The point of this chapter is to launch the "biology part" of this book. We'll start with the origins of cells, simple minds, and selves and with the mechanisms by which they persist and evolve. The chapter introduces some ideas in evolutionary theory, particularly the concept of *adaptation*. It then looks at how genetically programmed neural circuits of increasing complexity have evolved to drive behaviors that enhance survival and reproduction.

Origins of sensing and acting

Where in the last few billion years do we find the origins of our abilities to sense our environment—its chemicals, sounds, and lights—and then make appropriate movements or actions in response? When did selves and minds appear? The current idea is that the earliest steps toward life involved reactions in a primeval soup that brought together molecules that could make copies of themselves. *Evolution* then got to work, selecting and designing packets of organic material that had increasing potential for maintaining their own integrity and reproducing. Fascinating experiments have documented the spontaneous formation of simple organic molecules under conditions thought to have existed early in the life of our planet. The study of simple self-replicating molecules, possible precursors of our RNA and DNA, has become a new subdiscipline within chemistry. There is, however, debate over whether these processes all took place on earth. An alternative view is that early life forms appeared on other planets and that the earth was then seeded by organisms or molecules introduced when rock fragments from those worlds struck ours.

An epochal transformation came with the appearance of lipid molecules that could organize themselves into a thin film enclosing these self-replicating molecules, along with other systems that provided energy, which prevented their indiscriminate exchange with the external world. These membranes became the boundary at which exchanges of matter, energy, and information could take place. (The evolution of such an enclosure is an example of an emergent property of the sort represented in Figure 1–1: A level of structure appears that feeds back on lower levels of organization to contain and impose boundaries.) The biological cell, which we could call the simplest sort of self, had evolved. Only after this bounded structure appeared was it possible to distinguish "inside" from "outside," ultimately making possible the distinction between "What is happening to me?" and "What is happening out there?"

The enclosure of self-replicating molecules by a lipid membrane made possible the first simple cell, a "self" that had an inside distinct from the outside environment.

Why was there a progression from self-replicating molecules to self-replicating cells and thence (much later) to multicellular organisms? What underlying process might have caused the appearance of new and more complex forms? What permitted entities to persist, to reproduce themselves, and to adapt to changing environments? Charles Darwin's central insight was that a very simple mechanism can, in principle, account for the evolution and diversity of all living things. These things, single cells or complex animals, reproduce themselves and, in doing so, make occasional variations or errors that produce slightly different forms. A very tiny fraction of these different forms prove to be better adapted to their environment (perhaps they avoid predators better, use resources more effectively, or are more attractive to the opposite sex) and so are slightly more successful in generating copies of themselves. These more successful forms soon come to dominate the population and are thus poised for further adaptation. This process continues indefinitely and is sometimes referred to as the *Darwin Machine* (Figure 2–1). Its cycles of generating, testing, and replicating underlie not only biological evolution but also, as we will see, much of organismal development and behavior.

> *The idea of the Darwin Machine— with its cycles of generating entities, testing them, and preferentially replicating those that happen to work a little bit better—can be applied to many different self-replicating systems.*

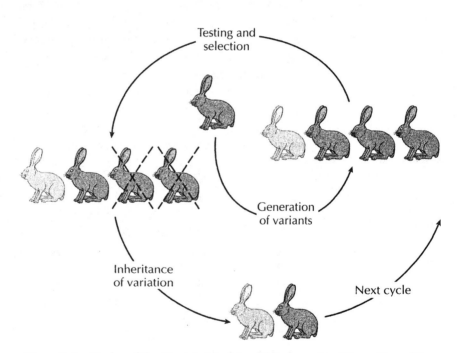

Figure 2–1   Cycles of the Darwin Machine. This example of the action of the Darwin Machine starts with a female member of a group of brown rabbits living in an area whose climate is becoming more cold and snowy each year. Most of its newborn are brown, but occasionally a genetic mutation may cause the appearance of an individual that is lighter in color. The darker brown rabbits are more likely to be eaten by predators such as foxes before they reach reproductive age, because they are easier to see against a snowy background (an X indicates a rabbit's removal). After a number of generations the lighter colored rabbits predominate in the population.

This model was wedded with modern genetics in the early 1900s by Fisher, Haldane, Wright, and others to form neo-Darwinism, which emphasizes the way mutations in individual genes result in the generation of variant adult forms (*phenotypes*). Phenotypes that are better adapted to their environment reproduce more successfully, leading to an increase in the fraction of the population that exhibits the newer gene combinations (*genotypes*). The emphasis has shifted, over the past 30 years, from individuals to genes as units of selection, and now it is increasingly believed that selection and adaptation can occur at many levels of organization: genes, groups of genes, individuals, and also families, populations, and larger social groups.

Simple forms of behavior

Returning to our simple cell, we can appreciate the origins of sensing and acting in terms of the Darwin Machine. Consider the primitive cells that we have just constructed, the precursors of modern bacteria. Cells that gained the ability to move, perhaps first by amoeboid motion and then by waving small propellers (cilia or flagella) could go to their food rather than depending on it coming to them. This mobility permitted them to reproduce more effectively, so motile cells came to predominate. The environment of these cells contained good things like food and also bad things like toxic chemicals. Any individual cell that began to develop some means of avoiding the bad things and approaching the good ones would be at an advantage. The eventual result was the appearance of *chemotaxis,* the ability to sense chemicals in the environment and move toward or away from them (see Figure 2–2). Individuals with this capability were better adapted to their environment than those without, and thus they could survive and reproduce at a higher rate. Over a time scale of billions rather than millions of years, the cells whose modern descendants are bacteria not only invented chemotaxis but also added a *nucleus* to contain their genetic material. Bacteria able to trap the energy of the sun, and others able to extract energy from complex molecules such as sugars, were incorporated into larger cells and became the power sources of modern plant and animal cells: chloroplasts and mitochondria.

Communication between cells

The invention of sex permitted the exchange of genes between different mating types in organisms such as yeast, and a new twist to the chemotaxis mechanism appeared. Cells of one type generated small molecules called *pheromones* to attract their opposite type (see Figure 2–3). Now the signal from the external environment came from another

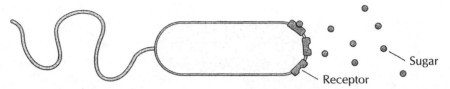

Figure 2–2 In the primordial sea (about 3.5 billion years ago), things to eat and things to avoid. Chemotaxis occurs when a specialized protein molecule called a *receptor* (one of the dark lines shown in the cell's membrane) binds to a small molecule such as a sugar used for food (the small gray dots). The receptor initiates a series of chemical reactions that instruct the cell to tumble about for a while and then take off in a new direction. If this new direction is the right one (the one that takes it toward higher concentrations of sugar), the cell keeps going straight. If it is not, the cell tumbles and tries again. Starting with this simple form of sensing and acting, we can reconstruct a sequence of steps that leads to the complex signaling systems used by our bodies.

organism, not just from food or things to avoid. Cells were talking to each other.

The basic chemical machinery that amoebae, bacteria, yeast, and multicellular animals use for sensing and responding to external stimuli has been preserved throughout evolution and functions in us today. In multicellular animals like ourselves, many of the molecules responsible for sensing and acting that once turned toward the external physical environment now turn toward the environment of other cells. The cells in our bodies use these molecules, which are called *hormones*, to sense and act on each other (see Figure 2–4).

Recall from Figure 1–1 that multicellular animals are composed of stable subsystems: Cells form tissues, tissues form organ systems,

Figure 2–3 Cells talking to each other (about 1.5 billion years ago). Molecules released by one yeast mating type (the small dots) are recognized by membrane receptors of another mating type, and slightly different molecules (the squares) released by the second type are recognized by the first.

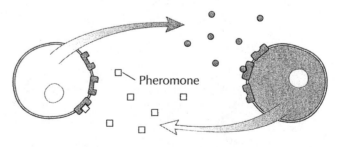

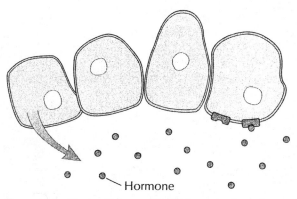

Figure 2–4   Communication within multicellular organisms (more than 700 million years ago). Hormones (the gray dots) released by one cell type, such as a cell in the head that senses food, might tell another kind of cell, such as a digestive cell in the gut, to release compounds that will help break down the food that is soon to appear.

organ systems form organisms. Each level of the hierarchy can be said to encapsulate, or contain, lower levels. There is a compelling reason why biological evolution has followed this route. The psychologist and computer scientist H. A. Simon has put it in the form of a parable about two watchmakers, Hora and Tempus. Hora puts together all 100 parts of a watch at once. Tempus puts together five separate stable subunits, or subassemblies, that are then combined to make the final watch. Given that there is a chance of dropping what one is working on and having to start over, who makes more watches? Which watch is easier to repair when broken? This pattern of constructing with stable subassemblies is fundamental in biological organization—and indeed in the construction of any complex entity.

The next step in the story line brings us from hormones to nerve cells and their signaling (see Figure 2–5). A cell, instead of releasing a hormone that diffuses a considerable distance to act on another cell, grows a long, thin process, called an *axon*, that comes very close to its target cell. An axon can be quite long: Think of the distance between the big toe and the bottom of the spinal cord in your own body—or better yet, in a giraffe. The signaling molecule that it releases, a *neurotransmitter*, is released from a swelling at the end of the axon (the *presynaptic terminal*). The neurotransmitter diffuses across a narrow cleft very rapidly to bind to *postsynaptic receptors* on the target cell. This causes the postsynaptic cell to generate a nerve signal. The whole complex is called a *synapse*, and the process is referred to as *synaptic transmission*.

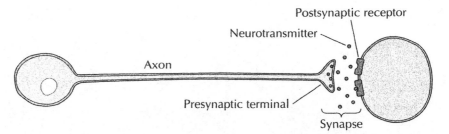

Figure 2–5   Rapid communication at a distance (more than 600 million years ago). The signaling molecules (the gray dots), now called neurotransmitters, are released from the end (presynaptic terminal) of a long, thin process (axon) and have only a small distance to move before they can bind to postsynaptic receptor molecules. This makes communication between the cells much more rapid.

Reflexes and interneurons

The process described in the previous section may seem a bit remote to you, but two-cell systems of this sort are a fundamental part of our own behavioral repertoire. Let the cell on the left in Figure 2–5 become the sensory neuron in Figure 2–6, sensitive to some external form of energy such as the stretch applied to your muscles when a doctor taps your knee with a small hammer. Let the cell on the right in Figure 2–5, to which the first cell talks, become a motor neuron in your spinal cord that triggers a compensatory muscle contraction that opposes the stretch, as when your knee jerks forward after the hammer taps it. This is an example of a *reflex arc*, the simplest multicell circuit found in animal nervous systems.

Two-cell units of this sort are used to construct the large array of *reflexes*, or harm anticipator–avoiders, that help us (and other animals) ensure a future for ourselves. Essentially the same kinds of circuits are used when a human withdraws a finger from a hot stove, and when a clam slams its shell shut when touched. Reflexes trade accuracy for speed: Better to be safe than sorry. They link sensitivity and responsivity on a rapid time scale, just as in our example of bacterial chemotaxis. They employ *receptor cells* that evolved to become responsive to external stimuli such as heat, light, sound, taste, touch, and smell. These stimuli became linked to an increasing range of possible behavioral responses carried out by *effector cells*, such as muscle cells and gland cells. In addition to receptors and effectors responding to and acting on the external world, an array of internal receptors and effectors have evolved to sense and regulate what is happening inside animal bodies—in our case, to monitor and control things such as temperature, blood pressure, digestion, and how our joints and muscles are moving. Virtually all of these circuits are hard-

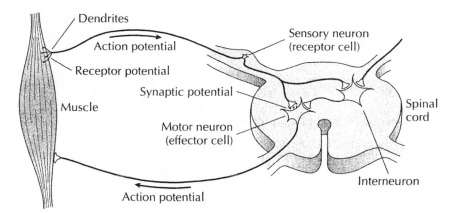

Figure 2–6 Structure of a simple reflex arc. The sensory neuron is activated by the stretching of tiny processes (*dendrites*) that thread among fibers of a muscle. An axon connects these dendrites to the cell body of a sensory neuron, which lies just outside the spinal cord. The axon continues on into the spinal cord to activate a motor neuron, which then sends a signal to the muscle that causes a contraction compensating for the stretch. Also shown is an interneuron, which can influence the activity of this reflex arc. See the text for an explanation of the other items labeled on this figure.

wired, which means that they are specified ultimately by our genes and are observed in a fairly stereotyped form in all individuals.

In these simple reflexes we observe the main nerve signals that regulate the mental life of all living creatures, plant and animal. They have maintained the same basic mechanism and form throughout millions of years. These signals are small, brief changes in the voltage across nerve cell membranes: *receptor potentials, action potentials,* and *synaptic potentials.* We will not be dealing with the exact forms and shapes of these voltage changes, but their locations are labeled in the drawing of the two-cell stretch reflex shown in Figure 2–6. A stimulus delivered to the receptor cell causes it to generate a local receptor potential, a decrease in membrane voltage that roughly corresponds to the duration and intensity of the stimulus. The cell then converts this to a series of long-distance signals—action potentials, each lasting only a few milliseconds—that travel rapidly (meters per second) along the axon to presynaptic terminals in the spinal cord. This causes the presynaptic terminals to release neurotransmitters, which diffuse across the synaptic cleft. Interaction of neurotransmitters with postsynaptic receptor molecules of the motor neuron generates synaptic potentials whose magnitude continues to reflect the intensity of the stretch. These synaptic potentials then cause the motor neuron to fire action potentials that travel to its presynaptic terminal with the muscle cell, resulting in activation of the nerve-muscle synapse and contraction of the muscle.

Most reflexes involve more than just receptor and effector cells, and the connections between these two are more complex than the previous

---

The basic signals of all nervous systems—signals that underlie our mental life—can be illustrated by the simple reflex arc. We can eavesdrop on these signals by placing a tiny sensing electrode inside or near the nerve cells. The small voltage pulses, or action potentials, that travel along the axon and pass by the electrode can be displayed on a computer screen or through a loudspeaker. Because individual action potentials are so fast (only a fraction of a millisecond to a few milliseconds in duration), they are sometimes referred to as spikes. It is an interesting experience to observe an experiment in progress while nerve cell activity is being monitored. You can actually listen to or see action potentials as their voltage signals are converted to clicks on a loudspeaker, or the voltage pulses are displayed on a viewing screen.

---

discussion indicates. All nervous systems, from the simple nerve nets of a hydra to our own, consist mainly of *interneurons*. These are cells that intervene to process information the receptors send to them and then modulate or control the actions that result. Such a cell is included in Figure 2–6. For example, if you are feeling stubborn while in the doctor's exam room, interneurons permit your brain to override the anticipated reflex and inhibit your lower leg from kicking forward when the hammer taps your knee.

The vast majority of nerve cells in our bodies are interneurons. They account for virtually all of our brain cells. In the brain, most of the action is going on constantly in the 1–10 trillion interneurons (the brain and central nervous system) that connect 100 million or so sensory cells to the 1–10 million motor cells. Your brain is mostly sending messages between different parts of itself. Changes in the environment that alter sensory cells result in perturbations of the ongoing activity of interneurons. These interneurons then alter activities in motor cells, which can cause perturbations in the environment. This is how we are structurally coupled with our environment: we act on the environment, sense the effects of that action on us, and then initiate the next action. We are continuously embedded in an action-reaction loop.

Evolution of the nervous system

Things were a bit simpler when the most complicated animals around were essentially cavities for ingesting and expelling food, similar to modern hydra and jellyfish. The nervous system was a diffuse fabric of cells (see Figure 2–7). The *enteric nervous system* that regulates the

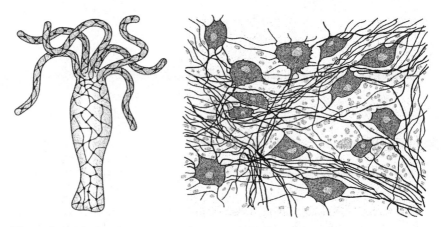

Figure 2–7   A simple *nerve net.* The nervous system of the hydra, shown on the left, is a uniform and diffuse collection of nerve cells that make multiple contacts with each other to form a net-like structure that can regulate contractions to move food in and out of a digestive cavity. A similar network of neurons, shown on the right, regulates contractions of the wall of our gut.

actions of our gut is derived from this primitive beginning (see "Origins and structures of the vertebrate nervous system" in Chapter 3).

The next step in evolution was for sensory cells to cluster in the food-intake or head end of simple animals, and bodies began to be designed in segments. The movement of each segment came to be regulated by clusters of nerve cell bodies, or *ganglia.* A central cord of nerve fibers connected ganglia to each other and to the head (see Figure 2–8). A larger clustering of nerve cell bodies, called a cerebral ganglion, appeared in the head, where a "command central" for integrating sensory input and directing the body to move began to take shape.

Invertebrates and vertebrates share a common segmental body plan, but at some point in the evolutionary line that led to vertebrates, the nervous system turned upside down with respect to the gut so that ventral structures became dorsal, and vice versa (see Figure 2–8). This is why the central nerve cord of a lobster runs along the abdominal side, or ventral, surface of its body, whereas our spinal cord runs along our back, or dorsal, surface. In both vertebrates and invertebrates, increasing numbers of nerve cells in the head region are characteristic of more complicated nervous systems.

The segmental structure of both vertebrate and invertebrate nervous systems is generated by a similar set of genes, called *homeotic genes,* which are important in determining body pattern. In parallel with the increasing complexity of nervous systems, the number of genes that living organisms carry seems to have undergone three major jumps.

Invertebrate

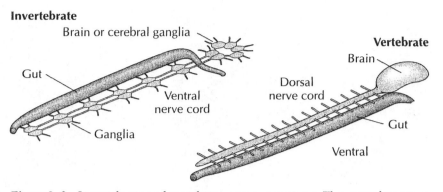

Figure 2–8   Invertebrate and vertebrate nervous systems. The central nervous system of an invertebrate consists of paired clusters of nerve cell bodies, or ganglia, running along the belly of the animal underneath the digestive tube (gut), with a larger cluster in the head that deals with sensory input and coordination of the whole body. The central nerve cord of a vertebrate runs along its back and is encased in bone; more of the neurons of the nervous system are clustered in a brain.

The most complex single-cell organisms with a nucleus have fewer than 10,000 genes. Invertebrates have at least 25,000 genes on average, and vertebrates average at least 50,000. The total gene set, or *genome,* is organized into substructures (chromosomes) that offer highly organized alternatives for selection. During these increases in complexity, some excess baggage appears to have accumulated. Random events and the mechanisms by which component subassemblies of genes are plugged together have led to the accumulation of stretches of "junk DNA" for which no function has been determined. What is even more curious, more than 50% of the genes that code for body proteins can be deactivated by mutation without blocking the development of viable organisms. Some of these genes surely reflect functional redundancy. Evolution has given us backup systems for many functions. Having arrays of genes that code for similar things allows organisms to be more resilient when subjected to environmental insults.

During evolution, different segments of the bodies or nervous systems of invertebrates and vertebrates were duplicated, mixed, and matched as though they were pieces in a molecular Lego set.

Think of how different we humans, along with other vertebrates, seem from the vast array of invertebrates on this planet—animals like worms, lobsters, and cockroaches. Our evolutionary line has been diverging from that of the cockroach for at least 500–600 million years, when our common ancestors were probably flatworms with very primitive nervous systems. Some estimates place the divergence of chordates and invertebrates as far as a billion years ago. Since then, both lines have independently invented some advanced features, which include sensory maps, parallel processing, population vector codes, central pattern generators, neuronal plasticity, spatial learning, and memory. (These concepts are covered in later chapters.) We tend to apply the yardstick of our human intelligence to conclude that vertebrates are much "smarter" than invertebrates. However, if we gauge smarts by environmental fitness, humans come out a distant second to the hordes of insects that have so successfully colonized every conceivable ecological niche on earth. Cockroaches will probably still be around if our species manages to do itself in.

An example of a successful invertebrate that, like ourselves, has evolved to become an unspecialized but successful exploiter of complex environments can be found in the octopods. People who study octopus behavior report experiencing these animals as fellow creatures, recognizing different animals and establishing individual relationships with them. Some animals seem timid, others curious and even trusting. It is tempting to treat them as aquatic cats and dogs. They watch you, come to be fed, display simple play behaviors, and will flee with the appearance of fear if you are mean to them. They can be curious about their reflection in a mirror, send out an exploratory arm and then rush in apparent distress back to their hole. In writing such descriptions, observers are implicitly interpreting octopus behavior in human terms. With dogs or cats there is a certain resonance in doing this because we are all mammals, but the octopus is an alien. Its brain anatomy bears virtually no resemblance to ours, and there is not yet a hint that its motivation would be adjustable in the same way that it is in mammals.

Adaptations and increasing complexity

We rationalize increases in the complexity of genomes and nervous systems as adaptations to the environment that made individuals more successful in passing their genes on to future generations. The idea of adaptation is a central one, and it offers an after-the-fact explanation for intricate, apparently purposeful designs that would otherwise seem to require crafting by divine engineers. We can use adaptation to explain why we have image-forming eyes; why birds have hollow, light bones; and why some moth wings have eye markings. The central idea is that each of these complex structures emerged over many generations in incremental stages, each refinement conferring slightly more advantage than its predecessor in fitting the organism to the environment (see the section on "Consciousness and the evolution of sensory organs" below for a more detailed example of this concept). In this sense, an adaptation is a form of knowledge about the environment. Adaptations such as chemotaxis and nervous systems arose through constant interactions of organisms and environments. This relational quality has given them the appearance of being goal-directed, or teleological, but there is no actual goal here—just a drift toward greater complexity because every incremental advantage, however small, might be grabbed and put to use in the next generation.

Adaptations are not just responses of passive organisms to implacable forces of the environment. Living creatures also can change the world in which they live in a variety of ways. The composition of the earth's atmosphere is affected as plants and animals generate oxygen and carbon dioxide. Trees cast shadows, dump leaf litter, suck water and nutrients from the soil, and exchange carbon dioxide for oxygen in the air. They are acting on the earth even as the earth is acting on them. Because organisms and their environments shape each other, it makes sense also to view adaptations as relations—as interactions between the two—rather than viewing them only in terms of how they influence the fit of an organism with an unvarying environment. Organisms and the environment in evolution, in organismal development, and during normal behavior form a unity that we often do not appreciate.

> *The concept of adaptation provides an explanation for the appearance of complex, seemingly purposeful designs in the absence of an omniscient designer.*

Not all adaptations reflect perfect functional solutions to current demands. Structures such as feathers were selected because they served one purpose—temperature regulation—and then were recruited to another—flight. Vertebrate jaws may have originated as skeletal arches that enhanced breathing. The bones of our inner ear were once a piece of the jaw. Swim bladders in fish developed from primitive lungs. In these cases a latent potential was recruited for a new use. During evolution there have been frequent reinventions of similar adaptations, and there have been losses, shifts, and even reversals of function. For example, the wings of birds and the wings of bees are *analogous traits* that perform the same function but arose independently on different branches of the evolutionary tree. In contrast, the limbs of vertebrates descended from a common ancestor and are referred to as *homologous traits*. The fins of ancestral fish, used for swimming, evolved into the legs of ancestral reptiles, birds, and mammals, used for running or hopping on land. The front legs of certain ancestral mammals and reptile-birds then evolved into the wings of bats and modern birds, respectively, and came to be used for flying. Bird wings and mammalian legs then evolved independently into the flippers of penguins and whales, respectively, thereby reverting to a swimming function and effectively reinventing the fins of fish. At least two groups of fish descendants independently lost their limbs to become snakes and legless lizards.

Evolutionary change is constrained by the building materials on hand. Because genes interact and regulate each other so extensively, there is little room for variability. Phenotypes and genotypes become so complex that they have only limited tolerance for deviation, beyond which they lose their functional integrity. A complex system like a human or a mouse is extremely limited in the direction in which it can change, because it is a hierarchy made up of subcomponents that also have limited room for change, because they themselves are made of further subcomponents. Thus the chance of a mouse evolving into a human is vanishingly small. It would require not only the right sequence of selection pressures, but also the right array of genetic variants and, just as important, the right conditions for driving viable and functional structural change. In the past 500 million years, few new structural types have appeared, and more than 99.9% of all evolutionary lines have become extinct. They were too complicated to change suddenly in response to new demands in the environment. Thus the probability that any present-day life form should exist is extraordinarily low, but it obviously is greater than zero!

The fossil record appears to have major gaps and does not document intermediate forms in the transitions between major groups. "Punctuated equilibrium" theorists believe that the transitions do not appear because they are essentially instantaneous on an evolutionary time scale. They grant the importance of genetic mechanisms, selection, and adaptation as part of the evolutionary process, but they also believe that

Most adaptations are compromises— not optimal solutions but practical, satisfactory ones.

speciation and the maintenance of species once they are formed also involve evolutionary processes acting at a higher level than individual organisms. Neo-Darwinians disagree. They maintain that gaps in the fossil record still cover periods of time sufficient for major changes and formation of new species to occur. Recent studies have shown that changes leading to new species can involve only a few genes and can occur over a relatively small number of generations.

Classical descriptions of evolution contain such phrases as "evolutionary drive" and "evolutionary progress," which imply an inevitable march toward more complicated forms. More recent studies on the complexity of shape—for example, how mollusk shells or mammalian backbones change over periods of millions of years—suggest, rather, that evolution drifts randomly toward both more and less complexity. With increasing time, this drift causes more complicated forms to appear. At the same time, however, some complicated forms become simpler.

Biological diversity

Biological reality isn't one story line; it is a cacophony of many stories all jumbled together, and there are many possible histories. In an explosion of biological diversity that occurred about 550–570 million years ago, during the Cambrian period, 20 fundamentally different groups of animals appeared. Some have body plans that look different from the forms we know today. It was during this period that complex nervous systems arose, supported by a modular method of construction that employed complicated gene circuits. No new phyla have appeared in the half-billion years since this Cambrian radiation produced the basic set of body plans present today in vertebrates and invertebrates, but each of these body plans has produced an enormous range of variations.

If we had been present 600 million years ago, before the Cambrian explosion, could we have predicted the present diversity of species on this planet? Certainly not. There are too many other scenarios that might have unfolded. We know that sudden changes in patterns of species have been caused by unpredictable geological upheavals such as volcanic action, continental drift, meteor impacts, and climate changes. The survival of our vertebrate predecessors was just one of several possible histories. The appearance of modern humans like ourselves could have been the result of accident or luck that distinguished our line from the many competing *hominid* lines that existed 500,000 years ago. It also might have been the result of adaptations, such as improved communication or language, that permitted our species to outcompete other hominids for limited resources. We simply don't know which alternative, or what mixture of the two, accounts for our emergence.

Survival of the luckiest, as well as survival of the fittest, may have been a factor in the appearance of modern humans.

Origins of minds, perceptions, and affect

The complicated architectures of animals evolved for the same reason that chemotaxis first appeared: to help animals ensure a future for themselves. The purpose of these systems is to generate behaviors that lead to survival and reproduction. Our brains evolved mainly to keep us out of trouble, not to think about themselves. Most of what they do is housekeeping: regulating blood pressure, body temperature, hunger, thirst, digestion, sexual drive, and so on. The brain is an organ, like a kidney or a liver, that plays a specialized role in putting together our complicated machinery and keeping it in one piece. At what point can these nervous systems or brains be said to involve mind, consciousness, or feelings of the sort discussed in Chapter 1? We can approach this question by offering an account of how new functions appeared over time.

The simplest form of mind

In the simplest behavior systems, such as chemotaxis or the reflex arc, a stimulus represents an action. Sensing, whether at the point of stimulation or more centrally in the brain, has little meaning apart from action. An itch is something you scratch, frequently without even thinking about it. In multicellular animals, a stimulus might not only elicit a local reaction but also be relayed to other parts of the body, allowing more complex approach or avoidance movements. In time, animals became more sophisticated, and the sensory side was partially decoupled from the response side. A central site evolved where the action pattern could be held back, in the form of some kind of representation, before being put into effect. (Thus we can suppress an urge to scratch an itch.) This holding, or representational, facility is nervous tissue.

At what point do we say that *mind* appeared? The definition of mind offered in Chapter 1, mainly in the context of thinking about ourselves, is a global one that offers little guidance on this question. Does a simple stimulus-response system like a bacterium performing chemotaxis have a mind? Does a mechanical thermostat containing a bimetallic element that bends with temperature to activate a switch have a mind?

One approach to answering these questions has been to attribute minds to animals when they first became capable of storing—and possibly recalling and reworking—action-based representation of the effects of environmental stimulation on their own bodies (see Figure 2–9). This function is localized in a ganglion or brain in higher animals. Thus the "center of gravity" of mind is the brain, both in humans and in simple invertebrates, but the brain's activities have little meaning outside of its embodied context.

With the appearance of a central holding facility, then, sensations can register in some part of the brain without automatically triggering action of the body surface; hence the action can be confined to the brain. It is known that the sensory cortex feeds back on incoming sensory nerves, so an initial stimulus might set up a self-propagating loop. Such a circuit presents us with a possible origin of *affect*, or emotions. Perhaps to like a stimulus is to respond to it in such a way as to keep up or increase the stimulation, and to dislike it is to respond in such a way as to keep down or reduce it. We can next imagine a multiplication of the circuits for holding *representations* of sensing and acting and the appearance of superimposed machinery to choose the representations that are most appropriate.

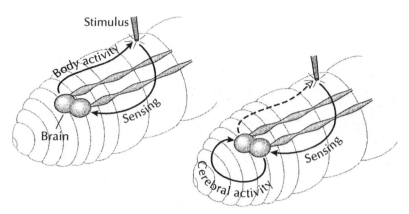

Figure 2–9   Some have suggested that animal minds originate in the transition from an automatic linking of sensations at the body surface and responding actions (left) to the ability to hold patterns of sensation or action in the brain (right).

Consciousness and the evolution of sensory organs

This brings us to the question of when consciousness appeared, particularly the simpler kinds of conscious awareness mentioned in Chapter 1, such as having sensations. The psychologist Nicholas Humphrey suggests that this kind of awareness might correspond to the activity of recurrent feedback loops that can create an extended present outside of physical time. This kind of consciousness can be set apart from the whole range of higher mental functions (perceptions, images, thought, beliefs, and so on). In this view, to be conscious is to have sensations, affect-laden mental representations of something happening to us here and now. Sensations occur in the province of one of the five external senses (sight, sound, touch, smell, and taste) or in the monitoring of our internal bodily states. All other mental activities are outside of consciousness, unfelt and not present to the mind, unless they are accompanied by reminders of sensation, as happens in the case of mental imagery or dreams. This is no less true of conscious thoughts, ideas, and beliefs. Narrative conscious thoughts are typically "heard" as images of voices in the head—and without this recollection of their sensory component, they would drop away.

We make a fundamental distinction between our internal sensations or subjective experiences of "What is happening to me?" and our perceptions or analysis of "What is happening out there?" How might we account for the appearance of this distinction during evolution? How did the signals from sensory organs come to be interpreted as signs of something in the external world? A reasonable hypothesis is that two distinct kinds of mental representations developed in simple nervous systems. One eventually led to subjective feelings and first-person knowledge of the self, the other to the objects of cognition and objective knowledge of the external physical world. The evolution of these dual modes of representation might go a long way toward explaining why we now have an apparent standoff between two classes of phenomena: subjective feelings and the phenomena of the material world.

The evolution of image-forming eyes that has led to our human visual systems is only one of many examples of the development of a distinction between sensation and perception (see Figure 2–10). We can think of the origin of vision in primitive, single-cell organisms as the "taste" or "touch" of light. Molecules in the cell membrane that

More complicated nervous systems began to make a distinction between internal sensation (What is happening to me?) and perception (What is happening out there?).

evolved for reacting to chemical attractants and repellents were further modified to become light-sensitive. This allowed organisms to distinguish "good" from "bad" levels of light. These molecules collected in cells that eventually became the *photoreceptor cells* (*rods* and *cones*) of our own eyes. These photoreceptors (indicated schematically as the vertical bars in Figure 2–10) next clustered together in eyespots sensitive to sudden changes in illumination that might indicate the presence of a predator. The beginnings of a genuine eye came when a patch of photoreceptors was transformed into a cup or depression in the membrane. The edge of the cup cast a shadow when light came from an oblique direction, thus causing a gradient of illumination across the inside of the cup. When the cup was further transformed into a spherical cavity with a narrow aperture at the surface, a pinhole camera was invented. Now the direction of the light was precisely correlated with the position of the image. It was only a small further step to fill in the pinhole with a translucent droplet, producing a full-blown camera with lens. In modern invertebrate and vertebrate eyes, a layer of receptor cells at the back of this camera can report a full image of the external world as signals to the brain.

This sequence provides an illustration of the process of adaptation mentioned earlier in this chapter: A series of small, increasingly useful, or adaptive, changes eventually yields a complicated structure that one might think could have been crafted only by a master designer. Recent studies suggest that image-forming eyes have been independently invented between 40 and 60 times in various invertebrate groups, and the estimated time for the transition from a patch of light-sensitive skin to an eye is under 400,000 generations, a mere eye-blink in geological time!

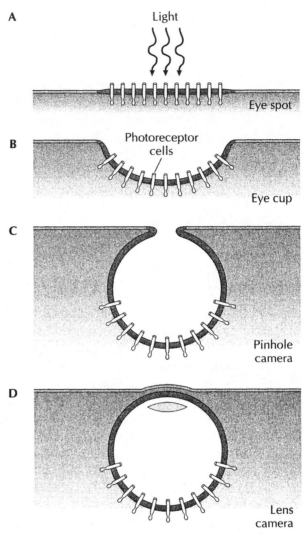

Figure 2–10   Evolution of the modern image-forming eye. Four stages in the transition from an eye spot to an image-forming lens camera are shown: (A) Eye spot (B) Eye cup (C) Pinhole camera (D) Lens camera.

Perceptions and new behaviors

The invention of the image-forming eye opened up a new world for more sophisticated perceptual analysis. Different objects at different distances cast different shapes on the retina, and stimulation by light of the "seeing skin" had become a source of information about the external world that could be stored by a brain or internal nervous system. By developing a separate channel for visual perception, alongside the already existing channel for visual sensation, animals could take advantage of the defining properties of light (What is happening out there?), while retaining interest in light as an intimate event affecting their own bodies (What is happening to me?).

The option of holding sensations in mind, as well as developing interpretative perceptions of what is happening in the external world, creates a variety of new options for behavior. An early step toward increasing subtlety would be to not just react to the immediate environment, as sensed by touch or taste, but also to develop short-range anticipation over a period of seconds—like the ability to avoid some quickly appearing threat. Humans and very simple invertebrates have circuits, whose hardwiring has been refined over millions of years, for getting out of the way without thinking about it if something suddenly looms and grows larger in our fields of vision.

Our response to light still can contain an affective, or subjective, component. Red light, for example, can sometimes induce physiological symptoms of arousal: Blood pressure rises, and breathing and heart rate speed up. Blue light has the opposite effect. These responses are innate; a 15-day-old human infant is more readily quieted by blue light than by red. Numerous psychological studies show that blue and green reinforce calm, whereas red and yellow can cause agitation. Monkeys show the same affective responses to colored light. On a longer time scale, seasonal affective disorder in humans seems to be caused in part by the lowering of ambient light levels that naturally occurs during the winter months.

Brains evolved to react to features in the environment that were salient to survival and reproduction. Our visual systems, like those of virtually all vertebrates, are most sensitive to patterns with a vertical axis of symmetry, the sort provided by the bodies of other animals. Being informed that other animals are looking at you is frequently important and is often followed by some sort of orienting response: Are you looking at your supper, or are they looking at theirs? A hierarchy of hardwired detectors go into action evaluating "friend, foe, food, or prospective mate." Regions of our brain respond to faces and to whether their attention is directed toward or away from us. One speculation is that orienting responses that began as reactions to alarm signals proved so useful in provoking a generalized update that animals began to go into the orienting mode more and more frequently.

This intermittent regular vigilance may have gradually turned into regular exploration, and a new behavioral strategy began to evolve: the strategy of recruiting information for its own sake in case it might prove useful. If you have ever watched a cat explore, you know that some mammals are hungry for information about the environment. Primates carry this to an extreme. Why did rationality or behaviors arising through learning and intelligence evolve at all? Probably because performing complicated tasks through thought and memory is a more effective and flexible use of our machinery. By generating complex internal models of the world and what to expect in it, we improve considerably on the repertoire that purely instinctive behaviors would permit.

SUMMARY   Starting with the simplest kinds of self-replicating entities that we now call cells, we find, several billion years later, a planet whose dominant species is a two-legged animal with a brain that thinks and enables the animal to write about it all. We picture throughout these eons, the relentless cranking of a universal Darwin Machine. Its cycles—of generating entities, testing them, and preferentially replicating those that happen to work a little bit better—underlie not only biological evolution but also, as we will see in later chapters, many aspects of organismal development and behavior. The Darwin Machine, however, is not the only engine of evolutionary change, and an expanded list must include factors such as accident, serendipity, and dumb luck. The origin of our own nervous systems lies in the signaling molecules that free-living single cells seized on to communicate with each other and then retained when they clumped together to become multicellular organisms. In the form of hormones and neurotransmitters, these molecules are intermediaries in organizing the array of electrical nerve signals that are the currency of our mental life.

In even the simplest animals, the vast majority of neurons are not cells that directly sense the environment or command an action on it. Rather, they are the cells called interneurons that intervene, making it possible for the organism to "think about" or hold information, so that sensing and acting can be coupled in less automatic and more varied ways. These cells cluster along a central nerve cord that runs the length of the body, and they also form the brain. More complicated nervous systems began to make a distinction between sensation (What is happening to me?) and perception (What is happening out there?). Varied sensory structures evolved, such as the image-forming eye, along with brains that could interpret sensory input to make a representation of what is happening in the external world. Brain regions appeared that were predisposed to respond to features of the environment crucial to survival and reproduction, such as suddenly appearing objects or faces. In the next chapter, we will consider more specifically the structures of vertebrate brains and nervous systems, designs laid down 400–500 million years ago. ∎

1. If you had just 5 minutes to summarize the theory of evolution for a friend, what would you say?

2. This chapter gave an account of how our image-forming eyes might have evolved in a series of very small steps, each step being a change that conferred on the organism some benefit that might render it slightly better at making copies of itself. Can you think of an analogous series of steps that might have led to other complicated structures in our bodies?

3. Some schools require that a religious account of human origins be given as much time and credibility as are accorded to the description offered by evolutionary theory. Do you think that such a position can be defended on rational or scientific, rather than religious, grounds? Why or why not?

4. Some scientists believe strongly that humans are the most advanced animal ever to have appeared on this planet and that our presence was foreordained—an inevitable consequence of evolutionary progress. Do you agree or disagree with these views? Why?

Suggestions for further general reading

Dawkins, R. 1996. *Climbing Mount Improbable.* New York: Norton. (This is an engaging account of evolutionary processes. Chapter 5 describes the evolution of image-forming eyes.)

Dennett, D.C. 1995. *Darwin's Dangerous Idea: Evolution and the Meanings of Life.* New York: Simon & Schuster. (This book describes the adaptationist point of view and provides a summary of the debate on mechanisms of evolutionary change.)

Humphrey, N. 1992. *A History of the Mind.* New York: Simon & Schuster. (Speculations in this chapter about the origins of sensation and perception, and about the increasing complexity of nervous systems, are largely taken from this book and from the Dennett (1991) book cited in Chapter 1.)

Reading on more advanced or specialized topics

Gerhart, J., & Kirschner, M. 1997. *Cells, Embryos, and Evolution.* Cambridge, MA: Blackwell Science. (This is an informative review of genes, development, and the evolution of animal forms.)

Keller, E.F., & Lloyd, E.A. 1992. *Keywords in Evolutionary Biology.* Cambridge, MA: Harvard University Press. (This volume provides a series of essays on the key ideas in evolutionary biology and the words used to describe them.)

Price, P.W. 1996. *Biological Evolution.* Orlando, FL: Saunders College Publishing. (This volume is a college text that provides a historical view of studies on evolution since Darwin's time.)

Chapter 3

Structures of Mind

In Chapter 2 we traced the story of nervous system evolution as far as the appearance of vertebrates and invertebrates and also covered some ideas in evolutionary biology. In this chapter we move on to deal with the evolution and structures of vertebrate nervous systems and brains, and we begin to discuss how to study the functions of the brain. Some of the material on brain structures and functions may strike you as being a digression from our emphasis on evolution, but it is only a temporary one, necessary for continuing to tell our evolutionary story in subsequent chapters.

Origins and structures of the vertebrate nervous system

Vertebrates and their nervous systems appeared 400–500 million years ago. The human nervous system, like that of fish, amphibians, and reptiles, has two major subdivisions. The *central nervous system* (CNS) includes the brain and spinal cord; the *peripheral nervous system* (PNS) is everything else (see Figure 3–1). Input occurs both at the periphery, as with touch receptors in our fingers, and at the level of the brain. The retinas in our eyes are parts of the brain. Output can involve moving a peripheral limb, but it also might consist of regulating the diameter of a blood vessel inside the brain. The sensory branch of the PNS deals with stimuli that impinge on our skin, as well as internal visceral stimuli such as those associated with digestion, excretion, and other regulatory functions. The motor portion of the PNS is conventionally divided into

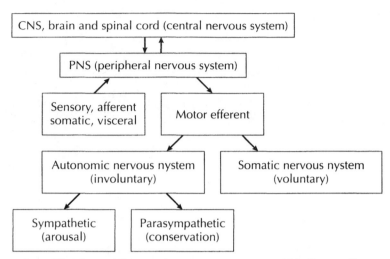

Figure 3–1 Divisions of the vertebrate nervous system. This figure offers an oversimplified description of the major divisions of the vertebrate nervous system. The first distinction is between brain and spinal cord (the central nervous system, or CNS) and any other parts of the nervous system that are peripheral to these structures (the peripheral nervous system, or PNS). The PNS then consists of a sensory branch (information coming into the CNS) and a motor branch (information leaving the CNS to regulate muscle movements). The further divisions of the motor portion of the PNS that are shown are described in the text.

a voluntary or *somatic nervous system*, which regulates movements of striated muscles of torso and limbs; and an involuntary or *autonomic nervous system*, which is concerned with involuntary functions such as digestion and blood pressure regulation.

The autonomic nervous system becomes increasingly complex in the transition from lower to higher vertebrates, mirroring the increased sophistication of behaviors associated with the four basic F's (fighting, fleeing, feeding, and fornicating). It comprises two sets of motor systems that act on our body organs with opposing effects. Activation of the *sympathetic nervous system* correlates with arousal and energy generation: The heart beats faster, the liver converts glycogen to glucose, bronchi of the lung are dilated for greater oxygen transfer capacity, digestion is inhibited, and secretion of *adrenaline* from the adrenal medulla is stimulated. Activity of the *parasympathetic system* is approximately the mirror image of this: a calming and a return to emphasis on vegetative, self-maintenance functions. The heart rate decreases and energy storage and digestion are enhanced.

The activities of our sympathetic and parasympathetic nervous systems correlate with our two major areas of activity: engagement and arousal versus rest and rebuilding of resources.

We also have a secondary brain in our bodies: the gut brain or enteric nervous system. It has an ancient origin, for the first nervous systems occurred in tubular animals that sat on rocks and waited for food to pass by. As more complex brains and central nervous systems evolved for finding food and sex, the gut's nervous system stayed where it acted, rather than moving to the newer central structures. This is the "brain" that gives us butterflies in our stomachs when we are about to go on stage. When the central nervous system gets anxious, the enteric brain mirrors this agitation. The enteric brain forms independently of our central nervous system during our early embryonic development and only later becomes connected to the brain proper via a cable, the *vagus nerve*.

Layers of the brain

The deepest structure of the vertebrate brain, which evolved over 500 million years ago, is the enlargement of the top of the spinal cord that consists of the *hindbrain,* which generates the *medulla, pons,* and *cerebellum,* and the *midbrain,* which forms the *tectum* (see Figure 3–2). This part of the brain handles breathing, heart rate, and other basic bodily functions necessary for survival. It also regulates general levels of alertness and monitors important environmental information such as the presence of food, predators, or a potential mate. We share with primitive vertebrates a so-called "little brain," or cerebellum, which attaches to the rear of the hindbrain and is important in coordinating movement and memories for learned responses. In our brains it also participates in some of the higher cognitive functions. Like our cerebral cortex and many other structures in the brain, it is bilateral, having a left and a right lobe. Finally, the forward portion of the brain, the *forebrain,* consisting of the *thalamus, hypothalamus,* and *cortex,* is much smaller in fish and reptiles than it is in higher vertebrates.

The tiny hypothalamus serves as the Health Maintenance Organization of the body, regulating its *homeostasis,* or stable state of equilibrium. The hypothalamus also generates behaviors involved in eating, drinking, general arousal, rage, aggression, embarrassment, escape from danger, pleasure, and copulation. It does an amazing number of housekeeping chores for such a small piece of tissue. Its lateral and anterior parts seem to support activation of the parasympathetic nervous system: drop in blood pressure; slowing of pulse; and regulation of digestion, defecation, assimilation, and reproduction in such a way as to contribute on the whole to rest and recovery. The medial and posterior hypothalamus regulate activation: acceleration of pulse and breathing

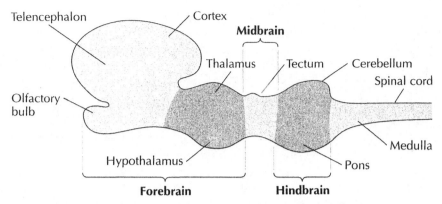

Figure 3–2   Major divisions of the vertebrate brain. The hindbrain comprises the medulla (which contains centers that regulate several autonomic visceral functions such as breathing, heart and blood vessel activity, swallowing, vomiting, and digestion), the pons (which also participates in some of these activities), and the cerebellum. All of the sensory and motor information that is communicated between brain and body passes through the medulla and pons. The cerebellum plays a central role in sensing and regulating movement and posture. The midbrain has centers for receiving and processing sensory information, particularly auditory and visual information, and is important in regulating states of arousal. The forebrain consists of the *diencephalon* (which contains the thalamus and hypothalamus) and the *telencephalon*. The thalamus controls access to the cerebral cortex, and the hypothalamus performs regulatory functions described in the text. The bottom portion of the telencephalon forms the *olfactory cortex*, the *hippocampus*, the *amygdala*, and other components of the limbic system. In mammals the top of the telencephalon forms the "new cortex," or *neocortex*.

rates, high blood pressure, arousal, fear, and anger. Stimulation of specific groups of cells in these areas can elicit pure behaviors. For example, rats placed in an experimental situation where they can press a lever to stimulate a pleasure center will do so to the exclusion of eating and drinking. Stimulation of another area can produce rage.

We can be described, to use a model proposed by the neuroanatomist Paul MacLean, as having a three-part brain, or *triune brain*, consisting of a reptilian *brainstem* core, an old mammalian brain called the *limbic system*, and the neocortex. Figure 3–3 shows MacLean's symbolic representation of the model, and Figure 3–6 (see next section) indicates how the inner limbic portions of the cortex are overlaid by the external neocortex. The limbic system appeared between 200 and 300 million years ago and was initially dominated by smell input. Corresponding structures are found in reptiles and birds. One compo-

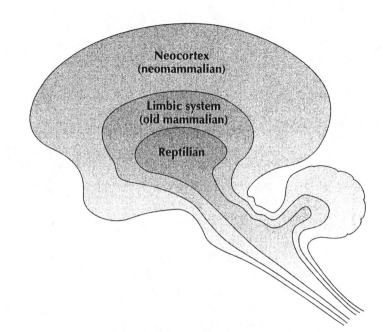

Figure 3–3 The model of the triune brain proposed by Paul McLean, indicating brain areas added during vertebrate evolution. The reptilian brain is the main seat of innate or instinctive behaviors regulating primitive survival issues. The old mammalian brain, or the limbic system, expresses innate motivational value systems that interact with the newer cortex, or neocortex, which manages propositional information and declarative knowledge about the world.

nent of the limbic system, the hippocampus, plays a key role in storing memories. Another, the amygdala, mediates emotional reactions relevant to survival.

The triune brain model suggests that we think of ourselves as having a hierarchy of three brains in one. These can act semi-independently but still are interconnected and functionally dependent on each other. During evolution, the newer structures have both encapsulated the older ones and led to their alterations. At the core is a reptilian brainstem, the reticular formation, and striate cortex. It is the seat of basic survival behavior patterns of the species that have strong genetic specifications. This is the brain that is crucial in basic hunting, feeding, and reproductive behaviors. This deep structure in our brains is analogous to the major portion of a reptile's brain, and it roughly resembles that of a 45-day-old human embryo, before the development of higher structures. A second system,

Our brain is constructed of layers that reflect stages in our evolutionary history.

the old mammalian brain, or the limbic system, is the seat of motives and emotions and is capable of responding to present information in the light of memories of past information. It is sometimes called the rhinencephalon to indicate that its regions evolved from structures previously associated with the sense of smell. (To be sure, many anatomists consider this model an oversimplification, perhaps even a misleading one, but its underlying evolutionary perspective is appropriate.)

In trying to understand a structure as complicated as the brain, scientists have attached names to portions that can be distinguished by position or shape and then have suggested functions for these named structures. Although it is hard to imagine proceeding in any other manner, this approach has been criticized as leading people to accept the structure-function assignments as established, when in fact they usually have been informed speculations. Emotions, for example, involve much more than the limbic system, and parts of the limbic system serve functions not related to affect, such as declarative memory. Thus it is important to be aware that terms like "limbic system" are in fact oversimplifications—broad anatomical names used to substitute for detailed physiological explanations. It is most useful to make reference to smaller functional neuronal groups whenever possible, further subdividing currently defined subregions of structures such as the amygdala, hippocampus, and other functional groups of cortical and visceral neurons.

The older core structures of the brain, such as the brainstem and limbic system, are somewhat analogous to a liver or a kidney in that they are organized less for thought than for automatic action, and for analysis that determines body temperature, blood flow, digestion, heartbeat, and every blink and swallow, as well as rapid emotional reactions. The hominid cortex sends cortical projections back down to these lower centers to generate more "top-down" regulation of pathways that in monkeys and lower mammals are relatively autonomous. Thus voluntary movements, especially of the hands, come under more cortical control.

Newer structures of the brain encapsulate older ones. Their feedback to lower levels of the brain can modulate the way in which more ancient structures regulate homeostasis, emotions, and movement.

The cerebral cortex

In lower mammals the cerebral cortex that overlays the limbic system is a simple, smooth structure, but in the sequence rat → cat → monkey → human, it increasingly arches into a complex horseshoe shape as a temporal lobe emerges. This process is shown in Figure 3–4. (The

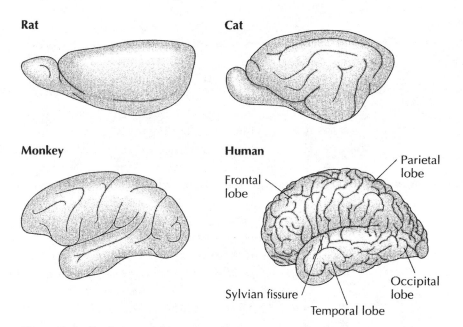

Figure 3–4 Evolution of the mammalian neocortex, illustrated by drawings of the brains of the rat, cat, monkey, and human. The most striking changes are the emergence of a temporal lobe, progressive infolding of the cortex that increases its surface area, and an increase in the size of the frontal lobe. The drawing of the human cortex shows the four major lobes of the brain, which are discussed in Figures 3–5 and 3–6.

newer cortex, or neocortex, in mammals is frequently referred to as the cerebral cortex, even though, properly speaking, the cerebral cortex also contains older, deep-lying structures such as the limbic system.) The rat neocortex is largely devoted to primary visual, auditory, and sensorimotor activities. More complicated brains, as in the cat, introduce more *crenulations*, or infoldings of the cortex, and association areas appear that deal with several sensory modalities rather than just one. Crenulations increase the brain's surface area enormously; the effect is rather like that of crumpling a piece of paper into a ball so that it can fit in a small space. Our human cortex, which is deeply furrowed, carries this to an extreme. Increasing complexity of the cortex seems to correlate with the development of social interactions within mammalian species, where a need arises to assess the probable reactions of others to close approach, to compete for food or mates, to distinguish among individuals, and perhaps remember who is reliable and who is not. Even though our brains are vastly more complex than rat brains, the myriad anatomical subdivisions in brainstem, midbrain, and forebrain are similar.

Figures 3–5 and 3–6 illustrate the four major divisions, or lobes, found in each hemisphere of our cerebral cortex: the frontal, temporal, occipital, and parietal lobes. The *frontal lobe* is concerned with our working memory, planning for future action, and control of movement. The *temporal lobe*, the horseshoe bend that points forward, deals with hearing as well as aspects of learning, memory, and emotion. The rear portion of the cortex, which consists of the *occipital lobe*, deals with vision, and the *parietal lobe* in the middle plays a role in somatic sensation, body image, and analysis of spatial relationships.

The cortex is an extensively folded sheet of nerve cell bodies and their connections that is only about ⅛ inch thick. The crests of the foldings are called gyri (*gyrus*, singular); the grooves are called sulci (*sulcus*, singular) or fissures. In the human brain, primary motor, somatic sensory, visual, and auditory cortexes take up only a relatively small area, as shown in Figure 3–5; the remainder is association cortex (see the

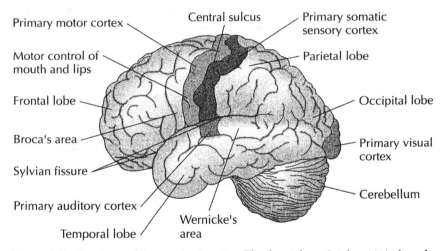

Figure 3–5   Regions of the cerebral cortex. The frontal, parietal, occipital, and temporal lobes are shown. Primary areas involved with just one modality (such as vision, hearing, sensing the body, or moving the body) are shaded. The rest of the cortex, the *association cortex*, integrates different functions. Also shown are two important functional areas that we use for understanding and generating speech: *Broca's area*, near the *primary motor cortex*, which controls the mouth and lips, is required for speaking; and *Wernicke's area*, near the *primary auditory cortex*, is involved in comprehending spoken words.

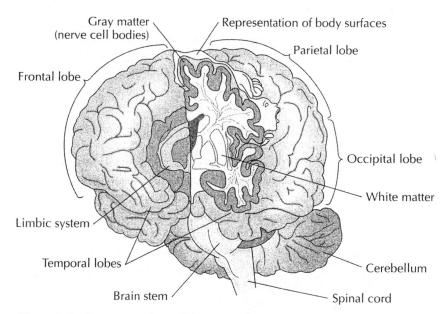

Figure 3–6 A cutaway view of the cerebral cortex shown in Figure 3–5, with the extent of the frontal, parietal, and occipital lobes indicated by brackets. A portion of the left hemisphere in front of the central sulcus has been cut away to show what the interior looks like. The drawing of the little homunculus, or person, along this cut indicates how regions of the body are represented along the surface of the cortex. The neocortex lies on top of the old mammalian brain, the limbic system, and brainstem. The internal part of the cutaway reveals the *white matter.* Its color derives from the fatty insulating myelin sheaths that cover masses of axons going to and from the cortex and connecting different parts of the cortex. These axons connect to the gray-appearing neurons of the cerebral cortex, or *gray matter.*

"Association of functions with different brain regions" section below). The *parietal-temporal-occipital association cortex* located at the junction of these lobes integrates somatosensory, visual, and auditory input and is involved in language. The *limbic association cortex*, comprising adjacent parts of the frontal and temporal lobes, is important in emotion and memory. The *prefrontal association cortex* is required for cognitive behavior and motor planning. It is apparently a locus of *working memory*—the temporary storage of information used to guide a future action. In all mammalian brains, the cortex contains four major connectional clusters formed by visual, auditory, somato-motor, and frontal-limbic

> *Different areas of the brain may specialize in one kind of activity, but they never work alone. Generating behavior requires the collaboration of many different centers; function is spread throughout the brain.*

areas. Each of the sensory systems is hierarchically organized, with a primary sensory area sending information on to higher stations more closely associated with the frontal-limbic complex.

The cerebral cortex is divided into two hemispheres, each of which is responsible for the opposite half of the body. The left hemisphere receives information from, and controls the movement of, the right side of the body, and vice versa. The two hemispheres communicate with each other via a band of nerve fibers called the *corpus callosum.* In the central top third of each of our cerebral hemispheres, the *central sulcus* separates a precentral gyrus concerned with motor function—the primary motor cortex—from a postcentral somatosensory gyrus that deals with sensing our body surfaces—the *primary somatic sensory cortex.* The central sulcus divides our "past" from our "future" in that posterior sensory areas are registering events that have occurred, whereas activity in anterior motor areas corresponds to responses that are about to occur.

Several structures shown in Figure 3–6 contain maps of our body surfaces or of our visual world. (These structures are central to the discussion of brain plasticity in Chapter 6.) A map of the opposite side of the body is represented along the cortical folds of both the precentral and postcentral gyri in each hemisphere. This map of the body surface, which is usually referred to as a somatotopic map, spans from head to foot and is shown in Figure 3–6. We know exactly where to insert an electrode in the left precentral gyrus to command a particular finger of the right hand to move, and we know where in the right postcentral gyrus to record the sensory response to scratching a finger of the left hand. Moving toward the rear of the cortex, we find that another kind of map, a *topographical map,* or representation of the external visual world, is plotted along the folds of the *primary visual cortex* occupying the rearmost portion of the occipital lobe. In this case we know, for example, exactly where to place an electrode to record the response to a small object in any portion of our visual field. This visual map is duplicated many times across the brain, and over 30 distinct areas deal with aspects of visual processing. We are very visual animals, and more than half the cells in our brains process visual information.

As you can see by now, brain anatomy is fiendishly complicated. It used to be said that it takes about 10 years of study for a bright and eager young person to learn what is known about the development and position of the various brain nuclei (here a *nucleus* is a clearly distinguishable mass of nerve cells). This rule of thumb no longer applies,

SELF-EXPERIMENT

In our brains, as in those of all vertebrates, the two sides of the body are sensed and controlled separately. The right side of the cortex moves and senses the left side of the body, and vice versa. You can gain some appreciation of your own bilateral nature by performing a very simple exercise on yourself. Close your eyes and for several minutes pay attention just to relaxing the left side of your face, especially the muscles around your left eye. Please do this before reading further! Now, note the rest of your left side. Does it feel more relaxed also? If so, it is probably because changes in the face region of the right precentral and postcentral gyri spread to include the brain regions that represent the rest of the left side of the body. Now compare your left and right sides. I suspect that you will notice a clear difference, the left being more relaxed than the right. Changes in muscle tone tend to spread along one side of the body, but not necessarily to the other side. Later, you might like to see whether this exercise works the same way when you start with the right side of your face.

because new information is accumulating at such a rate that any normal human who tries to keep up with it will merely fall farther and farther behind. Furthermore, it is easy to put considerable effort into learning some finer details of brain anatomy—and then discover that you have forgotten them within a few months unless you use them constantly. Rather than trying to keep it all in our heads, we now go look it up in brain anatomy databases on the Internet. In this book, we will mostly avoid the problem of knowing and naming structures. Apart from naming major landmarks, we will not delve into anatomical detail.

Modern studies of brain function

The brief introduction to brain anatomy that we have just offered permits us now to begin discussing how brain function is studied, a topic that will engage us in subsequent chapters of this book. Modern studies on brain function began in the 19th century against the backdrop of the phrenology fad, which purported to map different areas on the head and brain the phrenologists supposed were responsible for complex human traits such as spirituality, hope, firmness, destructiveness, and the like (see Figure 3–7). Phrenology was discredited toward the end of the century, when observations on animals and humans with brain damage revealed the association of more elemental functions with specific areas of the cerebral cortex. In 1861, Broca described patients who could understand language but could not

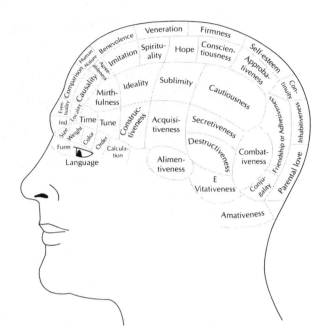

Figure 3–7   The 19th-century phrenologists thought that different contours on a person's head, such as bumps and dips, were related to different personality traits. Although phrenology was shown to warrant little credence, it spawned the view that different parts of the brain may be responsible for different functions and actions. This view is central to our efforts today to discover how the different parts of the brain control different aspects of our lives.

speak, even though they sometimes could utter isolated words or sing a melody. They were found, on postmortem examination, to have a lesion in posterior regions of the frontal lobes of their left hemispheres, now called Broca's area (see Figure 3–5).

In 1876, Wernicke reported a new kind of *aphasia*, or loss of the power to use or comprehend words, that involved language comprehension rather than execution. Patients could speak, but they could not understand. The cortical lesion responsible was located on a posterior part of the temporal lobe now called *Wernicke's area* (see Figure 3–5). Wernicke proposed that Broca's area controls the motor programs for coordinating speech, for it is located just in front of motor areas that control the mouth, tongue, and vocal cords. Wernicke's area is related to word perception, the sensory component of language. It is located near the auditory cortex and near the association cortex that integrates auditory, visual, and somatic sensation into complex perceptions. Wernicke predicted that a further type of aphasia would arise if the communication between the two areas was compromised. This is indeed found in *conduction aphasia,* which is characterized by an incorrect use of words, termed *paraphasia.* Patients with conduction aphasia have lesions in the fiber pathways that connect Broca's and Wernicke's areas. They can understand words that are heard and seen but cannot repeat simple phrases. They omit parts of words, substitute incorrect words, jumble grammar and syntax, and are painfully aware of their own errors.

In Germany in 1870, Fritsch and Hitzig showed that characteristic movements of the limbs can be produced in dogs by electrically stimu-

Studies in the 19th century on patients with brain lesions led to the identification of areas that are important in the comprehension and generation of speech.

lating certain regions of the brain. This sort of work was refined in this country, in the 1930s, by Woolsey and Rose. They surveyed a large number of different mammalian and marsupial brains to show that tactile stimuli elicit responses from discrete regions of the cerebral cortex—fields of cells that could be defined unambiguously. In the 1950s, Wilder Penfield used small electrodes to stimulate the cortex of awake patients during brain surgery, carried out under local anesthesia, for epilepsy. He tested specifically for areas that produce disorders of language to ensure that the surgery would not damage the patient's communication skills. He confirmed from patients' own reports the localizations assigned by Broca's and Wernicke's studies. He also mapped areas associated with specific sensory modalities and areas the stimulation of which elicited specific strong memories.

In studying human brains, we have the considerable advantage that humans can verbally report on what they are doing, whereas monkeys, cats, and rats cannot. Animal studies are not useless, however, for if we compare the detailed anatomy of a rat's brain with ours, we find that over 90% of the same basic groups or clusters of nerve cells are present in both, even though their shapes and sizes can be quite different. We can use indirect tricks to show that these clusters appear to serve roughly corresponding functions—for example, that working memory is located in the frontal lobes, and that spatial visual representations require the right parietal lobe. Although areas that represent functions such as these can always be found in our brains, the variation among different humans is much larger than is usually realized. The area occupied by primary visual cortex in some individuals can be double or half the average. The elements of the motor strip aren't always in the same order, and patches of sensory cortex are sometimes found in front of the motor strip. This variation can blur our sense of the overall average organization, but the point is that if we could map one individual brain in some detail, we might get the impression of considerable specialization, each little patch of cortex doing a somewhat different job. Such specialization has been found during neurosurgery and by imaging the activity of living brains.

Association of functions with different brain regions

Early mapping studies were most effective in identifying areas that are the early recipients of sensory information or the final direct generators of action. They didn't reveal much about the sophisticated thinking and processing carried out by the various association areas we have mentioned. Clues to what each of the areas might be doing have come from studies on people in whom physical trauma, strokes, or cancer have caused damage confined to a specific region. Such clues have to be interpreted with some caution, because the effects of brain lesions often are not simple. For example, we cannot conclude from a brain lesion that alters a particular behavior that the region the lesion affects is the sole generator of that behavior. The region might be an essential processing subsystem or might regulate connections among subsystems. It might reduce overall activation or lead to compensatory changes. Given these caveats, it is gratifying that many conclusions about the functions of different brain areas based on lesion studies have now been confirmed by direct imaging of our living brains (this is described in the section "Imaging the Activity of the Brain").

Let's begin with the frontal lobe, where injury can cause a variety of both obvious and subtle defects. Damage to its rear portion along the central sulcus, the primary motor cortex, can cause weakness or paralysis of specific body parts (see Figures 3–5 and 3–6). The *premotor cortex* in front of the motor strip has several maps of the body surface. The lateral portion just in front of the motor strip's area for mouth and face is Broca's area, where lesions impair speech generation. Premotor areas, sometimes called *supplementary motor areas*, interact with numerous other brain regions to plan sequences of actions, as in linking movements together. Musicians and athletes couldn't do without them. If you imagine making a movement but don't actually move, the premotor cortex works a lot harder than the rest of the brain. If you actually move, the motor strip also becomes active. Patients who have had strokes that injured the supplementary motor cortex usually have trouble with skilled movements such as speech and gestures. They might be able to perform each action of a sequence separately, but they still have trouble chaining the actions together into a fluent motion. A

When we remove a resistor from a radio, a howling sound may result, but this does not prove that the resistor served the function of being a howl suppressor. Similarly, loss of a behavior by lesion to a brain region does not prove that this region is the sole generator of the behavior.

common neurological test is to ask patients to tap their fingers rapidly and then change rhythm, or to draw a pattern and then switch to drawing a different pattern. Sometimes patients with premotor problems cannot easily change from one rhythm to another or switch from drawing one pattern to the next.

The prefrontal cortex is almost everything in front of the premotor cortex and motor strip. Distractibility and confabulation are the foremost signs of injury here. For example, a patient might set out to say something or do something and get easily distracted into saying or doing something else. *Confabulations,* a term used in this context to mean spurious comments or explanations, occur mainly with injuries to the frontal lobe's inside surfaces, not with injuries to the side or top. Prefrontal functions include strategy and evaluation, abstract and creative thinking, fluency of thought and language, volition and drive, selective attention, capacity for emotional attachments, and social judgment. Patients with prefrontal lesions sometimes get "stuck" in an ongoing strategy or sequence. Damage to the bottom surface of the frontal lobe causes storytelling that meanders or gets obsessive. These localizations of function are vague—not at all comparable, for example, to the predictable location of hand function in the middle of the motor strip.

The limbic association cortex is involved in emotion and memory. Lesions in the frontal lobe portion of the limbic association cortex, such as prefrontal lobotomy, have been used with psychotic patients to reduce affect and anxiety. This procedure, along with other forms of psychosurgery, has now been largely discontinued. Lesions in the temporal lobe portion of the association cortex impair the formation of long-term memory. Chapter 10 describes how the limbic association cortex plays a central role in integrating our rational and emotional minds.

The association areas of the parietal lobes are involved in attention to the spatial aspects of sensation and in the manipulation of objects in space. Different lesions cause many different striking deficits, including abnormalities in body image and perception of spatial relations. A partial list includes *agnosia,* the inability to perceive objects through otherwise normally functioning sensory channels; *optic ataxia,* a deficit in using visual guidance to grasp an object; *dysgraphia,* writing disability; and *dyscalculia,* the inability to carry out mathematical calculations, sometimes along with left-right confusion. Lesions of the nondominant (usually the right) parietal lobe can cause *anosognosia,* denial of a part of the body. Patients with this deficit fail to dress, undress, or wash the affected side, and they deny that the affected arm or leg belongs to them when the limb is passively brought into their field of vision. Such patients have lost a sense of self with respect to these parts of their bodies.

Specializations of the cerebral hemispheres

One of the most fascinating stories about association of separate functions with different brain areas comes from observations demonstrating that the two cerebral hemispheres have distinctive specializations. (Experiments showing that the two hemispheres can in some circumstances act as separate selves are described in Chapter 7.) The hemispheres are asymmetrical, the left slightly larger than the right in most humans. One means of revealing differences between the hemispheres has been to inject sodium amytal, a fast-acting barbiturate, into the left or right internal carotid artery. The drug is preferentially carried to the hemisphere on the same side as the injection and produces a brief period of dysfunction of that hemisphere. The effects of this procedure on language have revealed some relationships between handedness and speech functions. Nearly all right-handed, and most left-handed, people use the left hemisphere for speech, but 15% of the lefties have right-hemisphere speech, and some left-handed people (about 5%) have control of speech in both the right and left hemispheres. Sodium amytal tests have an interesting effect on mood. Left injection tends to produce brief depression, and right injection, euphoria. These effects occur at doses smaller than those needed to block speech. This observation suggests that functions related to mood may be lateralized, and further experiments have confirmed that this is so (see Chapter 10).

Many studies have now demonstrated functional specializations of the two hemispheres. The left hemisphere is most adept at language, math, logic operations, and the processing of serial sequences of information. It has a bias for the detailed, speed-optimized activities required for skeletal motor control and processing of fine visual details. The right hemisphere is stronger at pattern recognition, face recognition, spatial relations, nonverbal ideation, the stress and intonation component of language, and parallel processing of many kinds of information. It has a visceral motor bias and deals with large time domains. It appears to specialize in perception of the relationship between figures and the whole context in which they occur, whereas the left hemisphere is better at focused perception. While working with their hands, most right-handed people use the left hand (right hemisphere) for context or holding and use the right hand

A number of our faculties appear to be concentrated more in one hemisphere than in the other. The left hemisphere has a bias for focused and detailed, high-speed serial processing, whereas the right specializes in pattern recognition, nonverbal ideation, and parallel processing.

(left hemisphere) for fine detailed movement. Understanding and generating the stress and intonation patterns of speech that convey its emotional content is a right-hemisphere function, as is music. Several famous composers have had strokes in the left hemisphere that rendered them unable to speak, but they were still able to compose music. It is worth pointing out that cerebral asymmetry of cognitive abilities is not confined to humans but is observed in other mammals and also in birds.

Pop psychology in the 1970s carried the idea of cerebral specialization to such an extreme that one heard people referring to themselves as "left brain" or "right brain" thinkers, depending on whether they were more intellectual, rational, verbal, and analytical, or more emotional, artistic, nonverbal, and intuitive. It is curious that the latter group of people tend to sit on the right-hand side of classrooms, whereas the former sit on the left. The situation is not really so black and white, because it now is clear that in normal brains, interactions between the hemispheres are required for all major cognitive functions. There is much evidence that the capacity of one hemisphere to perform a particular task deteriorates when the corpus callosum connecting the two hemispheres is cut. Thus, even though lateral specializations are observed, full competence and expression of these specializations require crosstalk between the hemispheres and other parts of the brain. The fact that a particular brain region is required for an activity or competence does not mean that this region is the sole locus of that activity. It is more likely to be a necessary part of a larger chain of loci throughout the brain, all of which must cooperate.

Imaging the activity of the brain

Until recently, almost everything we knew about localization of language and other functions came from clinical studies of patients with brain lesions. Now, however, metabolically or electrically active regions of the normal living brain can be monitored with noninvasive procedures such as *positron emission tomography* (PET scanning), *magnetic resonance imaging* (MRI), and *electromagnetoencephalography* (MEG). These techniques all monitor some aspect of the metabolic changes that accompany nerve cell activity, and their variety and sophistication are increasing each year. As shown in Figure 3–8, activation of the visual cortex can be observed during the reading of words. Listening activates the temporal cortex. Broca's area and supplementary motor areas become more active during speaking. Thinking tasks recruit the inferior frontal cortex. Brain regions that become more active during

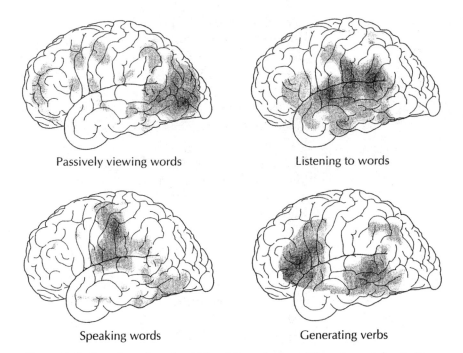

Passively viewing words

Listening to words

Speaking words

Generating verbs

Figure 3–8   Imaging of cerebral blood flow during different mental activities, shown by positron emission tomography (PET). Stippling indicates areas that become more active when the subject is viewing words, listening to words, speaking words, and generating a verb that indicates a use for a noun that is presented. (Adapted from Posner & Raichle, 1994.)

memory, perception, attention, orientation, emotions, and overall vigilance are being mapped. Imaging studies suggest that the cortex consists of many small "fields," cortical processing units between 600 and 3000 cubic millimeters in volume that contain approximately 4×10^7 neurons and 10^{12} synapses. There is great enthusiasm for the prospects of imaging studies, and popular magazines routinely print beautiful pictures of brain areas that light up during the performance of different activities. However, experts are questioning a number of assumptions and raising technical issues that make these studies less definitive than they may appear at first glance.

Later chapters in this book raise numerous questions for which imaging experiments provide an answer. For example, does a word that is read also have to have an auditory representation before it can be associated with a meaning, or can visual information be transferred directly to Broca's area? The latter is the case. Wernicke's area becomes active only when words are heard. The conclusion is that words presented visually or orally use different brain pathways to reach Broca's area, which is associated with language output. The PET technique has generated interesting studies on language localization (indicated in Figure 3–8). A word recognition task, involving visual input alone, lights up the occipital lobe. Instruction to speak—that is, to output a word—lights up the temporal-parietal-occipital association area, and instruction to associate a word with some use lights up frontal lobe association areas. Active cognitive processes, such as detection, identification, and use association, can be highlighted by subtracting from them the activity related to passive recognition of the stimulus being used.

During the use of short-term memory to retain a list of letters, the left supramarginal gyrus (near the junction of the parietal and occipital lobes) become more active, and during subvocal rehearsal (making rhyming judgments for letters), Broca's area is stimulated. During the viewing of an object, the processing of the color, motion, and form components of the visual image can be associated with separate areas. Imaging techniques reveal a convergence of what we see and what we think. The psychologist Stephen Kosslyn has shown that imagining what a telephone looks like can activate the primary visual cortex, just as though the same telephone were actually observed. Imagining a movement can activate the premotor cortex that is active when the movement is actually carried out.

Imaging studies demonstrate that the hyperactivity of frontal brain regions observed in patients with obsessive-compulsive disorder can be diminished by drug therapy or by behavioral therapy that trains the patient to regard symptoms as "a part of my brain that is not working, that is giving out false brain messages." When the patient's attitude in response is "I'm not going to let this bothersome part of my brain run the show," a systematic change in the metabolic activity of the frontal cortical regions involved occurs.

Imaging studies are being used to understand mental disease and to follow the effects of clinical intervention. Drug or behavioral therapy for obsessive-compulsive disorder, which involves dysfunctional repetitive behaviors such as constant hand washing, can decrease activity in forebrain structures associated with habit learning and complex movements. Depression can be correlated with increased activity of the amygdala (see Chapter 10). In schizophrenic patients who report auditory hallucinations (hearing voices), Broca's area becomes active.

This observation suggests that auditory hallucinations have more to do with the generation of words in the brain than with listening to them (which involves Wernicke's area).

Imaging experiments performed on humans as well as other animals suggest that all behaviors, including higher cognitive and affective mental functions, can be localized to specific regions or constellations of regions within the brain. We experience mental processes such as perceiving, thinking, learning, and remembering as continuous and indivisible. Each is in fact composed of several independent information-processing components and requires the coordination of several distinct brain areas. A central idea is that functions localized to discrete regions in the brain are not complex faculties of mind (the model of the old phrenologists), but rather are elementary operations. The more elaborate faculties are constructed from the serial and parallel (distributed) interconnections of several brain regions. This is why damage to a single area need not lead to the disappearance of a specific mental function. And even if the function does disappear, it may partially return because the undamaged parts of the brain reorganize to some extent to perform the lost function.

Our information on the association of different brain regions with different kinds of mental activities is becoming so overwhelming that no one individual could recall it all or keep all of it in mind at one time. For this reason, several efforts are under way to make databases on the brain accessible over the Internet, just as databases of DNA and protein sequences are now available. Thus an investigator who has conducted some PET scan experiments correlating increased blood flow in a particular area with a distinct mental activity will be able to find out readily whether lesions in that area are known to influence the same activity.

SUMMARY Present-day humans function with peripheral and central nervous systems whose basic design was laid down 400–500 million years ago. A system for voluntary action works alongside a more autonomic system whose two branches regulate arousal (sympathetic system) and restorative (parasympathetic system) functions. Hindbrain and midcortical regions regulate housekeeping, memory storage, and emotional behaviors. In higher mammals, the cortex becomes much larger and infolded as its regions specialize and collaborate in generating more complicated social communication and, finally, forethought and language. Frontal, parietal, occipital, and temporal lobes specialize in carrying out different sensory, motor, and integrative functions. In general, the posterior portions of the cortex register events that have occurred, and the anterior portions process what we are about to do in reaction to these events. The two cerebral hemispheres contain corresponding sensory, motor, and integration areas that control the opposite side of the body, but at the same time, they exhibit distinctive global specializations.

Damage to specific regions of the brain caused by tumors, strokes, or mechanical trauma has yielded important insights into the functions of different cortical areas. A large number of behavioral deficits in vision, hearing, movement, decision making, and socially appropriate behavior, which are described in more detail in Part III of this book, have now been correlated with damage to different brain areas. The recent development of sophisticated technology for imaging the activity of living brains is bringing about a revolution in our understanding of brain function. It is now possible to demonstrate directly the activation of functional areas suggested by brain lesion studies. Brain changes associated with depression, drug use, schizophrenia, and other disorders are being documented at increasing levels of detail.

The toolkit of basic facts that we have now assembled about brain evolution and brain function can serve as a foundation for our consideration of the minds of animals. We begin this examination in Chapter 4, where we consider the kinds of intelligence that might be attributable to monkeys and apes. In this way, we will seek an understanding of the platform on which subsequent stages of hominid intelligence are built. ■

Questions for Thought

1. Structures such as the brainstem and limbic system have been present throughout mammalian evolution, whereas the extensive prefrontal cortex characteristic of hominids has appeared only over the past several million years. What functions seem to be served by the newer structures, as contrasted with the older? Do these differences justify a generalization that the newer structures are more "advanced" than the ones that have been present longer?

2. The "triune brain" model depicts our lower brain structures as being reptilian in origin, the middle limbic structures as early mammalian, and the extensive neocortex of primates as later mammalian. Several commentators have suggested that this means we are run by three brains in parallel, any one of which might be in ascendance at a given time. What arguments supporting this idea and what arguments opposing it can you think of?

3. What are the major functional specializations of the four different lobes of our brains? Suppose it is demonstrated that a lesion of a discrete brain area causes a deficit (for example, say a lesion in the occipital cortex abolishes the ability to see colors). Does this tell us that the region in question is responsible for our color vision? When you read about the attribution of a function to a particular brain area, what cautions should you keep in mind?

4. A patient with a small lesion in the right parietal lobe loses the ability to comprehend or speak language. Given the known specializations of the left and right hemispheres, is this expected or is it surprising? What functions appear to be distinctive to the two different hemispheres?

Suggestions for further general reading

Calvin, W.H. 1990. *The Cerebral Symphony.* New York: Bantam Books. (This is an engaging account of how the brain works, and it is the source of some of the material in this chapter on localization of different brain functions.)

Greenfield, S.A., ed. 1996. *The Human Mind Explained.* New York: Holt. (An elementary, accessible, encyclopedic, and well-illustrated presentation of brain structures and functions.)

Posner, M.I., & Raichle, M.E. 1994. *Images of Mind.* New York: Freeman. (This book provides a fascinating introduction to the new brain-imaging technologies and what can be learned from them.)

Reading on more advanced or specialized topics

Deacon, T.W. 1990. Rethinking mammalian brain evolution. American Zoologist 30:629–705. (This is a detailed and thoughtful consideration of changes that occurred during the evolution of the mammalian brain.)

Gazzaniga, M.S., Ivry, R.B., & Mangun, G.R. 1998. *Cognitive Neuroscience—The Biology of the Mind.* New York: Norton. (This recent book provides an introduction to some of the areas of cognitive neuroscience mentioned in this chapter.)

Hanaway, J., Woolsey, T.A., Gado, M.H., & Roberts, M.P. 1998. *The Brain Atlas.* Bethesda, MD: Fitzgerald Science Press. (This is a new full color atlas of the human brain and central nervous system.)

Kandel, E.R., Schwartz, J.H., & Jessell, T. eds. 1991. *Principles of Neural Science.* New York: Elsevier/North-Holland. (If you want to invest in one heavy medical neuroscience textbook, the most recent edition of this work would be a reasonable choice. It is the source of some of the historical material mentioned in this chapter.)

Kosslyn, S.M., & Koenig, O. 1992. *Wet Mind—The New Cognitive Neuroscience.* New York: Free Press. (This is a graduate-level introduction to how the functions of different brain areas are elucidated by a variety of approaches, such as imaging and studying the consequences of brain lesions.)

Kosslyn, S.M., Thompson, W.L., Kim, I.J., & Alpert, N.M. 1995. Topographical representations of mental images in primary visual cortex. *Nature* 378:496–498. (A demonstration that areas of the visual cortex that become active during viewing of an object are also activated by imagining that object.)

Zigmond, M.J. (ed.) 1999. *Fundamental Neuroscience.* New York: Academic Press. (A comprehensive overview of all the neurosciences; suitable for graduate students.)

Chapter 4

Primate Mind

L et's take a few steps back from our discussion of human brains and consider the minds and brains of simpler animals. This will set the stage for describing the transition from monkeys through apes to the hominids of about 2 million years ago (we will save more recent times for later chapters). We can then consider the minds of contemporary monkeys and apes in the search for types of intelligence that might have antedated ours. We share with chimpanzees and some other great apes mental attributes that appear to be unique in the animal kingdom, reflecting the appearance of new brain structures and processes.

The question of animal consciousness

Consciousness is a device for focusing awareness through the linking of emotions and feelings to sensing and acting. It is an emergent level of organization that can coordinate and direct the neuronal assemblies from which it is derived. If we take consciousness to be an increasingly refined evolutionary adaptation, it seems reasonable to grant other animals a kind of consciousness that correlates with the complexity of their brains—to consider it a matter of degree rather than an all-or-nothing phenomenon.

The minds of animals very different from ourselves can do some amazing things that may cause us to wonder how special our intelligence really is. The language of humans is impressive indeed, but so is the sonar communication of bats and the celestial navigation of birds.

Dolphins not only use sonar but also communicate with vocal calls. These mammals have been aquatic for 60 million years and have brains larger than our own. They exhibit complex social organization and can spontaneously acquire new signals and use them appropriately. Bird brains, which have an anatomy less like our own, can perform prodigious feats of memory and carry out a variety of cognitive tasks. For example, in one study, an African Gray parrot named Alex was taught to recognize over 50 objects and could apply same-different distinctions based on color, shape, or size (up to six). If the parrot wanted a cracker and was given a nut, he would say no, implying *intentionality,* or knowledge that his word for "cracker" was about something: crackers, not nuts. He had very limited abilities to recombine words in new ways to indicate different goals, as in "I want . . . [*object*]" and "I wanna go . . . [*place*]."

Consciousness is an emergent property that is a product of biological evolution. It confers selective advantage by making it easier to adapt to rapidly changing features of the environment.

It is tempting to assume that what is going on in these animals' heads is similar to what we think would be going on in our own heads in the same situation. The actual observations of their behaviors, however, don't indicate that these animals are self conscious in the way that we are. For example, we cannot assume that the parrot was thinking about what was going on in the experimenter's mind. A simpler explanation is that he was producing behaviors that had, in the past, resulted in food rewards. In an example drawn from a more natural setting, we cannot assume that a mother bird that feigns a broken wing to distract a predator from her young knows that she is deceiving her foe—only that experience or instinct has instructed her that this behavior has the desired result. To know that she was deceiving the predator, she would need to represent the mental state of the predator. This is the same thing as saying that she would be attributing a mind to the predator and imagining what it was thinking—that it was being fooled by her trick. This process is usually referred to as having a *theory of mind.*

Although it seems natural to do so, we cannot regard the cleverness of animals—beavers building dams, dolphins saving drowning comrades, ants building nests, or chimps or pigeons noticing a spot of dye painted on their bodies—as evidence of self-awareness. Sophisticated information processing might be accompanied by self awareness or it might not. The problem is that we don't know in most of these cases whether detailed analysis would show that a simpler explanation might account for an observed behavior. Rather than attributing to an animal behavior our notions of believing, wanting, knowing, or seeing, might it be possible to prove that some kind of *associative learning* explains the behavior? Animals might respond to observable cues, categorize them, form associations among them, make inferences about them, and develop routine behaviors reinforced by rewards, all without any sense of self.

We need to remain open-minded in the face of the elephant that cries after being punished for stupidity and the astounding array of human-like emotional behaviors that have been documented for chimpanzees. We cannot prove that attributing these animal behaviors to human traits such as intentionality is incorrect, and it is a convenient way to organize descriptions. However, we must remember that what is actually going on may not be this complicated. The problem with virtually all of the popular accounts of love, hope, fear, grief, joy, rage, compassion, shame, and so on in animals is that simple hypotheses attributing these behaviors to something like reflexive conditioning have not been tested and ruled out. Rather, we forge an "explanation" by ascribing human traits to animals. This risky practice is referred to as *anthropomorphism.* The fact that there are strong physiological similarities between the emotional brains of humans and those of other animals does not mean that our emotional experiences feel the same as theirs. Given the empathy we can feel for our pets when they exhibit emotional behaviors that appear to be similar to our own, this point seems a bit alien and hard to accept, but it is true nevertheless.

As a subdiscipline of the field of *ethology,* the study of animal behavior, *cognitive ethology* attempts to deal with some of these issues by asking whether mental concepts such as representation and intentionality are useful in our efforts to understand animal behavior. Representation, for example, might be inferred from the behavior of sentries posted to look for predators of a group. The frequency of scanning for predators in some groups of birds depends on the geometry of the group, which suggests that the sentry has some sort of internal representation of this geometry. Play behavior in many animals seems to involve a clear set of signals and intentions. For example, in canines, a bow can signal "I want to play, do you?"

> *If a simple model or hypothesis can explain a behavior without reference to higher-order intentionality or a theory of mind, then we should not accept any more complicated explanation without proof.*

A number of techniques developed by cognitive psychologists to study human memory or imagery can be applied to animals, but designing animal experiments to prove unambiguously the existence of such mental experiences as intentionality, awareness, and conscious thinking is very difficult. (It's not easy to do with humans, either!) Looking for objective evidence for a faculty such as self-awareness in animals provides an example. Potential evidence on this comes from experiments with mirrors. Only chimpanzees, gorillas, orangutans, and humans more than about 18 months old consistently show curiosity about their reflection in a mirror or engage in mirror-guided behavior without training. But it turns out that pigeons and monkeys that have had mirror exposure and show no curiosity still recognize a change in themselves if, in a mirror, they observe a part of their body that has been colored by an experimenter. How do we distinguish whether this awareness comes with or without a sense of self?

At least one of the several different kinds of conscious awareness we mentioned in Chapter 1, the direct and unreflective kind of experience (such as what it is like to taste an apple), seems likely to be ubiquitous among higher vertebrates. Direct experimental measurements demonstrate that we also share with many animals the faculties of awareness, perception, attention, orientation, movement, memory, learning, thinking, emotions, energy, and mood. The contents of their consciousness or ours at any given moment consist of the brain's awareness of a small fraction of what these faculties are doing. These contents change continually, depending on demands of the current environment. There may be a sort of consciousness comprising all these elements that we all share, which might not require such things as a sense of self, language, or strategic planning. This consciousness is included in, but simpler than, our fully human version.

In examining the behavior of monkeys and apes, we start to have the uncanny feeling that very kindred spirits are at play. The next section offers a brief review of our primate precursors. We start by tracing the time line of the transitions from monkeys to apes and hominids, and then we review what we have learned from studying present-day monkeys and apes. It seems possible that distinct discontinuities, or cognitive chasms, may distinguish the minds of the great apes from those of monkeys and other vertebrates, and the minds of humans from those of apes. Current experiments suggest that the concept of a self occurs only in the great apes and humans and that the attribution of mental states to others occurs in humans alone.

Transitions from monkeys to hominids

Our ancestors of 30–60 million years ago were arboreal (tree-dwelling) creatures rather like lemurs and tarsiers, and we ourselves exhibit many of their most distinctive features. In these animals, who have many representatives in the present, bones and muscles are specialized for swinging between branches; thumbs and big toes are separate from the other digits (this makes grasping possible); and the shoulder girdle and pelvic girdle are looser than in most terrestrial mammals (see Figure 4–1). The gyrations that human joints can go through in modern ballet performances are far greater than other higher vertebrates can perform. Arboreal existence places extreme demands on the nervous

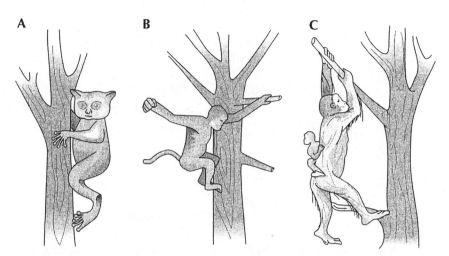

Figure 4–1 Early arboreal mammals. (A) Lemur (B) Monkeys (C) Apes
The limbs are specialized for the tension-bearing required to grasp tree
branches and move about in them.

system. The coordination required among vision, gravity sensing, and
motor actions is intricate. Many arboreal primate societies are socially
stratified, and individuals recognize each other and communicate emotions via facial muscles corresponding to those we use. These animals
also draw on a large repertoire of nonverbal communication (body language) and of noises and shouts.

SELF-EXPERIMENT

Y ou might stop for a moment to compare your own body to that of a
pet dog or cat and note the much greater freedom of movement you
have in your limbs.

The earliest *anthropoids*, the monkeys and apes, appeared in Africa
during the Oligocene epoch about 30 million years ago. They usually
have single births, the newborn are largely helpless, and the young
depend on parental care during a long period of growth and maturation. There is now general consensus that the hominid and chimpanzee line diverged from a common ancestor about 5 million years
ago, whereas the gorilla and the orangutan split off at least 9 million
and 12 million years ago, respectively. The evolutionary writer
Richard Dawkins has illustrated this process by suggesting that you
imagine yourself holding your mother's hand, and she her grandmother's, and so on for a chain of generations that stretches in a

straight line as far as the eye can see. Alongside this line stretches another one: a line of mother and daughter chimpanzees. If you now let go of your mother's hand and walk for many miles down the aisle between the two lines, the chimp and human faces will become more and more similar. Finally, your walk will be blocked by your joint ancestress who is standing at the fork of the two chains. If we assume 3 feet per generation, this is a walk of about 300 miles, which doesn't seem all that far.

Upright posture

A distinguishing characteristic of the early hominids (australopith-ecines) that appeared approximately 4 million years ago was the bipedal stance that permits an erect posture—an adaptation that is energy-efficient and enables us to walk long distances. This happened in animals the size of modern chimpanzees, well before the brain began to enlarge (see Figure 4–2). Ideas about what adaptive advantages might have been associated with standing include better dissipating body heat, extending the range beyond forest to open savanna, reaching higher in foraging, seeing farther over tall grasses, and carrying food or infants over long distances. In addition to direct evidence of erect posture and the use of simple stone tools, there is indirect evidence for division of labor (sexual dimorphism), shared food, nuclear family structure, larger numbers of children, and longer weaning periods.

Figure 4–2   Changes in the skeleton accompanying the transition to an upright posture. (A) Chimpanzee (B) *Australopithecus afarensis* (C) Modern human

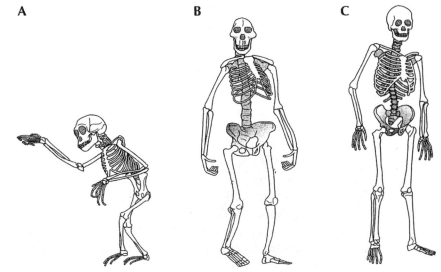

A   B   C

We are built for moving, not for standing. Our body structure has a high center of gravity, and walking is essentially a controlled falling forward. The humanoid frame can move in many more ways than the frames of other vertebrates. Some have speculated that the intelligence related to sensing and moving in these new spatial coordinates was a precursor to more advanced analytical capabilities.

SELF-EXPERIMENT

You can get a direct sense of the difference between the carriage of human skeletons and those of monkeys and apes by trying this simple exercise. (If you are worried about looking silly, you should probably do this when you are alone!) Stand up, and then crouch down by bending at your knee and hip joints. Your behind should stick out as you lower your torso forward and let your head and arms hang down. This may feel strange, because social conventions in Western cultures dictate that we never move the hip joint in isolation (torso and leg muscles are always included) and also require that we lock together movements of the shoulder, head, and neck. In this crouching, simian position, see if you can shake your head and shoulders a bit to let them come loose so that your arms dangle down. Bounce on your knees and let your behind go even further back. If you go ahead and do this, you can feel the stress taken off your back and the tension in the abdominals relieved as your gut hangs down. You're ready to go banana hunting! Note that turning about is a bit more clumsy, because your moment of inertia about the vertical axis is larger than it was when you were upright. Now slowly rise to your normal, upright, standing position and note the difference between this and the ape-like posture in an activity such as turning. The moment of inertia about the vertical axis is smaller in humans than in monkeys and other animals. We use less energy when we turn.

As you stand up, note the following differences that have appeared in the transition from chimpanzee to human skeletons: The human chest is compressed and the head moves back. The tail shrinks to a tailbone that forms a basin for our internal organs, and a curve is introduced in our lower backs. Our shoulder blades are lengthened for a wider range of upper-body movement. Our legs are lengthened and our feet are narrowed to support walking and running. Muscles around the pelvis arrange themselves for striding rather than power lifting. Vertebrae are wedge-shaped rather than square as in monkeys, which permits more flexible movement of the spine. The front of the pelvis in humans, at the center of gravity, is a triangle of weakness. Our front flexors usually do not match the strength of our back extensors. This weak area at the center of gravity is recognized and accomodated by athletes, dancers, and martial artists.

Larger brains

The upright posture achieved by the australopithecines was not accompanied by an increase in brain size. Larger brains appeared in the various *Homo* lineages, such as *Homo habilis* ("handy, or skillful, man"), whose brain size had increased to 600–700 cubic centimeters (cc) by approximately 2 million years later. Stone tools for cutting as well as mashing are found at *Homo habilis* fossil sites. These are crude tools of the sort created by slamming two rocks together until you get a sharp edge. Between 1.5 and 2.5 million years ago, as *Homo erectus* ("standing man") was becoming more prominent, brain volume increased to 900–1100 cc (see Figure 4–3) and more elaborate tools were being made, along with fire, shelters, and seasonal base camps. Migration out of Africa began. The second major increase in brain size, to approximately 1400 cc, occurred around 300,000 years ago, with archaic sapient humans, and the vocal tract started to assume its modern form. No later than 100,000 years ago, our fully modern version of *Homo sapiens* ("wise man") was present.

Lower primates have approximately the same ratio of brain size to body size as hundreds of other mammalian species. If this is assigned a value of 1 for the purpose of comparison with higher primates, the ratio increases from a value of 1 in the lower primates to over 2 in the great apes, to 4 in *H. habilis*, 5 in *H. erectus*, and 6–7 in *H. sapiens*. That is, we have six to seven times as much brain as the average mammal with a similar body weight. The increase in the mass and the energy consumption of the hominid brain is balanced by a reduction in the size of the gastrointestinal tract, made possible, perhaps, by a higher-quality diet. The prevailing idea is that the main cause of this relative increase in primate brain size was selection for the intellectual ability required to participate in large social groups and for the memory capacity required to handle many different relationships within groups. The increase in brain size correlates with group size in a number of primate species. Extrapolated to humans, the data suggest an ideal group size of slightly over 200. A survey has shown the average size of human hunter-gatherer groups and nomadic societies to be 150–180 individuals.

Figure 4–3 Changes in the shape and volume of the skull in the transition from (A) *Australopithecus,* through (B) *Homo erectus,* to (C) *Homo sapiens.*

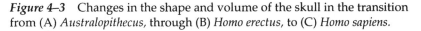
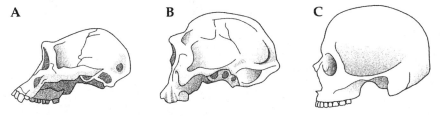

A   B   C

An alternative ecological theory suggests that a larger brain is required for the cognitive skills involved in coping with larger home ranges and seasonal migrations. An implicit assumption here is that bigger is smarter, but we have little firm evidence from other animal species that size correlates strongly with intelligence. Some fish species with brains the size of pinheads are much brighter than others with brains a thousand times larger. Elephants have big brains because elephants are big; they are not strikingly smarter than other animals. Another idea about our big brains, perhaps a bit far-fetched, suggests that they are a consequence of the heat stress on the brain that is caused by our upright posture. Heat that is dissipated from the exposed back of a quadruped or crouching ape rises to the head in hominids. Perhaps the brain got bigger to provide the increased blood flow needed for radiative cooling! The extra nerve cells that went along with this change in plumbing might then have been recruited for other purposes. Perhaps when hair was lost from the rest of the body, it was retained on the head because it reduced radiative heating from the sun. In short, no theory of what drove the explosive evolution of the hominid brain has gained complete acceptance.

Stages in hominid emergence

It is commonly supposed that the social behaviors and divisions of labor that we now observe in chimpanzees, such as male hunting groups and limits on female mobility associated with the period before weaning, might have become more pronounced with the transition to bipedal posture. Some available fossils suggest sexual dimorphism in australopithecines. The scenario of "man the hunter" as a driving force in early hominid social evolution has passed from favor as evidence for "man the scavenger" has accumulated. Animal bones found together with hominid remains also suggest that hominids may have been prey as well as predator. One possibility is that a distinctive evolved hominid behavior was cooperative scaring away of predators such as lions (by throwing rocks or using fire), thus making it possible to scavenge their kills. There is evidence that *H. erectus* tamed fire and thus could have used it both for this purpose and for cooking to counter spoilage. During the development of the genus *Homo,* many behaviors strikingly different from those of monkeys and chimpanzees appeared. These included feeding children after the age of weaning instead of leaving them to find food on their own, most adult men and women associating in couples, fathers as well as mothers caring for children, living long enough to experience grandchildren, and females undergoing menopause.

The course of hominid evolution was emphatically not a simple sequence of *Australopithecus* → *H. habilis* → *H. erectus* → *H. sapiens.* Rather, it was more like a pagoda tree with at least five layers of branching limbs representing radiations of australopithecines, habilines, erects, archaic moderns, and moderns. The erects and habilines could have independently derived from different branches of the australopithecine line. Moderns (including the Neanderthals) could have descended from early erects. (This point is taken up further in the next chapter. See Figure 5–3 for an illustration of the hominid evolutionary tree.)

> *Early hominids may have been scavengers more often than hunters, and predators less often than prey.*

Discontinuities, or pulses, in the evolution of hominids appear to correlate with abrupt cooling periods and contractions of rain forests that occurred in Africa about 5 million, 2.5 million, 1.7 million, and 900,000 years ago. At these times, major changes in the fossil remains of other animals have been observed. Antelope horns, used in species-specific mating recognition, have proved to be a useful marker for changes in nonhominid species. One hypothesis is that a cold spell and shrinkage of forested habitat 5 million years ago forced tree-dwelling quadrupeds to forage as bipeds on the savanna. The next major cooling, about 2.5–2.8 million years ago, may have caused a permanent shift to grasslands and a splitting of prehumans into *Australopithecus* and *Homo.* The cold spells of 1.7 and 0.9 million years ago may have reinforced the emergence of *H. erectus.* Definitive proof of the "evolutionary pulse" idea is difficult to obtain, however, and recent work examining in more detail the mammalian fossil record in East Africa has been interpreted to indicate slower, continuous changes.

On balance, the observations are consistent with the idea that slow evolution in the Darwinian mold has been "punctuated" when sudden changes in global climate have occurred. An animal species stressed by the disappearance of its accustomed environment will have one of three fates. It will migrate to an environment similar to the old one, adapt to the new environment, or become extinct. The chaotic and uncertain nature of these environmental changes makes it possible that the appearance of fully modern humans, perhaps in response to one of these changes, had a large element of chance and certainly was not foreordained. Forms like ourselves might just as easily never have appeared, or they might have arisen only after several million more years.

Origins of human intelligence

Having laid out a time line for the evolution of humans from a chimpanzee-like precursor, what can we say about the changes in mental machinery that were going on? Unfortunately, the paleontological record tells us very little about what was going on inside those fossilized skulls as they increased in size in the transitions from australopithecines through *H. sapiens,* alongside the increasing complexity of tools and artifacts. Cranial endocasts of fossil *H. habilis* skulls, made by using the skull as a mold for a plaster cast of the brain it once contained, do reveal one interesting feature: Bulges appear over Broca's and Wernicke's areas (see Chapter 3), which are involved in the generation and comprehension of language, respectively. This observation indicates a relative increase in the sizes of these areas, and perhaps language competence increased along with it. Apart from evidence like this, the best way we can obtain clues to the origins of our modern human intelligence is to study the brains and behaviors of modern monkeys and apes.

Primates have larger frontal cortexes than other mammals, and the prefrontal cortex contains a unique layer of small granular cells. The most striking increase in brain size during the monkey, ape, and hominid transition is in the prefrontal cortex, which occupies about 24% of the cerebral mantle in humans, compared with about 14% in the great apes (see Figure 4–4). PET imaging studies suggest that the left medial frontal lobe is an important locus of theory-of-mind tasks (see the section "Awareness of the mental states of others" near the end of this chapter). It is also central to foresight and planning mechanisms that are absent in the apes. Expansion of the cerebellar cortex in humans is also larger than extrapolation from primate trends would predict. A phylogenetically newer part of the human cerebellum called the *dentate nucleus* makes connections with the frontal lobes and may be correlated with distinctively human language and cognition.

Figure 4–4 The brain of modern humans (A) is larger, is more densely folded, and has a more prominent prefrontal cortex (shaded areas) than that of modern apes (B).

A   B

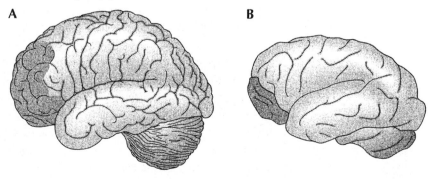

Because genetic data make it clear that our closest ancestor is a creature similar to the modern chimpanzee, it is commonly assumed that we can take chimpanzee behaviors as possible precursors of our own. We have to keep in mind, however, that evolution is not like a ladder, with one character always building on a previous, similar one. It is more like a tree, in which similar characters may have appeared independently on several different branches. Thus some present-day behaviors of humans and chimps (such as genocide) may have arisen quite independently, in response to the selective pressures of their separate environments. If we humans had chosen to study bonobos (pygmy chimpanzees) intensively for many years, rather than other species of chimpanzees or baboons, we might have concluded that early hominids lived in societies in which warfare was rare or absent, social life centered on females, and promiscuous sex facilitated a large array of social interactions. Or, to put the point another way, the fact that pygmy chimps are so totally different from other apes in their social structure and sexual, nonaggressive behaviors raises the possibility that we might have turned out that way rather than being genocidal and xenophobic. Thus the undesirable behaviors that we share with chimps may or may not have been our own separate invention.

> *Evolution is a tree, not a ladder. Human brains did not evolve "from" chimpanzee brains. Rather, hominid and chimpanzee evolution have been proceeding independently in the 5–6 million years since our evolutionary lines diverged.*

Episodic intelligence

Bearing in mind the foregoing cautions, we do see intelligence in monkeys and chimps that would appear to be an appropriate foundation on which to build, in stages, our more complex minds. Merlin Donald, a Canadian psychologist, has proposed a sequence comprising four main stages of cognitive evolution in primates and hominids: the episodic, mimetic, mythic, and theoretic. He suggests that these stages correlate approximately with apes and australopithecines, *Homo erectus*, archaic moderns, and modern humans. The central idea is that older systems and their associated brain structures are encapsulated by newer ones, all operating in parallel. We can at different times be operating from one or from a combination of these intelligences. There is debate over the validity of these stages, but they offer a useful context and are generally accepted. It is Donald's earliest stage, the *episodic intelligence* he attributes to monkeys and apes, which is relevant to our current discussion. The other stages are covered in later chapters.

An episodic intelligence lives in the present—in a series of concrete occasions. Single events and sequences of events or episodes can be remembered, and retaining these as well as remembering complex sets of social relationships, requires a large memory capacity. The *episodic memory* system stores and recalls perceived events. Many animals demonstrate the ability to analyze and recall situations, but they show no evidence of being able to re-present them for reflection. The closest we might come to understanding what is meant by episodic intelligence, when it is suggested as a component of our current brand of human awareness, is to conceive of it as being present in those moments when our minds are momentarily devoid of internal narrative chatter, when we are attentive only to what is happening in the immediate present—having sensations but not reflecting on them, letting memory associations triggered by current perceptions rise spontaneously. In this frame of mind, we might find, for example, that we know (remember) where a purse or comb is without thinking about it.

SELF-EXPERIMENT

Try putting aside this book and your language mind for a moment to test whether the idea of an episodic mind makes sense to you. Pause and see whether you can put yourself in a mental space of "just being," letting your mind become quiet and noting only the sensing and acting happening in the immediate present, along with any nonverbal memory associations that are triggered by your current perceptions.

Some of the most thorough studies attempting to define the nature of episodic minds have focused on East African vervet monkeys, which are not as advanced as chimps. These monkeys show complex social interactions, classify relationships into types, and also classify sounds according to the objects and events they denote (such as leopard alarm, snake alarm, and eagle alarm, each associated with specific behaviors). They have a laser beam sort of intelligence focused on a very narrow region. There is no evidence that these monkeys attribute mental states to each other. They are skilled observers of each other's behavior but can't be said to analyze each other's underlying motives. The monkeys exercise subtle and penetrating discrimination in social matters, yet they don't seem to transfer this capacity to other contexts. They do not seem to have knowledge of their knowledge (to know that they know), in the sense of being aware of their own states of mind and using this awareness to explain or predict the behavior either of themselves or of others. The lack of such awareness may be why they can't transfer very specific pieces of knowledge or procedures to similar appropriate occasions (for example, they do not use the "leopard sound" process to invent a sound for a new danger that appears). Even so, we must be cautious in generalizing about the behavior of monkeys, for very intelligent behaviors have been noticed in some exceptional individuals.

One Japanese macaque monkey, for instance, devised a variety of physically sophisticated strategies to extract an apple from a transparent tube.

The great apes: selves and others

The chimpanzees and other great apes mark a major increase in cognitive abilities. Chimpanzees are socially the most advanced of the non-human primates and have greater than 98% genetic similarity to us. This is more similar than the red-eyed and white-eyed vireo songbirds are to each other. Jared Diamond, a student of human evolution, points out that a zoologist from outer space would classify us along with the two species of chimpanzees as three species of the genus *Homo*. The genetic differences between humans and chimps, although small, are obviously very important. Detailed explorations of the genetic differences between humans and chimps imply that chimps and humans may be different by only a few hundred genes, and that less than 100 genes account for the cognitive differences.

Socialization and other skills among the chimps

The chimp life cycle starts with a long period of socialization, and loose bonds are maintained between females and their adult offspring. Societies of 30–80 individuals occupy a persistent and defined home range over a period of years. Males cooperate during hunting and sharing of meat in a way that is unique in nonhuman primates. The social organization shows flexibility; different subgroups form on different days for hunting forays. Chimps employ complex visual and auditory communication, and at least 35 different sounds have distinct meanings. When two groups meet, they sometimes share a feeding site. At other times they use exaggerated movements and shouts in a territorial display, then withdraw. Genocide has been documented, as in, for example, one troop of chimps wiping out another in a slow and systematic way. We don't know whether this is a precursor or a separate invention of similar behavior shown by humans. This chimpanzee behavior raises the possibility that one rationale for hominid group living was defense against other hominid groups. Group living would enhance both the effectiveness of defense against other human groups and aggression toward them.

Chimps have highly developed manual skills, can solve problems, can use natural tools, and have elementary tool-making ability. However, their ability to look ahead and plan appears to be very limited. For example, no chimp spends an evening collecting a supply of sticks to use in fishing for termites the next day. It is interesting that species other than ourselves haven't come up with a faculty as useful as foresight. This faculty appears to be correlated with the enlargement of the frontal lobes, which is distinctive to our hominid brains.

Groups of chimps show political and moral behaviors that are strikingly similar to our own. They follow prescriptive social rules and anticipate punishment for infractions. Their rules of reciprocity involve giving, trading, and revenge, and they exhibit moralistic aggression against violators. Groups learn to adjust to, and give special treatment to, disabled and injured individuals. The status hierarchy is modulated by complex alliances, peacemaking, and negotiation. We can also recognize analogs of our entire range of human emotions, as individual chimps move between moods of being happy, sad, angry, lonely, tired, embarrassed, and so on.

Groups of chimps geographically isolated from each other develop different tools and grooming rituals and pass these on through teaching and imitation.

Chimps in captivity have even been trained to do simple addition with Arabic numerals. They can classify objects into types and sets and can arrange differing numbers of objects in correct numerical order. (Rhesus monkeys have also been shown to have this capacity.) Although chimps and monkeys can use simple signs or symbols presented by humans, they do not spontaneously invent them. Some bonobo chimps, upon watching others use a board of symbols, have used the board in simple communication tasks. The animals will perform language-like operations that some investigators claim reveal a grammar equivalent to that of a human infant, showing some sensitivity to word order and syntactical rules, but this is done only in response to extensive molding, drilling, and reinforcement by the researcher. They don't seem to have a genuine feel for what language is about. To be sure, it is an anthropocentric distortion to be prompting chimps to try various human-style tasks as though these abilities were a measure of biological worth. Focusing on human syntax and speech can divert our attention from understanding the rich intelligence that chimps actually display in their interactions in the wild. Critics of animal language research say that trying to teach chimps language is like trying to teach humans to fly, for they have nothing analogous to the language instinct that humans have.

Developing a concept of self

As we have noted, chimps, orangutans, and human infants after about 18 months of age are unique among the primates in their reaction to mirrors. Monkeys and other vertebrates, upon encountering a mirror image of themselves, never move beyond treating the image as another member of the species and frequently make threatening displays. Chimps who look into a mirror act at first as though they have encountered another chimp, but they soon begin to perform simple repetitive movements, like swaying from side to side, while watching their images. Perhaps they are learning that they can control the movement of the *other* chimp. They then appear to grasp the equivalence between the mirror image and themselves and start to explore body parts such as their genitalia, which they can't ordinarily see (see Figure 4–5). If a spot of dye that can't be smelled or felt is placed on a chimp's eyebrow ridge during anesthesia, the animal will notice the dye when it first encounters a mirror after waking. More telling, the chimp will touch the dyed area and then smell and look at the fingers that have contacted the mark, behaviors that suggest self-recognition—a sense of self.

Awareness of the mental states of others

Although chimps show behaviors more consistent with having a sense of self than do monkeys and less complex vertebrates, there is debate on whether they can perform a further operation characteristic of humans: to appreciate others as also having selves to which beliefs can be ascribed. Do chimps, like humans, have a theory of mind? Observations of deceptive behaviors shown by chimps in the wild seem most easily explained by assuming that they are ascribing beliefs to the animals they are deceiving, but the fact that chimps know how to deceive does not prove they know they are doing so. Studies on autistic human children suggest a dissociation between having a sense of self and being able to ascribe beliefs to others. Autistic children begin using a mirror to inspect themselves at the same age as normal children, but they appear to develop only a rudimentary ability to attribute a mental life to others. They appear to suffer a sort of "mind-blindness" with respect to other humans.

Figure 4–5   Chimpanzees display active curiosity when encountering a mirror, exploring parts of their body that they cannot otherwise see. Their behavior suggests that they have a sense of "self" somewhat akin to our own.

The most critical experimental tests of whether chimps can attribute mental states to others have involved vision. The effort has been to determine whether for chimps seeing is believing, as it is for humans. The experiments usually involve at least two humans. One, the knower, observes food being placed in one of several cups screened from the chimp's direct vision, while the second, the guesser, has left the room. The guesser returns to the room and points at an empty cup while the knower points at the baited cup. The chimp is allowed to search one cup and keep the food if it finds it there. Animals quickly learn to select the container indicated by the knower more often than that indicated by the guesser. However, because the chimp might not be making an association based on the knower's visual access to the baiting, but rather associating "the one who stayed in the room" with food, more complicated experimental designs are tried. For instance, the guesser remains in the room with a paper bag over his head while a third person enters the room and baits a cup in the view of the knower. Chimps learn to choose the cup subsequently pointed at by the knower, but this could reflect a further associative rule that has nothing to do with seeing as knowing—for example, "pick the cup pointed at by the guy who didn't have a bag over his head."

In another set of experiments, chimps are exposed to two trainers, one able to see and one whose vision is occluded by a blindfold, screen, or food bucket placed over the head. The chimps are rewarded with food for making a begging gesture in front of the trainer that a human would judge able to see the chimp. The fact that the chimps show no disposition, either immediately or during early training, to prefer the person whose vision was unblocked suggests that they may not understand the relationship between seeing and attending. A problem with this experiment is that even if chimps have a learned or unlearned tendency to beg from people with visible eyes, this might reflect the unconscious associative rule "begging from people with visible eyes is more likely to lead to reward," rather than requiring an explanation in mental terms, such as "seeing is knowing." More subtle experiments are needed to determine whether a chimp employs the concept "see." There is no ambiguity about this issue in human infants, who between the ages of 3 and 5 years begin to use their visual experience to attribute real and false beliefs to others. (See "Stages in the development of human selves" at the beginning of Chapter 7.)

Human children seem to understand desires before they understand beliefs, which suggests that chimps might do better when examined for

Humans and chimps display many similar behaviors. However, we cannot know whether these similarities in behavior reflect similar subjective experiences.

evidence of understanding desires or goals rather than beliefs. Chimps watching actors try to solve a problem are more likely to select photographs depicting achievement of the actors' implicit desires or goals. More interestingly, they can cooperate with a human partner on a task that requires different roles, and they can switch roles. However, we cannot know whether these similarities in behavior between chimps and humans reflect similar subjective experiences. Because humans can do so much without self-consciousness (later chapters discuss examples such as blindsight, procedural learning, and cognition outside of awareness), and because our consciousness of self is so labile, an extrapolation to what it is like to be a chimp is not in the cards. We have to remember that the brains and minds of chimps are not simply steps on the ladder to humanity but alternative products of the evolutionary process.

SUMMARY

The question of what kind of consciousness animals have is a difficult one, because we don't have the tools to look into those minds and know what it is like to be an insect, a bird, a dog, or a chimpanzee. What we can observe are behaviors and nervous structures that show a continuous thread of increasing complexity throughout vertebrate evolution, leading us to assume that we share fundamental faculties like awareness, attention, memory, and emotion. However, the temptation to attribute our human style of experience and motivation to animals such as our pets must be tempered with the realization that simple associative learning—as when animals learn by trial and error which behaviors produce food reward, affection, or punishment—is sufficient to explain very complex behaviors; there is no need to invoke a "self" such as we experience. It is in the anthropoids that appeared about 30 million years ago and now form our closest link to the rest of the animal world that we observe structures and behaviors that are clearly antecedent to our own. The transition to an upright posture that evolved at some point after the hominid and chimpanzee lines split about 5–6 million years ago was bad for our backs but freed our hands for manipulative use and gave us a greater range of movement than other vertebrates enjoy. The rapid radiation of a series of different lines, such as *Australopithecus, Homo habilis,* and *Homo erectus,* tested different hominid designs as brain size steadily increased. Archaeological sites with hominid remains show that simple tools and fire were in use by approximately 2 million years ago.

As a starting point for describing distinctively hominid intelligences, we make the assumption that the minds of monkeys and apes have changed much less rapidly than ours during the past few million years and that they thus represent a base on which further changes are built. We attribute to monkeys, apes, and many other animals a sort of intelligence that is episodic and present-centered, has very little sense of past or future, and is largely unaware of its own state. It is only in the great apes that we see the first compelling evidence of an appreciation of "self" more like our own. A final transition, from the sense of having a self to the attribution of such a self to others, appears to be a distinctively human feature. Experiments with chimpanzees suggest that their ability to attribute beliefs to others, if present at all, is extremely rudimentary. Although we share with animals a host of cognitive abilities—such as perception, memory, and learning—there is no evidence that any animal comes close to humans in generating an internal "I" that fills a mind-space with stories of past and future and imagines the minds of others. Stages in the development of these hominid innovations are the subject of Chapter 5. ■

Questions for Thought

1. Think of a seemingly intelligent behavior that you have observed in a pet animal—a behavior that might well lead you to assume that the animal knew what was going on in your mind. Can you think of ways to explain the pet's behavior in more simple terms that don't rely on its interpreting your mental state? What would lead you to choose the simpler or the more complicated explanation?

2. It is widely believed that humans are the only species that shows foresight—that is, can plan ahead. Do you think this is true? What kind of experiments would you design to look for foresight in an animal?

3. A chimpanzee that is familiar with its face in a mirror is briefly anesthetized, and a small, odorless spot is painted on its face. If the chimp looks in a mirror after waking, it notices the spot in the mirror and points at the spot on its face. This experiment was originally interpreted to suggest that the chimp had a notion of self similar to our own. However, the same sort of experiment also works with a pigeon, an animal with which we feel much less kinship. Is there an interpretation of these results that does not require postulating the sort of awareness of self that we experience?

4. Genocide and xenophobia are observed between groups of chimpanzees and also between groups of humans. What conclusions can we draw from this about the origins of human behaviors?

Suggestions for further general reading

de Waal, F.B.M. 1996. *Good Natured: The Origins of Right and Wrong in Humans and Other Animals.* Cambridge, MA: Harvard University Press. (A description of many animal behaviors, particularly those of chimpanzees, that mirror human behaviors. The author argues that the gulf between animal and human consciousness is not as wide as some people think.)

Gould, J.L., & Gould, C.G. 1994. *The Animal Mind.* New York: Freeman/ Scientific American Library. (This book is a well-illustrated survey of animal minds and behavior. It gives many examples of the sort mentioned in the first section of this chapter, describes Pepperberg's experiments with the African Gray parrot named Alex, and reviews attempts to train apes in language use.)

The next three books discuss changes in cognition and structure that accompanied the transitions from monkeys to hominids. They are equally relevant to the subject matter of Chapter 5.

Diamond, J. 1992. *The Third Chimpanzee.* New York: Harper Collins.

Donald, M.D. 1991. *Origins of the Modern Mind.* Cambridge, MA: Harvard University Press.

Kingdon, J. 1993. *Self-Made Man—Human Evolution from Eden to Extinction?* New York: Wiley.

Reading on more advanced or specialized topics

Deacon, T.W. 1997. *The Symbolic Species—The Co-Evolution of Language and the Brain.* New York: Norton. (A masterful description of mammalian brain evolution and the specializations that might have provided a foundation for the hominid invention of symbols.)

Grier, J.W., & Burk, T. 1992. *Biology of Animal Behavior.* St. Louis: Mosby Year Book. (This comprehensive college text covers many of the points in this chapter.)

Povinelli, D.J., & Preuss, T.M. 1995. Theory of mind: Evolutionary history of a cognitive specialization. *Trends in Neurosciences* 18:418–424. (This article provides more information on the question of whether apes can attribute mental states to others.)

Seyfarth, R.M., & Cheney, D.L. 1992. Meaning and mind in monkeys. *Scientific American* 267:122–128. (This article provides a description of monkey intelligence and its limits.)

Chapter 5

Hominid Mind

We now have an outline of some of the major steps in the transitions from monkeys to apes and from apes to hominids, as well as some information on how their minds are distinctly different from ours. In this chapter we continue to trace the stages through which the minds of early hominids developed, approaching ever nearer the appearance of our own modern human variety. We will pick up the story at the stage of *Homo erectus,* approximately 2 million years ago, and then follow one model of the evolution of human intelligence up to the period before the invention of agriculture and cities. Over this time, hominids were evolving psychological mechanisms that are shared by all races of modern humans. Further, the advent of language was making possible the transmission of the rules and ideas of cultures, allowing adaptive behavioral changes to occur at a much faster rate than genetic evolution would permit. This brings us to modern human brains and minds, which were fully present by about 100,000 years ago. These modern brains and minds are the subject of Parts II and III of this book. The more recent shaping of our minds by the invention of writing and other complex social innovations is discussed in Part IV.

The mimetic intelligence of early hominids

At the time of the appearance of *H. erectus* major changes were under way. More complex facial musculature suggests a richer range of emotional expression than the present-centered and nonreflective episodic minds of monkeys and apes could generate. This emotional expression was probably supported by increased complexity of both the phonetic (sounds or calls) and the prosodical (volume, pitch, tone, and emphasis) components of vocalization. Changes in the skull and jaw permitted the generation of more varied sounds. *H. erectus* had a larger brain, made more elaborate tools, used fire, had seasonal base camps, and spread out from Africa to Eurasia. Its culture mediated the transition from ape to human.

Merlin Donald, the psychologist whose ideas were mentioned in Chapter 4, uses the word "mimetic" to describe the intelligence of hominids at this stage of evolution and suggests that mimetic intelligence remains embedded in the modern human mind. He believes this intelligence is similar to that seen in prelinguistic children, illiterate deaf-mutes, and patients seen in a clinical setting who have lost language but retained social skills and communicate by mime. *Mimetic intelligence* is the kind of cognition needed to learn music, crafts, and sports—largely by imitation and without language. This stage of archaic hominid cognition resembles the extra-linguistic features of the modern mind.

The ability to produce conscious, self-initiated, representational acts that are intentional but not linguistic is different from mimicry or imitation, for intentional representational acts are used to reenact, or present again, an event or relationship. This happens in games such as charades and is the basis of arts such as pantomime, ritual dance, and visual tableaux. A central feature is the modeling of social structure. Chimps learn only how to react to each individual in the larger group. Human children model the group structure, playing role-acting games. Group mimesis is what we call ritual. A single mimetic performance might include manual signals, postural attitudes, facial expressions, nonverbal vocalization, and gesture.

SELF-EXPERIMENT

To have a feel for mimetic intelligence in your own experience, pause for a moment and imagine that you have suddenly lost the use of language—not only can you not hear and speak it, but you also cannot construct internal narrative sentences. That is, try to restrict your thinking to visual and mechanical images of the sort you might need, for example, to build a wall from stones. Internal words and sentences are not necessary, only images of the process and its goal. Now, feel the many ways in which you would still be able to communicate the process and goal through gesture and movement. In the same way try signaling that you are hungry, wish to go outside, want to meet someone, and so on.

Donald suggests that mime, play, games, skilled rehearsal, nonlinguistic gesticulation, tool making, other instrumental skills, and many other expressive devices used in social control are products of the mimetic system as it continuously models the episodic world. This system is an elaboration, or summary, of episodic experience dealing with skills, social roles, and emotional events. It is a distinctive hominid invention, a kind of cognition that is distinguishable from language even in modern humans. A simple drawing can be used to illustrate the idea that mimetic mind orders and encapsulates the outputs of episodic mind (see Figure 5–1).

The emphasis here is on mimetic intelligence as antedating verbal linguistic abilities, but we cannot rule out the possibility that the two underwent a slow and continuous evolution alongside each other. Whichever interpretation is correct, there is abundant evidence that sophisticated conscious concepts can exist without language. Adult humans who have been without language can describe a rich mental life after they have learned language. Most word learning is attaching words to preexisting concepts, objects, actions, collections, and social institutions. Deaf people who have been isolated and have not learned sign language exhibit advanced spatial knowledge and skills, can handle money, and can pantomime narratives. In patients with brain lesions that disrupt language, mimetic skill usually survives, and doctor and patient can communicate by sign or body language. Destruction of mimetic abilities always takes language with it, and such patients are much more out of touch with human reality.

> *Sophisticated conscious concepts can exist without language. Adult humans who have been without language seem indistinguishable in many of their cognitive skills from adults with language.*

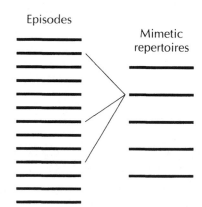

Figure 5–1   This drawing illustrates the idea that mimetic intelligence is built by collecting isolated chunks of episodic, present-centered information, indicated by the lines on the left, into sequences of meaningful activity such as a set of instructions on how to do something. Thus each mimetic routine, indicated by the lines on the right, encapsulates a series of isolated actions that have not previously been linked together.

Episodes

Mimetic repertoires

Kinesic communication

The mimetic intelligence we have been describing underlies our body language, the nonverbal communication that is signaled by kinetic motions—the *kinesic communication*—of our faces or limbs. This usually has emotional significance, as when we open up our faces to communicate affection or contract them if we are rejecting someone. These gestures, along with many others, recur across cultures. We join company with other higher vertebrates in using nonverbal communication to model and set social roles. Detailed time-lapse movies can be analyzed to document the fact that this nonverbal communication proceeds in many parallel channels. Our mimetic exchanges usually occur within a larger framework that includes linguistic expression, but words don't necessarily alter the nonverbal elements of the exchange. Language can carry on in parallel, without disturbing the fabric of spontaneous mimetic communication (see the accompanying self-experiment). Different parts of our bodies, different movement patterns, are essentially organs of social behavior. Social status is regulated by confidence, age, size, and sex. (Is your chest puffed up or collapsed? Is your pelvis thrust forward or pulled back?) Posture signals social rank, sexual attractiveness, and emotional support. The signaling of social status by body carriage reaches its most complex development in our species. For humans, as well as other social vertebrates, an individual's relations with other members of the population is a central factor in determining that individual's survival and reproduction.

SELF-EXPERIMENT

Y ou are aware of parallel channels of communication from your own experience, especially when verbal and nonverbal messages conflict. As an exercise, pretend that you are delivering the following mixed messages (parentheses indicate the physical action that is occurring while the preceding words are spoken).

- I'd like to know you better (drawing back).
- I don't want to intrude on your space (moving forward).
- I really am happy to be here (looking apprehensive).
- I don't understand why people never approach me (frowning).
- People are always trying to take advantage of me (looking seductive).
- I don't want to tell you what to do (with commanding voice).

Social cohesion and body language

An overriding controller of our movements is our social self-image. It is decisive in determining the most intimate details of how we move in public. Get up from reading this book for a moment and move about as though you were a person of the opposite gender. If you are a man, imagine yourself moving as a woman, and vice versa. How does it feel? The point here is that you carry your body in only one of many different possible configurations, which are all indicative of social status and role. We can become conscious of these configurations and can deliberately change them, but usually they are unconscious, regulated by nonverbal social cues. The postures we assume are emergent properties of our social group—of a sort of "group mind." The complex and varied personalities that we act out require distinctive holding patterns of postural muscles, as well as characteristic individual configurations of our neuroendocrine and autonomic nervous systems.

We are programmed by our kinesic context. Are you aware, in yourself, of the moments when you are imitating the expression on a face you are looking at? This is a universal human tendency. Synchronization of mood is crucial to smooth interaction, and it involves the linking and orchestration of physical movements. The next time you are listening sympathetically to someone else, note what happens if you suddenly stop the subtle motions of your body or face whose rhythm is matching the speaker's. We all tend to seek feedback and the company of others to confirm either our current mood or the mood we have a disposition to be in.

We nonverbally transmit moods as though they were viruses, and some people are more likely to be senders, and others receivers. Have you ever noticed yourself imitating the expression on a face you are looking at?

To be a member of a group you must mimic its behaviors, whether you are a seagull or a human. Carried to an extreme by humans, complementary body language helps to define and cement the members of a group together. The stereotyped evolved behavior of laughter also reinforces group cohesion. Bonding, affiliative, and maternal behaviors are under the influence of hormonal and autonomic mechanisms just as hardwired as those that control fighting or fleeing. In many vertebrates they are enhanced by the hormone oxytocin and correlate with energy-restoring and energy-building activities of the parasympathetic nervous system. What we are dealing with here is an integrated ensemble of mind, body, and world.

Origins of language

To continue our story of hominid evolution, we must now add language to these complex systems of emotional and kinesic communication. Think about the constant narrative within our heads. We use this narrative to communicate with ourselves and by vocalizing part of it, with others, but what is its origin? No one would claim at this point to have the definitive answer. It is hard, however, to observe the alarm calls of the vervet monkey—different calls for eagles, for snakes, or for leopards—or the body language and calls of chimpanzees without imagining them as signals that might come under voluntary cortical control and that are strung together in sequences to describe more complex events.

Language excels at organizing categories in our natural and social world, even if it is not very good at conveying the types of information that faces, smells, and emotions are able to convey. Although there is evidence that a sudden flowering of language occurred around 50,000 years ago, this may well have been preceded by a long, slow adaptive evolution of brain mechanisms underlying speech generation and comprehension. Language mechanisms in australopithecines and in *H. erectus* may have been much more sophisticated than we suppose from their simple stone tools.

The postulated base we are building on is the episodic intelligence of the monkeys and apes (see Chapter 4) and the mimetic intelligence of early hominids. In the former, current aspects of the environment appear to control what an animal does next; there is no thinking about long-term projects. Decisions to fight, flee, feed, mate, or just scan the environment appear to be based on a present-centered reality. The later stage we call mimetic intelligence adds the more extended communication of social procedure and rituals. Language may have originated from oral reinforcement of symbolic gestures used in communication, such as the facial expressions that signal anger, sadness, puzzlement, derision, and disapproval, as well as the body gestures of shrugging shoulders, waving, clenching the fist, and the like. Linguistic and mimetic pathways could thus have developed in parallel, the linguistic pathway enriching and reinforcing the mimetic, even though it is possible to dissociate them (as in the self-experiment on page 92).

> *The cognitive changes underlying language did not necessarily develop to support spoken language as we now experience it, because there would have been no language acquisition support system. The words and symbols of language probably originated outside of language, with symbols initially invented for nonlinguistic purposes.*

Internal narrative

How, then, might spoken language have arisen from the sets of 20–50 vocal signals that we see in some social primates? The philosopher Daniel Dennett has speculated that an early step may have occurred when vocalizations that were used to share information ("tiger coming," "no food here,") began to be used for communication by an individual with itself as well as for communication between individuals. An example might be "Food here?"—a question that was originally addressed to others but then began to be asked by the individual in isolation, talking

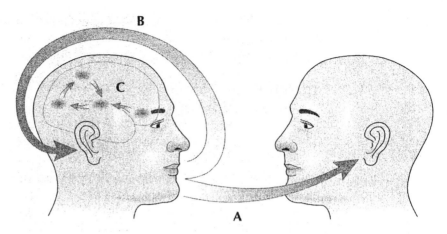

Figure 5–2   Dennett speculates that the activities of speaking and hearing, which originated in one individual signaling another (A), might have then proved useful to individuals in isolation, first as they spoke aloud and listened to themselves (B), and then as they developed internal brain pathways that could accomplish this without peripheral vocalization and audition (C).

to itself. Perhaps a system that evolved for communication with other individuals—your mouth speaks, other ears listen, others speak, you listen—could change into communication within the individual: speaking and listening to oneself (Figure 5–2). The virtues of talking very quietly to oneself and then silently answering, would be recognized. The loop of self-stimulation would be maintained, but the peripheral vocalization and audition portions would be dropped because they weren't contributing much. "Talking to oneself" aloud would be slow and laborious, compared to the swift unconscious cognitive processes it was based on, because it had to make use of large tracts of nervous system designed for other purposes—in particular for the production and comprehension of audible speech. Furthermore, it would be just as linear (limited to one topic at a time) as the social communication it evolved from. The idea of inventing new paths of internal communication is quite reasonable and is observed clinically in human patients with brain damage. The damaged area is not repaired, but new ways of performing the necessary tasks are discovered.

Language as an adaptation
Perhaps the most influential hypothesis is that language is an adaptation that developed because it supported the distinctions that need to be made in increasingly complex social organizations. One possibility is that early hominid alliances based on grooming became impractical

as the increasing amount of time spent on grooming in a complex society interfered with other activities. Language then evolved as a grooming substitute. Kinship, marriage, and lineage tracing certainly became much more complex in the transition from primate to hominid cultures. Social institutions grew more formalized and were given names. Rather than language being a difference that gave rise to culture, the stages of its formation are more likely to have been an outgrowth of culture.

Social structures are made up of relationships based on learned information about other group members. Social status plays an important role in the organization of kinship and marriage in both nonhuman and human primates. Information about social relationships can be communicated with far greater precision with language than without, making it easier to distinguish among close kin, kin at some remove, and individuals in other lineages. Naming individuals and relationships can make it possible to articulate the rules of social interactions between clans.

Evolution of brain structures supporting language

What happened, in terms of brain circuitry, to support the appearance of a human competence so distinctively different from the vocalizations of other vertebrates? No other species, including apes, has mastered the process of language production, although some chimpanzees raised in captivity have shown a capacity to learn the meaning of some human words and the syntax of simple sentences. Animal communication systems fall into three classes. They can be the sort of random variation on a theme observed in birdsong, a continuous signal that indicates the magnitude of some variable (as when the liveliness of a worker bee's dance indicates to its hivemates the richness of a food source), or a set of calls in which each serves a discrete purpose, such as warning of the presence of a predator. The distinctively different feature of human language is that an infinite number of meanings are made possible by the combinatorial system called grammar. Thanks to grammar, the number of complex words or sentences in a language is unlimited. Discrete elements are arranged into combinations whose meaning derives from the meanings of their parts.

Hominid language is a distinctive feature of the cerebral cortex, whereas the vocal calls of primates and other animals are controlled by older neural structures in the brain stem and limbic system that generate emotional behaviors. These older structures also control human vocalizations other than language, such as laughing, sobbing, and shouting in surprise or pain.

In modern monkey brains we observe areas, presumably present in our common ancestor, that appear to be homologs of the Broca's and Wernicke's areas in humans, which are involved in the generation and comprehension of language, respectively. The Broca's homolog is involved in movements of the face, mouth, tongue, and larynx; the Wernicke's homolog deals with sound sequences and vocal calls. As we saw in Chapter 4, cranial endocasts of *Homo habilis* fossil skulls indicate enlargement of these regions, and some investigators think that the neural preconditions for language are first met in this species. The most plausible idea is that these modules were slowly co-opted by other functions, or perhaps they were duplicated, with some of the duplicates taking on new inputs and outputs. In one of the several hominid species (*H. habilis*, *H. erectus*) that existed from 3 to 1 million years ago, an expansion or rearrangement of these brain areas would have permitted a transition from gestural and sound communication (mimetic intelligence) to phonemic language, in which the same sounds can be combined in different ways to make sound units (words) with different meanings. It has also been suggested that increases in the size of the frontal and parietal cortex and the appearance of cerebellar structures unique to the human brain are correlated with the development of language. It is a pity that we cannot document stages in these transitions. Our soft hominid brains leave no fossil records of the sort we find for skulls.

Language and the evolutionary tree

One might be tempted to ask "How did chimpanzee brains change into human brains with language?" but that approach is inappropriate. Implicitly, we would be assuming that evolution is like a ladder, with one species leading to the next. Rather, evolution is like a bush or tree, and the hominid evolutionary tree is a complex one with most of its branch points shrouded in mystery. Figure 5–3 depicts some of the origins, breaks, and branches in the hominid transitions discussed both in Chapter 4 and below. In the roughly 5 million years since our branch split from that of present-day chimpanzees, there have been 300,000–400,000 generations during which we could have evolved brain structures supporting a universal grammar while the chimps did not do so. The issue of whether "language" in chimps and that in humans have similarities is largely beside the point. Even if some chimps were taught to produce real signs and to group and order them consistently, this would not show that the human ability derived from the chimp's. The central point is that in the evolutionary tree, traits such as eyes, hands, and vocalizations have appeared several times on different branches, most of which did not lead to humans. Some of these animal adaptations, such as the Doppler radar used by bats and the celestial navigation capabilities of some migratory birds, rival human language in their sophistication and complexity.

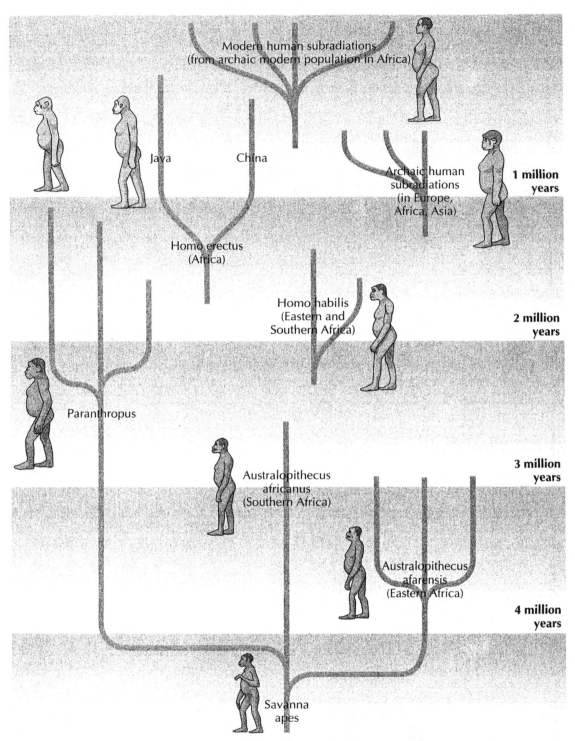

Figure 5–3 Hominid evolution depicted as a "pagoda tree" in which each level diverges into regional branches. The clusters of hominids at each level are poorly understood. Archaic moderns include groups distinctive to Africa and Europe (they are sometimes referred to as Heidelbergs, the group from which Neanderthals arose) and groups distinctive to Asia (Mapas). Fully modern humans diverged from a Heidelberg population in eastern Africa. Adapted from Kingdon, *Self-Made Man.*

The emergence of modern humans

What were hominids doing during the mimetic and linguistic transitions we have discussed? There is evidence of several waves of migration from Africa to the Eurasian continent over the past 1–2 million years. Archaic humans were firmly established in the Far East between 1 and 2 million years ago and in Europe no later than 700,000 years ago. An *H. erectus* site in Java has been dated to 1.8 million years ago. The rest of the globe was populated much more recently (Australia 50,000 years ago, Siberia 20,000 years ago, the Americas 11,000 years ago, and the Pacific Islands 30,000–1500 years ago).

A controversial question has been whether *H. erectus* evolved into *H. sapiens*, or a separate line that became *H. sapiens* displaced *H. erectus* worldwide as it did the Neanderthals in Europe. Two main hypotheses have been proposed. One hypothesis argues for a multiregional evolution of humans whereby *H. erectus*, *H. neanderthalensis*, and other populations semi-independently became the modern races of *H. sapiens*, with some gene flow between them. The other hypothesis contends that all modern humans derive from a small group of common ancestors that lived in Africa. These individuals evolved into the modern races of humans during their emigrations from Africa and displaced all other hominid lines. The genetic evidence in favor of this second scenario is now very strong.

Compelling genetic evidence suggests that all modern humans derive from a small group of common ancestors that lived in Africa between 100,000 and 300,000 years ago.

Evidence for the out-of-Africa hypotheses

The first data to point toward an African origin of all modern humans generated great excitement several years ago. It consisted of information on the genes of mitochondria, which are passed on to offspring almost exclusively by the mother. Such genes have higher mutation rates than nuclear genes, and the genetic distances between different human groups can be inferred from the number of mutations. Groups that have evolved independently of each other for a longer period of time should have accumulated greater numbers of different mutations. A computer algorithm was used to construct the most parsimonious sequence of changes that could have led to the genetic differences observed today. The first attempts at applying this algorithm suggested that mitochondrial DNA has been evolving for the longest time in Africa, with the ancestral lineage of all current DNAs traced to a single woman—the "mitochondrial Eve." Many other women presumably lived at the same time, but their mitochondrial lineages simply went extinct; that is, at some point they no longer had any descendants in an unbroken *female* line. (Subsequent analyses have shown that the same data set is also consistent with multiple genealogies, so it really doesn't prove the existence of a mitochondrial Eve.)

A second line of evidence, however, has supported the idea that all modern humans derive from a common ancestor who lived 100,000 to 300,000 years ago. A portion of the male Y chromosome (passed from father to son) contains the only genetic material besides mitochondrial DNA (passed from mother to daughter) that is inherited from just one parent and so is not recombined in ways that make it more difficult to reconstruct an evolutionary history. The fact that it shows very little variability across different races of modern humans suggests that modern *H. sapiens* could have descended from a small group of male ancestors who lived about 270,000 years ago. Another group of studies has now tackled nuclear DNA, focusing on a piece of chromosome 12, which has a great variety of patterns in sub-Saharan Africa, loses many patterns in Northeast Africa, and is dominated by just one type in the rest of the world. This evidence implies a series of small populations continually "budding off" from larger ones, losing variety as they go. These data suggest an African origin, dating to approximately 100,000 years ago, for all non-African human populations. Studies of one site on the Y chromosome suggest also that it was carried back into Africa from Asia, such that migration occurred not only out of, but also back into, Africa.

Genetic and linguistic differences between modern humans have been used to construct family trees describing the radiation and diversification of current races of humans from an original African stock. One branch separates African from all other populations; a second splits Europeans from the remainder of the non-Africans, and the relationships among the Native Americans, East Asians, Australians, and Melanesians are controversial. Because genetic, migrational, and linguistic family trees are so controversial, any particular story seems to unravel within a few years. Most linguists believe that after 10,000 years, little trace of a language remains in its descendants, which would make it very unlikely that traces of the most recent ancestor of all contemporary languages could be found.

Co-evolution of humans and their tools

The advent of tools caused the circumstances of hominids to be more and more "self-made," essentially turning us into artifacts of our own artifacts. (*H. erectus* was making sharp stone flakes for cutting meat about 2 million years ago and bifacial stone tools about 1.4 million years ago.) The fundamental mechanism, termed the "Baldwin effect" after its discoverer, is that new procedures or behaviors that increase reproductive success are followed more slowly by evolved forms that support them. It seems likely that we adapted to new technology (fire and tools) both physically and psychologically. Thus cooking and processing food removed the need for massive jaws and allowed us to colonize colder parts of the world. Similarly, boats made possible our migration to distant lands and islands.

More sophisticated technology was presumably a major factor in Pleistocene population explosions that occurred in separate parts of the world. Africa's population increased rapidly approximately 80,000 years ago, whereas Europe's exploded about 40,000 years ago—a much later date. This coincides with a large leap in the sophistication of tools, and with the appearance of decorated artifacts and cave art. One unsolved puzzle asks why the stocky Neanderthals, about 30 percent larger than modern humans, coexisted with modern humans in Europe and the Middle East for over fifty thousand years and then disappeared. (Recent analysis of DNA from Neanderthal fossil bones shows in fact that modern humans and Neanderthals evolved independently over a period of more than 500,000 years.) The

Humans have become "tools of their tools," as slow, adaptive changes in body and brain design have supported new technologies and behaviors.

supposition is that the Neanderthals must have lost some kind of evolutionary competition, perhaps as moderns developed more elaborate social systems or superior tools and better food procurement. The main challenge to survival faced by groups of humans during these periods was probably other groups of humans competing for the same resources.

The origins of mythic intelligence

The mind-tool of words permitted the evolution of language, the formulation of ideas, and the birth of a new kind of culture. Donald suggests that just as mimetic cognition collected episodic event perception into more extended and instructive patterns, the next transition to an intelligence (which he terms mythic) collected the scattered repertoires of mimetic culture under the governance of integrative myth—a story of how things are (see Figure 5–4).

Here we are talking about the middle Paleolithic, 200,000 to 40,000 years ago—the time of archaic *H. sapiens*. This is when the second major increase in brain size occurred and the vocal tract began to assume its modern form. The suggestion is that during this period, humans were all enveloped by a mythic participatory reality, without the sense of self and other that is characteristic of modern Western culture. We feel only vestiges of this today, as when we are overcome by powerful public emotions, such as patriotism or civic pride, during song or chanting.

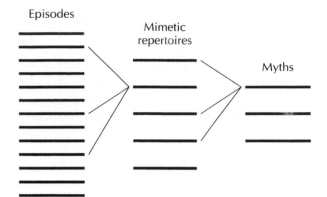

Figure 5–4   This drawing expands Figure 5–1 to the next proposed stage of hominid intelligence, the collection of sets of mimetic repertoires into the different continuous stories that are the foundation of a *mythic intelligence* supported by language.

Symbolic devices such as the vocabulary of a language supported mythic invention and the integration of shared knowledge. Thus the separate repertoires of mimetic culture were collected under the umbrella of integrative myth. Constructing histories of the past and models of the human universe required both symbolic invention and phonological adaptation. The story line of a myth could specify the proper places of plants, animals, humans, and tools in the natural order. A collective mind could be governed by myth, and it still is today in the arena of social values.

What caused the transition to upper Paleolithic culture?

Why does the archeological record show a relatively sudden appearance of artifacts and inventions long after the brain of *H. sapiens* had attained its present size? The really great leap in human tools and art didn't occur until 40,000 or 50,000 years ago—with spear throwers appearing before harpoons or bows and arrows, beads and pendants before cave painting. During this period, the appearance of ornaments and images seems to signal the emergence of new forms of social organization. Some suggest that this "big bang" of cultural activity and development correlates with a final gelling of language capabilities, as the anatomical basis for modern spoken language and complex vocabularies fell into place. Although many studies have emphasized a European center (southwestern France) for this sudden flowering of human culture, more recent evidence from archeological sites in Africa suggests that advanced stone tools and blades were appearing in

Africa as early as 240,000 years ago. This evidence raises the possibility of a slower evolution, rather than a revolution, in human culture, tools, and language.

Evolutionary psychology—the search for a universal mind

The story we have told so far is now being viewed from a new perspective—one that many believe may affect our thinking about ourselves as profoundly as the Freudian revolution did toward the beginning of this century. The newly emerging field of *evolutionary psychology* claims to describe and explain human behavior in a fundamentally new way. Instead of Freud's picture of the mind as a bunch of squabbling persons—conscious versus unconscious, superego versus ego versus id—it postulates a complex array of behavioral modules evolved as adaptations to our Paleolithic ancestral environment, modules that all modern humans share. We will review some of the background for this model, keeping in mind that it is highly controversial. Information presented in several subsequent chapters of this book in fact argues against it, so it is important to outline both sides of the debate.

A brief history of recent trends leading up to evolutionary psychology might be useful at this point. A number of books popular in the 1960s argued that we should look to sex, aggression, territoriality, pair bonding, or other socially evolved behaviors as the real mechanisms that determine the form of human society. The authors of these books did not see the history of our ideas and institutions as an explanation of our current society but rather viewed them as the outcome of interactions between individuals determined by blind biological processes. All of these arguments were flawed, because each selected one aspect of what it assumed to be the behavior of primitive humans and made that single aspect account for the whole of culture. And the "drives" that were postulated were often at variance with the facts.

Evolutionary psychologists picture the brain not as a general-purpose problem-solving machine but as something closer to a Swiss Army knife, a gadget that includes separate tools that evolved for specialized purposes.

The 1970s saw the appearance of *sociobiology,* defined by its proponent E.O. Wilson as "the systematic study of the biological basis of all social behavior." Early sociobiological arguments frequently took contemporary human motivational terms such as "aggression," "sex," "dominance," and "caste" and assumed they were natural categories instead of mere projections of our fertile minds onto those of animals. Evolutionary psychologists, as the intellectual heirs of sociobiology, have maintained that early attempts at sociobiology tried to skip psychological mechanisms and assumed a link too direct between genes and complicated behaviors. Thus sociobiologists missed crucial causal links by ignoring how evolved psychological mechanisms, whether genetic or nongenetic, might play out in individuals and groups.

Genetic arguments for an evolved psychology

Some core ideas in evolutionary theory suggest reasons why social modules of mind would have been a plausible evolutionary adaptation for humans. A starting point was the realization that males and females face different situations in trying to pass their genes on to their offspring. For many animals, including humans, males can reproduce hundreds of times a year, females only once. Thus for a woman there is

In many species, males and females need to follow different strategies for getting their genes into the next generation.

little (genetic) point in mating with multiple partners, but each new partner offers a man a chance to get more of his genes into the next generation. Women must sacrifice much more for reproduction than men do. Hence women's reproduction is best served by their being selective about sexual partners, judging the male's fitness and commitment and his potential to contribute to or invest in the offspring. Sexual selection thus works in two ways: Males evolve to compete for scarce female eggs, and females evolve to compete for scarce male investment. The idea is that in many species there is an evolutionary "arms race," wherein natural selection favors male brains that are good at deceiving females about their future devotion, and female brains that are good at spotting deception. (One might call this the "sweet-talking" theory of evolution.)

Comparative anthropological studies show a universal pattern of women being more selective about sex partners than men are, and men desiring sex with many partners. It appears that in all known cultures, women with unrestrained libidos are judged more harshly than comparable men. Thirty-seven different cultures have been documented in which males focus on younger mates (better able to produce babies), whereas women prefer older mates (better able to provide resources). Most evolutionary psychologists would argue that it is implausible for all peoples to have arrived at these similar customs independently, without significant genetic encouragement. They assert that it is unlikely that these behaviors were present for 200,000–500,000 years, before modern humans radiated out of Africa, and were transmitted purely by cultural means without being extinguished in a single culture.

What other selection pressures might have acted on men and women to generate sexual differences in brain and behavior? One approach to understanding the factors that may have shaped human evolution during the Paleolithic is to observe existing hunter-gatherer societies. Men generally are responsible for foraging over long distances and for the construction of weapons used in war. Women specialize in food gathering near the camp, making clothing, caring for children, and preparing the food. In men this division of labor might lead to selection for long-distance route-finding ability and targeting skills. In women it might favor short-range navigation, perhaps using landmarks, fine motor capabilities, and subtle perceptual discriminations.

Some of the behavioral adaptations that were appropriate to conditions in the Paleolithic may be damaging to us today. All humans show dietary preferences for salt, fat, and sugar. These are important nutrients, and they are likely to have been very scarce in our ancestral environments, so unrestrained tastes for them would have been a useful adaptation. Now, however, they are so easy to obtain that many of us get sick from eating too much of them. Also of dubious value in modern times is the evolved behavior of male aggression, reflecting pressures of sexual selection common to most vertebrate species. Another vestige of our ancestral behavior in modern human society is the vertebrate male trait of raising the odds that his genes will be passed on by having not just a spouse or mate, but

The fact that natural selection gave the human brain mechanisms appropriate for action in the Paleolithic world is no guarantee that these mechanisms are still useful today.

other partners as well. That these behaviors, both dietary and sexual, are "natural" does not excuse them; being predisposed to a certain behavior doesn't mean that the disposition should be indulged. Knowing we have such a predisposition does help, however, if we want to change our behavior.

Evolution of cooperation

In the foregoing description, we have been following a gene-centered argument, which rationalizes evolutionary changes in terms of strategies used by our "selfish genes" (a term popularized by Richard Dawkins) to propagate themselves. A next step is to realize that it is not essential to pass on the genes that happen to be in one's own body, so long as copies of those genes are transmitted. They can be carried by close relatives whose reproduction one helps to ensure. Thus genes that enhanced cooperation between family members would be favored by natural selection. This process, referred to as *kin selection*, is found throughout the invertebrate and vertebrate phyla, and chemical cues are frequently used in recognizing one's kin. Extended families—

several generations living together—occur in about 3 percent of avian and mammalian species. Families that control high-quality resources are more stable over time, and that goes for an extended family of birds controlling a granary of seeds hidden in trees as well as for a human aristocracy with its hereditary land holdings. Poorer families tend to disintegrate over time, so their genes are more likely to be diluted.

For humans the kin selection mechanism may have given rise to the sympathy, empathy, compassion, and love that bond family members together. Further, this may have provided a platform for a further development: *reciprocal altruism,* or cooperation between genetically unrelated members of the same species. A series of careful mathematical arguments has demonstrated that the genes of groups of cooperating individuals should be passed on more successfully than those of groups whose members do not cooperate. Thus the appearance of genes that promoted the development of cooperative behaviors would be favored. Reciprocal altruism is fundamental to all human cultures and also in animal societies—especially chimpanzees—where individuals and their past deeds are recognized and recorded. Selection for behaviors that support cooperation could be an evolutionary force underlying the appearance of a sense of obligation, sensitivity to betrayal, friendship, enmity, sympathy, dislike, and gratitude.

Does the suggested origin of our more noble behaviors from our "selfish genes" mean that our selfless behaviors are really selfish—that we are being hypocrites? Not at all, the evolutionary origins of our motives must be distinguished from the motives themselves.

What evidence is there that any of these behaviors are modules of a "social mind" common to all humans? One line of support comes from brain lesion studies. Stroke or cancer in certain parts of the brain, especially the frontal lobes, appears to compromise social behaviors while leaving many other faculties intact. Some intriguing evidence also comes from psychological experiments showing that people are good at solving difficult logical puzzles when these are cast in the form of social exchange, particularly when the object is to find out whether someone is cheating. Is there a "cheater-detection" module among the mental organs that govern reciprocal altruism? Does a "group-forming module" enhance the capacity for identification with other people as parts of a unified hunting or working group, so that individuals make sacrifices for the group as a whole? To carry these ideas to their extreme, reciprocal altruism might be rephrased as the Golden Rule: "Do unto others as you would have them do unto you." Thus it may provide us with a predisposition toward moral behavior, just as each of us has, in the presence of other humans, a predisposition to learn a language.

A further element in building up a story line for evolved psychologies in humans rests on looking not at the origins of cooperation but at the consequences of competition. A wide variety of both vertebrates and invertebrates have dominance-subordination hierarchies. These result from compromises made by individuals in their competition for mates, food, and other resources. Status hierarchies achieve their ultimate sophistication in primate and human societies. Rank is signaled by a complex set of facial, vocal, gestural, and body language cues that function essentially as organs of social behavior. A significant part of the human male ego may result from the same forces that produced the stag's massive antlers: sexual competition among males.

It is fascinating, then, that human societies display two highly developed, and frequently conflicting, adaptations—competition (status hierarchies) and cooperation (reciprocal altruism). Think how large a fraction of your own conscious thought is spent in these two arenas, considering what groups you belong to, what your status is, and whether to cooperate or compete. The fundamental argument here is that although different cultures show astonishing variation in the surface behaviors associated with either cooperation or status competition, the underlying modules of behavior are the consequence of a genetic and developmental environment that all humans share.

SELF-EXPERIMENT

Think for a moment about the activities you engage in during a typical day. How many of them are colored by your sense of your relative status with respect to others and by the question of whether you will cooperate or compete with them? All social vertebrates face such choices.

Evidence from cross-cultural studies

The preceding discussion has a very specific context for modern humans. We are all descendants of the humans who constituted the final successful radiation out of Africa that began approximately 200,000 years ago, replacing all other hominid groups. Our minds are adapted to the way of life of hunter-gatherers, not to modern circumstances such as the invention of agriculture, which occurred only within the last 10,000 years. Psychological solutions to problems faced by hunter-gatherers were crafted over the past 1–2 million years, not the past 10,000. A "bottom-up" approach to evolutionary psychology asks what these problems were (finding nutritious foods, finding a mate, avoiding predation, communicating with others, detecting cheating) and considers options for solving them. In contrast, a "top-down" approach is useful in asking whether common motifs across cultures suggest universal mechanisms, and it is to this approach that we turn next.

A significant problem with this approach has been that anthropologists are generally rewarded when they find differences between cultures, not similarities. Many accounts of unusual behaviors have proved to be mistaken, such as Margaret Mead's claims that Samoans had free sex. Also incorrect are claims that the Native American Hopi have a different concept of time; Trobriand islanders have a different notion of cause and effect; and the Inuits' proximity to snow makes them better able to distinguish varieties of white than most of us, even though more words for varieties of "white" are used. These misunderstandings have all been taken as evidence that fundamental categories of reality are not "in" the world but are imposed by culture. An extreme is the view of many cultural anthropologists that science is just another culture to be studied, a culture that attempts a form of cognitive colonialism. A vigorous debate exists in the American Anthropological Association and in many academic departments, between biological and cultural anthropologists. The biologists search for evolutionary and physiological bases for social behavior, while cultural investigators deconstruct cultural texts and tracts by applying postmodern criteria.

> *Using the idea of reverse engineering, one approach to understanding our brains is to find out what they were designed to do. It is the mechanisms that serve these purposes, and not necessarily expressed cultural behaviors, that we might expect to be universal.*

Listing and evaluating human universals

Many candidates for universal human behaviors suggested by cultural studies are related to language: metaphor, narrative, poetry, myth, rituals, and words for units of time, body parts, plants and animals, kinship, logical relations (same, different, not, in, part/whole), and so on. Others are oriented more toward social structures, including such generalizations as "hierarchical social organization results in economic inequality," "labor is divided by sex and age," "male and female natures are different," and "men dominate the political sphere." We do not necessarily look for genes that dictate these traits; they do not have to be instincts or innate psychological tendencies. They are the result of complex interactions between developing human brains and their social environments and are only abstractly related to a universal mind.

> *Comparative cultural studies have generated lists of human behaviors that seem to occur in all societies, and the evidence for a core set of behaviors is compelling.*

Here is a list, offered by the psychologist Steven Pinker in his book *The Language Instinct,* of suggested instinctual modules, aside from language and perception, that might eventually pass the test of universality.

1. Intuitive mechanics: knowledge of the motions, forces, and deformations that objects undergo.

2. Intuitive biology: understanding how plants and animals work.
3. Number.
4. Mental maps for large territories.
5. Habitat selection: seeking safe, information-rich, productive environments, generally savannah-like.
6. Danger, including the emotions of fear and caution; phobias for stimuli such as heights, confinement, risky social encounters, and so on.
7. Food: what is good to eat.
8. Contamination, including the emotion of disgust, reactions to certain things that seem inherently disgusting, and intuitions about contagion and disease.
9. Monitoring of current well-being, including the emotions of happiness and sadness and the moods of contentment and restlessness.
10. Intuitive psychology: predicting other people's behavior from their beliefs and desires.
11. A mental Rolodex: a database of individuals, with blanks for kinship, status, or rank; history of exchange of favors; inherent skills and strengths; plus criteria that rank the value of each trait.
12. Self-concept: gathering and organizing information about one's value to other people and packaging it for others.
13. Justice: sense of right, obligations, and deserts, including the emotions of anger and revenge.
14. Kinship, including nepotism and allocation of parenting effort.
15. Mating, including feelings of sexual attraction, love, and intentions of fidelity and desertion.

How do we begin to evaluate such a list of proposed universals? Among the varieties of human behaviors, there are some with clear genetic components (facial recognition and language generation) and some that seem much less likely to be genetically determined (the writing of language and the control of vehicles such as horses and airplanes). In between lies a large gray area populated by more or less plausible ideas like the "social function of intellect" hypothesis, which suggests that reasoning and thought (as opposed to learning and memory) evolved to hold human societies together (making their members more likely to survive), not for learning facts or skills. Cognitive psychology has turned up a number of interesting deviations from what would be ideal reasoning—deviations that would make sense if we had an innate predisposition to finding quick and dirty solutions to problems posed by the logic of social exchanges. Unfortunately, plausibility is not enough, and we will have to wait some time for fundamental tests of the existence of instinctual or genetically influenced modules of social mind.

Some geneticists and developmental biologists are very critical of efforts to explain so many of our common behaviors as evolutionary adaptations, and they would quarrel with the amount of space devoted to the topic in this book. One of their points is that we cannot exclude the possibility that a given behavior arose not as an adaptation, but rather by accident. Testing the hypothesis that each of the universal behavioral modules—the naive early physics, biology, psychology, and so on—is a semi-independent adaptive module almost like a body part is difficult. To understand where a body part (such as a heart, a kidney, or an opposable thumb) came from, we need to see how it varies or is shared by groups who descend from a common ancestor. The proposed "mind modules" of evolutionary psychology leave no fossils, they appear in only one instance (all modern humans), and there are no creatures that have more or fewer of these proposed modules of mind to compare ourselves with. Thus we simply can't know how they arose; we can only speculate.

Cognitive and developmental neuroscientists are still in the early stages of formulating and testing plausible theories of cellular mechanisms by which genetic instructions could be translated into "deception detectors" or other social modules. Perhaps the situation will be clearer when we better understand the brain circuits that underlie these behaviors. It does not seem unreasonable to suggest that genetically determined developmental programs of our brains incline us to learning social strategies influenced by the local social environment, just as the product of our language "instinct" is determined by the language spoken by individuals around us. The results have elements that are universal across known cultures. The fact that a behavior is universal does not imply some sort of direct link between a gene or genes and that behavior. All that is required of the genetic structures is that they allow the development of behavior modules that form as human brains evolve in a social dialog with other humans as well as through interaction with the physical environment. That the result may be a module of social behavior present in all humans may attest to the uniformity of the developmental environment of those humans and not to genes directly establishing that behavior. Just as feral children raised by animals in the wild are unable to develop language, so they also presumably fail to develop the array of social modules of behavior

> *To describe a modern behavior in terms of its presumed adaptive significance in the Paleolithic may be the equivalent of making up a "just so" story, for we have few means of proving the point.*

suggested by the evolutionary psychologists. We will discuss the roles of genes and environments further in Parts II and III of this book.

The evolution of ideas and customs

In thinking about either universal minds or culturally specific minds, we need to consider the time scale over which the relevant processes are occurring. Until now, we have mainly emphasized genetic and evolutionary mechanisms that underlie both constancy and change between generations over many millennia. Body language and verbal communication introduce a vastly more rapid way of ensuring both constancy and change within cultures and a means by which cultures distinguish themselves from each other. Ideas and customs, in addition to our genes, can act as units of information transfer that regulate behavior and pass from one generation to the next.

Students of animal behavior use the term "phenotypic cloning" to describe the process by which parents can so firmly impress behaviors on their offspring that the behaviors (phenotypes) seem to be inherited. (In spite of what we like to think, we all act remarkably like our parents as we grow older.) A core point is the argument that differences in behavioral styles between one family line and another provide a context for natural selection. The behaviors that work best are passed on because of differential reproductive success, and less adaptive behaviors are lost from the "phenotypic pool" analogous to the gene pool of genetics. This mechanism acts also at the level of humans and animal cultures, and in this context it is termed *group selection*. Over longer periods of time, genetic changes in individuals that facilitate the adaptive behaviors adopted by a group might then be selected for. This is the Baldwin effect mentioned in the section "Co-evolution of humans and their tools" and is a scenario offered by some evolutionary psychologists.

> *In humans and other animals, learned behaviors can be passed on as reliably and reproducibly as though the information were in the chromosomes.*

Human cultural groups are adaptive responses, just as are birds' feathers and mammals' fur. They are vehicles of selection and have the effect of reducing the importance of differences in fitness between individuals within the group. Groups of humans organize and defend themselves as though the groups were individual organisms, with homeostatic mechanisms and defense strategies. They have a sense of "I," with childish and adult components. A fascinating array of adaptive and maladaptive behaviors have been cataloged by social psychologists. For instance, self-deception on the part of individuals, tribes, and nations is so pervasive that it is tempting to speculate that it has a biological ultimate cause—as though trying to do (or avoid) things that rationally shouldn't be done (or avoided) in some cases generates variation that benefits the species.

The concept of memes

To describe the propagation of cultural ideas, the biologist Richard Dawkins has used a genetic analogy and coined the term *meme* (rhymes with "cream"). Dawkins gives the opening four notes of Beethoven's Fifth symphony as one example of a meme. He also notes, as an example of a meme in animals, that in 1920s Britain, birds learned to open milk bottles on people's doorsteps. A few titmice then learned that they could puncture the foil caps to drink, and this information was passed on to several other species. The philosopher Daniel Dennett points out that one of the first major steps a human brain takes in postnatal self-design is to provide an environment for specific cultural memes. It gets adjusted to the local conditions that matter the most—in a few years, it becomes a Swahili- or Japanese- or English-speaking brain. Newborns can form sounds characteristic of any language, but they begin to specialize in the language they hear and lose the ability to form "foreign" sounds. The idea is that once our brains have built the entrance and exit pathways for the vehicles of language, they swiftly become host to entities—the memes—that are mostly specific to different cultures and have evolved to thrive in just such a niche.

The term "meme" refers to a unit of cultural information that replicates itself reliably. The meme is a replicator, the cultural equivalent of the gene.

The evolution of memes such as creation myths could not begin until animal evolution had created species such as the advanced hominids, with brains that could provide for their shelter and habits of communication that could provide for their transmission. The access that individuals have to the ideas of their cultures (we don't have to reinvent the wheel) probably swamps most individual genetic differences in brain design and largely removes the advantage from those who are born slightly more inventive.

Evolution of memes

Darwinian mechanisms are at work: There is variation (different ideas or concepts), replication (ideas or concepts passing between humans via language and imitation), and differential fitness (passing on some ideas, like a warning signal, is more useful than transmitting others). However, in the world of memes the best ideas do not always win; accident, timing, and marketing may be more important. We persist, for example, in using the present-day typewriter keyboard, even though other designs are much more efficient. Memes, as replicators, propagate at blinding speed compared with the pace of gene evolution. Another important distinction is that memes do not have the clearly defined, independent nature of genes, so we can't quantify and analyze their transmission in the same manner. Another crucial distinction is that ideas are not passively replicated and transmitted. Instead, each individual or group passing them on can "add value," or creatively alter them during transmission. The success of an idea is measured by the spread of its influence in the face of competing ideas.

The evolution of memes should be visualized not with the tree metaphor that we have used for the diversification of biological species, but rather as a joining, parting, and interconnecting of lineages— like the streams of a river delta running apart, and then sometimes back together, as they move toward the ocean.

SUMMARY The origins of our distinctly *Homo sapiens* intelligence, how it is that hominids came to develop the ability to use symbols and language, will always remain shrouded in uncertainty. We will never have a direct view of the brain anatomy and physiology of 2 million years ago. Still, some very strong clues suggest the progression of intelligences as outlined in this chapter. The appearance of new facial muscles that we now use to communicate meaning and emotion, much more complex than those of chimpanzees, probably reflects the development of a new kind of mimetic hominid intelligence. This intelligence supported social interactions through more sophisticated emotional kinesic communication, incorporating complex facial expressions and other body language. As hominids developed skills and social structures that permitted them to migrate out of Africa over the rest of the globe, the intellectual challenge of coping with ever more complex environments and social interactions was met in part by the invention of symbol use and spoken language.

We are the descendants of a small group of modern humans that originated in Africa approximately 200,000 years ago and then moved out of Africa to displace all other contemporary hominids, including the Neanderthals in Europe and the Middle East and the remaining *H. erectus* in Asia. This restricted origin of modern humans lends support to the idea that an evolved "social mind" underlies a universal human nature—that in spite of the amazing diversity of human cultures, we do not start with a completely blank slate. Evolutionary psychology portrays us as influenced by universal psychological mechanisms that are adaptations to our ancestral environment—to our past as hunter-gatherers in Paleolithic Africa. The engine that has driven the blinding speed of modern human evolution has been the evolution of ideas and customs. Culture determines in part what our brains become, how they specialize during their development to perform particular skilled motor activities, devise languages, and engage in rituals. Our biology and our culture shape each other through a never-ending feedback loop that operates during individual development and is transmitted from generation to generation by teaching. These developmental processes that shape our individual and social selves are the subject of Part II of this book. ■

Questions for Thought

1. Hand axes that have two faces crafted to make a sharp cutting edge have been found at *H. erectus* sites dating back to about 1.5 million years ago. Try to list the different kinds of intelligence, such as the ability to plan ahead, that would be required for such a task. Can this list be described as a set of capabilities intermediate between those of modern apes and humans?

2. What evidence might you look for to develop further the idea that humans become tools of their own tools—that technologies such as spoken language or making spears facilitate adaptive supporting changes in brain and body structures?

3. Imagine that you have discovered a hidden mountain valley in Java in which a population of *H. erectus* has lived for the past million years, isolated from contact with all other hominids. Individuals communicate with sounds and gestures that bear no obvious relationship to modern language but are obviously much more complex than the communications used by modern apes. How would you go about determining whether this group had yet invented symbols (things that represent something else because of a relationship, convention, or resemblance)?

4. The mating habits of humans that are observed across many cultures, such as the preference of younger women for older, financially secure male partners, and the designation of symmetrical faces as "attractive," is taken by some as evidence for an evolved universal psychology in humans, strongly influenced by genetics. Can you think of other explanations? Devise experiments to evaluate the relative importance of innate biases and cultural instructions (including possible thought experiments that, for ethical reasons, you wouldn't actually carry out with real humans).

Suggestions for further general reading

The first three books deal with the origins of language.

Deacon, T.W. 1997. *The Symbolic Species—The Co-Evolution of Language and the Brain*. New York: Norton.

Donald, M.D. 1991. *Origins of the Modern Mind*. Cambridge, MA: Harvard University Press. (This book is the source for the descriptions of mimetic and mythic intelligence presented in this chapter.)

Pinker, S. 1994. *The Language Instinct*. New York: William Morrow. (A number of points in this chapter are taken from this book, which is a sheer pleasure to read. Chapter 13 discusses human universals.)

Dawkins, R. 1976. *The Selfish Gene*. New York: Oxford University Press. (An introduction to the gene-centered view of evolution that provides a basis for some of the ideas in evolutionary psychology; also an introduction to the idea of memes.)

Kingdon, J. 1993. *Self-Made Man—Human Evolution from Eden to Extinction?* New York: Wiley. (This book provides a detailed account of hominid evolution and is the source of the information in Figure 5–3.)

Wright, R. 1994. *The Moral Animal*. New York: Pantheon Books. (The description of evolutionary psychology in this chapter draws heavily on this stimulating introduction to the area.)

Reading on more advanced or specialized topics

Barkow, J.H., Cosmides, L., & Tooby, J. 1992. *The Adapted Mind*. New York: Oxford University Press. (A series of essays on evolutionary psychology.)

Brown, D.E. 1991. *Human Universals*. Philadelphia: Temple University Press. (A more detailed presentation of potential universals in human behavior.)

Sober, E. & Wilson, D.S. 1994. Re-introducing group selection to the human behavioral sciences. Behavioral and Brain Sciences. 17:585–608. (This essay deals with groups of animals or humans as units of selection, arguing that the gene-centered view presented by Dawkins is too restricted.)

Sperber, D. 1996. *Explaining Culture: A Naturalistic Approach*. Oxford, England: Blackwell. (A consideration of the evolution and epidemiology of cultural ideas.)

Part II
Developing Mind

Chapter 6

Plastic Mind

We now leave general descriptions of the evolution of hominid minds, psychology, and culture to turn to a more detailed account of how those minds develop, the next theme we need in assembling a description of the biology of our minds. The first part of this book has outlined the increasing sophistication and complexity of animal and human minds over evolutionary time, focusing mainly on the adult forms that mate and pass their genes on to future generations. These minds and brains start out as a mere blueprint, or template, provided by their genetic history, and then their adult forms arise only through a complicated sequence of developmental steps. To change the final product, the building blocks and/or the steps in their construction have to be changed.

It is remarkable how labile, or plastic, the construction of brains and minds can be. It varies because the intimate details depend on the actual environment provided by other cells in the developing embryo, on interactions between embryo and mother, and finally on interactions of the brains and bodies of growing children with their physical and social environment. Each of us has a unique brain whose formation is directed by our early surroundings, language, and culture. The structures described below form in a stereotyped and fairly constant way during embryonic development, but after birth they continue to grow and can be molded and shaped by their interaction with the outside world. This ensemble of evolutionary and individual developmental history forms the adult "society of mind" that is the subject of Part III of this book.

This chapter offers some evolutionary arguments for why brain development has become more malleable in more complicated animals, and it also describes the amazing plasticity that we can observe in developing as well as adult brains. This plasticity underlies the effects that both social experience and sexual differentiation have on brain processes, and it is required for the changes in nerve connections that support memory and learning. Our ability to remember facts and procedures—perhaps the most striking example of our brain plasticity—is considered in this chapter. This type of cognitive neuroscience is emphasized later, in Part III, but there are two reasons for discussing it briefly here. First, similar changes in nerve cell synapses seem to occur during nerve development and during the storage of some kinds of memories. Second, the human "selves" whose construction we consider in Chapter 7 are built from memories.

An outline of brain development

Development consists of an intricate sequence of cell divisions and migrations that create local environments whose different chemistries turn different sets of genes on or off. Early development is dominated by axial information systems (dorsal-ventral, head-tail) that span the whole embryo and cause localized gene actions in different parts of the growing embryo. Events at this stage show considerable developmental flexibility and thus are a target for adaptive changes during evolution. Midway through development, an intricate interconnectivity occurs between elements that will later come to represent separate modules such as organ primordia (of brain, heart, lung, liver, and so on). This developmental path restricts the flexibility of the system because changes in one module can alter many others. By late development, however, more developmental flexibility is seen again because the body has been highly modularized. At this point, adaptive changes in a liver, for example, don't have to cause changes in nervous tissue. Similarly, a genetic change that improves the effectiveness of a brain module doesn't have to affect the kidney.

The enormity of the problem we face when we try to understand the development of our brain can be illustrated with some simple numbers. Our brains contain at least 10^{10} neurons with an average of 10^4 nerve connections or synapses to each, yet the human genome contains less than 10^{5-6} genes. Thus there is no way that the position of each nerve cell, much less each of the many connections made by that cell, could be uniquely specified by a single gene. The problem is compounded by the need for instructions to form all of the other organ systems of our bodies.

We share with all vertebrates an embryo that in its early stages is a flat plate made up of inner, middle, and outer layers: *endoderm, mesoderm,* and *ectoderm.* Figure 6–1(A–C) shows cross sections of an early embryo that indicate the way these layers fold to form the *neural tube* from which the central nervous system develops. Figure 6–1(D) shows a view of the neural tube from above, cut horizontally so that you can see its interior. You can imagine this neural tube as a sausage-shaped balloon filled with water (*cerebrospinal fluid,* or CSF). Three swellings at the front end of the balloon form forebrain, midbrain, and hindbrain (you might find it useful to refer to Figure 3–2, which offers a side view of these structures). The forebrain further subdivides into a central portion (diencephalon) and two vesicles (telencephalon) that sprout from it to form eventually the two cerebral hemispheres that constitute our cerebral cortex. (Throughout this bulging and folding process, the central CSF-containing channels are maintained and become the *ventricular system* of the adult brain.) Two smaller vesicles that sprout from the diencephalon become the *optic nerve* and *retina.* The diencephalon finally differentiates into the thalamus and hypothalamus. The thalamus is the gateway for information going to and from the cerebral cortex. The telencephalon folds onto itself to form the hippocampus and olfactory cortex on its internal and bottom surfaces. These structures are two cell layers thick. Then, only in mammals, the top external part of the telencephalon forms the "new cortex," or neocortex, which has six layers of

Figure 6–1 Formation of the neural tube, neural crest, and brain vesicles. (A) The three basic cell types of the early embryo. The endoderm generates many of our internal organs, the mesoderm generates our bones and muscles, and the nervous system and skin come entirely from ectoderm. A part of the ectoderm gives rise to the nervous system by forming a flat sheet of cells called the neural plate. (B, C) A groove forms in this plate, and the walls of the groove join to form the neural tube. The whole central nervous system (CNS), consisting of spinal cord and brain, develops from this tube. As this happens, some neural ectoderm pinches off just to the sides of the neural tube. This is the neural crest that gives rise to the peripheral nervous system (PNS) described in Chapter 3. (D) A view of the neural tube from above, showing forebrain, midbrain, and hindbrain. Adapted from Figures 7.8 and 7.9 in Bear et al. *Neuroscience: Exploring the Brain.*

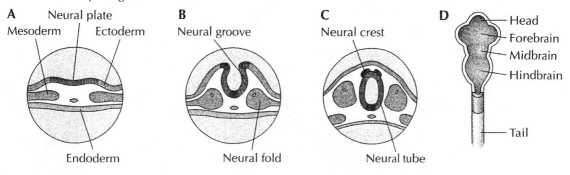

nerve cells. When people speak of the cerebral cortex, they usually mean the neocortex, even though "cortex" properly refers to all of the structures derived from the telencephalon. Figure 6–2 provides simple summary drawings of the developing human brain, from the stage of the neural tube shown in Figure 6–1 to the formation of the neocortex.

These brain structures, along with those described in Chapter 3, provide us with a basic hard-wired ensemble of automatic, reflexive, and instinctive mechanisms shaped by genetic trial and error over many generations. If we put our hand on a hot stove, we need not think about escaping as withdrawal reflexes take over, jerking it out of harm's way. We share with other vertebrates hardwiring for fighting, fleeing, sex, aggression, sleeping, and eating. Such hardwiring is centered in the primitive mammalian brain, the limbic system, and in such other structures as the brainstem, thalamus,

We are born with brains wired to attend longer to stimuli that look like human faces than to other stimuli, and our own faces register appropriate emotional responses.

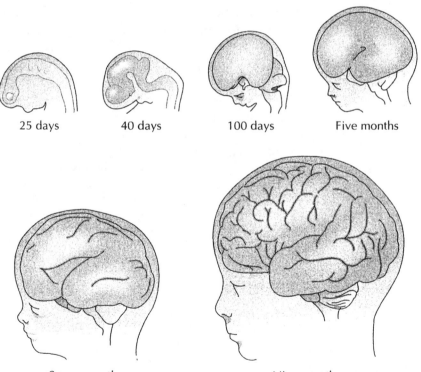

25 days   40 days   100 days   Five months

Seven months   Nine months

Figure 6–2 Changes in the structure of the developing human brain. The first three drawings, which indicate the swellings of the neural tube during the formation of forebrain, midbrain, and hindbrain, are shown enlarged with respect to the later stages. These later stages show the cerebral hemispheres overgrowing the midbrain and hindbrain, as well as partly obscuring the cerebellum.

and hypothalamus. The inferior temporal cortex of 5-week-old monkeys contains neurons that respond to faces and complex geometrical patterns. Our short-term and longer-term behaviors can be under instinctive control. We act out daily, monthly, and annual cycles as we sleep and wake, produce fertile eggs once a month, and undergo seasonal changes in mood and affect.

There is a problem, however, in relying only on hardwired, or inflexible, behavioral routines that have been crafted over millions of years of evolution. Just as they evolved slowly, they can change only over many generations, as genes and developmental mechanisms are altered, and numerous features of the environment change much faster than that. The solution that evolved as brains became more complicated during evolution was to make their formation more plastic—patterned by the actual surroundings in which they must function. This permits human adaptation to an environment to occur on the time scale of a single life span, rather than the many generations that would be required for genetic selection within the population's gene pool.

Origins of plasticity

Having a nervous system whose design is completely predetermined by a fixed set of genes and developmental sequences has one major drawback. If the environment changes suddenly, the animal may be left with inflexible behaviors appropriate to the environment that shaped its evolution but quite dysfunctional under the new conditions. A solution, or adaptation, to this problem would be to have genes specify not one fixed nervous system, but rather a starting array of options that can be tested for their appropriateness as developing nerve connections and pathways are used in the real world. Organisms with the ability to select among developmental options should have an advantage over those that cannot easily adapt to changing circumstances. Organisms that have more plasticity should more effectively move toward a desirable adult form—and so reproduce better. Their technique for achieving more plasticity should then be passed on. A Darwin Machine mechanism of the sort described in Chapter 2—preferential duplication of forms that work best—could act on a developmental, rather than a generational, time scale to select and amplify growing nerve pathways that work, at the expense of those that do not work as well.

These options appear to have been taken during the course of evolution. Pathways and competencies that do not prove to be relevant during development do not mature. In the case of feral human infants raised by animals in the wild, normal language and bipedal locomotion do not develop. The close matching of their behavior with that of their surrogate animal parents shows how little distinctively human behavior is obligatory in the absence of a normal human cultural environment. In the right selective environment, however, the brains of these children could have become the brains of airplane pilots. Similarly, songbirds have a genetically programmed template that specifies a range of sounds that can be learned, but the song actually performed is usually learned from other birds. The rule seems to be "use it or never develop it," a variant on "use it or lose it."

In more complicated animals, interaction between the environment and neural growth leads to a flexible, constructive kind of learning that minimizes the need for detailed prespecification of structures. Selection dictates which of the many possible pathways are chosen and become permanent.

As birds learn to sing, and as human babies learn to walk and produce language, there is room for variation and change, but after this learning period, the design laid down becomes relatively permanent. Thereafter, further learning is much more difficult. Once we have learned to walk or ride a bicycle, we usually don't forget how to do it. But learning to ride a bicycle after adolescence is much more difficult than when we are under 10 years old. Similarly, a young human infant is a polyglot, able to utter the sounds of any human language. But much of this potential range is lost as soon as the language actually learned fixes the design of the infant's language "pathways."

During brain growth there is a constant sorting and juggling of nerve cells and connections. Those that make a match with their environment thrive, and the others wither. Imagine what it would be like to move in a visual world that consisted mainly of *vertical* lines and contours—to be unable to see the horizon; experiments on cats and monkeys that we will soon describe suggest that this might happen to us if we were shown only vertical stimuli for a year or so after our birth. Cells that process vertical stimuli would grow to prevail over cells that deal with horizontal lines, because our visual brains wire themselves to be most responsive to the stimuli actually encountered early in life. There are critical periods during which not only our visual brains but also many other areas, including our social brains, are wired to conform to and accommodate the external environment. If that early environment is degraded, so is the development of our mental capacities.

A hierarchy of developmental circuits from innate to learned

We would expect innate circuits that shape basic survival behaviors, such as approach/avoidance, to influence circuits that can be modified by experience. Clusters of nerve cells, present deep in our brainstem and common to all mammals, distribute neurotransmitters such as serotonin, acetylcholine, dopamine, and norepinephrine to large areas of our cortex and influence both the growth of the brain during development and its behavior, as well as plasticity, in the adult. These older innate circuits are responsive to what is happening to more modern sectors of the brain and can signal the "goodness" or "badness" of different situations. They are crucial components of the chemistry underlying motivation. They react by influencing how the rest of the brain reacts, and how it is shaped, so that it can become wired in the way that most effectively supports survival. For example, it is most relevant to grow a brain that is predisposed to register associations between illness and taste (rather than between illness and place, sound, or temperature) and then, through learning, to determine which foods with which tastes actually lead to poisoning or illness.

What we are describing is a hierarchy of primary (genetic) and secondary (developmental) problem-solving devices. The primary genetic mechanism acts on a generational time scale, and the secondary process comes into play during postnatal development. This is the distinction made by references to ultimate and proximal causes of human form and behavior. The secondary, or proximal, process involves the growth and reinforcement of neuronal pathways and connections that work best, as well as the atrophy of those that are not found useful. This reinforcement comes not only from our learning to move about in the immediate physical world but also from cultural and social influences that guide our behavior and development.

A human child cannot be genetically equipped with knowledge of who will be nurturing and who dangerous, but it can be "told" by its genes that facial characteristics are important indicators of this distinction.

Human genes and environments interact on at least four levels in the construction of brains and selves: (1) Genes instruct, and are instructed by, the complex internal environment of the fertilized egg and by subsequent interactions between groups of dividing cells and tissues. (2) They can be regulated by hormonal and other interactions between the developing fetus and the maternal chemistry of the uterus. (3) Gene expression after birth in infant humans, as in other animals, is patterned by the development of sensing and acting routines appropriate to the species' typical physical environment. (4) Individual social interactions among infant, caretaker, and peers then pattern the learning of more complicated behaviors. Thus the influence of genes is expressed through a long, tortuous, and indirect pathway.

The wiring of developing brains

We now need to consider what is known about brain developmental processes, and the ways in which they are shaped by environmental changes. As we have noted, the brain originates as a swelling at the head end of the spinal cord. Then a series of bulges and folds give rise to the eyes and the lobes of the cortex, as nerve cell bodies migrate to their final positions. Axons then grow out to make interconnections between appropriate groups of nerve cells. A variety of mechanisms guide the growth of axons as they find their targets in the brain. One mechanism is derivative of the chemotaxis described in Chapter 2. A nerve cell body, or rather the growing tip (called a growth cone) of its axon, can be attracted to move toward a target that is releasing a particular growth factor to "call" the growth cone (Figure 6–3). Physical cues, such as those that promote growth along grooves or alongside other nerve cells, are also used. Some cells serve as guideposts for the turnings or migrations of others. Ongoing neural activity—the firing of nerve signals—is crucial in both the growing cells and their potential targets.

When a final target is encountered, such as when a motor nerve axon finds the muscle that it will control, the searching "fingers" retract, and both nerve and muscle respond by making the pre- and postsynaptic structures that are required for a synapse. A growing axon may make many temporary connections with other cells, acting as though it is testing them for appropriateness, before moving on to its final position. An important factor appears to be the functional appropriateness of the tentative connections being made and remade. Are they useful in correlating the input and output of the whole animal? Are they appropriate for the environment in which the organism is functioning?

Figure 6–3   The growth cone. If we look in the microscope at the growing tip of an axon, we observe what appears to be very intelligent purpose, just as in bacteria exhibiting chemotaxis. Delicate little finger-like projections wave about and literally reach out to touch and taste other cells in the growth path of the axons. The growth cone is repelled by some such cells and attracted by others.

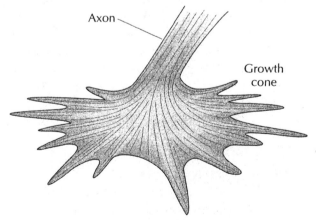

Pathways to the cerebral cortex

To consider what is happening in more detail, we need a simple description of how sensory cells in the eye, ear, or skin ultimately get their information to the cortex. Virtually all of them connect to cells that pass through the thalamus, which has separate nuclei or groups of nerve cells devoted to different kinds of input. The lateral geniculate nucleus carries visual input to the visual cortex, the medial geniculate nucleus carries sound information to the temporal cortex, the ventral posterior lateral nucleus carries somatosensory information from the body to the parietal cortex, and so on (Figure 6–4). The flow of information is bidirectional, for the cortex also sends information back to the thalamus. There is strong evidence that axon pathfinding between major structures such as the eye and the thalamus, and the thalamus and the cortex, is under the control of genes. This pathfinding also appears to require constant nerve activity.

It is currently thought that the early cortex is not regionally specified and that the specialized areas form as axons from the thalamus grow to them, bringing different kinds of stimulation from the external world. It is almost as though various sensory surfaces—with their specialized receptor cells sensing light, sound, pressure, and so on—impose themselves onto the brainstem, then onto the thalamus, and finally onto the cortex itself.

The cortex develops in two directions, radially and tangentially. In the radial direction are six layers of nerve cell bodies; layer 1 is on the top, and layer 6 on the bottom. Information coming into the cortex goes primarily to layer 4, the "in box" of the cortex. Cells of layers 5 and 6 send information back out to subcortical brain regions (functioning as the "out box" of the cortex), and cells in layers 1, 2, and 3 connect different cortical regions to each other, sort of like an interoffice network for sending memoranda back and forth. As we move across different regions of the cortex tangentially, these six layers might be found to be supporting vision, hearing, commanding movements, and so on. Their detailed structure varies in accordance with their different roles.

Functional plasticity in the formation of cortical areas

During the formation of these thalamus-to-cortex pathways, dramatic plasticity at the cortical level can be observed, and specialized cortical regions expand, contract, or take on functions other than their normal ones if unusual circumstances are encountered. A number of experiments of the sort shown in Figure 6–5 demonstrate that areas of cortex can switch from one sensory mode to another. If one sensory modality

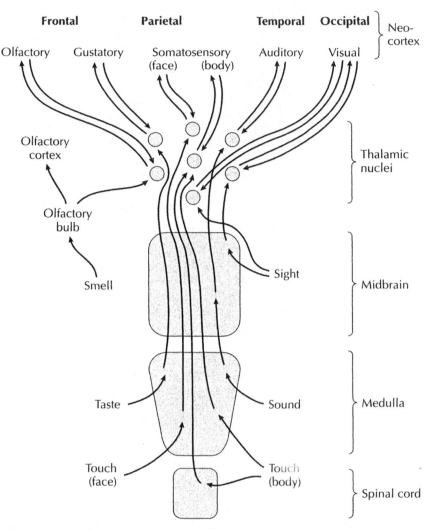

Figure 6–4 Pathways from peripheral sense organs enter lower brain areas and then pass through different nuclei of the thalamus on their way to areas of the neocortex that are specialized for different sensory modalities.

is blocked at birth, areas of cortex that normally serve it can be invaded by other sensory modes. Thus in cats deprived of visual input, the parts of the parietal cortex that are usually predominantly visual are taken over by auditory and somatosensory input, and these animals show greater sound and tactile discrimination than normal animals. Another striking observation is that in some congenitally blind humans, the visual cortex is activated by reading Braille. This shows that input from the hand that normally goes primarily to the

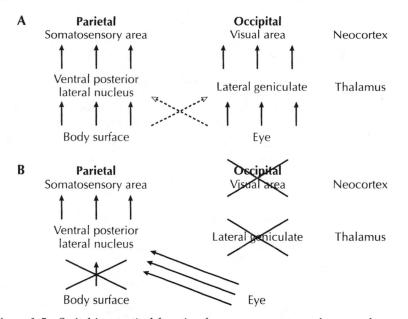

Figure 6–5 Switching cortical function from one sensory mode to another. (A) Most of the input from the eye to the brain goes through the *lateral geniculate nucleus* of the thalamus to the visual cortex located at the back of the brain, but early in cortical development, a few connections are also made to other parts of the thalamus (dashed line); these connections normally are eliminated later in development. Similarly, sensations at the body surface are sent mainly to the ventral posterior lateral nucleus of the thalamus and then to somatosensory cortex in the parietal lobe located in front of the occipital lobe, but again, some connections are made to other parts of the thalamus and are later eliminated. (B) The experiment, begun early in development, involves placing lesions in the lateral geniculate nucleus and the visual cortex, as well as blocking input from the body surface to the thalamus (as shown by the Xs). Now input from the eye has lost its normal targets but still has the few connections made to other areas of the thalamus (dashed line, top). Also, the ventral posterior lateral (VPL) nucleus of the thalamus and the somatosensory cortex are without their normal input. What is observed is that the visual connections to the VPL nucleus of the thalamus (shown as the dashed line in part A) can multiply and become a permanent visual input (solid lines) directed via the VPL nucleus to somatosensory cortex. This somatosensory cortex takes on the function of visual cortex. In the same sort of experiment, visual information can also be rerouted to the auditory cortex, which then converts from representing the pitch and frequency of sound to representing the locations of objects in the external world.

somatosensory cortex can also be directed to visual areas in the occipital lobe. One model is that at birth the human cortex has *synesthesia*, mixing of the senses, and that the senses become clearly separate only after about 4 months. Before this, in human babies, electrical responses to spoken language are recorded not just over the auditory regions of the temporal cortex but over the visual cortex as well. In the small number of human adults who have synesthesia, such as those who see colors when they hear sounds, the normal separation of the senses apparently has not occurred.

Other types of experiments further demonstrate cortical plasticity. In the newborn rodent cortex, visual areas can be transplanted to somatosensory areas to take on somatosensory function, and the reverse transfer also works. Auditory and visual cortex transplanted onto each other also change their function. However, the transplants never function in exactly the same way as the normal structures, which suggests that they may have already been patterned by some thalamic input. Most of these examples involve primary sensory areas, but a striking plasticity in higher cortical functions is observed when, in newborn monkeys, the portion of the temporal cortex responsible for visual object recognition (see Chapter 8) is removed from both left and right cortexes. This function moves a considerable distance, i.e., to the part of the parietal lobe that normally deals with the movement and orientation of objects in space.

Transplant experiments have demonstrated cortical plasticity by showing that a cortical area that normally serves one sensory modality can be transplanted and take on the functions of another.

Plasticity in forming the visual cortex

Studies on the development of the visual system, particularly the wiring of the cells in the occipital cortex at the back of the brain, have provided several fascinating examples of how labile the wiring-up process is and how susceptible it is to being changed by distortions in the environment. Similar phenomena are found in all parts of the brain, but the visual system has proved so accessible to experimentation that many basic and pioneering studies have used it.

The primary visual cortex in the occipital lobe of one hemisphere receives input from both eyes. If we move an electrode along the surface of this cortex in adult cats or monkeys, we find alternating rows of cells that respond mainly to one eye or to the other. Studies on kittens and monkeys have shown that cells of the primary visual cortex are driven by both eyes at birth, but one eye tends to dominate. During the first 6 weeks of life, as the young animals learn to move about and use their visual world to guide body movement, much clearer domains of cortex are formed that respond mainly to one or the other eye. However, if visual information from one eye is blocked during a critical period after birth (4–6 weeks in the cat), either by putting an opaque contact lens in the eye or by temporarily sewing the eyelids shut, the normal adult pattern is changed. Input from the eye that remains open now expands to occupy a larger area of cortical surface, while the area occupied by input from the closed eye contracts.

The playing out of this competition requires that the cortical targets themselves also be actively communicating. If their nerve signals are silenced by chemical inhibitors, inputs from the closed eye expand. There appears to be a push-pull mechanism of synaptic plasticity: When target cells are working (are giving postsynaptic responses), the active eye has the advantage just described, but without postsynaptic activity, the inactive inputs have an advantage. One possible explanation is that activity from the active eye causes its target cells in the cortex to release molecules (neurotrophins) that stimulate proliferation of the active inputs.

> *There seems to be an active competition between the two eyes for cortical targets. Diminished input from one eye tells the cortex that the active eye is more important and deserves more connections. In other words: Use it or lose it!*

Figure 6–6 Ways in which altering nerve pathways from different sources, such as suppressing input to the visual cortex from the left but not the right eye, might influence the competition of the two eyes for targets in the visual cortex. (A) The normal balance of input from left and right eyes, via the lateral geniculate nucleus. (The example is simplified to show only a few synaptic connections between cells. In reality, the axon from a cell in the lateral geniculate nucleus might branch to make synapses with hundreds to thousands of target cells in the cortex.) After suppression of input from the left eye, increased activity might improve the effectiveness of existing connections (B), disuse might lead to atrophy of the unused pathway (C), and axons of the more active pathway might sprout branches that form new synapses (D).

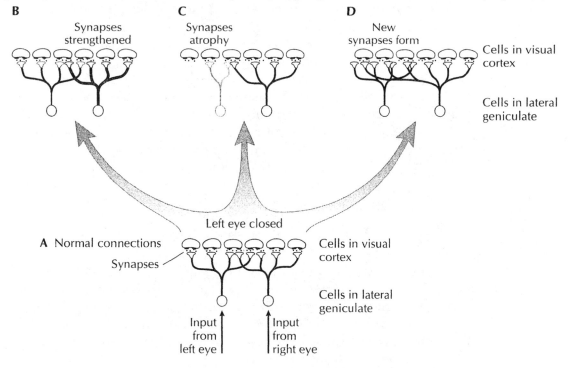

There appear to be many ways in which the number and strength of synaptic connections between cells can be altered. Figure 6–6 outlines some of these ways in a very simplified form.

The story becomes even more interesting as more subtle properties of visual cortical cells are examined. Most of these cells are sensitive to the orientation of a visual stimulus, and cells that respond to all directions of the compass are found at birth. If, however, a young cat is exposed to an environment that contains mainly vertical bars during the critical period when connections are formed, then cells sensitive to vertical bars predominate in the adult visual cortex. As is the case with the ocular dominance areas, a crude, genetically specified pattern present at birth can be profoundly altered by the visual experience actually encountered during the postnatal growth and development of the visual system.

Experience guides the formation of successful connections

Two processes appear to be central in wiring up our brains: the pruning away of initial, exuberant overgrowth of axons into their target areas, and elaboration of the complexity of the connections that remain. The first process has been likened to a Darwinian competition, including replication of pathways, testing of their appropriateness, and enhanced survival of those copies that work best. This selective process also probably works to test the results of the invention, or construction, of the complex circuits used to solve the problems specific to different kinds of information processing (visual, auditory, somatosensory, and motor) throughout an extended period of brain maturation. An example of a selection process—one that might guide both the formation of new connections and the elimination of unnecessary ones—might be the effectiveness of getting food from hand to mouth, which requires elaborate circuits for hand-eye coordination. We are born with hard-wiring set to do it in a primitive and clumsy way. The pathways then grow and are refined through testing. Another example is offered by development of the visual system. We are born with cortical cells that detect stimuli of all orientations, but the ability of human adults and many terrestrial animals to detect vertically or horizontally oriented contours is superior to their ability to perceive oblique angles. The prevalence of vertical and horizontal orientations in natural indoor and outdoor settings apparently leads to increasing stimulation and growth of visual cortical cells that specialize in those orientations. A further example of how nerve cell wiring is influenced by functional testing is outlined in the experiment shown in Figure 6–7.

What a brain is apparently doing during the wiring up of its nerve cells is testing the functional appropriateness of connections that are present or are being formed. Do those connections work in guiding behavior in the real world?

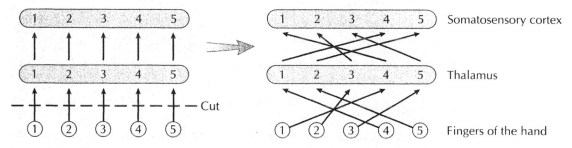

A Normal pathway

B Pathways after disorganized regeneration of nerves to hand

Somatosensory cortex

Thalamus

Cut

Fingers of the hand

Figure 6–7 The sorting out of appropriate nerve connections. An example of the determination of nerve connections by functional testing comes from experiments in which a bundle of sensory nerves running to the hand of a young monkey is severed. (A) Before the nerve to the hand is cut, nerves in the fingers ultimately report, via the thalamus, to adjacent parts of the somatosensory cortex: finger 1 goes to area 1 of the thalamus and then to area 1 of the brain, and so on. (We made these numbers up, just to make our point. They don't refer to existing anatomical designations of the sort used by professional neuroanatomists for thalamus or cortex.) If the bundle of nerves to the hand is cut (dashed line), its distal end (the end farther from the attachment) degenerates, but then its axons can be regenerated from the ends of the nerves above the cut that are still connected to their cell bodies. (B) These axons grow back to connect to the hand in a disordered fashion. Now the axons reporting from finger 1 to the thalamus might be those that used to report from finger 4, and so on, as shown by the crossed connections on the right. Adjacent areas of the cortex should no longer represent adjacent fingers. Quite to the contrary, however, the representation of this reinnervated hand in the primary somatosensory cortex develops in a orderly fashion. The developing brain is able to sort things out and create order, despite the fact that its sensory inputs were temporarily scrambled. This suggests that the pattern of sensory stimulation from the fingers is the most crucial cue for establishing neighbor relationships in the part of the somatosensory cortex that represents the hand, where adjacent areas of the cortex represent adjacent fingers. The nerves from adjacent fingers will be active together more frequently than the nerves from the first and fifth fingers. Cells that fire together are then more likely to wire together! Synapses that use the main excitatory transmitter of the brain, glutamic acid, appear to play a central role in these examples of plasticity.

It is not clear how much of the circuitry for higher mental functions is determined beforehand by genetic instructions, and how much is discovered by each growing brain as it bootstraps its way to maturity, growing through a series of stages of increasing complexity, each of which makes use of the solutions to problems devised in earlier stages. From what we now know about the molecular details of how nerve cells work, we can see how such factors as the speed of nerve signals and the density of connections between nerve cells might be directly controlled by genes, but we have very little idea how higher functions such as language might be linked to genes. The prevailing view is that the linkages are very indirect, and the examples we have given show that developing cortical areas are very flexible in the functional assignments they will accept.

Perhaps the most amazing example of this comes from clinical observations on infants with intractable epilepsy who have undergone removal of an entire cerebral hemisphere. One might expect that this would completely block normal development, during which competing language-related and other functions displace each other into opposite cerebral hemispheres. (Thus the left hemisphere normally has a skeletal motor bias and is optimized for speed, syntax, and visual details, whereas the right hemisphere has a visceral motor bias and deals with large time domains, the prosody component of language, and spatial relationships.) In defiance of all such predictions, however, in children with one hemisphere removed, all of these operations can collect and develop in the hemisphere that remains.

Adult brains can change their nerve connections

Until recently, it was assumed that brain cells and wiring change very little after puberty, when the final form of the adult brain has taken shape. Thus many studies emphasized the slow decay in cognitive function that frequently occurs in aging: loss of openness to new experiences and so on. We still have to explain, however, why some people can show striking recovery from brain damage and why it is that if we put on eyeglasses that magnify or shrink the visual world we perceive, our ocular reflexes and hand-eye coordination soon adapt as though nothing had happened. Changes in the nerve cells that regulate these reflexes in monkeys have been monitored, and brain imaging experiments in humans have shown the posterior parietal cortex to be involved. Even more striking, we can wear glasses that either turn our visual world upside down or reverse left and right, and within a few days our perceptions change so that we can function almost normally, even throwing and catching a ball. (After we take off the glasses, it takes a day or more for appropriate function to be restored.) It is difficult to reconcile these observations with the assumption of a fixed adult structure.

Consider the intriguing case of the woman who spoke both Italian and English and went to work as a United Nations translator. Before she began her new job, her left hemisphere, the normal locus of language, was used for both languages. After she had been in the job a few months, Italian switched to the right hemisphere!

Expansion and contraction of cortical areas

A large number of direct experiments have now demonstrated that the adult cortex can remodel itself within localized areas. There is debate over whether these changes involve the actual growth of new axons and connections over long distances, or whether existing horizontal connections between cortical regions, normally silent, become active. Probably both events occur. The most detailed work has been done in monkeys and entails making direct electrical recordings from the somatosensory cortex. More recently, imaging techniques have permitted similar observations in human brains. When performance of a particular sensory or motor activity is emphasized (such as reading Braille with one finger or developing a repetitive and skilled motor activity with one finger), the portion of sensory and motor cortex devoted to that activity expands. Conversely, when input from a digit is suppressed, for example by taping one digit to the next, the area of cortex that usually represents that digit is appropriated by adjacent digits. A similar phenomenon occurs in the visual system. When a small area of the retina is damaged, the area of visual cortex that represents that area is invaded by adjacent retinal areas, a process called "filling in." This is what normally happens with the blind spot on our retinas, a small area where photoreceptors have been pushed aside by optic nerve fibers gathering to project into the brain.

Brain changes that occur during filling in or shifts in hand-eye coordination happen in only 10–30 seconds—much too fast and far for new connections to grow. Changes that occur over periods of days or weeks as new motor or sensory skills are acquired can involve distances of more than a centimeter of cortex and may involve new growth of axons. The ability of a cortical area that represents one of our fingers to either expand or contract probably reflects a continuous competitive give and take between neurons. If one neuron becomes much more active because it is needed for some skilled task, it can begin to encroach on areas used by other neurons. If it becomes more silent because fewer cells are talking to it, its sphere of influence contracts. These changes might be of the sort shown in Figure 6–6, altering the strength of existing synapses and/or forming new synapses. Such plasticity enables us to adapt to and learn new situations.

A change in somatotopic organization of the hand area in humans has been observed by means of magnetoencephalography after surgical separation of webbed fingers (syndactyly). The presurgical maps displayed shrunken and disordered hand representations. Within weeks after surgery, the cortex had reorganized to reflect the functional status of the newly separated digits. This finding is consistent with the results of the experiment shown in Figure 6–7. The somatosensory cortex appears to use the timing of arriving information to create spatial representations of the fingers. Because input from one finger is usually synchronous and separate from input from the other fingers, the cortical representation of that finger is separate.

Blind people who read Braille literally reconfigure sensory cortex for the fingertips. The area devoted to the finger used for reading is several times larger than the corresponding area in sighted people. The expansion of this area as Braille is learned can be followed in imaging experiments. String players exhibit an increased cortical representation of fingers of the left hand. During the training of fingers to tap out a particular sequence, the area of primary motor cortex activated by performing the sequence expands, and the changes persist for several months. In one experiment, one group of adults was given a daily five-finger exercise to play, up and down a keyboard, and another group was told just to press the keys randomly. The brain's representation of hand muscles in the subjects who learned the piano exercise increased threefold compared with subjects who randomly operated the keyboard. The biggest surprise came from subjects who were taught the exercise but then told just to rehearse it mentally, not manually, while looking at the keyboard. This mental exercise achieved the same result as manual practice.

Mental rehearsal of a finger exercise can increase the area of cortex that represents the hand just as effectively as actual manual rehearsal can. This may be why imagining movement as a way of learning and refining it has been developed into therapies for rehabilitation and techniques for training of dancers and athletes.

Cortical plasticity and the phantom limb phenomenon

Cortical plasticity appears to play a central role in "phantom limb" phenomena observed after amputation of an upper limb. Patients experience sensations such as itch or pain in their no-longer-existent limb. The invasion of an area of somatosensory cortex that had been responding to a now-absent limb may underlie the sensations involved. The amount of phantom limb pain correlates with the extent of neuronal reorganization in the somatosensory cortexes. In some patients who have undergone upper limb amputation, the face area invades the area that had been responding to the limb. (The area of cortex representing the face lies just next to the area representing the limb; see Figure 3–6.) Stimulation of the face is then experienced as sensation arising from the hand as well as from the face. A systematic, one-to-one matching is reported between specific regions on the face and individual digits of the hand. A drop of warm water allowed to trickle down the face is felt also as warm water trickling down the phantom limb. In the case of an amputation just above the elbow, stimulating either the face or the remaining upper arm can cause feeling "in the fingers." This is presumably because in the somatosensory body map, the hand area is flanked on one side by the face and on the other by the upper arm and shoulder.

Another striking example of plasticity after limb amputation is seen when a tall mirror is placed vertically on a table and perpendicular to the patient's chest, so that a mirror reflection of the normal hand is seen "superimposed" on the phantom. Moving, touching, or vibrating the normal hand now causes a corresponding sensation in the phantom hand, but heat, cold, and pain are not transferred. This suggests that there is a normally latent link between brain areas in the right and left cerebral cortexes representing the two hands whose activity can be brought to awareness if visual input is provided. In some cases, viewing movement of the mirror image relieves chronic spasms and pain in the phantom limb, perhaps by providing sensory feedback for motor commands that usually register as pain because they lack such feedback.

Social experience can alter brain structure

Given the plasticity of our sensory and motor cortex, it would seem reasonable to look for plasticity in parts of the brain that regulate our more complicated social and emotional behaviors. Here there are very little data, apart from studies on behavioral effects of impoverished early environments (these studies are mentioned in Chapter 7). We know

If the wiring of our adult sensory and motor cortex can be altered by training, what about the parts of our brain that control social and emotional behaviors?

much less about the brain pathways underlying these more complex behaviors than about more primary sensory and motor parts of the brain. Imaging studies have shown complex changes in brain activity correlated with schizophrenia and other psychopathologies, but interpretation of the data is in its infancy. We are not yet able, for both ethical and practical reasons, to induce a behavior change in human subjects (such as the change from a dominant to a submissive personality) and then examine the effect on the activity of nerve cells in the hypothalamus.

Animal studies, however, provide evidence for a feedback loop between wiring of the adult brain and complicated social behaviors. It is very likely that increasingly sophisticated imaging techniques will yield similar information for humans. We would, in fact, expect that as evolution worked at the group level of animals to shape their social structure, brain plasticity appropriate for switching between alternative social roles would have been generated. This is presumably because role specialization increases the fitness of the whole group.

An example of such role specialization comes from studies of an African cichlid fish species in which aggressive males command large territories and keep other males at bay. These dominant males have enlarged nerve cell bodies in the region of the hypothalamus that regulates mating. If a dominant male is bullied by an even larger male, it becomes submissive and the hypothalamus cells shrink along with the size of the testes, which cease producing sperm. Dominant males have bright coloration unlike that of females and subordinate males, so they are more susceptible to predation. When a dominant male disappears, all the previously meek males rush into the area and start fighting. The winner then grows bigger and gains bright coloration, his hypothalamus cells and gonads enlarge, and sperm production begins.

Monitoring exactly how individual nerve cells are changing when social experience alters behavior is very difficult in vertebrate nervous systems, because these cells are extremely small and numerous, and their anatomy is not well understood. It has been possible, however, to take an analysis to the level of single nerve cells in studies on the invertebrate crayfish, whose nerve cells are much larger. A neurotransmitter (*serotonin*), which is known to be involved in the expression of aggression in many animals, acts differently on a neuron that controls the escape reflex in dominant and subordinate animals. This difference is due to a change in the postsynaptic receptor molecules on which serotonin acts.

Most relevant to humans, of course, are experiments on monkeys or apes. Numerous studies have documented neuroendocrine changes that correlate with dominance or submission in these animals. Removal of a dominant male usually results in competition, followed by behavioral changes in the winner. In many mammals, high dominance status correlates with increased *adrenocorticosteroid* levels. It is likely that similar changes occur in humans: If we change our group role either from "loser" to "winner" or from submissive to dominant, long-term changes in brain wiring probably take place. The increasingly powerful magnetic imaging techniques being developed may soon let us observe localized brain changes that correlate with such events.

Limits of brain plasticity

What are the limits of the plasticity of our brains? What can and what can't be changed? This is still unclear. The picture that has emerged so far is of critical periods during development when major pathways that regulate sensing and acting are laid down and can be modulated. Then, in adult brains, there is an ability to fine-tune these pathways if sensory or motor demands change. We don't yet have a link between direct observations made on our brains and more complicated aspects of our personality. Effective therapies exist for altering such things as sexual dysfunctions, panic, and manic or depressed moods, but other attributes (such as sexual orientation) are strongly resistant to change. Perhaps the brain areas that regulate some behaviors are simply less plastic than others.

Memory is a form of brain plasticity

An obvious kind of plasticity in our adult brains is revealed by our daily experience of remembering things—facts, faces, contexts, and manual skills. Each memory we can access reflects changes that have taken place in nerve connections in our brains. The remembering of phone numbers, facts, and places—which can be very rapid and may require only one exposure to the relevant item—seems likely to rely more on rapid changes in the strength of existing nerve connections. The slow learning and remembering of skills and procedures, such as your experience when you are trying to improve your tennis game, appear to involve cellular mechanisms very similar to those responsible for the plasticity discussed in previous sections. Nerve cells actually make new connections. An avalanche of exciting new experiments are documenting changes in gene expression and synaptic molecules that correlate with memory formation, and several pharmaceutical companies are rushing to use this information to develop memory-enhancing drugs.

A moment's reflection on our own experience makes it clear that there are several different kinds of memory. These memory types are common to mice and men and have been studied in both species. Working memory is what we access for very recent events, where it is appropriate for recall of these events to lapse after a short time. It is what we use to remember a telephone number we have just looked up until we finish dialing it. There is an important reason why most telephone numbers have seven digits. We can hold in awareness, or short-term memory, approximately seven chunks (meaningful units) of discrete information. About five seconds per chunk is required to commit these units to longer-term memory (as in memorizing a phone number). Regions of the prefrontal cortex appear to be most heavily involved in working memory, and different areas specialize in spatial locations, object identification, and verbal memory.

SELF-EXPERIMENT

Think about how long you remember a phone number that you have just looked up and will not use again. This is the duration of your short-term or working memory.

Long-term memory

The specifics of some of the events held in working memory, if they are perceived as important, might be passed on to one of the two major kinds of long-term memory displayed by animals: *procedural memory* or *episodic memory*. Procedural memories are the "recall" components of learned action patterns. They preserve general principles for action and ignore situation-specific details. Episodic memory refers to our ability to recall specific places, facts, numbers, or instances. Procedural memory and episodic memory involve different neural mechanisms. Birds can lose their songs (a procedural memory system) if lesioned in one part of the brain, and they can lose their ability to hide and relocate food (an episodic memory system) if lesioned in another. Some human amnesiacs can learn new motor skills (procedural memory) with no recall of having learned them (episodic memory). Other names are also used for these two kinds of memory: noncognitive versus cognitive, nondeclarative versus declarative, implicit versus explicit.

We will deal here with only a few of the different memory systems. At least six such systems can be distinguished and associated with different brain structures: (1) Episodic memory (sometimes referred to as explicit memory), the conscious recall of facts and events, is associated with medial temporal lobe and diencephalic structures. (2) Working memory, which is discussed in Chapter 12, is associated with prefrontal cortex. (3) *Priming*, which relates perceptual and conceptual representations, is associated with occipital, temporal, and frontal cortex. (4) Motor skill learning is associated with the striatum. (5) *Classical conditioning*, wherein we learn relationships between perceptual stimuli and skeletal motor responses, is associated with the cerebellum. (6) *Emotional conditioning*, which relates perceptual stimuli and emotional responses, is associated with the amygdala.

Episodic, or explicit, memory consists of our ability to recall specific places, facts, numbers, or instances (as discussed above). Some restrict episodic memory to the recall of events that happened to the individual and use the term *semantic memory* for recall of facts such as the location of cities. Several recent studies have suggested that the hippocampus and other parts of the brain play a role in the transfer of information from working, or short-term, memory to this kind of long-term memory. If the hippocampus is damaged (by anoxia or mechanical shock) or is removed, the ability to form new memory is lost. Work with many patients has shown that it is possible for acquisition of long-term memory to be lost completely, while all other intellectual powers remain intact. These subjects can read a newspaper, understand all its contents, and 20 minutes later have no recall of having done so. The kind of memory required to learn both mental and physical skills (procedural memory) remains intact. Furthermore, there is no damage to the working memory used in immediate recall.

Patients with bilateral damage to the amygdala but with intact hippocampus cannot acquire conditioned autonomic responses (such as a skin conductance response to a color that has been paired with an unpleasant noise), but they can recall the pairing of the conditioned and unconditioned stimuli. Conversely, patients with intact amygdala but bilateral damage to the hippocampus learn the autonomic conditioned response without grasping the facts about the conditioning stimuli. The storage of both explicit factual memories and emotional memories involves the medial temporal lobe as well as frontal and other areas. Imaging studies show that activity not just in the hippocampus portion of the medial temporal lobe, but also in a surrounding area called the parahippocampal cortex, correlates with whether novel items are remembered. Imaging studies further suggest that memory storage processes involving words are associated with enhanced activity in the left prefrontal cortex, whereas the right hemisphere becomes more active when visual images are involved. Memory retrieval is accompanied by enhancement of right prefrontal activity. Both imaging and brain lesion studies suggest that memory retrieval is under the executive control of the prefrontal cortex.

Damage to the hippocampus can abolish explicit recall, whereas damage to the amygdala can abolish emotional memory. The idea is that our hippocampus and adjacent structures link the separate parts of a long-term memory as they are formed, making it possible for all to be evoked when the memory is recalled.

A famous example of a complex memory occurs in Marcel Proust's novel *Remembrance of Things Past*. It is the flood of recollections stimulated by eating a small, rich pastry called a madeleine. The event being recalled originally started with perception: the narrator's feeling and seeing his cup of tea, the spoonful he raised to his lips, along with other visual, olfactory, and motor qualities engaging different parts of the cortex. These would have passed their sensations to the hippocampus, and the hippocampus would then have orchestrated the formation of an associative net linking all the perceptions into a multifaceted experience. At a later time, reenacting just one of the events of this scene (eating the madeleine), like pulling a single strand of the net, would draw up behind it all the other strands with which it is connected. Figure 6–8 may help you visualize what may be going on here.

Providing enough cells in the hippocampus to support forming new memories may require the violation of a long-standing "law" about

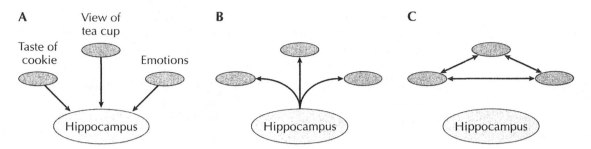

Figure 6–8   Model of the role of the hippocampus in forming memories. (A) Features of a scene such as taste, vision, and emotional feeling—processed in different areas of the cortex—all send signals to the hippocampus. (B) Networks of nerve cells in the hippocampus reassociate the separate features and send signals back to the cortex. (C) As a result, the areas of the cortex become linked in such a way as to form a long-term memory that unites the separate features of the scene.

brain cells: that in the adult human brain they do not divide. Division of cells in the hippocampus has recently been observed for the first time, even in aged adults. It has also been discovered that the decay of memory abilities observed in patients with Alzheimer's dementia correlates with MRI measurements showing a decrease in the size and volume of the hippocampus.

Researchers have measured the activity of the hippocampus in lab rats while the rats are exploring and learning a new environment. Simultaneous recordings from 100 or more nerve cells show that their firing patterns correlate with the position of the animal and that these firing patterns change when the animal's position changes. Even more interesting, the correlated activity of the cells during sleep sometimes repeats the activity of those cells during earlier spatial exploration. This may reflect memory consolidation of the exploration. A role for the hippocampus in mice learning their way around mazes is suggested by "knockout" experiments that use genetic manipulations to delete specific synaptic components in the hippocampus. In mice with such deletions, learning is compromised. Brain imaging studies in humans have now shown that locating and navigating accurately in a virtual-reality town presented by a computer display are associated with activation of the right hippocampus.

Why do we not remember events before we were 3 or 4 years old? Studies on children show that from the time they begin to talk, at around age 2, they have both *generic memory* (recall of repeated episodes) and episodic memories (recall of single episodes). Amygdala and hippocampus have developed sufficiently to support emotional and factual memories. But the kinds of memories that last a lifetime are initiated only when children begin to weave together autobiographical memory—a story line—at around age 3½. It is at this same age that children begin to show strikingly different approaches to their daily experience, different ratios of introversion/extroversion, and patterning versus dramatic behaviors.

Memory is not like a fixed filing system. It is not recording information like a camera. What creates memory is a semblance or approximation of the original events, sometimes with many biases and errors. We know too that the strands of memory are not complete, much information is filtered out. The strands are not always accurate; they can be distorted by personal goals, current knowledge, or social conventions. A given memory changes over time to resemble previous experiences of a similar nature, corresponding to the mental templates into which we fit our experiences. Numerous experiments demonstrate that false memories do indeed occur.

SELF-EXPERIMENT

You can perform a demonstration of false memory by simply reading out loud to a friend a list of similar items (such as bed, rest, awake, tired, dream, wake, snooze, doze, slumber). If you then ask your friend whether an unspoken but related word (such as sleep) was on the list, he or she is very likely to report that it was there, even though it was not.

Models of recognition and memory

Models of interactions between cortex and hippocampus during recognition and memory have been constructed by using computer *nerve nets* that are very simplified versions of systems of real neurons. A nerve net that models a first-stage attentional subsystem (like the hippocampus) learns and forms short-term memory traces that are relayed to a second stage (like the medial temporal lobe), where long-term traces are formed. These are relayed back to the first stage. Learning occurs when a mismatch between bottom-up and top-down patterns occurs. Thus seeing a familiar face does not trigger learning (that face is already present in the top-down patterns), but seeing an unfamiliar face does. Efforts are being made to correlate such nerve net models with brain imaging experiments. Activation of left dorsal, frontal, hippocampal, and other medial temporal brain areas is observed during the encoding of words, whereas the encoding of unfamiliar faces activates corresponding areas in the right hemisphere.

Imaging studies demonstrate that our learning and memory engage areas of the cortex that deal with sensory input and motor output. Anatomically separable regions in the left hemisphere tend to process words for distinct kinds of items, such as animals, persons, or tools. At least 15–20 different categories for storing knowledge have emerged from brain lesion studies, the lesions being spread mainly over the occipitotemporal axis of the left temporal lobe. Among the categories are plants, animals, body parts, colors, numbers, letters, nouns, verbs, proper names, faces, facial expressions, and categories of foods such as fruits and vegetables, and they all seem to have separate visual and verbal storage areas. The category an object belongs to acutely affects how it registers in the brain.

Work with amnesiacs suggests that parallel brain systems exist for remembering specific items and remembering the categories to which they belong. In some amnesiac patients, if a series of related items are displayed, knowledge of the relationship is formed by some sort of procedural memory process, but recall of specific items is impaired. Thus an item might not be remembered, but it can be assigned to a category. This suggests that the neocortex can gradually acquire classification knowledge independently of the hippocampus and related bodies that are damaged in amnesia.

One study on a patient who had sustained cerebral damage shows evidence for (1) a major division between visual and linguistic higher-level representations and (2) processing subsystems within language. The patient could not name animals, regardless of the type of presentation (auditory or visual), but had no difficulty naming other living things and objects. Accuracy of the physical attributes of animals could be distinguished (such as whether animals were correctly colored), but the color of a given animal could not be stated. In this case, knowledge of physical attributes was strictly segregated from knowledge of other properties in the language system. In other cases, patients are unable to generate visual images "in the mind's eye" but have reasonably intact recognition of what they see. The opposite is also observed: Recognition is impaired but internal imagery is intact. This observation suggests that functionally (and perhaps anatomically) distinct routes to a central store of visual templates can be selectively damaged.

In thinking about a cow, we apparently must use the circuitry for the category "animal" in order to come up with a color, size, and so on. Objects in a different category, such as "fabricated objects" can pass through a different set of processing channels.

We have talked about changes in nerve nets, areas becoming linked, and regions where information is stored, but in this book we will not examine the details of what goes on at the level of individual nerve cells and the synapses they use to "talk" with each other. Most investigators assume that memories ultimately have to correspond to long-term changes, either strengthening or weakening, in the information transmitted by individual synapses. They probably also involve both the formation of new synapses and the destruction of existing ones (as in Figure 6–6), processes central to the development and wiring of brain regions described earlier in this chapter. An enormous amount of contemporary research is focused on trying to describe the cellular mechanisms that can cause such changes. There is now evidence that nearly every aspect of synaptic function can be altered in a long-term way: how much neurotransmitter is released when an impulse reaches a presynaptic terminal; the sensitivity or number of postsynaptic receptor molecules that are activated by the neurotransmitter; and the tightness and surface area of the synaptic contact. Formation of new synapses during memory consolidation has also been documented. In many of these cases, the neurotransmitter glutamic acid and its several postsynaptic receptors appear to play a central role.

Procedural memory

The formation of our procedural, implicit, or nondeclarative memories and habits are associated with regions of the cortex, thalamus, and basal ganglia that are largely distinct from those involved in the formation of explicit memories. This system can sometimes step in to replace functions that a damaged explicit memory system can no longer serve. Procedural memory is used in learning complicated motor sequences associated with manual skills, and as we noted earlier, plasticity in the adult brain is associated with such learning. For example, when a novel finger exercise is taught to the right hand, imaging studies show increased activity in left motor, premotor, supplementary motor, sensory areas of the cortex, and in the right anterior lobe of the cerebellum. The idea is that the initial stages of motor learning are related to somatosensory feedback processing and internal language for guidance of the finger movements. As skill is acquired, the areas of activation become less global.

PET imaging studies on the processes underlying procedural memory have made use of the phenomenon of priming, a change in the ability to identify or produce an item as a result of a specific prior encounter with it. A standard procedure is to show, on a screen, during the hour before a conversation with the subjects, a word or picture for which there is no conscious recall, and then ask subjects to say the first word that comes to mind when a list of approximately ten word beginnings appears on the screen. For "mot-," the subject might reply "motor" or "mottle" or "motive." Those who have seen the word "motel" on their screen within the past 30 minutes recall it without knowing why. When they are asked just to finish the word, the visual cortex lights up, so the process seems more like perception than thinking. This suggests little understanding of the word, only a perception of its letter shapes.

Patients with a damaged hippocampus perform this task normally. By contrast, asking subjects to try to recall, from a previously presented list, words that match the stem currently being presented causes the frontal lobe to light up, which implies that conscious, higher-level thinking is needed in the memory search. The simplest tasks that can be devised light up several parts of the brain at once, which suggests many little "processors" or agents that are linked together.

Olfactory memories

Smell is one of our most powerful and primitive memory systems. You may have noticed this when a smell distinctive of your childhood unleashed a flood of memories. Olfactory input links directly to primitive brain centers in the hypothalamus, and manipulation of this system is the goal of a new aromatherapy industry that aspires to influence mood through smells, with different odors facilitating alert, calm, or refreshed moods. In addition to the primary olfactory system that responds to smells, higher vertebrates, including humans, contain a second system, the *vomeronasal system,* that responds to sexual attractant molecules (pheromones). Although this system is very important in the mating of many mammals, it has been assumed to be vestigial in humans. But perhaps this is not so. The vomeronasal system does project to regions of the hypothalamus that are involved in sexual and affective behavior. And only recently it has been found that odorless compounds from the armpits of women in the late follicular phase of their menstrual cycles can shorten the menstrual cycles of women exposed to the compounds. Some biotechnology companies are now working on what they think are pheromones extracted from human skin that can regulate affect. Another random and curious point about what may be a genetically encoded smell memory: A woman, when asked to sniff T-shirts that men have slept in, tends to prefer the smells emanating from men who have histocompatibility complexes (genes involved in generating our immune systems) that differ from her own. Mating with such men would confer a wider array of immunity options on the offspring.

The sexual brain—plasticity induced by hormones

This chapter has emphasized how malleable the brain is to shaping by the external environment. A final example of this plasticity is a topic that has inspired much debate: the sexual differentiation of our brains. A crucial environment during the brain's plastic development is the uterus, where the developing embryo is exposed not only to its own hormones but also to those of adjacent embryos and its mother. This environment shapes the development of sexually differentiated brains and behaviors. There is intense interest in this area, and few topics excite livelier debate than the issue of nature versus nurture in determining sexual behaviors.

After the internal and external genitalia, the brain is the most significant area of sexual differentiation. The hypothalamus contains separate centers for male-typical and female-typical sexual behavior and feelings. The medial preoptic area (just in front of where our optic nerves cross each other) plays a vital role in male-typical sexual behavior. It has a high level of receptors for testosterone (released by the gonads). Damage to this region in male animals of many species can cause a reduction in or cessation of heterosexual copulatory behavior and sometimes causes those males to perform more female-typical behaviors in approaches to a stud male. If this area in normal male animals is electrically stimulated, they begin mounting and pelvic-thrusting behaviors. At least one cluster of nerve cells in the medial preoptic region is sexually dimorphic; that is, it differs between the sexes. The third interstitial nucleus of the anterior hypothalamus is threefold larger, on average, in males than in females. This is the area that has been suggested to vary with sexual orientation in males, being smaller in gay men. The formation of the sexually dimorphic nucleus depends crucially on the circulating levels of testosterone during a critical period just prior to and just after birth. During this period in females, neurons of the nucleus die, and this can be prevented by adding testosterone. It takes a specific external signal, the presence of sufficient circulating levels of androgens, to reprogram development in the male direction.

Androgen receptors are found throughout the brain, and their stimulation by testosterone during development appears to play a large part in superimposing male features on the brain's intrinsic female developmental program.

Two further brain regions that show sexual dimorphism are the corpus callosum and the anterior commissure. The anterior commissure is a bundle of nerve fibers connecting the two hemispheres that appeared early in vertebrate evolution; the larger corpus callosum that connects the hemispheres is unique to placental mammals. Both of these structures have been reported to be a larger part of the total brain in women than in men, which suggests richer connectivity between the hemispheres in women. This difference may account for women's greater verbal fluency and for the fact that language seems to be restricted to the left hemisphere to a lesser extent in women than in men. A number of other differences between men and women in brain organization have been suggested. Brain damage studies show that for language and control of hand movements, women depend more than men on anterior regions of the brain.

Hormonal influences on behavior

The organizing effects of testosterone have major consequences for behavior. Prenatal testosterone levels in male monkeys influence their levels of rough-and-tumble play. Human girls who have congenital adrenal hyperplasia, and thus are exposed to unusually high androgen levels prenatally, can show play and toy preferences more typical of males. There is considerable variability in sexual behavior even among animals of the same sex, and this can sometimes be traced to natural processes during development. Female rats sometimes mount other females and perform pelvic thrusting. The propensity for this male-typical behavior is strongly influenced by the position of the female when it was a fetus in the uterus. Female fetuses that happen to lie between male fetuses are more likely to display mounting behavior as adults than those that lie between female fetuses. This appears to be because they take up testosterone from the adjacent male fetuses. In human female-to-male transsexual operations with testosterone administration, aggressive tendencies, sexual motivation, arousability, and visuospatial ability increase and verbal fluency declines. The results for male-to-female subjects after androgen deprivation are changes in the opposite direction.

A masculinizing effect can be seen in the auditory systems of women who have a male twin. Normal human cochleas (inner ears) generate very weak sounds that propagate back through the middle ear, where they can be recorded. Women exhibit more of these weak sounds than men, a sex difference that exists from birth. Females who have a male twin generate about half the average number of sounds observed in same-sex female twins and in female non-twins, about the same number as seen in men. Prenatal exposure to high levels of androgens has apparently had a masculinizing effect on the auditory systems of these women.

The trait of male aggressiveness in mammals correlates with greater levels of testosterone from puberty onward. Males castrated before puberty (including human eunuchs) are more docile. The relationship between testosterone and behavior is not a simple one, for testosterone and its related group of androgens can be both causes and effects of aggressive behavior. Nothing is ever simple when we are dealing with hormones, and the testosterone = aggression equation is no exception. Deficiency of testosterone can also be linked to aggression. (Targeted at men over age 50 who worry about their declining energy and libido, an "Androderm patch" sold by a pharmaceutical company releases 5 mg a day of testosterone into the bloodstream. It is reported to boost libido, increase muscle mass, and lower the voice! There are concerns, however, about the long-term effects of such hormone therapy.)

The amygdala is important in sexual behavior and aggressive behavior, which involve the corticomedial and basolateral nuclei, respectively. The corticomedial nucleus links to the medial preoptic area, and a corticomedial lesion can interfere with sexual behavior. The basolateral nucleus connects to regions farther back in the hypothalamus that play a role in aggressive behavior, and a basolateral lesion can reduce aggressive behavior and rough-and-tumble play. Bilateral ablation of the amygdala has been performed on very aggressive adults and children who have not responded to other forms of treatment and has resulted in reducing their aggressive behavior.

> *The greater aggressiveness of human males is perhaps the most striking example of a sexually differentiated trait. The trait is observed in most mammals and is presumably the result of sexual selection during evolution.*

Hormonal influences on visuospatial skills

The other most widely studied difference between male and female brains involves spatial or visuospatial skills. On average, males (rat or human) are better at mazes than females, and human males are better at visualizing rotating objects. (We don't know how to test rats for this latter capability!) Conversely, women tend to outperform men on some tests of verbal ability and fluency. Human women (and female rats) have a greater tendency to use landmarks in spatial learning tasks, whereas males use geometric cues. Are these cognitive differences inborn or learned? Probably both, but it is striking that women who were exposed to high levels of androgenizing hormones while they were fetuses (either as a result of congenital adrenal hyperplasia or because their mothers were given the synthetic steroid diethylstilbestrol) score better than other women on spatial tests. Similarly, the maze-running performance of female rats given androgens around the time of birth is better than that of untreated females. In androgen-insensitivity syndrome, chromosomal males have testes that secrete testosterone, but these males have a mutation in the gene for the androgen receptor. The body acts as though no androgens were present and develops as female; individuals usually are raised as girls. They do worse on visuospatial tasks than their male relatives and have verbal skills similar to their female relatives. During the menstrual cycle in women, as estrogen levels increase, spatial abilities decrease and articulatory abilities increase. In men, a lowering of testosterone levels in the spring correlates with an increase in spatial abilities.

In all of these examples, hormones apparently modulate the synaptic pathways that underlie our higher cognitive faculties.

Cognitive patterns may remain sensitive to hormonal fluctuations throughout life. Recent animal studies have shown that steroid hormones can cause cellular changes and synaptic reorganization in the adult hypothalamus. Estrogen administration stimulates memory and the growth of axons and dendrites in the hippocampus.

SUMMARY   The examples of brain plasticity that have emerged from studies on the sexual differentiation of the brain and on the mechanisms of learning and memory paint a picture of our developing and adult brains as plastic devices that are constantly re-forming themselves. The evolutionary rationale for this plasticity is that it permits us to wire up our brain circuits in response to the world in which we actually grow up and function, rather than the world of our ancestors. This description represents a revolutionary change in perspective, for as recently as 30 years ago, it was widely assumed that development was rigidly programmed and that adult brains remained constant through life. At the level of individual cells and complex systems of cells, what we see instead is a constant testing of what works best and an ability to overcome even extraordinary perturbations or lesions in normal development. A most dramatic example is provided by the near-normal development of human infants that have had an entire cerebral hemisphere removed. We will consider some further examples of brain plasticity when, in Chapter 11, we discuss the effects of genetic mutations and brain lesions on the development of areas of the brain crucial to language.

Each of our systems, from fundamental visual and motor mechanisms to the higher functions of socialization and personality formation, appear to have a critical period, or window of time, during which their habits are laid down. Once the structures are formed, we are pretty much stuck with them. Even so, our adult brains have abilities to rewire themselves when new tasks of discrimination are required or when areas of brain tissue have been damaged. Changes in the brains of some animals have been observed to accompany changes in social status, and it is not unreasonable to suppose that analogous processes might occur in humans. Subtle changes in nerve connections underlie the memory systems that permit us to recall places and events and to remember skilled action sequences. Interactions with the internal hormonal environment also pattern brain plasticity, as in the sexual differentiation of the brain. The immersion of each of our developing brains in a particular physical, linguistic, and cultural environment generates in each case a physically unique structure. This structure, broadly similar in all humans but differing for each individual in the details, supports the generation and definition of the human selves that are the subject of Chapter 7. ■

Questions for Thought

1. Permitting a nervous system to wire up in a flexible way, depending on the environment that the organism actually encounters, seems like such a good trick; one might expect animals such as insects, who are less able to do this, to have lost out in the evolutionary competition. Why, then, are beetles perhaps the most varied and numerous animal species on this planet?

2. There is debate about whether complicated nerve circuits—such as those that coordinate hand and eye movements—are formed by processes akin to Darwinian evolution or by an active, constructive learning process. Are the nerve pathways selected from existing options or invented? Can you design some thought experiments that would determine whether either of these alternatives (or both) is (or are) correct?

3. Suppose you were curious about observing the plasticity of your own adult cerebral cortex, and suppose you had a friend who was willing to let you play with her MRI or magnetoencephalography equipment. This machinery allows you to observe what brain areas become most active during a given task. What experiment would you design, and what result might you expect to see?

4. Storage in memory of the objective factual components and the emotional components of an experience appears to require the activities of two different brain structures. What are these structures, and what kinds of observations have demonstrated their importance?

Suggestions for further general reading

Bear, M., Connors, B., & Paradiso, M. 1996. *Neuroscience: Exploring the Brain.* Baltimore, MD: Williams & Wilkins. (Chapter 18 of this book discusses the wiring of the brain.)

Deacon, T.W. 1997. *The Symbolic Species: The Co-Evolution of Language and the Brain.* New York: Norton. (Chapters 6 and 7 discuss brain development and its plasticity.)

LeVay, S. 1993. *The Sexual Brain.* Cambridge, MA: M.I.T. Press. (This book is one of the sources for the section on the sexual differentiation of the brain.)

Schacter, D.L. 1996. *Searching for Memory: The Brain, the Mind and the Past.* New York: Basic Books. (An engaging description of memory mechanisms and how they can be distorted.)

Reading on more advanced or specialized topics

Deacon, T.W. 1990. Rethinking mammalian brain evolution. *American Zoologist* 30:629–705. (This article summarizes the experiments, described in Figure 6–5, that demonstrated that cortical function can be switched from one sensory mode to another.)

Florence, S.L., Jain, N., Pospichal, M.W., Beck, P.D., Sly, D.L., & Kaas J.H. 1996. Central reorganization of sensory pathways following peripheral nerve regeneration in fetal monkeys. *Nature* 381:69–71. (This is the article on which Figure 6–7 is based.)

Milner, B., Squire, L.R., & Kandel E.R. 1998. Cognitive neuroscience and the study of memory. *Neuron* 20:445–468. (A description of the history and current status of studies on the mechanisms of memory.)

Ungerleider, L.G. 1995. Functional brain imaging studies of cortical mechanisms for memory. *Science* 270:769–775.

Yeh, S., Fricke R., & Edwards D. 1996. The effect of social experience on sero-tonergic modulation of the escape circuit of crayfish. *Science* 271:366–369. (These experiments demonstrate a link between social experience and the chemistry of specific synapses.)

Chapter 7

Minds and Selves

The discussion of mind development in the previous chapter placed emphasis on the developing brain selecting what works best, given its particular genetic background and the physical and social environment it encounters. In recent years, however, more and more experiments have revealed that the human brain is a curious and active creature, exploring its world and actively constructing responses. This chapter starts with a description of early stages in the formation of human selves—stages that correspond to maturational processes in our developing brain hardware. What emerges in the first few years, distinctive to us human animals, is the child as a storyteller, a narrative autobiographical self. The second part of the chapter examines, from several points of view, the question of what a human self is: how it might be distinct from the selves of other animals and how its nature has been revealed in clinical studies of brain-damaged adults. The third section describes the self as a modular entity, containing different classes of intelligences and even different personalities. In the final section, we shall try to pull together some ideas on nature and nurture in the formation of selves. Evidence has linked genetic factors to complex behavioral traits, and our fundamental working model of what a self is can be influenced by cultural surroundings.

Stages in the development of human selves

During the first few years of life, human infants are in the process of growing brains that look very similar to other primate brains. There is no evidence that humans have neuron types or circuits that are fundamentally different from those of the great apes, for example, although more of the cortex is occupied by association areas. Frontal lobes and regions of the cerebellum are also relatively larger. Brain imaging studies show that subcortical structures are most active at birth; then occipital, temporal, and parietal activity corresponding to sensory-motor development increases most rapidly between 3 and 6 months; and a rapid increase in frontal lobe activity occurs between 8 and 10 months. At this time, long-range connections between major brain regions are being laid down. These may be the anatomical basis of an array of correlated changes that are taking place in language, communication, and cognition. During this period, faculties such as tool use, intentional communication, imitation, and retrieval of hidden objects are coming into play. Words are comprehended, and nonnative speech sounds are suppressed. Between 9 and 24 months, the density of synaptic connections between brain cells reaches 150 percent of adult levels, as a rapid acceleration occurs in the acquisition of vocabulary, grammar, symbolic play, and categorization abilities. By 48 months, overall brain metabolism has peaked, most grammatical structures have been acquired, and a period of stabilization begins. Brain metabolism and the density of synaptic connections then begin to decline, and they continue to decrease until, after puberty, they reach adult levels. The elimination of connections may be driven by a competition that favors the survival of those that are working best. Superior frontal cortex, involved in higher functions, continues to increase in volume from 8 to 25 years of age.

By the age of 12 to 18 months, humans have become little natural scientists, expressing an instinct to learn. Dolls that don't follow physical rules cause startle reactions, and basic aspects of objects are understood: how objects set in motion continue to move, how one object can support another placed on top of it, and how an object still exists even if another object blocks its view. A human baby looking in a mirror takes his or her image to be another child until the age of about 18 months, when it recognizes the image as its own. At this age humans also recognize any conflict between the tone an adult often uses when speaking to a child and the content of the spoken message (for example, saying "don't touch that" in a cooing, calm, and smooth voice). At around 2 years of age, the entire grammar of a language blossoms over a period of about 6 months. A simple experiment demonstrates that between the ages of 3 and 4, others are assigned a separate mind. At age 3 a child who observes matches being put in a crayon box says that a toy rabbit that was absent when this was happening also knows the box contains matches. The child is not able to conceive of the mind it attributes to the rabbit as being different from its own mind. At age 4 the child will say the rabbit thinks the box has crayons because the rabbit didn't see the matches being substituted for them. This is clear evidence for the development of an ability to ascribe minds holding beliefs (in this case, a false belief) to others.

Contemporary studies, all influenced by Piaget's work on child development, have given rise to several different descriptions of stages in mental development. One model suggests that the ability to ascribe mental states to others develops in four sequential cognitive stages: an intentionality detector, an eye-direction detector, a mechanism for sharing attention to an object with another person, and a theory-of-mind mechanism. Using this scheme, autism might be described as a sort of "mind-blindness" caused by breakdown of the transition between the second and third steps, such that autistic people are largely unaware that other people have minds. Another description presents the child as physicist, then mathematician, then psychologist, annotator, and linguist, proceeding from unconscious knowledge through conscious knowledge to verbally expressed knowledge. Each of these areas is suggested to be an internal module present in all humans. A further categorization is of the sequential development of a so-called point mode (2–3 months) for sensing and controlling present environments, followed by a line mode (8–10 months) that adds future and past to the present. Then follows a construct mode (1–2 years) that detaches from specific places or time to generalize away from the "I." A transcendent mode (8–10 years) then makes it possible for the child to analyze patterns and relationships outside of a specific place and time.

> *It appears that we all begin as "little scientists" who pass through a sequence of stages in discovering facts about the physical world and the minds of other humans.*

Effects of rich versus impoverished environments

Development of many areas of the brain both in humans and in other developing animals is a function of the presence (or absence) of rich and varied interaction with the environment. Rats raised with multiple (rather than single) families or with toys (rather than without) have 10–20 percent thicker cerebral cortexes. Their brain nerve cells are larger and have many more connections. The effects of environment can persist in the adult; adult mice living in cages that contain toys, nests, tunnels, and play wheels have more hippocampal neurons than mice kept in a standard laboratory box that contains only food and water. Many young animals devote 20 percent or more of their energy to play activities such as leaping, jousting, pouncing, chasing, and nipping. In these activities they expose themselves to predators, at some risk to their health and safety. Synapse formation, particularly in the cerebellum, is at its height during this play period, which also serves as rehearsal of many of the moves needed as adults: mock flight, stalking, and biting. In highly social species like monkeys, the young spend half their waking time at play, with males engaging in rough-and-tumble play while females emphasize chase games. How to win and lose and rules of submission and dominance are worked out. In humans and other animals there appears to be a critical period extending into early adult life for the formation of self-image and social skills. Nerve connections in the frontal lobes continue to multiply during this time. An important function of culture is to program young brains in social rules and procedures during this critical receptive period; those internalized social routines then remain relatively constant throughout adult life. There appears to be increasing acceptance of the idea that peer relationships are more important than parental or adult models in patterning social behaviors during this critical period. Adolescents are much more interested in being like other adolescents than in being like adults.

Impoverished environments appear to have the opposite effect of rich and varied surroundings: They suppress brain development. In humans exposed to early stressful or abusive conditions, retarded development of the hippocampus and impairment of short-term verbal memory have been observed. Brutality and cruelty to children can cause changes to their brain chemistry, altering the levels of neurotransmitters such as serotonin. Romanian orphans who experienced profound overcrowding and deprivation of adult touch and holding exhibited changes strikingly similar to those observed in baby monkeys removed from their mothers after birth and reared without parental care. Growth is stunted and social behavior profoundly disturbed. The message here is that there are critical periods in human development during which not only primary sensory and motor pathways, but also pathways regulating complex social behaviors, are laid down. After these windows of opportunity for plasticity have passed, the brain becomes unreceptive to further major changes. Language, if not mastered by the time of adolescence, is never learned.

> *In humans exposed to early stressful or abusive conditions, retarded development of the hippocampus and impairment of short-term verbal memory have been observed. Brutality and cruelty to children can alter their brain chemistry.*

The role of language

The learning of verbal language plays a central role in the development of human selves. The amazing plasticity of the brain allows this process to take place also in congenitally deaf children of normal intelligence, who have no difficulty learning a highly sophisticated sign language. Recent studies suggest that the amount of language to which an infant 6 months to 3 years old is exposed each day—from an engaged and attentive adult human, not TV or radio—is the most reliable predictor of later intelligence and social competence. One suggestion is that language ability forms during human development out of mimetic social sharing of signs and communicative behavior (see Chapter 5). Event representations are taken to be the fundamental units of memory; very young children demonstrate quite good memories for recurrent features of common events. The basic idea is that the social communicative capabilities of the infant constitute the preparation for language. An autobiographical and narrative self then arises to make sense of reality.

The philosopher Daniel Dennett emphasizes that the fundamental tactic of human self-protection, self-control, and self-definition is telling stories—concocting and controlling the story we tell others and ourselves about who we are. This storytelling derives from the mythic personality discussed in Chapter 5. Just as spiders don't have to think consciously and deliberately about how to spin their webs, and just as beavers, unlike human engineers, don't deliberately plan the structures they build, we do not consciously and deliberately figure out what narratives to tell and how to tell them (unless were are professional story-tellers or con artists). Our tales are spun, but for the most part we don't spin them. They spin us. Our human consciousness and our narrative selfhood are their product, not their source. The making of stories and myths leads humans to do something that no other animal does: to deceive themselves in a sustained way. All groups of humans create imaginary worlds and myths about life after death. This requires going against empirical reality and physical evidence. Different cultures do this in different ways, but they all do it.

Human selves and groups are suspended in webs of significance that they themselves have spun. We make sense of the world by telling stories about it, using a narrative mode to construe reality.

The cerebral hemispheres as selves

Fascinating insight into the composition of selves comes from clinical studies of brain-damaged patients. Some such studies have shown that our two cerebral hemispheres can act as separate selves and that one's normal sense of oneself as a coherent being is achieved by neurally connecting a family of distinct operations carried out semi-independently in each hemisphere. Recall that each of these hemispheres senses and influences the opposite, or contralateral, side of the body. They talk to each other via a thick bundle of nerve fibers called the corpus callosum. One treatment for epilepsy has been to cut this bundle. The surprising finding is that each hemisphere carries an independent awareness of the self.

Each hemisphere of a split-brain patient is aware of tactile stimuli applied to the opposite side of the body but is unaware of those applied to the same side. Conflicting or opposing commands can be given to each hemisphere, because the left ear reports to the right hemisphere and the right ear to the left hemisphere. The cognitive neuroscientist Michael Gazzaniga and others have shown that distinctive features of the two hemispheres can be revealed by experiments on visual performance. They make use of the fact that our left hemisphere sees the right part of our visual world while the right hemisphere sees the left. Figure 7–1 shows how this happens. The left sides of our two retinas, which see the right visual field, send their information to the left hemisphere. The right sides of the retinas see the left visual field and send information to the right hemisphere. If we fix our gaze on the dotted line running through the word HEART in Figure 7–1 and arrange it so that the HE is projected on our right retina and the ART on the left retina, we report the word HEART because the two cortexes communicate, via the corpus callosum, to figure out the whole word.

If asked to name what is seen, however, a split-brain patient says ART because the left hemisphere is the seat of language and can issue a report. The HE part of the word cannot be expressed because it is shown to the right hemisphere, which cannot speak. The mute right hemisphere does know what is going on, however, because the subject will select a picture of a man from a series of photographs if asked to match what is seen. If the letters DOG are flashed to the right hemisphere, the subject can select a model of a dog with the left hand. These simple language operations can be carried out by the right hemisphere, but more complicated ones cannot. Although the right hemisphere cannot talk, it can perceive, learn, remember, and issue commands for motor tasks.

SELF-EXPERIMENT

Imagine for a moment what it must be like to be the right-hemisphere self in a split-brain patient. There you are, trapped in the right half of the brain in a body whose left side you know intimately and still control and whose right side is now as remote as the body of a passing stranger. You want to tell the world what it is like, but you can't. You are cut off from verbal communication, which is generated from the left hemisphere of the brain, to which you have lost your direct connection.

The splitting of the visual world between the two hemispheres has been used as the basis for a series of experiments with what are called chimeric photographs. If the right visual field contains, say, a woodland

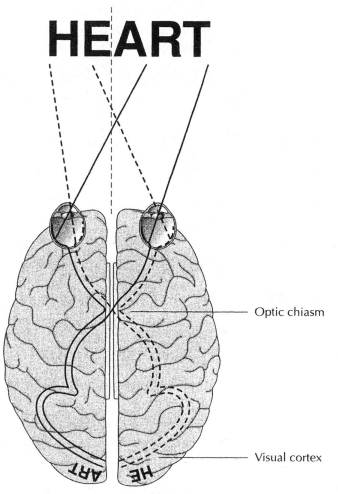

Figure 7–1   This schematic drawing illustrates how it is that information from the right and left sides of our visual world is sent, respectively, to the visual areas of the left and right cerebral hemispheres. The left side of the left retina and the left side of the right retina, shown as the solid lines, send information about the right visual world to the left occipital cortex, and the right sides of the retinas, shown as the dotted lines, send information to the right cortex. If the bundle of fibers connecting the two hemispheres, the corpus callosum, is cut, then one side does not know what the other is seeing.

scene and the left shows an erotic nude, the subject verbally reports seeing the woodland but becomes agitated without knowing why. Sometimes an explanation for this arousal is invented, or confabulated. In such a case, the left hemisphere is using its language competence to report the best story it can make up, given the circumstances. Conflicts between the two hemispheres can become even more dramatic. One patient who was prone to aggressive emotional outbursts, which are usually associated with the right hemisphere, used this hemisphere to command his left hand to pick up a hammer to attack a researcher. A struggle then ensued between the two functional selves present, as the right hand, controlled by the left hemisphere, moved to restrain the left! We could not ask for a clearer demonstration of two selves in one brain.

Self-boundaries

The entity that we call our self can expand or contract. In expansion of the self-boundary, we take something "out there" as though it were part of ourselves: a car, job, house, or reputation. Any threat perceived to that entity then is felt as a threat to our very survival. Simple to say, but very basic. Perhaps you recall how you felt when the first scratch appeared on the finish of a new car you were extremely proud of. You may also recall instances of self-boundary contraction. "I didn't do that! That wasn't the real me talking. Yes, the words came out of my mouth, but I refuse to recognize them as my own." These boundaries are influenced by whether we are feeling good or bad about ourselves. When asked to identify their own voices from a series of recordings, subjects with high self-esteem claim to own other people's voices, whereas depressed subjects claim too few voices as their own. And all the while, in both cases, the galvanic skin response shows that the information is being tallied correctly by the autonomic nervous system.

SELF-EXPERIMENT

You might try the following experiment with a group of friends: Put a paper sack on the desk and ask the group to imagine that something very important and valuable to them is in the sack, perhaps a gift from a loved one. Carefully close the top of the sack as though to seal in its value, and then—without warning—suddenly smash your fist down on the sack to crush it. You might hear an excited gasp or two. After apologizing for causing this discomfort in the service of the demonstration, ask your friends what they felt. Did they experience contraction of their chest and front flexor muscles, and a slight feeling of pain and loss?

Observations on patients with brain lesions suggest that the experience of self and self-boundaries requires a continuous sensing of body states. Most patients commonly experience the loss of an ability (such as the ability to recognize faces, to see colors, or to read) as something happening to them and describe it in the sorts of terms one would use in describing a back problem. They see the problem afflicting their selves. However, in extreme cases of anosognosia (denial of a part of the body, frequently associated with damage to the right parietal lobe), the problem is not referred to the self; it is denied. When a right-hemisphere lesion blocks sensing and movement of the left side, the existence of the left arm can be denied, or a story can be fabricated to explain its presence. One suggestion is that the emotions associated with monitoring discrepancies and anomalies are located in the right hemisphere. This perhaps underlies the fact that some anosognosic patients with right-hemisphere lesions who deny the existence of parts of their bodies are much more likely to engage in elaborate and fanciful rationalizations than either normal individuals or those with left-hemisphere damage. The idea is that the job of the left hemisphere is to make up plausible stories. If something goes wrong, it denies or confabulates to try to make aberrant information fit in. The right hemisphere detects anomalies and, if they become serious enough, forces the left to start from scratch with a new story line. Damage to the right hemisphere can delete this editorial function.

SELF-EXPERIMENT

Our self and body image can be altered by sensory incongruities or conflicts. Here is an experiment you could try with some friends: Sit at a table with your left arm resting on the table to your left but hidden from your view by a screen. Have another person sitting to your right place his or her left arm on the table directly in front of you (alternatively, a rubber model of a left hand and arm can be placed in front of you). Now, a third accomplice uses two small paintbrushes to stroke both your hidden hand and the hand of the arm you can see in front of you, synchronizing the timing of the brushing as closely as possible. If you are like virtually all of the people who try this test, you will soon start to feel as though the touch you can *feel* is in the position of the hand you can *see* and that this visible hand is your own! Your brain has altered its representation of your body in space, and you are feeling a phantom limb, just as amputation patients sometimes do. You are literally having an "out of body" experience. If a drop of cold water is applied to your hidden hand, the cold can sometimes be felt in the location of the new hand.

Variations on this experiment show that we can similarly displace our experience of our nose—or even of our entire head. These demonstrations show how our body image, despite its apparent durability and constancy, is a transitory construct that can be altered by the stimuli we actually encounter.

Experiments on split-brain subjects of the sort we have mentioned also reveal the role of the self as a presentation manager, a story-line generator. In split-brain patients, an instruction to "walk" can be flashed to the right hemisphere (some patients, especially left-handed people, retain the ability to understand simple linguistic commands with their right hemisphere). The linguistic, speech-generating left hemisphere has no knowledge of this instruction. When the patient gets up and begins to walk about the room and is asked why, a rational (though bogus) explanation is generated, such as "Uh, I'm going to get a Coke."

Similar behavior can be elicited from normal subjects in hypnosis experiments. A subject under hypnosis can be given a posthypnotic suggestion for a trivial activity, such as an instruction to crawl about on the floor. After coming out of hypnosis, the subject might be engaged in a normal activity, such as drinking coffee with the experimenter, and then suddenly say something like "What a fascinating floor pattern" or "I want to check out this rug" and then proceed to crawl around on the floor. It would appear that programs in the brain, on the basis of the information available to consciousness, present a plausible story to account for the subject's actions. "I'm acting out a hypnotic suggestion" is not part of the available information.

Selves are modular constructions

From a variety of sources, we obtain clues that human selves consist of several semi-independent modules. Genetic and developmental studies reveal a set of core intelligences that together assemble an "I." The psychologist Howard Gardner has suggested that several intelligences should be distinguished as basic to our different areas of competence: logical-mathematical, linguistic, spatial, musical, bodily kinesthetic, and personal-interpersonal. Evidence for the distinctiveness of these intelligences comes from studies of their development and also from observations on geniuses and on *idiot savants* (who are born with some exceptional abilities but are retarded with respect to others).

To take just a few examples, evidence for logical-mathematical intelligence comes from the demonstration of innate mathematical ability in human infants, who can perform simple addition and subtraction at the age of 5 months. It is also supported by the existence of individuals who are precocious by genetic endowment. Pascal was forbidden by his father to speak about mathematics. Therefore, he made simple geometrical drawings on the walls of his playroom, devised his own mathematical terms and axioms, and rediscovered the propositions of Euclid. The presence of a genetic component in musical competence is suggested by infant prodigies such as Mozart, Mendelssohn, and Saint-Saens. Nijinsky, Barishnikov, and Marcel Marceau offer examples of precocious kinesthetic intelligence. Note, however, that the argument for a genetic component in the exceptional behavior of these individuals has to be tempered by that fact that some were exposed to distinctively different early experiences, preferences, opportunities, habits, training, or practice.

The multiple-intelligences model suggests an array of core computational capacities, such as phonological and grammatical processing for language, and tonal and rhythmic processing for music, rather than the general intelligence, or so-called *g* factor, of the IQ psychologists. In some cases, these computational capacities might be largely localized to specific regions of the brain, for some are compromised by damage to specific brain areas. Others might be spread more widely across different areas. Recent genetic studies, mentioned below, do provide support for a heritable component of general intelligence, perhaps due to variations in very basic parameters that influence the whole brain, such as nerve signal conduction or the ease of making new nerve connections.

The example of musical intelligence

Let's focus on music for a moment. It is tempting to compare human music to bird song, for which there are definite brain specializations. The function of bird song is communication, and song may have preceded speech in humans, as a component of the mimetic intelligence that existed before the appearance of grammatical language. As we all know, music is strongly linked to emotion. The first musical instrument was the human voice, but there is evidence for musical instruments (pipes and flutes) dating back to 50,000 years ago, and there is presumptive evidence of the role of music in organizing work groups, hunting parties, and religious rites. The development of musical skills, like that of the other proposed modules of intelligence, follows a stereotyped course, so that, for instance, 4-month-old babies are sensitive to consonance versus dissonance, 6-month-old babies detect musical patterns, and 2-year-old children spontaneously pick up and sing songs to themselves during play.

Clinical evidence points to a modular musical faculty. There are numerous cases of brain-damaged children, some autistic, who have exceptional musical ability. Injuries to the right frontal and temporal lobes can cause difficulties in discriminating tones and reproducing them (*amusia*). In some subjects who have damage to areas in both the left and the right temporal lobes (where auditory circuits dealing with pitch reside), speech and auditory faculties seem normal, but the subjects cannot recognize specific music or songs. However, they still can follow rhythm and the emotional content of the music. The Russian composer Shebalin developed a severe Wernicke's aphasia but remained able to compose competently. In the last 4 years of his life, Maurice

Ravel lost the ability to compose or play music, but he could listen to and appreciate musical pieces.

The mechanisms for apprehending and storing pitch, like a set of tones, are separate from those used for the sounds of language. Remembering a set of tones is not compromised by random verbal interference, but it is disrupted by random competing tones. Musical composers describe themselves as constantly having tones in their head, generating musical phrases without thinking about it. These lines of evidence for functional and anatomical modules of musical competence cannot be taken to mean that it is an isolated faculty, however, for musical activity interacts with other intelligences. Listening to Mozart results in better performance on spatial tasks, and 3-year-old children given weekly piano lessons register 80 percent higher scores in spatial and temporal reasoning than average.

How many selves to a customer?

While we are considering information on known or proposed modules of selves, let's look at the variety of selves or intelligences that we might contain from another angle: the idea that each of us is not one self but many different semicomplete selves. You probably have been jarred occasionally, when in a critical mood, upon realizing that the style of your speaking and criticism is very similar to the way in which you were corrected by your parents. Or, after being subjected to sudden criticism, you may find yourself cringing just the way you did as a child. We all seem to have a continuous experience of an "I," but the "I" in place (the resident self) can change from moment to moment. It is as though we are made up of a club, or a board of directors, one of whom is in command at any given time. Members of this board can include our present and past personalities, as well as the personalities of others who are (or were) important in our life. The hint that our continuous experience of an "I" is a fiction is its troublesome instability: the fact that we can act as though we were different people at different times and often seem relatively powerless to control who we are and when. This is because the "I" consists of a succession of emergent personalities, and which one presides at any particular time depends on the circumstances.

SELF-EXPERIMENT

Can you recall moments when, with a start, you realized that you were feeling and speaking not from a present-centered adult perspective, but rather exactly as you did when you were a small child. And at other times, have you suddenly thought while you are speaking, "I sound just like my parents"?

Descriptions of how we develop these processes, from Freud's analysis to the present, have a number of common themes. Although different schools use different jargon to describe the process and generate therapies that typically come into vogue for 5–10 years, they all share the theme of modeling the expression of several humans, sometimes called ego states, within us. As an example, you may have heard of "transactional analysis," a popularized incarnation of Freudian therapy that peaked in the 1970s. It describes a parent ego state that is imprinted on our brains when we are young and that has two main components: a nurturing, caretaking parent and a critical, judgmental parent. This parent ego state contains the rules for outward behavior toward others. Rituals seen in the parents are internalized, as are the parents' inward instructions to self. The child ego state consists of permanent records in our brain of the way we experienced our own impulses as a child and how we felt about the world. It contains at least three components. A "natural child" is affectionate, impulsive, sensuous, uncensored, curious but also fearful, self-indulgent, self-centered, rebellious, and aggressive. A "little professor" is intuitive, creative, manipulative, and playful. Finally, an "adaptive child" accommodates to the demands of parents and the social world, being courteous and compliant, avoiding confrontation, procrastinating, and withdrawing. Finally, an adult ego state is meant to be the "reality-testing machine" that is centered in the present rather than being a read-out of the more primitive parent state or child state. This adult ego state is the executive that chooses whether a novel output or one from the parent or child state is appropriate. It is this component that psychotherapies attempt to strengthen.

This sort of description of the self as made up of many selves does not explain how any particular self works. Indeed, the field of psychology has entertained a series of theories that have rarely outlived more than a few generations of their proponents. Most psychological explanatory theories, such as psychoanalysis and the postulating of the Freudian unconscious, have not been cast in a form that can be either proved or refuted. Some psychologists have been criticized for inappropriately trying to imitate the quantitative analyses that are often possible in biology and physics. One example, mentioned on page 169, is the attempt to describe a very complex and modular phenomenon— intelligence— by a single number, the IQ or intelligence quotient.

Yet another perspective on the issue of how many selves each of us contains comes from considering apparent fractional as well as multiple personalities. There is the case of the twin sisters in York, England, who live together in a hostel and seem to act together as one individual, collaborating in single speech acts in sequence or in unison. It seems natural to regard "them" as more of a "her." Oliver Sacks describes two brothers, identical twins with IQs of 60, who, only when together, and communicating by a variety of tics, twitches, head bobbing, and rolling eyes, could perform prodigious feats of mental calculation.

More striking are the many purported cases of multiple personality disorder. The model has been that traumatic childhood experiences such as physical or sexual abuse cause a child to decide that the horror is happening to someone else and thus generate several independent personalities. In the case of Billy Milligan, an Ohio jury determined that he could not be punished for the crime (rape) committed by one of his parts. There are anecdotal reports of changes in patterns of allergies, phobias, and movement habits between different personalities. The newer name for this condition, dissociative identity disorder, reflects uncertainty over whether a patient identifying himself in multiple ways is really displaying identities that constitute personalities. Indeed, handing down the diagnosis of multiple personality disorder, which started in the 1950s, has proved to be a fad that has subsided. The condition appears mainly to have been the product of suggestible patients, misinformed diagnoses, and incompetent therapy involving suggestive techniques such as hypnosis. Several well-publicized epidemics of altered behaviors, in addition to dissociative identity disorder, have the curious feature of being reported largely for Northern American and European populations. While some of these (such as seasonal affective disorder, attention-deficit/hyperactivity disorder, chronic fatigue syndrome) appear to have a biological basis and probably occur more widely, others are more problematic (such as the numerous cases recently reported of recovered memories of sexual abuse, satanic ritual abuse, and alien abductions).

Selves, genes, and environments

This and the previous chapter have cited numerous examples of how the human mind can end up in different possible configurations. To what extent are these configurations captive to the genetic instruction we are born with, and to what extent are they patterned by our physical and social environments? Numerous studies have argued that several components of human personality tend to remain constant throughout an individual's life and have a heritable component. Such stable traits include novelty seeking, harm avoidance, reward dependence, persistence, extraversion/introversion, emotional stability, and sexual orientation. Most of the work to date has correlated overall genetic constitution with behavior, but more recent studies have noted correlations between mutant forms of single genes and behaviors such as nurturing, novelty seeking, and drug addiction. Studies on identical twins raised apart sometimes reveal similarities in detailed mannerisms that may reflect their shared genetic and intrauterine hormonal environment. There is clear evidence from studies that compare identical (monozygotic) with nonidentical (fraternal, dizygotic) twins that genetic factors account for at least 50 percent of the difference in general cognitive ability (including social cognition) between individuals. It may be that variations in a higher faculty such as social cognition are actually the consequence of more general underlying differences in attentional or motor mechanisms of the brain. Although there is some evidence that general intelligence correlates with higher brain metabolism, faster conduction velocities, and bigger brains, there are no generally accepted links between differences in most cognitive performance and variance in underlying brain mechanisms.

Framing the issue of nature and nurture

We need to be aware of a potential fallacy lurking in the debate over whether certain character traits, and, in particular, general intelligence as measured by the IQ test, have a genetic basis. That possible fallacy is the assumption that a complicated behavior such as intelligence can be measured by a single number, and that it has been described precisely enough to be measured. Intelligence probably consists of several dozen abilities influenced by many different genes, each affecting more than one character. Until we understand this complexity, we can't even begin to sort out roles of nature and nurture. IQ tests are a crude estimate of intelligence in the same way that pulse, blood pressure, and body temperature provide an overview of general health. A physiologist or physician can proceed to tests of liver function, heart function, and so on, but the ability of a psychologist to dissect the components of intelligence is much more crude.

In many studies, the implicit assumption is that some fraction of our behavior is caused by heredity and some fraction by environment and that the problem is simply to assign the proper percentage to each. Unfortunately, this assumption frames the issue in a misleading and oversimplified way. A more appropriate description of what is going on is that *our genes generate options that are tested as an environment provides input that results in behavior.* The usefulness of the behavior in enhancing survival and reproduction determines what supporting neuronal pathways become permanent.

The author Robert Wright puts this in more simple language by using an analogy: Heredity provides us with a set of genes for different traits that you could imagine as being like control knobs on a stereo amplifier. At different times during development, different sets of knobs appear and then disappear. The important thing is that which knobs are selected for use and how these knobs are tuned depends on constant interactions with the environment—what settings are most successful in guiding our behavior, seeing food, getting it to the mouth, communicating with other humans, avoiding predators, and so on. There is genetic variation among humans, which leads to slightly different sets of knobs that are tuned more or less broadly.

We must also consider that there are random events in the development of cells and nervous systems that are neither genetic nor environmental influences in the usual sense. One example, given in Chapter 6, is the relative placement of male and female embryos in utero that can influence female testosterone levels and brain development. Knowing the genetic basis of a character does not enable us to predict how changeable that character might be by random, individual, or social circumstances. This means that mere proof of the heritability of a trait yields very little information about how malleable it might be.

It is not practical or useful to try to separate the contributions of environment and genes to our behavior, because they feed back on each other in an intricate dance that begins in utero and continues through puberty.

Finding a correlation between a behavior and a gene is emphatically not the same thing as finding a gene for the behavior. The philosopher Elliott Sober gives the example of people who knit and people who do not. With few exceptions, knitters have two X chromosomes (are females); people with one X and one Y chromosome (males) almost never knit, at least in contemporary American culture. This does not mean that we have discovered genes for knitting. Finding a gene or collection of genes that incline an individual to a given behavior means that the behavior in this sense is "natural," but it says nothing about its relevance, usefulness, or acceptability in prevailing circumstances.

Physical environments and selves

The influence of physical environment, social environment, and language on the formation of human selves is perhaps easier to appreciate than the influence of genetics, and it is especially striking when one notes the different cognitive habits and constructs of self that are found across the world. An illustration of the effects of different physical environments comes from noting the relativity of more complex sensing and acting. Those who grow up in "right-angle" cultures with rectangular rooms and shapes are more susceptible to the illusions shown in Figure 7–2 than are those in Stone Age cultures who live in circular dwellings in the rain forest. People raised in dense forest, where the relevant visual world is mainly within 50–100 feet, can become alarmed and confused upon seeing savanna for the first time. Distances of miles cannot be processed, and a herd of buffalo in the distance is likely to be interpreted as a colony of ants.

Cultural influences on self

Different cultures can define self, others, and their interdependence in strikingly different ways. In many Asian cultures, interactions among people predominate in the experience of cognition, motivation, and emotion. The definition of self emphasizes the relatedness of individuals to each other. The role of a self is to blend into harmonious relationship with others. American and European cultures downplay this interdependence to construe the self as an independent entity with unique inner attributes. The role of a self is to discover and express its distinct potential. Not surprisingly, notions of what are healthful and

Figure 7–2   (A) The Müller-Lyer illusion. The vertical lines are the same length. Most people, however, report that the left vertical line is longer than the right, because the left figure is taken to indicate a corner receding from the viewer and the right figure to indicate a corner projecting toward the viewer. (B) The Ponzo illusion. Here the horizontal lines are the same length, but because the lines are between converging straight lines (like a railroad track), the top line is usually reported as being longer. This is a reasonable interpretation of cues supplied to a nervous system that has been trained to interpret perspective and distance involving lines and edges. (C) The Devil's tuning fork. Most Westerners cannot reproduce this drawing, but African tribespeople who don't share Western conventions about interpretation can reproduce it with little difficulty.

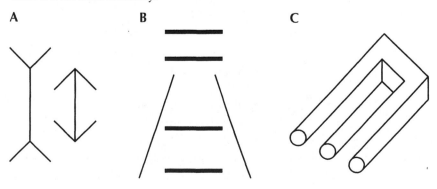

A   B   C

what are abnormal behaviors vary between cultures. Anorexia nervosa seems as culture-bound to America as *amok* (acting wild and crazy) is to Malaysia. The Japanese malady *taijin kyofusho*—a morbid dread that one will do something that embarrasses other people—has no counterpart in Western culture or diagnostic systems. Hopi Indians define five different types of depression that do not match those enumerated in the American Psychiatric Association's *Diagnostic and Statistical Manual of Mental Disorders*.

Our nervous systems form in an ecological dialog with our physical and social environment. Our brains are shaped by the particular world they grow up in, just as they in turn shape that world. Their cognitive structures are heavily influenced by culture. The regions of the brain engaged by ideographic Chinese and those engaged by phonetic English are different. The premotor cortex of a professional football player is different from that of a biblical scholar.

Many of you reading this book have a sense of individualism and self-consciousness patterned largely by Western European civilization since the 17th century. All human minds were in a somewhat different world before then, and many still are. It is striking that the idea of the self as "a permanent subject of successive and varying states of consciousness" doesn't appear in the *Oxford English Dictionary* until the 17th century. This is not to say, however, that the actual nature of human selves was different before that time. Older classical essays suggest that the writers had selves very similar to our own, but the great majority of people were immersed in a more collective group identity, just as in the contemporary Asian cultures mentioned previously. A number of preindustrial societies have little notion of a person as a separate entity. Both the Old and the New Testament of the Bible often portray humans not as active agents of individual decision or choice but rather as passive pawns of an active God.

By the same token, many patterns of modern life that you might assume to be "natural" are actually of recent origin. The Western idea of "home" as an enclosed nurturing space for one family derives specifically from Amsterdam in the late 17th century. The work week, with its rigid separation of work and leisure, is an artifact of the Industrial Revolution. Homosexual culture as a distinct social category was an invention of the late 19th century. Our cultural arrangements have an overriding influence on what we consider normal, and we frequently (and mistakenly) overextend this concept to include "natural" or "biological."

The relativity of thought systems

A discussion of this sort is not complete without some reference to current discussions of the relativity not just of selves, languages, and social customs but of all knowledge. One extreme position has been to label Western science as just another system of magic that has only as much legitimacy as any other social construct. Popular forms of irrationalism have become so pervasive that conferences of concerned scientists have met to address the issue. Because we are immersed in our world and our nervous systems are shaped by a complex interplay between our whole bodies and that world, how can anything we know be considered absolute?

Our view of reality is framed by the limitations and peculiarities of our sensory apparatus, the prejudices of our presuppositions, and the restrictions of our language and culture. We form our ideas of what is correct or true from a network of unconscious, as well as conscious, bits of information taken in from the environment.

The relativistic position is that we frame our understanding in terms of very restrictive and culturally specific metaphors—that the way we have been brought up to perceive our world is not the only way. Still, even the most severe social constructionist would probably grant that there are indeed immutable facts about the natural world, even if our accounts of them can depend on capacities and vocabularies that are socially constructed. It isn't terribly useful for different cultures to try to step outside of some core perceptions such as "rocks are hard," "two plus two is four," and "gravity defines up and down." On the other hand, there is no obvious reason why different cultures should not arrive at different conventions of a more superficial sort, such as those reflected in gender roles or metaphors like "time is money," "labor is a resource," "love is a journey," and "problems are puzzles."

The coherence of any system of thought rests on its stability. Does it work? Is it useful? Science distinguishes itself from mystical or magical traditions in that it seems to meet this criterion of stability, or usability, better. Most of us probably believe that cultures based on some kind of scientific rationalism will be more adaptable—and thus more stable—than those based on magical world views.

SUMMARY   We have now patched together part of a picture of the active construction of developing selves. Starting from the activity-dependent early wiring of our brains, discussed in the last chapter, we all proceed to develop as "little scientists." A human child's increasing competence in dealing with its physical and social world passes through a set of stages so stereotyped that it is hard to escape the conclusion that these stages rely on genetically specified components. However, the expression of these components—the competence and connectivity of the brains that actually grow—can be enhanced by rich physical and social environments or inhibited by impoverished ones. The contributions of specific brain areas to determining the nature and boundaries of the self are revealed by brain lesions that can cause a dissociation of the "selves" sensing and controlling the two sides of the body, or that can cause denial of a physical part of the self. The left hemisphere is revealed as a "presentation manager" that can sometimes go awry and confabulate bogus explanations in order to make sense of contradictory experiences or sensations.

Genetic and developmental studies suggest that several semi-independent core intelligences contribute to our repertoire of abilities, and psychological studies present the model of each of us as a "committee of selves," only one of which is usually the spokesperson at a given moment. An appreciation of the complexity of selves and their molding by physical and cultural influences reveals that much of the public discussion over genes and behavior is simplistic and misguided. Debate over learned versus innate mechanisms comes into sharpest focus in studies on language development, and we will conclude our discussion of this topic when we cover brain mechanisms of language in Chapter 11. The great variety of selves that humans can form, and the significant cultural differences in perception, mental categories, and selves construed as independent versus interdependent entities, show the importance of social factors in constructing selves. To proceed further in describing human minds and selves, we must now examine more of the details of their structure and function. Therefore, in Part III of this book, we will expand on the metaphor of each of us as a society of mind. ■

Questions for Thought

1. The philosopher Daniel Dennett makes the point that our brains spin stories about who we are, just as spiders spin webs or beavers build dams, without consciously and deliberately thinking about how to do it. Our narrative selfhood is the product of this process, not its source. Do you agree or disagree with this? Why?

2. Suppose you meet a person whose hemispheres you know to have been separated by surgery to cut the corpus callosum. Say you ask this person to look straight ahead and then, without glancing to the side, name a common object you hold up at the right edge of his or her visual range. Could the person do it? Why?

3. This chapter discusses the ideas of multiple intelligences and multiple selves within an individual human. What kind of evidence supports these models? Do you think one of these concepts is more plausible than the other?

4. Cultures vary in the relative value they place on the independence and the interdependence of individuals. Try to imagine yourself living and experiencing first one, and then the other, extreme end of these options. From each perspective, what sorts of explanations might you offer for your behaviors? What might be the roles, from each perspective, of personal introspection and awareness of personal motives ?

Suggestions for further general reading

Dennett, D.C. 1991. *Consciousness Explained.* Boston: Little, Brown. (The discussion of the boundaries of selves is drawn from Chapter 13 of this book.)

Donaldson, M. 1992. *Human Minds.* New York: Penguin Press. (One account of stages in the development of the human mind.)

Gardner, H. 1993. *Multiple Intelligences: The Theory in Practice.* New York: Basic Books. (This book discusses evidence for the existence of semi-independent intelligences, such as logical-mathematical, linguistic, spatial, musical, and so on.)

Gazzaniga, M.S. 1998. The split brain revisited. *Scientific American* 279(1): 50–55. (A review of studies on patients whose separated cerebral hemispheres act as two semi-independent selves.)

Pinker, S. 1997. *How the Mind Works.* New York: Norton. (Chapter 5 of this book discusses some of the evidence that humans come equipped with genetic predispositions to learn intuitive physics, biology, and psychology.)

Reading on more advanced or specialized topics

Bouchard, T.J. 1994. Genes, environment and personality. *Science* 264: 1700–1701. (A brief review of evidence that genetic factors influence behavior.)

Elman, J.L., Bates, E.A., Johnson, M.H., Karmiloff-Smith, A., Parisi, D., & Plunkett, K. 1996. *Rethinking Innateness: A Connectionist Perspective on Development.* Cambridge, MA: M.I.T. Press. (This book reviews several human developmental sequences and argues that they reflect powerful learning capacities rather than detailed genetic specifications.)

Kempermann, G., Kuhn, H.G., & Gage, F.H. 1997. More hippocampal neurons in adult mice living in an enriched environment. *Nature* 386:493–495. (One account of how environment can influence brain growth.)

Markus, H.R., & Kitayama, S. 1991. Culture and the self: Implications for cognition, emotion, and motivation. *Psychological Review* 98(2):224–248. (A discussion of the cultural relativity of the construal of self as independent versus interdependent.)

Ramachandran, V.S. 1995. Anosognosia in parietal lobe syndrome. *Consciousness and Cognition* 4:22–51. (A further discussion of the left hemisphere as the story-maker that imposes consistency on the world, whereas the right hemisphere contains a "questioning" mechanism that monitors anomalies and discrepancies.)

Part III

Society of Mind

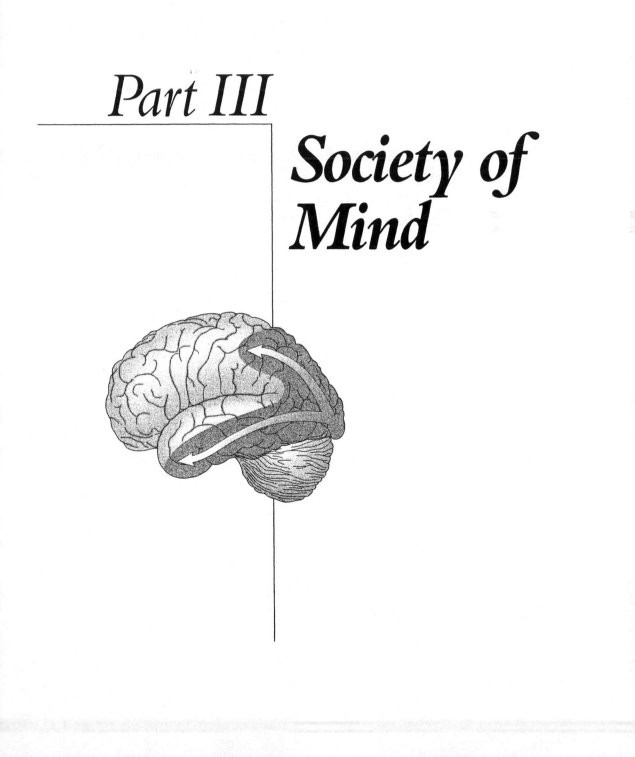

Chapter 8

Perceiving Mind

T his chapter, the beginning of Part III of this book, launches our exploration of how the different agencies of our minds work and how they are assembled into a coherent whole. These agencies arise from the evolutionary and developmental histories discussed in Parts I and II. We have noted many examples of the modularity of our brain functions but have addressed only a fraction of the experimental evidence. This chapter and Chapters 9 through 11 deal with our everyday experiences of sensing, acting, having emotions, and using language, respectively. Breaking up the discussion into these chunks helps us sort things out somewhat; however, these faculties interact so extensively that to view them as separate is really an oversimplification.

Ecology of sensing and acting

What animals like ourselves are able to perceive is shaped by a long history of adaptation and co-evolution with a particular environment, a particular ecology. We have receptors for visible (to us) light between about 400 and 700 nanometers in wavelength. We are unable to see patterns of ultraviolet light visible to the moth, we do not have receptors for the infrared light that some snakes use to sense heat given off by prey, and we do not have the acute long-distance vision of a hawk. We cannot hear the sound of a dog whistle or follow the scent of an escaping prisoner. Compared to most mammals, our sense of smell is quite poor. On an evolutionary time scale, we, like other animal species, have developed sensing and acting routines that are suitable for our particular physical and social niches. From the flood of physical information that impinges on us—light, sound, smell, and so on—we generate the perceptions we need to answer the question "What do I do next?" In humans, as in the most simple animals, perception serves action. The two are so intimately linked that it is a bit arbitrary to present them in two separate chapters.

Faculties such as visual perception and movement are linked in a continuous loop both during the developmental wiring of the brain and in the adult brain. Motion informs and refines vision, which informs and refines motion. Vision has little meaning apart from its use in behavior. One striking example of this has been provided by experiments in which two groups of newborn kittens were treated differently. One group could move about normally, and each of its members was harnessed to a simple carriage and basket that contained a member of the second group. The kittens in the second group had the same sort of visual input as the first, but they were passive—unable to test the relationship between their own movement and the environment. After a few weeks of this treatment, the first group behaved normally, but those who had been carried around failed several visual tests, such as avoiding steep drops. This experiment suggests that gaining knowledge of how to act in response to what is seen requires testing by the visual guidance of action and that such knowledge cannot be obtained just by passively extracting visual features from the environment. The elaborate reciprocal testing among developing brain, body, and external environment installs the filters and interpreters of our sensory world that are described in this chapter.

> *The ultimate purpose of our perceptions is to make it more likely that we will act in ways that help transmit our genes to future generations. Perception serves action.*

Perception focuses on change

Perception involves much more than just the brain, with its picture-like images and talking-to-oneself thoughts. What we know of external reality we learn through the way that reality affects our entire bodies. The outside world is registered in terms of the internal modifications it causes as we move about, changing the state of our viscera, our skin, and our autonomic nervous system, as well as our central nervous system. Our brains register what is happening "out there" as a set of rapidly flickering maps spread across our somatosensory and motor cortexes, as well as less topographical representations of our viscera in the brainstem and hypothalamus. One grounding reference for a sense of "self" appears to be a constantly renewed primordial representation of the body in action.

Our sensory systems are most interested in rapid changes in our environment, for it is these that we must respond to in order to survive. Think of how quickly you react when an unexpected shadow suddenly falls across your path. It is characteristic of our sensory receptors that dramatic alterations in a stimulus, such as onset and offset, are detected more easily than equal changes along a continuum. Recall the times when you have turned on a three-way lamp and then turned it off again. The sequence would have been something like: darkness → 50 → 100 → 150 watts of light → darkness. You notice dark → 50 watts as a big effect; 50 → 100 and 100 → 150 seem much less; off is again a big effect. Similarly, you have a very clear response to first touching your finger to your forearm. If you then apply a slowly increasing steady pressure, and occasionally press harder briefly to notice the amount of change you can just detect, the brief press must become larger as the background pressure is increased. Each bit of stimulus has made your skin receptors less responsive to the next bit of stimulus. The system "resets itself" to a new level of sensitivity (in other words, it adapts) so that its response is appropriate to the background.

Our perception of a stimulus is seldom absolute but, rather, depends on what has gone before. For example, if you move your hands among hot, cold, and tepid bowls of water, tepid feels warm or cold depending on which direction you come from. (The same sort of demonstration can be done with a set of three increasing weights.) Although we are good at perceiving changes on the time scale of these moment-to-moment behaviors, we usually don't notice changes that are much slower. You might not be aware, for example, that air pollution in your city has increased slowly over a period of several years, until a friend who visits after being away for a long time says, "Boy, the air is a lot more polluted now than when I left."

Perception is filtered and directed by many factors

Most of the sea of sound, odor, gravity, and light in which we are immersed is known to our brain/body but not explicitly perceived. What we are aware of perceiving is only a small fraction of the information registered by our sensory organs and processed apart from consciousness. In fact, imaging studies have revealed brain regions that are responsive to novelty outside our awareness. Numerous psychological studies have documented that unconscious perceptions can influence subsequent cognitive and affective reactions. Our perceptions are formed as primary sensations pass through an elaborate series of filters and interpreters installed by our evolution and our individual development, as well as by the attention, arousal, and expectations at hand. What we perceive is a mixture of what is there and what we expect.

The filtering processes of our brains help to guarantee that what gets through is relevant to the moment (when we are hungry, we look for restaurants, not gas stations, as we drive along). Anticipating a particular kind of stimulus actually increases blood flow to the part of the brain that processes that sensory modality. Our perceptions can be heightened or suppressed by powerful ascending pathways that rise like a fountain from the brainstem and shower the cortex with arousal-regulating neurotransmitters such as serotonin, acetylcholine, dopamine, norepinephrine (also called noradrenaline), and histamine. Our alertness and attention can be enhanced by drugs that stimulate norepinephrine release in the brain. Brain imaging studies reveal locations in the cortex that are components of networks of attention and that also regulate orientation and vigilance.

Our stream of conscious awareness is just a fraction of a larger intelligence that selects what perceptions make it into awareness—an intelligence of which we are usually unaware.

As an example of filters and censors that can act on our vision and language, consider being asked to finish the words S_X, SHI_, and F__K. If you reported six, shin, and fork, was the censorship bias in the reception or the response? Probably a mixture of both. Think of all the parts of your cortex that were lighting up during this exercise! Or consider the "cocktail party effect." When several conversations are going on around you, and you hear your name mentioned in one, you attend to that conversation immediately and tune out the others. Filters and censors like these ones suggest the presence of a feedback loop between cognitive processes of the frontal lobe and the more primary sensory cortexes that are registering all of the input.

Our assumptions and expectations can color our interpretation of what we hear and see. Consider the statements "I went to the nudist play" versus "I went to the new display" or "the prince of whales" versus "the prince of Wales." In this case, context enables us to differentiate between phrases that sound identical. Figure 8–1 offers an example of a shifting visual interpretation. In seeing the object shown on the left, we make the most simple assumption, that it is a hexagon, unless prior expectations tell us that it is another view of the object on the right.

Distinguishing between sensation and perception

Look again at the object on the right in Figure 8–1. Most people initially register this experience as looking at the top of a square with the lower set of vertical lines defining a surface that stands nearest the observer. However, if we stare at the figure long enough, it will flip so that we seem to be looking up at the bottom of the box, with the same vertical

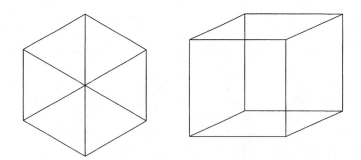

Figure 8–1 Drawings that illustrate the distinction between sensation and perception. The figure on the left is usually taken as an octagon, but it could be interpreted as the cube on the right rotated to a different position. The cube on the right, which is usually called the Necker cube, can be seen as having its top surface receding either to the left or to the right.

lines now defining its back side. Of course, neither the object itself nor its image on our retinas is changing. This is only one of many examples that can be used to demonstrate the distinction between sensation (the direct sensory recording) and perception (what we take that recording to mean). Recall that in Chapter 2 we discussed the evolutionary origins of this distinction, as more complicated animals began to separate the pathways of "what is happening to me" (sensation) from "what is happening out there" (perception).

Such distinctions are now being observed at the level of the firing of single nerve cells whose activity can be correlated with the way an object is perceived. It seems most likely that the rules for sorting out ambiguous visual images or linguistic utterances are formulated during the postnatal development of our brain circuitry. It is very unlikely that an *a priori* set of rules that evolved as adaptations to our ancestral paleolithic environment could anticipate and accommodate the visual and linguistic ambiguities generated by our modern surroundings. Perception of three-dimensional forms requires experience and learning. The sophisticated scene and feature analyses carried out by our visual brains (discussed below) are apparently constructed during development, as top-down processes determine which analyses work best in meeting changing environmental demands.

A more dramatic demonstration of the brain's ability to generate perception distinct from sensation can be observed in blind humans by attaching to their backs a patch driven by a video camera that the subject controls, a camera whose output to the patch causes the stimulation of multiple points on the skin. Each point represents one small area of the image captured by the camera. Within hours, some subjects can learn to recognize common objects such as cups and telephones, to point accurately in space, to judge distance, and finally to use perspective and parallax to perceive external objects in a stable three-dimensional world. The patterns projected onto the skin develop no such "visual" content unless the individual is behaviorally active, directing the video camera via head, hand, or body movements. After a few hours, the person no longer interprets the skin sensations as being of the body but projects them into the space being explored by the body-directed "gaze" of the video camera. What develops is not necessarily understanding but a strategy for responding appropriately. Test subjects do not locate objects as lying up against their skin—any more than those of us with vision locate objects as lying up against the retina of our eyes. Instead, they perceive objects as being out there in space. Thus a tactile sensation of "what is happening to me" is converted into a vision-like perception of "what is happening out there." More recently another form of sensory substitution, the conversion of visual images to sounds, has proven partially successful.

A vivid demonstration of the plasticity of sensation and perception comes from experiments in which blind subjects can learn to "see with their skin."

Perception of spatial relationships

Our brains use context to shape our perception of relationships. Consider the example shown in Figure 8–2. The two central circles are the same size, but they look different because of the relative size of the surrounding circles. In this case, there is a fascinating corollary: Although we consciously experience the central circles as differing in size, if we are asked to pick up the center discs, our grip immediately

Figure 8–2   Our subjective experience of the size of the middle circle is influenced by the size of the surrounding circles.

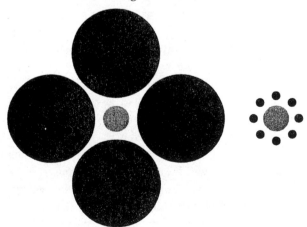

matches the true size of the objects. This demonstrates that the visual pathways in our brain that are required for skilled actions are separate from those that mediate our conscious perception. These two pathways are described in more detail below.

Perceptions frequently do not correspond to reality. Our stored images of familiar objects can be so strong that we see or hear what we think should be present rather that what actually is present. We (and all other animals) can act on the basis of caricatures of reality. Just a few aspects of a stimulus are usually sufficient to enable us (and induce us) to identify an object. (We are not unlike the male stickleback, a fish that will attack any object that vaguely resembles the red belly of another male.) We base our perception on best bets about what is out there. The point of having perceptions is not to be a perfect physical measuring device; it is to participate promptly in appropriate behaviors.

If you are ready to see a black ace of spades or a red ace of hearts, when a red ace of spades is shown, you are likely to see one of the two choices you have set for yourself rather than the card actually before you.

These examples illustrate that sensing is seldom naive but, rather, depends on context and comparison with a history of similar sensing. The brain specializes in rough-and-ready detection of what's probably important, not necessarily what is really there, and it is willing to make a lot of mistakes. We can extrapolate from such simple examples to our more complicated behaviors. Bias and hunches born of our history influence the scanning mechanisms we use to watch out for changes or danger in the environment. In people who are constantly apprehensive, those mechanisms seem to have taken on a chronic and inappropriate negative bias. Even the most benign events are interpreted as threatening. The converse of this situation is the Pollyanna syndrome, where negative input is denied. Humans, as individuals and groups, frequently deny the relevance of information they don't want to deal with. On a larger scale, we see this response in the muted reactions that many people have to ethnic genocidal wars and to the environmental and population crises.

Visual systems

The five major sensory systems (vision, olfaction, audition, sensation, and gustation) not only process separate sensory modalities but also extensively interact with and influence each other. For example, sound can alter our perception of visual motion, the auditory cortex is activated during silent lip reading, and vision and touch are closely linked in analyzing objects in our surroundings. We'll focus on vision here, though. Humans are visual animals, and at least 60 percent of our cerebral cortexes are involved in some aspect of processing visual information. In the visual system we face directly the question "Where does it all come together—where is the I?" We study vision from the top down (psychological experiments) and from the bottom up (electrophysiological experiments), and the area where the two have not yet met provides some fascinating puzzles. Here we are touching on something not fully understood: the link between neuronal firing and our conscious experience.

Not only does vision interact with our other senses, but it also forms an ensemble with movements of body muscles in which perception and action are linked. Vision involves much more than passive perception. Contractions of muscles that move the iris, rotate the eyes, control the face muscles around the eyes, contact neck muscles, and bring about other somatic movements can all be integral components of the experience of vision.

Self-experiment: a look at vision and its muscular correlates

We can use a simple exercise to illustrate the linkage of vision to muscle movements and tension. The following is best done if you can have someone else read the instructions to you, but it will probably work if you read through the instructions yourself, paying attention to the places where you are asked to pause before continuing. Take it slowly; don't rush.

Start by trying to focus and concentrate very hard on the following line, imagining that you will have to reproduce it from memory and that you are given only 10 seconds to learn and remember the characters:

#*$%)@!?

Now, stop. Move your forehead muscles. Are you frowning? Expand and contract the muscles around your eyes. What is their position now, and what was it when you were looking at the characters? Open and shut your jaw gently. Are the muscles loose or slightly clenched? Shrug your shoulders up and down. Are they relaxed or slightly elevated? Move your head slightly forward and back to stretch the muscles along the back of your neck. How tense are they? Now note your breathing. Take a deep breath, let it out, and see what pace of breathing seems natural as you resume.

You are likely to note numerous muscle contractions of which you are not usually aware. These patterns of contraction go along with your paying close, focused attention to a stimulus such as the characters you memorized.

Now, let's move on to another set of instructions, but try to remember the patterns of muscle tension that you just experienced. Read the following three instructions several times so that you can remember them, but do not read further. When you have the instructions in mind, you can continue with the experiment.

1. Rub your hands together to warm them, and then place your palms lightly over your eyes. Leave them there for at least 30 seconds. Let your eye muscles and breathing relax.
2. Place your hands in your lap, and, in your mind's eye, imagine a horizontal bar and slowly look back and forth from one end of the bar to the other. Then imagine a vertical bar, and do the same.
3. After several minutes of doing this, slowly open your eyes to receive the whole visual world without reaching out to focus on any particular item.

Once you have read these steps several times, do what they say before reading any further! Only then should you continue reading.

Now that you have taken all three steps, consider this question: How does your visual experience right now compare with what you were feeling just after you were asked you to focus on and remember the characters in the previous exercise? Are you more aware of the edges of your visual world? Does your vision feel more "open" than before? Check through the muscles you reviewed above. Do they feel harder or softer?

Some individuals who have completed this exercise with spoken instructions have reported that their visual world was very fuzzy, or even disappeared entirely, for a moment. This is similar to the experience most of us have had while listening to a boring sermon or lecture: We notice with a start that the visual scene was gone for a moment. If our eyes become completely still, the image of the external world on our retinas becomes stationary and we are temporarily blind. Seeing requires rapid saccadic movement of the eye muscles—that is, a constant darting about of the eyes that causes corresponding shifts of the visual field on the retinas. Visual sensing requires scanning and noting differences. We imagine we see a whole visual scene, but in fact our brains are attending to a series of rapid snapshots taken at each point where the eye rests as it shifts about. The point of the imagined movements along the horizontal and vertical bars was to get you to relax the chronic tonus of the muscles that usually move the eyes, in an effort to neutralize this scanning mechanism.

Perhaps you noted a difference between your focused vision at the start of the exercise and your more open vision at the end. A check of the muscles mentioned above would then illustrate some of the muscular correlates of vision focused on the details of a single object versus vision opened up to take in the whole visual world. In the former case, light is directed toward a small central region of our retinas called the fovea, which contains a high concentration of color-sensitive cone cells and is responsible for high-resolution vision (see Figure 8–3, page 190). In the latter case, the periphery of the retina is also engaged to take in the whole visual world, including its edges. Foveal vision is often correlated with the tensing of facial muscles and the contraction of flexor muscles along the front of the torso. The relaxing exercises were meant to engage input from more of the retina, letting more of the peripheral visual field that stimulates the edges of the retina be accessible. This more open vision can correlate with relaxation of facial muscles and the front flexor muscles of the torso.

Some athletes who must keep track of complicated movements over their entire visual field report cultivating a more open, or holistic, seeing of the sort we are getting at here. If instead, they focus, they must move their heads to see as much, and the act of focusing inhibits the flexibility of somatic muscle movement. This kind of visual experience may account for some athletes reporting that they enter a trance ("a zone") during periods of peak performance. The feeling is that an entity largely outside of conscious awareness has taken over and is running the show.

Our visual brain

Now let's consider our visual brain, the subject of the most intense contemporary research in cognitive neuroscience. Visual sensation and perception are the best understood of our mental faculties. This system manages the ordinary but amazing feat of keeping our perceptions of external objects constant as we move about, even as the size, shape, color, and brightness of the objects projected onto our retinas is constantly changing. The visual system must receive a flickering, two-dimensional image from the retinas and render this image into some sort of three-dimensional version that can guide appropriate action.

Our elaborate visual cortexes are the latest installment in the evolution of seeing. They follow upon the transitions we discussed earlier: from light-sensitive patches of membrane to image-forming eyes that send information to complex neural networks. Studying these cortexes in the cat and macaque monkey has revealed much of what we know about our own central visual pathways. Although we have been evolving separately from the macaque monkey for more than 15 million years, and thus must be cautious in comparing our visual brains, many areas of functional specialization seem to be similar in both.

The visual system has been studied more intensively than other parts of the brain for several reasons. For one thing, it is relatively easy to describe exactly the input to the visual system—the form, intensity, motion, and color of light that hits our eyes and is then transmitted to our retinas. (It is much harder to describe the quantity of an odor we inhale and to pinpoint exactly where it acts.) Another reason why interest has focused on the visual system is that the anatomy of the structures involved in visual processing is better understood than that of any other part of the brain. A series of relay stations can be followed from the retina to deep in the brain. At each stage of the relay, one can sample the activities of adjacent nerve cells and find that they are spread out in a topographical representation of the external world. In the occipital cortex, for example, this representation has become distorted, as though you had taken the retinal image on a piece of paper and crumpled it up to make it fit on the foldings and twistings of the cortex.

Humans are primarily visual animals, relying much less than most other vertebrates on touch, smell, and hearing.

The next section offers a brief description of visual pathways and the processing of visual information in parallel streams that deal with different aspects of visual images, such as form, motion, and color. This will set the stage for us to consider how visual perception is accomplished.

Visual information is processed in parallel streams

The lens of our eye projects an inverted image of the external world onto the retina, the thin film of nerve cells at the back of the eye (see Figure 8–3). This film contains millions of light-sensitive photoreceptor cells much like the grains in a photographic emulsion, and the pattern of their excitation corresponds precisely to the patterns being viewed. The photoreceptor cells then "talk" to a second layer of cells (bipolar cells), which in turn talk to a third layer of cells (*ganglion cells*) whose axons form the optic nerve that carries visual information toward the center of our brains. This nerve is a bundle or cable containing about a million ganglion cell axons. Electrical recordings show that each of these axons responds best to discrete small spots of light (or darkness); thus they are sometimes called spot detectors. Such recordings also show that the ganglion cells from which these axons derive specialize to report different kinds of stimuli.

Some ganglion cells with relatively large cell bodies (magnocellular cells, M) are especially sensitive to changes in a light stimulus and ultimately feed information to parts of the visual cortex that specialize in analyzing motion, location, size, and spatial relationships. Other ganglion cells with smaller cell bodies (parvocellular cells, P) specialize in

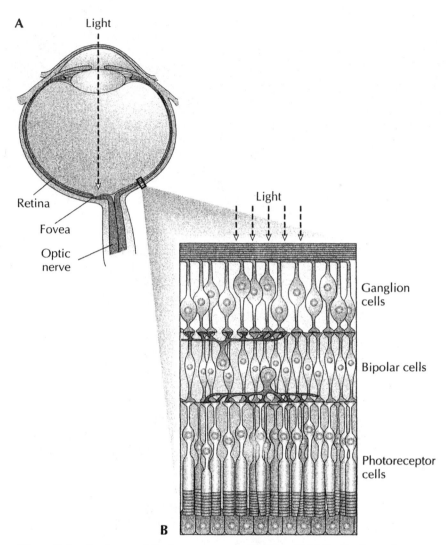

Figure 8–3   Anatomy of the human eye and retina. (A) Like the lens of a camera, the lens of the eye casts an inverted image of external objects onto the retina. The image of the object on which we are most directly focusing falls on a central part of the retina called the fovea, which contains color-sensitive photoreceptors (cones) and is most important in daylight vision. The scene surrounding this central object projects to more peripheral parts of the retina that contain fewer cones and more rod photoreceptors. Rod cells are important for vision in dim light. (B) The retina itself is a thin tissue consisting of three layers of nerve cells, and light passes through these layers before actually striking the photoreceptors. Axons of the ganglion cells form the optic nerve, which carries information from retina to brain. Also illustrated are a few of the cells that can transmit information sideways in the retina. Adapted from Figure 9.12 in Bear et al. *Neuroscience: Exploring the Brain.*

color and high contrast, and their information is finally used by cortical areas that are involved in object recognition. The distinction between M and P pathways arises at the first information relay between photoreceptor cells and bipolar cells and then persists into the visual areas of the brain. You will encounter further references to M and P pathways later in this chapter.

As the optic nerves from both eyes travel toward the center of the head, they follow the pathway outlined in Figure 8–4, meeting each

Figure 8–4 Information flows from retina to brain. Axons that report from the left sides of our two retinas, and thus relay information about the right-hand side of our visual world (our right visual field), proceed back toward our left hemispheres, where they connect to the left *lateral geniculate nucleus,* a part of the thalamus that is the brain's first nerve relay station for visual input. The axons that report from the right sides of our retinas (our left visual field) do the opposite, sending information about the left visual field to the right lateral geniculate nucleus. Alternating layers of the lateral geniculate structures get input from one or the other eye, and each of the layers is specialized to project information for either the M or the P pathway onto the visual cortex. Information about the left and right halves of our visual world remains segregated as the two lateral geniculate nuclei then send information back to area V1 of the occipital cortex, the primary visual cortex. In this drawing, the optic nerves and lateral geniculate nuclei are shown larger than their actual sizes for clarity. Adapted from figures in C. Shatz' 1992 article in *Scientific American* 267:60–7.

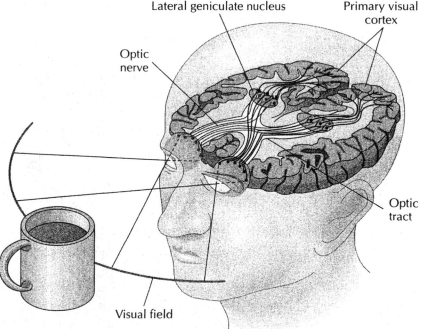

Lateral geniculate nucleus

Primary visual cortex

Optic nerve

Optic tract

Visual field

other in a crossing called the optic chiasm and then proceeding via the lateral geniculate nucleus to the V1 areas of the right and left hemispheres. (Look back at the view of these pathways shown in Figure 7–1.) Area V1 of the left visual cortex, which reports on the right visual world, and area V1 of the right visual cortex, which reports on the left visual world, would be just under your left and right forefingers if you placed them at the middle of the back of your head at about the level of the top of your ears. Recall from Chapter 7 that the two halves of our visual world are reconnected and integrated by means of the corpus callosum, the large bundle of nerve fibers that communicates information between the two hemispheres. We have already noted that cutting this bundle in some patients with intractable epilepsy caused them to become individuals who see the two halves of their visual world with two different "selves."

Certain developmental dyslexics who do poorly in tests that require rapid visual processing show abnormalities in the lateral geniculate magnocellular layers that process fast, low-contrast visual information. Also, imaging studies of such individuals show reduced activity in higher visual centers that process motion information. Some dyslexics have difficulty not only with rapid visual stimuli but also in processing sounds, which suggests a more general deficit in processing of rapidly changing sensory stimuli.

Form, motion, and color

Axons that have arrived at area V1 from the lateral geniculate nucleus make connections on neurons in the middle of the six cell layers of the cortex (at layer 4), and at this point they are still spot detectors, responding best to small spots of light or darkness just as ganglion cells of the retina and cells in the lateral geniculate nucleus do. However, a fascinating transformation can be observed by exploring the activity of cells in nearby layers of the cortex. An electrode inserted perpendicular to the cortex (into layers either higher or lower than layer 4) reveals cells that fire best not in response to a spot of light but, rather, when a small patch of retina is stimulated by a line of one particular orientation. Although the exact wiring that turns spot detectors into "line detectors" is not known, a simple hunch is probably the correct one. If a number of spot detectors arranged in a straight line (that is, cells that are ultimately getting information from a line of receptor cells on the retina) all "reported" to a single following cell, they would constitute a line detector. As the electrode that found the line detector is moved up and down through the cortical layers, it encounters cells with more complex properties. Some cells respond best not to lines of light but to dark-light edges; some distinguish whether those edges are moving from right to left or from left to right. Others respond best to right-angle corners between light and dark.

As we move into the cortex, we find cells that respond to more complex stimuli. Instead of being sensitive to spots, cells fire in response to lines of a particular orientation, movement from a specific direction, and edges of light or dark. The components of our visual world are being constructed one piece at a time.

The plot thickens as the electrode is removed and inserted into an adjacent area of the cortex. Now the preferred orientation for the line detectors has shifted slightly, as well as that for the more complicated cells. Moving across the cortex and lowering the recording electrode, we encounter a series of "orientation columns," each about 20–50 microns (micrometers) across, and each column's orientation preference is slightly different from the preferred orientation of the preceding column. These columns are driven mainly by one eye, but after the electrode has sampled across the cortex for 200–500 microns, columns are encountered that prefer the other eye. Thus mapping the surface of the visual cortex reveals stripes or bands of cortex 200–500 microns across that are driven mainly by one or the other eye. These orientation and occular dominance columns are shown in Figure 8–5. Finally, the cortex contains islands of cells that respond to the color of the stimulus.

The surface of area V1 of the cortex, then, is a rich mosaic of partially segregated subcompartments that contain, for each spot on the retina and in the visual world, cells whose firing corresponds to all possible orientations of the stimulus, whether the stimulus is presented to the right or left visual world, whether it is colored, whether the stimulus is rapid with low light contrast or slow with high contrast, whether the disparity of the same stimulus on the two retinas gives clues about its distance or depth, and so on.

Area V1 in the back of the cortex acts as a post office, sending information forward to an adjacent area of cortex, V2, and then (both directly and via V2) to the areas V3, V4, and V5 that occupy folds, or crenulations, in the cortex a small distance toward the front of the brain (Figure 8–6). Lesions in area V1, usually caused by strokes, result in a complete block of the ability to acquire visual information consciously. Both electrical recordings and brain imaging studies show that areas V3, V4, and V5 deal with distinctively different aspects of the visual

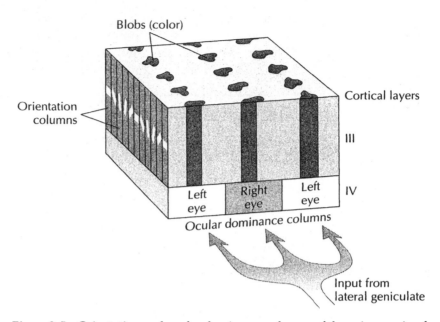

Figure 8–5   Orientation and ocular dominance columns of the primary visual cortex, area V1. For simplicity, this drawing represents the domains as rectangular in shape, but they actually are arranged in pinwheel configurations. Adapted from Figure 10.25 in Bear et al. *Neuroscience: Exploring the Brain.*

input. Area V5 (which is also referred to as the MT area) is most active in response to moving stimuli. Brain lesions in this area can cause *akinetopsia,* the inability to distinguish moving forms, without loss of color or form perception. Area V5 responds poorly to moving stimuli in dyslexic subjects who show deficits in reading and phonological awareness. A small area adjacent to V5, called MST, processes the visual motion, or optic flow, that results from movement of the observer through its environment.

SELF-EXPERIMENT

Recall sitting in a stationary train as another train slowly pulled past on an adjacent track and then feeling that your own train was moving backward after the other train passed. This is called a motion after-effect illusion. You may also have looked at a waterfall for a period of time and then, on looking to the side, observed that trees in the adjacent forest appeared to be moving upward. When normal subjects are presented with this motion after-effect, known as the waterfall illusion, they report seeing motion even though the stimulus is stationary, and at the same time their V5 areas are very active. This is an intriguing result, because it begins to provide us with a neural correlate of one of our subjective experiences.

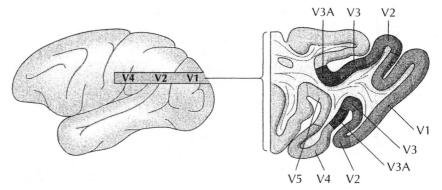

Figure 8–6 Location of different visual areas, shown using the macaque monkey brain (where these have been mapped with the most precision). Adapted from figures in Zeki's 1992 article in *Scientific American* 267:68–76.

Area V4 is most reactive to form-with-color input, such as a Mondrian painting. Lesions in this area can cause *achromatopsia*, the inability to distinguish between colors while form perception remains intact. Firing of neurons in area V4 can be correlated with visual attention directed either toward an area of space or toward a particular object. Surgical excision of area V4 in the rhesus monkey causes deficits in the recognition of objects that have been transformed either in their size, degree of occlusion, or amount of contour information provided. In general, increasingly complex functions are spared as lesions occur in consecutively higher parts of the human visual system. These areas correspond to several dissociable levels of conscious vision: phenomenal vision, object vision, and object recognition.

It seems that visual information goes from the post offices of areas V1 and V2 into a variety of pigeonholes where it is analyzed piecemeal. There are at least 32 visual areas in the macaque monkey, comprising approximately 50 percent of the cortex, and about half of these contain maps of the external world that are reported by the retina. As information flows toward association cortex and the front of the brain, visual information mixes with other sensory input (such as sound and somatosensory stimuli) and motor systems. There is such a melding of visual input with resulting motor output that it is difficult to say where it all comes together before action is taken. Action can be initiated well before visual processing is complete. As information flows from sensory input toward motor output, we would expect to find stages at which responses to stimuli began to correspond to the task about to be performed, rather than to the sensory input itself. Indeed, the activity of cells in the posterior parietal cortex of monkeys can correspond to actions about to be performed.

The "what" and "where" systems

The prevailing idea is that the distinction between *magnocellular* (M) and *parvocellular* (P) *pathways* persists as information flows from area V1 toward higher visual centers. The M pathway carries information about where a visual stimulus is and about its spatial relationships, size, and motion. This pathway projects from V3 (dynamic form) and V5 (motion) in a dorsal information stream toward the parietal lobe, where motor and somatosensory cortices are located (Figure 8–7). Cells in this stream respond rapidly to changes in stimuli, are not sensitive to color, have low resolution, report information from relatively large areas of the retina, and are very sensitive to changes in contrast (light intensity changes at edges). This is what one might expect for a system that is ultimately responsible for rapid guidance of muscular movements in response to visual stimuli. It is probably most appropriate to view this dorsal pathway as a visuomotor control pathway, not just a sensory or perceptual pathway. There is no clear demarcation of where vision ends and action begins.

The P pathway proceeds mainly from V3 and V4 in the direction of the temporal lobe (the inferotemporal cortex), sending a ventral stream of information that is most concerned with what a stimulus is. Cells in this pathway have high resolution (that is, they report information from a very small area of the retina), respond to color, are slower than M cells in responding to changes in stimuli, and are not very sensitive to changes in contrast. These are properties that seem appropriate for object recognition, and in fact, a part of the temporal cortex appears to be specialized for the detection of faces (see page 198).

The separation of these two major streams of information suggests that information about the identity of objects can be computed separately

Figure 8–7   Dorsal (where) and ventral (what) streams of information.

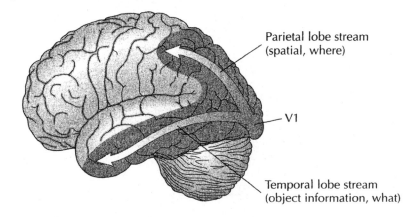

Parietal lobe stream
(spatial, where)

V1

Temporal lobe stream
(object information, what)

from the information needed to react to that stimulus. Occipital-parietal-temporal association areas might call up various memories relevant to a stimulus (such as the fact that apples can be used to make pies), and decisions related to the stimulus would also involve the frontal lobes. The dissociation of object-processing and spatial-processing domains persists into the prefrontal cortex in primates.

The distinction between dorsal and ventral streams has been studied most carefully in macaque monkeys, with their approximately 32 different visual areas. Imaging studies have so far differentiated ten human cortical visual areas with corresponding properties. Of course, the distinctions between the M and P, parietal and temporal, where and what pathways are surely not so clear and tidy as the simplified picture being presented here. There is segregation of information, but these pathways also interact continuously. This account does not cover further information streams that may sketch boundaries and paint in their color, nor does it describe how different information streams might converge and recombine.

> *The ventral "what" system (temporal lobe) might tell you that an object is an apple; the dorsal "where" system (parietal lobe) would tell you where it is and how to shape your hand to pick it up.*

Visual pathways outside the cortex

Axons from the retina also pass to at least ten other regions, including the pretectum and superior colliculus of the midbrain, areas that are important in regulating eye movements guided by visual input. Visual projections such as these, that do not pass through the cortex, may underlie the phenomenon of *blindsight*. Subjects with lesions in the primary visual areas have scotomas, or blind zones, in their visual fields. They cannot verbally report on visual stimuli in these areas, but when asked to guess whether a stick (that they can't "see") is held horizontally or vertically, they answer correctly. And, they can direct their hand to where a point of light is flashed in their blind area. This is an example of sensation being flawed while perception is partially intact.

SELF-EXPERIMENT

You can get a feel for what blindsight might be like by performing a simple exercise. Try looking about the room and then closing your eyes. Visual sensation will cease, but for a while at least, your knowledge of the room will persist, and you will be able to reach in the right direction for something. This is not surprising. But imagine what it would be like if you were to keep your eyes permanently closed and still had continuously updated knowledge of the position and shapes of objects as though you had just closed your eyes. You would feel that your perception was not legitimate, much as a patient with blindsight does, because you would not have ongoing involvement in the sensation of seeing.

Blindsight can be produced in normal subjects by a clever visual stimulus that places a square-shaped array of paired dots moving past each other in differing locations within a larger square array of similarly paired dots moving at right angles to the first. The dots are so closely superimposed that an observer does not consciously perceive two groups of dots. Still, subjects "guess" the location of the smaller set of moving dots correctly. The stimulus is one that is projected only poorly from area V1 to higher visual areas, which suggests that activation of these higher areas is required for subjective awareness of a stimulus. This correct performance in the absence of awareness might utilize subcortical pathways. There are many other examples, in both normal and brain-damaged subjects, demonstrating nonconscious or implicit knowledge of stimuli that cannot, however, be perceived explicitly or recollected consciously. This observation suggests that, in addition to the modules for explicit sensing and reporting, other distinct modules capable of sensory processing can still do their work when the first set of modules is out of order.

Ensembles of cells encode faces and other icons

Are there specific dedicated cells whose firing corresponds to a single complex image (such as your grandmother's face)? Apparently not. It is clear that cells in our inferior temporal cortex are active in facial recognition, but stimuli are represented by patterns across ensembles of cells, not by the firing of single cells. Face-selective cells are found to be members of ensembles for coding faces rather than detectors for a particular face. In the superior temporal sulcus, different populations of cells, located in patches 3–5 millimeters across, are selective for different views of the face and head. These cells may support a parallel analysis of different characteristic views of the head that combine to support view-independent (object-centered) recognition. Some neurons in the inferior temporal cortex can learn to respond to all views of previously unfamiliar objects, but most respond to only one view. Activities of these cells may be important as "social attention" signals, indicating where other persons are directing their attention. Such a process is required for social interactions.

Activation of face-sensitive cells can correlate with activity in both the hippocampus (declarative memory) and the amygdala (involved in emotional memory). PET scan studies show that large areas of temporal and occipital cortex are active during the processing of facial information. When subjects are asked to visualize internally the face of a famous person, the face area of the temporal cortex becomes more active. MRI studies using binocular rivalry show how activity in the face area can correlate with visual awareness: A subject whose left eye is shown a picture of a face and whose right eye is shown a picture of a house reports switching—experiencing one and then the other every few seconds. During intervals in which the face is reported, the face area becomes relatively more active, and when the house is reported, the region surrounding the hippocampus that is involved in spatial recognition becomes more active.

Brain lesions, particularly to the right hemisphere's temporal lobe, can cause face-recognition impairments, or prosopagnosias, while sparing the ability to recognize most other objects. Such a case is described by Oliver Sacks in his book The Man Who Mistook His Wife for a Hat. *The man in question had lost his ability to recognize faces, so he had to use recollection of the dress his wife was wearing to recognize her at a party.*

Electrical recordings from the monkey cortex have recently shown that columns of cells in the inferior temporal cortex are selective for a range of similar stimuli. One intriguing set of experiments started with a large collection of toy animals, vegetables, and natural objects as visual stimuli and then progressively simplified and abstracted the features necessary for eliciting the strongest responses of single neurons. Columns responsive to colored bars, hand shapes, ovals with gradients of luminosity, face shapes, T-shapes, and other iconic stimuli were found.

The inferior temporal cortex appears to use *ensemble coding,* with no one cell representing the detailed information being processed. Rather, the world we perceive emerges from the coordinated firing of sets of interconnected neurons. Examples of ensemble coding occur at all levels of the visual system. Color perception is an emergent property of a "committee" of photoreceptors. Depth perception is an emergent property of disparity-detecting cells in area V4 whose firing reflects how the position of an object on the retina changes as its distance from the eye changes. Individual cells are not sharply tuned for objects, say 8.0–8.2 meters away, but we can make this distinction by averaging the responses of large numbers of similar cells. Such estimates improve with the square root of the number of cells involved (such that quadrupling the number of cells doubles the precision). Similarly, any single cell in area V5 might not track the velocity of a visual stimulus with great accuracy, but the average response of a large number of these cells connected together might be very accurate indeed. We can resolve spatial differences in images on our retina that are smaller than the separation of the photoreceptors, presumably because the reports of many receptors on the retinal position of a stimulus are averaged.

Information streams flow forward, backward, and sideways

Work on the visual system is refining the simplistic classical distinction, still widely used in teaching physiology, between what goes into the brain (sensations, perceptions) and what comes out (actions). Lurking behind this idea was the incorrect metaphor of a clear chain of command: an input stream, then someplace where "it all comes together for decision making," and then an output stream. The initial stages of visual and other sensory input are indeed hierarchical and involve mainly the flow of information from peripheral receptors into the brain. (For example, our brains do not send information back to our retinas.) Information flow in the final stages of motor output also is mainly one-way. Between these more peripheral functions, however, visual information is flowing in the dorsal and ventral streams (mentioned above) through 30–50 different areas where it mixes with signals from other sensory and motor areas, with lots of cross-talk and feedback.

Even at the early stage of the lateral geniculate nucleus, which is usually described as a simple relay station passing information from retina to cortex, feedback connections predominate. The lateral geniculate nucleus gets only 20 percent of its input from the retina; the other 80 percent is feedback from the visual cortex and input from lower centers in the brains such as those that control eye movement. Recordings from the lateral geniculate body or area V1 in live animals show that the responses are very context-sensitive, changing with body tilt or posture or with auditory stimulation.

There are so many reciprocal and cooperative interactions between visual and other systems that the situation is better described as a cocktail party than as a chain of command.

Resonating neuronal ensembles link vision, posture, sound, and so on. Meaning resides in complex patterns of activity among the numerous units that make up these networks.

The projection of a later stage of processing back onto an earlier one is referred to as top-down, re-entry, or re-entrant processing. This re-entrant input is often more diffuse than the incoming information was. Thus the forward projections of V1 and V2 to V3 and V5 are very specific; thin stripes of V2 cells project to V4, whereas thick stripes of cells project to V3 and V5. Yet the return (re-entrant) input to V1 and V2 from the specialized visual areas is very broad. This input apparently allows V1 and V2, which are largely devoted to simple line detectors, to represent complex features that require feedback from higher cortical areas. Thus correlates of attention and figure-ground separation have been found in recordings from single cells and small groups of cells in areas V1 and V2. One example comes from cells that respond to the illusory edges of the invisible triangle (the Kanizsa triangle) shown in Figure 8–8. Cells in areas V1 and V2 that respond to an illusory contour or line at a border where no contrast exists must be receiving feedback from higher visual areas that have defined the whole figure.

The effect of top-down processing can be readily observed in both monkeys and humans when attention is focused on a particular aspect of a stimulus, such as its color, motion, or identity. Higher centers in the frontal lobes apparently feed back to enhance the activity of cells and areas dealing with that aspect of the stimulus, while suppressing others. Thus instructions to pay attention to the motion, shape, or color of a stimulus enhance the activity of V5, V4, and the temporal lobe "what" pathway, respectively.

Another example of a correlation between a sophisticated visual perception and nerve cell firing comes from neurons in areas V1, V2, and V4 whose activity follows perception during binocular rivalry experiments. Monkeys were trained to report their perceived orientation of a grating stimulus by pressing levers, and then gratings of different orientations were shown to the two eyes. Many cells, particularly in area V4, showed activity that correlated with the perceptual dominance of one, and suppression of the other, stimulus. When recordings moved on to the inferior temporal cortex, activity of nearly all the cells reflected the dominant perception.

A linking of perception and action at the single-cell level has also been observed. Monkeys can be trained to respond behaviorally to a set of light points moving together in a fixed direction in a field also occupied by randomly moving points (the human observer doesn't notice the coherent movement of the subset; everything just seems to be random). Activity in the V5 region is recorded that corresponds to this discrimination. Microstimulation of the circuit that encodes this direction of motion elicits the trained behavioral response (without stimulating the retina).

Figure 8–8 The Kanizsa triangle. Cells are found in areas V1 and V2 that can respond to the illusory edges formed by these shapes.

This work has been carried even further to show that the responses of some cells in the frontal lobe hold information about intended behavioral movement before it is actually carried out.

Re-entrant, or top-down, processing presumably underlies the activation of areas V1 and V2 that is observed in magnetic resonance and PET imaging studies when a visual stimulus is recalled. The areas activated by a visual stimulus can increase their activity during mental recall of the same stimulus. Brain imaging studies show that both motor areas and area V1 can become active when subjects are asked to rotate imagined visual objects. Numerous fields in parietal, temporal, and frontal cortex also become active during manipulation of images. PET studies show differential recruitment of the temporal ("what") and parietal ("where") pathways when subjects are asked to imagine an object or to imagine tracing a pathway between two familiar street locations. Damage to the right frontal lobes can compromise tasks that involve mental imagery in the (imagined) left visual field.

The fact that knowledge stored in higher centers can activate primary visual cortex might partially explain why our visual perception can be biased to report what we want to see. In the fascinating case of Charles Bonnet syndrome, damage to early parts of the visual pathway results in a blind spot in some part of the visual field. Subjects report vivid visual hallucinations confined entirely to the region of this blind spot. This suggests that the hallucinations may be generated by feedback from higher cortical centers—feedback that can no longer be compared with what is actually present in the subject's visual world.

As one might expect, the "what" and "where" systems are selectively compromised by damage in the temporal and parietal lobes, respectively. For example, a car accident victim with a lesion between the part of the brain that compiles images coming from the eyes and the library of images in memory could not recognize what he saw but could still draw on his library of images. He could not name an asparagus shown to him but could draw an asparagus when asked. His ability to recognize human faces was unaffected by the brain damage, which implies a separate system for face recognition. What emerges from all these facts is a picture not only of the bottom-up flow of information but also of top-down projection of higher brain areas back to earlier visual areas.

A binding process underlies visual perception

How are different aspects of the visual stimulus organized into perception? This is called *the binding problem*. Complex visual images are being processed by parallel pathways that specialize in color, form, motion, solidity, and so on. How does the brain associate the work being independently done by separate cortical regions? Different properties such as shape, color, and motion must be "bound" to the objects they characterize. An object and its motion must be distinguished from its background. These problems are among the most crucial in cognitive neuroscience. The binding problem is not just a theoretical worry. Some patients with bilateral parietal lobe damage miscombine colors and shapes and are unable to judge relative or absolute visual locations. Spatial information associated with the dorsal "where" pathway has been compromised.

Our visual consciousness starts building as our eyes dart about over the surface of a viewed object to generate a series of very rapid, focused snapshots. These are the saccadic eye movements mentioned in the discussion of the first self-experiment in this chapter. The information gathered during a saccade is delivered to a scanning and processing mechanism in the visual cortex; the process is complete in about 50 milliseconds. This mechanism registers distinctive boundaries that are created by elementary properties of brightness, color, or line orientation. We rapidly and automatically process the property of subjective closure of forms. A pop-out effect occurs for letters and digits: A letter target is detected more efficiently among digits than among letters, and vice versa. Because letter recognition and digit recognition are not innate, it is likely that the customary separate groupings of letters and digits in the environment leads to their separate encoding. For postal workers who routinely see letters and digits together, letters do not pop out so much from digits.

Our experience of a continuous visual world is an illusion. It could be arranged, by attaching a tracking device to your cornea, that small fragments of a text (from a whole written page) are displayed only during the brief times during which you are actually directing a saccade toward their position on the page. An observer not connected to this device would see only transient flickers of word fragments darting about the page, but you would experience a continuous page of text.

The scanning system encodes useful elementary properties of the overall scene (such as texture, color, orientation, size, and direction) into feature maps in different brain regions. An abstracting function may then compose key aspects of the image that distinguish the object of attention from its surround—a master or saliency map is formed. Thus the early stages of the visual pathway provide a faithful representation of the retinal image, whereas later stages of processing hold edited representations of the visual world modified to suit the immediate interest and goals of the viewer. If a key part needs further examination, then the brain refers to the individual feature maps.

How are salient features bound together into a master map? One suggestion is that visual attention may be mediated by subcortical structures such as the pulvinar, claustrum, and superior colliculus, as well as by the prefrontal cortex. Bursts of correlated action potentials in these structures may represent the saliency map. Evidence suggests that neurons in the visual cortex that are activated by the same object in the world tend to discharge synchronously. According to this theory, separate populations of cells—say, those responding to aspects of the color, shape, texture, motion, smell, and sound of a stimulus like a bus, along with those that hold memories of buses experienced in the past—all send out nervous impulses at the same rate for a fraction of a second. As the neurons all fire together, sometimes oscillating about a central frequency, the perception of the bus is created in the network. The binding is a matter not of where but of when. Thus the synthesis of the visual image in the brain would depend not only on the simultaneous activity of cells in the different specialized visual areas but also on the temporal synchrony of their responses. This synchronous activity would include areas such as V1 and V2 with which the specialized visual areas are reciprocally connected. To link visual perception and action, it would be necessary to synchronize also with motor areas of the cortex, and such synchronization has been observed. Synchronization of the firings of large ensembles of neurons could be important whether or not those firings were occurring in a rhythmic or oscillatory pattern. (Investigators' excitement about the joining of nerve cells in rhythmic oscillations being a possible answer to the binding problem has been muted somewhat by the discovery that the oscillations measured in the visual areas of the cat brain are not observed in visual areas of the monkey brain.)

The visual percept might not reside in any given visual area, even if that area is critical for certain features of that visual image, but might rather result from ongoing activity in several connected visual areas. It seems likely that the simultaneous activity of many visual areas is necessary for conscious visual perception. Stimuli do not reach visual awareness unless all these areas are stimulated, even if signals bypass area V1 to reach the specialized visual areas indirectly, as is observed in blindsight.

Neural correlates of visual consciousness

A goal of current research is to determine the neural correlates of our experience of seeing—our visual consciousness. It seems most likely that visual awareness and planning involve the frontal cortexes, which receive connections from the higher, specialized visual areas such as V4 and V5, but not directly from area V1. This argues against activity in area V1 by itself being the neural correlate of images we are aware of. It is possible that there are specific neurons, normally dependent on input from many areas, whose firing gives rise to the current content of our visual (or other) consciousness. If this is the case, one might be able—with some not-yet-invented technique—to stimulate these cells directly and generate in a human subject the same subjective experience that is associated with their normal input and firing.

SUMMARY

We are at the threshold of understanding how the array of modular processors that first transform and analyze different aspects of our sensory world—such as visual motion, form, depth, and color—proceed to interact and generate our conscious experience of a visual percept. Progress in understanding the perceptual worlds of hearing, tasting, smelling, and body movements is not so advanced. The great variety of line detectors, shape detectors, icon detectors, figure-surround discriminators, and so on represent parts of the solution to the central problem posed by the physical environments in which the visual brain evolved: how to process visual information in a way that leads to effective action in the world, action ultimately in the service of reproduction. Sensory information coming into our brains is arranged hierarchically at first but soon merges into regions of association cortex that specialize in "what" or "where" information—regions that blend sensory modalities and mix with motor, premotor, and prefrontal areas. These higher areas send information back to earlier stages of processing, and crosstalk between different information streams contributes to the binding together of percepts. The initiation of action, then, has a fuzzy origin that becomes more structured and hierarchical as actual movement repertoires are executed.

Higher vertebrates in particular use the past as well as the present in interpreting current sensory input. What has been seen in the past can influence what is seen in the present. Experience during development of the brain and in adulthood leads to the assembling of a whole repertoire of assumptions and interpretations that have proved useful in the past. These most often facilitate perception and actions, but they also can bias and confuse our responses if a past interpretation is not appropriate to the present. As we will see in the next chapter, systems that regulate body movement also acquire training and habits, which, though they are indispensable for skilled action, can also impede appropriate responses to novel situations. ∎

Questions for Thought

1. One approach to understanding perception is to ask, "What kind of machine would a good physicist or engineer build to render inside the head an accurate representation of the sights, sounds, and so on out there in the real world?" Another approach is to say, "Forget the omniscient engineer. What perceptual mechanisms have in fact been cobbled together during evolution to guide action in the real world, in the service of passing on our genes?" What do you think are the merits of each of these two approaches? Do they suggest different research strategies?

2. Many experiments demonstrate that most of our perceptions are not naive but are informed by a previous history of sensing that imposes biases and interpretations on what we think we perceive. Why do you think our brains would have been designed this way? What are the advantages and disadvantages? How might you try to determine whether such biases are learned or innate?

3. Would a lesion in your right inferior temporal lobe be expected to influence how you pick up an object with your left hand? If so, how?

4. Visual information flows from higher visual areas back to lower visual areas such as V1. What are some ideas about the role such top-down processing might play?

Suggestions for further general reading

Crick, F. 1994. *The Astonishing Hypothesis: The Scientific Search for the Soul.* New York: Scribner. (This book, like the book by Zeki, cited below, gives a description of information processing by the visual system.)

Goleman, D. 1986. *Vital Lies, Simple Truths: The Psychology of Self Deception.* New York: Simon & Schuster. (An accessible account of psychological studies that demonstrate how perceptual filters, self-deceptions, self-images, and the like are constructed. Several examples used in this chapter were taken from this book.)

Ornstein, R. 1991. *The Evolution of Consciousness.* New York: Prentice Hall. (Several examples of the relativity of perception cited in this chapter were taken from this book, which is an engaging account of some of the topics covered in this and subsequent chapters.)

Pinker, S. 1997. *How the Mind Works.* New York: Norton. (Chapter 4 of this book includes an interesting discussion of how the visual mind solves problems of shape, space, and perspective.)

Reading on more advanced or specialized topics

Gazzaniga, M.S., Ivry, R.B., & Mangun, G.R. 1998. *Cognitive Neuroscience—The Biology of the Mind.* New York: Norton.

Zeki, S. 1993. *A Vision of the Brain.* Oxford, England: Blackwell Scientific Publications. (A very accessible account of visual information processing by the brain.)

The next two volumes are collections of brief review articles that cover essentially all of the areas of modern cognitive neuroscience. They have material relevant to all the chapters in Part III of this book. Together with Gazzaniga's cognitive neuroscience textbook and the citations on the Web site for this book (see page xii of the preface for the URL), they provide more detailed primary references on the observations reported in this chapter.

Gazzaniga, M.S. (ed). 1995. *The Cognitive Neurosciences.* Cambridge, MA: M.I.T. Press. (Chapter 4, 5, and 6 of this comprehensive cognitive neuroscience textbook deal with different aspects of perception.)

Squire, L.R., & Kosslyn, S.M. 1998. *Findings and Current Opinion in Cognitive Neuroscience.* Cambridge, MA: M.I.T. Press.

Chapter 9

Acting Mind

Now we shift our emphasis from perception to action, to consider the nature of the body movements that make up our behaviors. This chapter starts by noting further how our minds, body actions, and environment are linked in a seamless whole and then considers how mind and consciousness might be defined from the point of view of movement. We next review some aspects of our experience of movement of which we are usually unaware, using several simple exercises to sense the hierarchical and habitual nature of the neuronal control of our motion, exercises that can also be used to refine and change that control. A further section takes a brief look at the neuronal pathways underlying action, and a final section considers how movement might be regulated by a Darwin Machine mechanism.

Action—the interface of mind and environment

As we go about our daily lives, a significant fraction of our experience consists of preoccupation with the thoughts flowing through our heads, the chatter of our internal discourse. Occasionally, this noise may diminish, as though the brain is taking a brief time-out from constantly talking to itself. At such times, we can quietly notice the rest of our body and its experience as we move through our activities. Do you ever feel as though an "it" rather than an "I" is doing the moving? And do you ever wonder if this is what it would be like to be an animal, not self-conscious, moving through its terrain? In this state of mind, you probably notice many small signals from your body, and also from the environment, that you usually ignore. When you pass either an attractive or a menacing person, subtle somatic episodes or emotions associated with approach or avoidance appear and then disappear. If the menacing person suddenly says, "Got any spare change?" you note a more obvious tensing of the whole body and an increase in heartrate, as though it is preparing for flight. These multiple body flickerings are present at all times, but normally you tune them out.

Such experiences reflect the processes going on as movement of your body leads to construction of a representation of the external world from the perturbations caused as that world touches it and showers it with odors, sounds, and light. It is easy to lose sight of this embodiment of our brain-mind because we spend most of the hours of our waking consciousness living in our heads—thinking about, reading about, and talking about ideas. Many of us usually tune out awareness of what is going on in the rest of our bodies as we move about and as our feelings change. The brain, however, does not tune out. Outside the narrow spotlight of our awareness, a massive and constant stream of information flows back

It is our whole organism—body and brain—that interacts with our environment. Mind is about the rest of the moving body, about what to do with it, about where to move next.

and forth between brain and body. The global state of parasympathetic/sympathetic activation in the peripheral autonomic nervous system that innervates our viscera is being monitored, and the outcome affects the emotional balance between approach and avoidance in every passing moment.

The image conjured up by science fiction writers and philosophers of a "brain in a vat," isolated but otherwise identical to the normal brain, is unrealistic in more than just the obvious ways. The vat makers would have to reproduce the subtle and myriad sensory inputs to this brain, its responding actions on the body, and the brain's subsequent sensing of the effects of those actions—a formidable proposition! It is unlikely that there are autonomous symbolic brain structures that do not require, or are not regulated by, the exchange of information with the rest of the body. The body is an essential component of the content of our mind.

Acting on and perceiving the environment require constant modifications of body musculature. Goal-directed movements are constantly checked and refined as sensory receptors monitor their progress. The body is constantly changing itself in accordance with the visual world that is present and the actions being contemplated in it, part of a massive background calculation that yields each moment's answer to the question "Do I like or dislike, approach or avoid this situation?" Perceiving is thoroughly about acting, and acting is completely about perceiving, a rich relationship that can be obscured by the arbitrary separation of the two in most accounts and textbooks. The self we all experience as we move through a day requires a continually reconstructed or updated image of our perceptions, feelings, and actions. What we think is going on "out there" is not just the photograph-like image we are most aware of. It is also a subtle symphony of brain representations of our viscera, our moving muscles, and the biochemical regulators of our hypothalamus.

Our minds are ensembles of physiological operations linking the muscular, endocrine, immune, and nervous systems (central, peripheral, voluntary, and autonomic). This ensemble has evolved to guide action specific to our species (over geological time) and our culture (over the lifetime of the individual). Our mind-brain must be defined in a way that considers the whole organism, its movement, and its feelings. It must also be described in terms of ongoing reciprocal interactions with the environment. Our actions change our environment, and those environmental changes in turn affect our actions in a continuous loop. This is the heart of cognition, and the explicit data storage and logical manipulation that are the focus of much cognitive neuroscience play the role of supporting this reciprocal interaction. Mind is much more than a filing cabinet or a logic machine. And we need to keep all of this in mind as we try to achieve an understanding of action or movement sequences, whether spontaneous or learned.

A movement-oriented view of mind and consciousness

Starting with the first twitches of a developing embryo, the constant currency of animal life is action and movement. The innate movements of the embryo are the earliest building blocks of motor behavior. Those movements begin before the development of the nervous system that will ultimately control them, and they help shape the formation of that system. It is through testing the appropriateness of action that motor and sensory pathways develop and are coordinated. Most textbooks offer a description of the sort shown in part (A) of Figure 9–1 to represent the basic relationship between acting and sensing. A linear path from sensing to acting is portrayed, and the effect of action on subsequent perception, shown by the dashed line, is not emphasized.

We could also present the sequence, in a subtly different but perhaps more useful way, as a circle or cycle wherein any point could be the start. For example, let's turn it around, as in part (B) of Figure 9–1, to make movement the primary step. Perception of the resulting perturbation of the environment then informs subsequent movement. In this view, we might consider consciousness a mechanism by which an

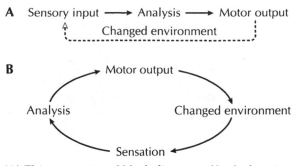

Figure 9–1   (A) This conventional block diagram of body function emphasizes a one-way sequence from perception through analysis to action. (B) A
more appropriate diagram shows a circular and continuous loop: Acting on
the environment perturbs it, and perceiving the effect of that perturbation
informs further action.

organism initiates movement to acquire information about its present
and past environment. The perceived unity of our consciousness may
have something to do with the fact that we are constantly generating
coordinated movement patterns in the face of diverse sensory stimuli.
Thus, in seeking the physical location of the neural correlates of consciousness, we might do well to look closely at the higher motor levels,
located in the frontal cortex and *cingulate* cortex.

Thinking can be viewed as the activity of deciding "what movements I make next." The most complex brains are found in animals that
make the most complex motions. The fact that motor
activity is commonly assumed to be a lower cortical
function than those subserving "pure" thought
reflects the tradition, found in many cultures, of sepa-
rating mind and body and assuming that the latter is
somehow lesser. But how can we say that the perfor-
mance of an acrobat is less "intellectual" than that of a mathematician?
Earlier in this century, investigators seriously discussed—but later dis-
missed—a motor theory of thought, which suggested that conscious
thought correlated with brain activity underlying actual or imaged
movement. Now modern brain imaging has revealed that conscious
planning and motor imagery engage the same brain areas, a result that
makes such ideas more plausible (see below).

*It is possible to view mental activity as
a means to the end of executing actions,
rather than depicting motor activity as
something subsidiary, designed to satisfy
the demands of the higher centers.*

Kinesthetic intelligence

An evolving *kinesthetic intelligence* may have led to our narrative self
consciousness. The neurophysiologist William Calvin suggests that
evolution of our motor skills, as in making and using tools and spears,

established sequence-handling machinery in the premotor cortex that became Broca's area, which is crucial for generating the sequences of syllables used in talking to oneself and others. Speaking is itself an intricate physical feat. From the point of view of the premotor cortex, articulating long strings of syllables might be a lot like climbing a rock face or pitching a baseball—or throwing a spear. Our fundamental kinesthetic experiences of up-down, right-left, inside-outside might provide a physical basis for the development of symbols and metaphors used in language (see Chapter 11 for more on this topic).

Consider the possibility that many of your conscious thoughts are associated with subtle acts of moving and sensing your musculature. Some experienced meditators report this to be the case. (Can you really think well without tensing your neck? Can you do math problems lying down?) We all know that feedback from muscle tension and limb position can affect our conscious feelings. Forming our facial muscles into the shape of a smile can actually lighten our mood, and making a frown can do the opposite. Calvin mentions the account of Oliver Sacks, who reported having his shoulder muscles electrically stimulated to generate the gesture of a shrug—whereupon he felt as though he wanted to raise his shoulders to express nonchalance, as in "So?"

Action repertoires

The consequence of a long developmental history that teaches effective patterns of acting and sensing is the construction of an elaborate hierarchy of neural agents that filter and process both output and input. Our brains are an archive of images or representations of both perceiving and acting, accumulated during our developmental history. The activity of the brain reflects expectations set up by years of experience. We have a large array of motor repertoires—movement patterns built up from simpler subunits that we automatically execute, altering them through feedback if an intended action was not accomplished. Luria, the famous Russian psychologist, has used the term *kinetic melodies* to describe such movement patterns. Many of us have such automatic routines for dressing, unlocking a door, or moving through a familiar house that we can be completely unaware of carrying out the actual movement sequences while we daydream about something else.

Parallel actions

With training, we can split ourselves into parallel streams of activity, becoming more muted versions of the split-brain patients mentioned in Chapter 7. One example of parallel streaming is the "automatic writing" that became a fad early in the 20th century. Gertrude Stein, working in

William James' laboratory, trained herself to write down dictated words while reading something else. She recalled the reading but recalled nothing of the words she had written down by dictation. A similar kind of parallel processing happens in kinesic communication, or body language, which we discussed briefly in Chapter 5. We can be aware of, and consciously respond to, the verbal content of a discussion with someone, while at the same time unconsciously reacting to signals sent by that person's posture and tone of voice, and all the time we are making equally unconscious movements of our own. During acting and sensing, we are conscious of only a minute fraction of the total information flow. If this were not the case, we would be overwhelmed—like someone who tried to watch everything on 50 different cable TV channels at once or to read every message going over the Internet.

Movement exercises that reveal underlying mechanisms

You can become partly aware of some of the complex layers of activity underlying an action—some aspects of the kinetic melodies that underlie our daily acts. This requires that you be willing to slow down enough to engage the subtle sensing requested in the exercises that follow. You can experience what we see reflected by modern imaging and electrical recording experiments that monitor the brain's activity during the planning and execution of discrete actions. The first exercise deals with the planning that goes on before movement actually is executed. Both imagining and initiating a movement happen over a time scale of about a third of a second.

SELF-EXPERIMENT

This exercise works best if someone is giving you these instructions, but you also can do it alone. Sit quietly with eyes your closed, letting both arms rest on the arms of your chair or on a desk. Try to relax your arms completely. Now imagine that someone is going to ask you to lift your right arm gently. Think about lifting your right arm, but don't actually do it. Then stop, and completely relax your right arm. Do you feel the "letting go" of the muscles you had already tensed slightly, the whole configuration you had prepared for lifting? It is really all there, planned before the gross movement occurs. Now repeat the experiment and actually go ahead and lift your arm. What do you feel?

MRI imaging shows that when subjects are asked to think about moving a hand, the premotor cortex and other areas adjacent to the motor cortex become most active; this indicates that there is a distinction between parts of the brain that prepare for movements and parts that carry them out. Just as imagining an object engages the same areas of visual cortex that actually viewing the object activates, so motor images engage regions that are active during actual movement. Recent work has shown that motor imagery and motor execution involve activation of very similar cerebral structures at all stages of motor control, except that the final motor output is not expressed during motor imagery.

A second exercise deals with noting the various components of a movement pattern in more detail. Many of our habitual movement patterns contain extraneous contractions, and you can learn about this in an interesting way. You can sometimes sense more about what goes into a movement pattern by imagining that pattern than by actually carrying it out.

SELF-EXPERIMENT

Repeat the previous arm-lifting exercise, but don't do the actual movements. Close your eyes and imagine yourself lifting your arm from the surface it is resting on. Gently note and feel all the muscles getting ready to lift the arm. Now note your neck muscles. Do you really need to tense them to lift your arm? No. The muscles that contract to lift your arms are down in your chest and back; the neck muscles are not needed. Imagine relaxing your neck while you lift your arm. Now, slowly, actually lift your arm.

The subtle sensing that you are using in these exercises is at the core of some training techniques used by musicians, dancers, and athletes to refine their movement—techniques that tell us much about the relationship between moving and sensing. They also enable us to detect chronic inappropriate movement patterns and retrain ourselves to move more efficiently. A further trick is to go beyond imagining a movement and to perform it very slowly and very gently (so that feedback can register to shape, in turn, the central program that is reading out). This works because our sensory receptors are most sensitive to stimuli of low to medium intensity. If a motion is made in a gross or more strenuous manner, the receptors don't report what is happening so effectively. In slow, gentle movements, one can sense and play with new configurations, instead of locking into a habitual pattern. If a task can be done by a group of, say, four muscles, but our habit is to let one muscle strongly predominate over the others, the brain listens to feedback from this one and ignores the rest. If appropriate use and interaction of these muscles are to be sensed, then small movements must be employed so that one senses tonus and stretch from all muscles more or less equally. You can feel this by trying the following experiment.

> **SELF-EXPERIMENT**
>
> Press your hand down hard on the arm of your chair, and note how much you can feel. Now release and shake out your arm and hand. Now press in the same way, but begin very gently and slowly—and see how much more you sense.

These exercises—imagining a movement or carrying it out very gently and slowly—can be a basis for retraining muscle movement patterns, for laying down new procedural memories and their corresponding long-term changes in the wiring of our brains. This is relevant to more people than just dancers and athletes. As we age and begin to have more difficulty jumping over fences and getting into the back seats of compact cars, it is in part because we waste so much energy and effort. We usually learn movement patterns when we are younger and more energetic, and we refine them only until they are "good enough." Only later do we discover that they really don't work very well. Retraining to refine our inefficient movement patterns can enable us to enjoy our customary activities for a longer time.

Neuronal pathways underlying action

How are appropriate action and sensing linked?—by specialized committees of neurons on many levels of organization, from the very simple to the very complex. Committees of such agents in the spinal cord can direct walking in the absence of the brain, but the higher centers are required for purposeful action. These committees, which often have overlapping memberships, can organize themselves if they are given some feedback about how well they are doing. Acting and sensing are linked by many feedback loops. Motor nerves descending from brain to spinal cord send branches to ascending sensory pathways, and these branches serve to adjust sensory bias or communicate an expected sensory input from the about-to-be-ordered movement so that it can be compared to what actually happens. This is the system that permits motor learning by trial and error. Think about learning how to write when you were very young. Can you remember how hard it was to get your hand to make fine motor movements—how your letters were very large and crude at first? Years of variation (trying different muscle movements) and then selection (noting which movements resulted in the best and smallest letters), went into establishing the stereotyped movements you now use when you write a letter by hand.

To exert motor control, our brains approximately reverse the transformations that we discussed in Chapter 8. Instead of building up an image of what is outside, we "realize," or carry out, the image of a desired action on the outside world. This process has to be instructed by the "what" and "where" systems of the temporal and parietal lobes mentioned in Chapter 8. These systems define the world in which the movement is occurring. World-centered and person-centered coordinates of movement must be established on the basis of maps of the environment in the parietal cortex and the hippocampus, which are themselves built from sensory input. These coordinates are used by the supplementary motor areas and the premotor cortex as they prepare instructions for the primary motor cortex and other movement centers in the brain. It is important to distinguish movement kinematics (the sequence of positions that a limb is expected to occupy at different times) from movement dynamics (the actual control of the movement plan as it is carried out under differing environmental conditions).

Whereas perception builds up an internal representation of the external world, action starts with an internal image of the desired outcome of a movement and then proceeds to execute that movement.

It is presently thought that the supplementary motor area contains an action programming subsystem that sends coordinates of each component movement, in the proper order, to an instruction generation subsystem associated with the premotor cortex, which then instructs a movement execution subsystem of the primary motor cortex. The location of these cortical areas is shown in Figure 9–2. The complexity of these processes is revealed by the variety of *apraxias* (breakdowns in skilled movements) that can be caused by brain lesions. Patients with *ideomotor apraxia* are able to perform a sequence of movements, but they have difficulty with the individual components. Individuals with *ideational apraxia* can perform an activity such as lighting a candle if the lights go out, but they are unable to follow an instruction to do so. Disorders sometimes focus on specific activities, as in dressing apraxia and oral apraxia (inability to make skilled gestures with facial muscles). The *agraphias,* a series of specific disruptions in the ability to write, can occur in the presence or absence of the ability to read. Some of these disorders reflect problems in producing the movements per se, and others are caused by problems in language processing.

A massive cable of axons carries instructions from motor cortex to motor neurons in the spinal cord that direct fine movements of our limbs, hands, and fingers. This direct pathway from cortex to the spinal cord appears first in mammals, and increasingly detailed motor and sensory maps of the body appear in the somatosensory and motor cortexes of higher mammals and primates. The human cortex differs strikingly from that of the chimpanzee in that much larger sensory and motor areas are devoted to the face and hands. Dominance of our motor activity by one cortex, usually the left, is much more pronounced than in monkeys and apes. We also go to greater lengths in

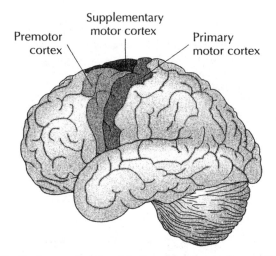

Figure 9–2   Cortical areas involved in the planning and execution of movement. Imaging experiments reveal that very simple habitual movements activate mainly the primary motor cortex. Activity in the supplementary motor cortex increases during more complex movements, whether they are actually carried out or are just mentally rehearsed without execution.

employing one arm and hand, usually the left, to support and provide context for fine movements, while the other hand, usually the right, carries them out.

The cortical system for voluntary movements is layered on top of two other levels of movement control: descending systems of the brainstem and the spinal cord. Medial (toward the center) brainstem pathways are important in combining somatosensory, visual, and vestibular (balance) information to control posture and the axial core muscles that must position themselves to support movement of the limbs. Lateral (toward the edges) brainstem pathways control distal muscles of the limbs and are important for goal-directed action. Thus it is the medial pathways that are most involved when your posture is automatically adjusting itself against gravity as you walk or turn, and the lateral pathways come into play when you reach out and pluck fruit off a tree. The spinal cord, the lowest level of motor control, contains local circuits that carry out rhythmic motor patterns, such as walking or running, and also reflexive withdrawals from aversive stimuli. These local spinal circuits are modulated by the higher centers.

The three-level hierarchy of cortex, brainstem, and spinal cord is regulated by two further subcortical systems that report back to the cortex via the thalamus (see Figure 9–3). These are the *basal ganglia* and

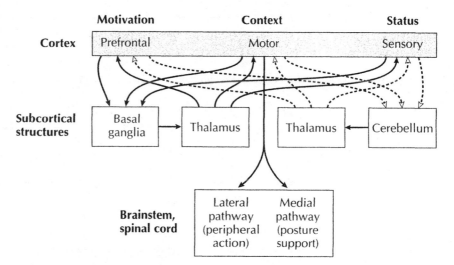

Figure 9–3 Modulation of the motor control hierarchy of cortex, brainstem, and spinal cord by subcortical systems. Most cortical regions send information to both the basal ganglia and the cerebellum. After being processed by the lower structures, this information is fed back via the thalamus to those same cortical regions. It may also be sent to other targets. The basal ganglia seem to deal mainly with the motivation and context for action, whereas the cerebellum monitors the status of action. Recent experiments implicate both the basal ganglia and the cerebellum in higher cognitive functions such as language.

the cerebellum. The function of these complex structures is not well understood. The basal ganglia are a complex set of nuclei that receive inputs from all cortical areas. Until recently it was thought that these nuclei sent information back mainly to the motor planning areas of the frontal cortex, but recent work has shown that they make specific closed loops with virtually all cortical areas. Electrical recording and brain imaging studies suggest that basal ganglia structures are involved in establishing the context for motor behaviors and also some purely cognitive operations. Activity is observed that corresponds to motivations, expectations, or rewards. Diseases of the basal ganglia cause motor abnormalities such as involuntary movements and loss of spontaneous movements. One of the nuclei, the *substantia nigra* (Latin for "black stuff") is dark because its neurons contain a derivative of the neurotransmitter dopamine. It is the death of these dopaminergic neurons that causes *Parkinson's disease.* Abnormality in the dopamine system of another center, the caudate nucleus, appears to be associated with the faulty neurological braking that causes the chronic tic disorder *Tourette's syndrome.*

Although the function of the basal ganglia is not well understood, several disorders result from abnormalities of these areas. Parkinson's disease results from the loss of dopaminergic neurons in the substantia nigra, and Tourette's syndrome can be traced to abnormalities in the caudate nucleus.

The cerebellum receives sensory input that enables it to compare actual performance with intended movements and to compensate when things do not go according to plan. Lesions here disrupt balance and coordination. A recent interpretation is that the cerebellum is not activated by the control of movement per se but rather serves as an error-checking device during motor, perceptual, and cognitive performances, processing sensory data related to those activities. There is strong evidence that the cerebellum is involved in motor learning, because such learning can be blocked by lesions in one of its three main subdivisions. Genetic manipulation of mice to remove a particular form of the postsynaptic receptor acted on by glutamic acid can make them deficient in one type of cerebellum-dependent motor learning. The cerebellum receives input from the periphery as well as from the sensory and motor cortexes and sends output mainly to the motor regions of the brainstem and cerebral cortex. The cerebellum's input and output happen at a fixed rate, 10 times a second, so we actually move in a somewhat jerky way at about this frequency. There is accumulating evidence that the cerebellum does much more than just effect motor coordination and control. Different regions of it become active during different cognitive tasks (matching verbs with nouns, for example).

If this is beginning to sound complicated, it is. We know much less about motor systems than about the visual system (this is why textbooks typically devote twice as much space to sensation as to motion). The descriptions of motor pathways that we have, of the last ten or so layers of synapses before a muscle contraction, are not as detailed (or as simple) as the description we can give of the first ten or so synapses of sensory input in the visual system. Recently, however, progress has been made in understanding the coordination of movement sequences at the cortical level. Electrical recordings from single neurons in the primary motor cortex of monkeys show that firing can correlate with several different aspects of a movement: its direction, its force, or the visual or other stimuli that are used as the instruction to move. In a monkey trained to move its arm in the direction of a visual stimulus such as a point of light or a spiral, the firing of cells that calculate the movement can be detected just before the actual motion begins. Although large areas of motor cortex are organized into areas of spatial representation (legs, arms, torso, head, and so on), finer-scale maps seem to represent combinations of muscles used in coordinated actions (for example, the muscles of the torso, shoulder, upper arm, and lower arm that must be activated in a precise and smooth sequence for the animal to reach out and grasp an object).

Recordings from the ventral premotor cortex of the monkey have demonstrated the existence of neurons that fire both when the monkey grasps or manipulates an object and when it observes the experimenter making a similar action. These neurons, which are sometimes called mirror neurons, appear to be part of a system that matches observed events to similar internally generated actions, and thus they form a link between observer and actor. Imaging studies on humans show corresponding activation of premotor cortical areas both when an action is executed and when another person is observed carrying out the same action. These mimetic phenomena may represent an observation-execution matching system, an information exchange mechanism that underlies the more complicated mimetic and linguistic human intelligences that we discussed in Chapter 5.

Movement generation by Darwin machines

How might the hierarchy of subroutines that go into making our movement be regulated and refined, especially those supporting movements that are very rapid? Reaching, throwing, and kicking are ballistic movements carried out so fast that there isn't time for feedback from sensory receptors. The minimum time for a nerve signal to make the round trip from our arm to our brain and back to our arm is about 110 milliseconds. A dart throw is over in about 120 milliseconds, so there is no time for us to receive and process feedback on how things are going. The instructions for the sequential muscle movements must be stored and then "read out" in some way. You got a sense of this "get set" storage in the first self-experiment in this chapter.

The neurophysiologist William Calvin describes a movement sequence as analogous to a row of railroad cars in a train, where each car represents a component of the movement. Each component could consist, for example, of a particular set of nerve cell firings that cause movement of a subset of the muscles engaged in the total movement sequence. How is the best movement sequence (arrangement of railroad cars) chosen? Imagine that many trains are lined up in parallel, each with a slightly different sequence of cars (movement instructions), as in a railroad yard that contains many parallel train tracks. (Figure 9–4 illustrates the oversimplified case of three tracks.) All of these tracks converge on a track that exits from the train yard (the movement sequence actually performed). Now, let each train be tested for how effectively its sequence of

A   Trial one

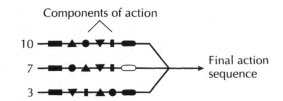

Components of action

10 ━━▲●▼┃━━
7 ━━●▲▼┃○
3 ━━▼┃▲●━━

Final action
sequence

B   Trial two

Duplicate ⟨
10 ━━▲●▼┃━━
10 ━━▲●▼┃━━
3 ━━▼┃▲●━━

C   Trial three

10 ━━▲●▼┃━━

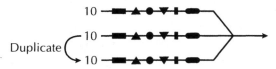

Duplicate ⟨
10 ━━▲●▼┃━━
10 ━━▲●▼┃━━

Figure 9–4   A Darwin Machine model for generating and refining a movement sequence. Let each symbol represent one stage in an overall movement
sequence. (A) These three sequences of symbols represent parallel but slightly
different routes to generating the overall movement. Each sequence is executed and "graded" in terms of its effectiveness in the current environment
and by comparison with memories of similar past sequences. This grade is
indicated by the number at the left of each sequence. (B) A sequence that is
ranked as less effective can be replaced by a duplicate of a more successful
sequence (arrow). Sometimes a slight alteration that occurs during this duplication might produce an even more effective sequence. (C) Repetition of this
process many times finally generates a unified "chorus" of parallel and similar sequences that, when executed together, can control a complicated movement with great precision. Of course, the brain would use a great many more
sequences than the three illustrated here.

cars works. Let those trains that worked best duplicate themselves, dis-
placing some trains that were less effective. Repeat the cycle until identical trains are running on every track. Finally, put all these tracks to work
together to provide refined control for a series of motions. (Another analogy might be that of a number of people starting to sing randomly but
eventually coming together into a chorus.) We are essentially describing
yet another version of the Darwin Machine.

Movement may be controlled by the application to neural networks of a version of the same abstract Darwin Machine that is used on the longer time scales of species evolution and organismal development. In all of these contexts, variation and selection act together as though to attain a goal.

Why do we suggest that there are many trains carrying out the same sequence of instructions? Because for any one train by itself, there is a problem. The range within which a nerve cell may fire after it is triggered is from 1 to 10 milliseconds. Calvin points out that this is too imprecise even for such an activity as throwing a rock at a stationary prey 4 meters away. There is an 11-millisecond launch window in which a rock can be thrown to hit a rabbit at 4 meters. A rock released too early will overshoot; a rock released too late will land in front of the rabbit. The launch window shrinks to 1.4 milliseconds if the target is 8 meters away. How do we guarantee a launch within a 1-millisecond interval using nerve cells that have a 1- to 10-millisecond "jitter"? Part of the answer may be that trains with identical sequences of cars can emerge simultaneously from the marshaling yard and have their firing times averaged. When the firings of many motor neurons are averaged, the motor effect is much more reliable than that elicited by the firing of any of the individual neurons. (Think of an engineer who wants to measure the time at which midnight occurs and has a 100 different clocks, each of which is off by a few seconds. Noting when half of the clocks have struck midnight gives a much more accurate estimate than listening to just one.)

Calvin further proposes that a cerebral Darwin Machine might underlie our ability to carry a small-scale model of external reality in our heads, all the while continuing to test it against various alternatives, continually revising our assessment of which is best, predicting future situations, and so on. His suggestion is that a random sequencer arranges templates into parallel strings, each of which is "graded" by memories of how similar strings performed in the past and weighted for emphasis by the present environment. Dozens or hundreds of such sequences might be tried out simultaneously, with the most appropriate new generation shaping up in milliseconds, thus initiating insightful action without overt trial and error. It is interesting that the shaping-up or selective mechanisms appear to be damaged in some patients with frontal lobe lesions. These patients can spin scenarios of action but cannot easily choose among them.

Ideas that flow through our heads could be selected as candidates for storage in long-term memory by similar mechanisms. Most of the candidate sequences would be held in our unconscious short-term memory and thrown away after use. Transfer to long-term memory would be necessary to establish the ability to recall such sequences. Only those that survived a thorough reality test would be retained. The sequences—at least those involved in the short-term generation of language—might contain about seven chunks of information each. (We can hold about seven digits, such as a phone number, in short-term memory long enough to repeat them or dial a phone.) This could be why, when deciding what to say next, we plan ahead by no more than about half a dozen chunks, words, or concepts. We usually don't know how our sentences are going to end when we start them.

SUMMARY   Trying to understand action is a more daunting task—and probably a more complex one—than we face with perceptions, the subject of Chapter 8. Our self-conscious cognitions rest on a vast background of moving muscles and viscera that are continually monitored as the organism moves about in its physical and social environment. The core event of our daily activities is a continuous feedback cycle in which we initiate movements of these muscles and viscera to acquire information about, and change, our internal and external environments, and perception of these changes instructs further action. Our habitual movements are regulated by a vast repertoire of automatic movement routines learned during development. These are orchestrated by a complex array of cortical mechanisms that proceed from an image of an intended action to its execution. Electrical recordings of brain cell activities and imaging studies reveal some of the building blocks of this movement control—a collaborating hierarchy that extends from cortex to subcortical, brainstem, and spinal cord mechanisms. Specific brain lesions can impair different aspects of the sequences involved in planning, instruction generation, and execution of movement. One model suggests that the generation and refinement of movement utilize a Darwin Machine mechanism in which more successful sets of instructions are duplicated at the expense of less useful ones.

The reasons that an array of nerve cells might have for firing in the supplementary motor or premotor cortex are much more numerous than those that affect an array of cells in the visual cortex. The visual cells, even though they are subject to feedback from higher centers, have the fairly definite job of analyzing information about visual sensory stimuli, whereas the motor cells may participate in the resolution of many decisions about why and how a reaction to a particular visual stimulus is taking place. Goals, memories, and intentions have more influence on actions than on perceptions. Further, as we consider the constant feedback between action and perception that links our brain, body, and world together, yet another set of actors must be integrated into our description: the array of emotions that provide rapid response systems and that also bias and pattern many of our behaviors. These emotions are the subject of the next chapter. ■

Questions for Thought

1. The first section of this chapter reexamines the idea of an extended definition of mind, first mentioned in Chapter 1, a definition encompassing body and environment. This can be contrasted with a definition that restricts the idea of mind to the activities of the brain. What are the merits of these two approaches? Which do you think is more useful?

2. This chapter gives several examples of our ability to carry out several sensory-motor sequences, or kinetic melodies, at the same time. Some we are conscious of, some not. Please continue the thinking about selves that we started in Chapter 7 and suggest how you might incorporate such information into your idea of what a "self" is.

3. Electrophysiological experiments have shown that nerve cell firing in preparation for a movement can begin slightly before our conscious awareness of intending to make that movement. How can you reconcile such information with the assumption that consciousness plays a role in controlling our actions?

4. Can you think of experiments that might test the Darwin Machine model that Calvin suggests underlies complex action sequences (including sequences of thought)? For example, could the complex sequence of speaking language provide a context for testing this idea?

Suggestions for further general reading

Calvin, W.H. 1990. *The Cerebral Symphony.* New York: Bantam. (The material on Darwin Machine models of movement is drawn from Chapters 10 and 11 of Calvin's book.)

Clark, A. 1997. *Being There.* Cambridge, MA: M.I.T. Press. (An extended discussion of how mind must be defined in terms of an acting body and its interactions with the external environment.)

Damasio, A.R. 1994. *Descartes' Error—Emotion, Reason, and the Human Brain.* New York: Putnam's. (The first section of this chapter draws on Damasio's Chapter 10, "The Body-Minded Brain.")

Minsky, M. 1986. *The Society of Mind.* New York: Simon & Schuster. (Minsky's book has interesting descriptions of the sorts of agents that are necessary to underlie and support action: hierarchies of stable subassemblies.)

Reading on more advanced or specialized topics

Bear, M., Connors, B., & Paradiso, M. 1996. *Neuroscience: Exploring the Brain.* Baltimore, MD: Williams & Wilkins. (Chapters 13 and 14 of this book review spinal cord and brain control of movement.)

Crammond, D. 1997. Motor imagery: Never in your wildest dream. *Trends in Neuroscience* 20:54–57. (This article describes experiments that monitor brain activity during the imagining of movement as well as during its actual execution.)

Gazzaniga, M.S., ed. 1995. *The Cognitive Neurosciences.* Cambridge, MA: M.I.T. Press. (Part IV of this volume is devoted to motor control.)

Kosslyn, S.M., & Koenig, O. 1992. *Wet Mind—The New Cognitive Neuroscience.* New York: Free Press. (Chapter 7 discusses brain control of movement.)

Chapter 10

Emotional Mind

The rambling internal narrative of our thoughts is like a swimmer in a sea of emotions, constantly registering the gentle rocking that goes with subtle changes in background feelings as well as the crashing waves that accompany fear or passion. What are our emotions? They certainly feel more rich, juicy, and energetic than "just thinking." We experience them as coordinated responses spreading through the whole body, frequently linked to a social context. Sometimes we may experience a sense of "losing it"—getting so caught up that rational processes aren't running the show. Could this be because a different brain has taken over at such moments, one adapted to our evolutionary past but not necessarily to our present world? Does this mean that emotion and reason are opposing forces?

An emerging consensus argues the contrary position–that our rational processes depend vitally on the "lower" brain structures that mediate emotion, and that lack of emotion can be just as damaging to reason as its excess. The apparatus of rationality is not layered on top of our basic regulatory and emotional processes, but rather rises and develops from within them. "I feel, therefore I think" reflects what happens in the brain better than Descartes' famous "I think, therefore I am." Modern clinical studies on human patients with brain lesions show that either an absence or an excess of emotions can prevent rational behavior. We might begin to think of emotions as the glue that binds together the modules of mind and as pointers to the contents of consciousness that are relevant to a particular moment. Emotions are a part of our evolved psychology and are every bit as cognitive as the more rarefied domains of mathematical and linguistic logic. This concept has been overlooked because emotions are so much harder to describe. There also has been a cultural bias, with intellectuals setting up an artificial opposition between reason and emotion in which the emotional sides of our natures are unstable and unreliable distractions from "real thought." Fortunately, the long-standing scientific taboo against studying subjective experience is being relaxed, and more weight is being given to *affective neuroscience* alongside, or as a part of, cognitive neuroscience. It is interesting in this regard that computer scientists who model cognitive processes are sometimes finding it useful to introduce global analogs of affect into their simulations.

This chapter begins with a brief discussion of the way we define emotions and then moves on to consider both their evolution and the brain structures and pathways that underlie our emotional behaviors. Lesions in some of these structures not only diminish affect but also distort rational processes, which suggests that emotional pathways must be intact for our rational faculties to work properly. Emotional pathways can work more rapidly than those involved in conscious reasoning, and this may give us some insight into why we don't always act the way hindsight tells us we should have. It is easy to misapply our emotional repertoire. We all face the problem of applying hardwired emotional machinery such as the fight-or-flight response to modern circumstances in which threats are much more subtle than a charging lion on the African savanna.

Defining emotions

Devising a reasonable system to describe the many emotional behaviors we experience is a daunting task, but this hasn't kept numerous different schemes from being launched. The examination of fear in the accompanying self-experiment, along with many other emotional situations, suggests that our emotional experiences have at least three different manifestations: (1) a physiological component that includes autonomic nervous system activity—changes in viscera, blood pressure, distribution of blood flow, digestive system, and so on; (2) our behaviors, such as facial expressions, that convey anger or sadness; and (3) our subjective feelings, such as love, fear, and hate. Some of our emotions reflect drives or desires basic to survival, such as hunger, thirst, lust, pain, pleasure, and aggression. These emotions, in some form, are shared by all higher vertebrates, especially mammals. Other emotions are more explicitly related to communication with our fellow humans: happiness, disgust, surprise, sadness, anger, distress, interest, fear, and jealousy. Measuring emotions is a challenge, because the same stimuli can be pleasant or unpleasant, depending on the context (e.g., if you have just had a huge candy bar, you may react negatively to a sweet soft drink, but if you are tired and thirsty, the same sugary drink is a pleasing relief).

SELF-EXPERIMENT

A useful place to begin a description of the variety of emotions is with our own experience. Let's take the example of fear. Pull yourself away from this focused reading for a moment and try to recall receiving a fright: perhaps you narrowly escaped being hit by a speeding car or became aware that someone was following you on a dark and dangerous street. Your heart pounded, your body tensed, your face contorted with fear, and a strong feeling of dread passed through your body. Probably you can actually experience a faint "replay" of these reactions just by recalling the situation.

It is interesting but not surprising that most studies on brains and emotions deal with negative affect, such as fear, anxiety, and anger. We don't go to doctors to seek cures for feeling happy, joyful, or optimistic. It is easier to elicit and measure fear or anxiety than happiness, and much of what we experience as positive emotions might be mainly the absence of negative ones. Further, happiness is linked not simply to the absence of a threat, but also to how we perceive our general well-being with respect to that of others.

We can't say which emotions are "primary" in the same sense that we know the primary colors are blue, yellow, and red—we can't even be sure the analogy holds. But the main candidates include anger, sadness, fear, enjoyment, love, surprise, disgust, and shame. Each of these emotions is made up of a family of related feelings. Anger, for example, might be expressed as fury, outrage, resentment, exasperation, acrimony, irritability, or hostility. Enjoyment includes relief, contentment, delight, amusement, sensual pleasure, rapture, euphoria, and (at the extreme) mania. An intense emotion usually does not last more than a few minutes, but we can experience its more muted form, mood, for many hours. Finally, each of us has a distinctive temperament—a readiness to evoke certain sets of emotions, such as those associated with being cheery or melancholy. Most of these temperaments remain remarkably constant throughout life. There is considerable evidence that some temperaments, such as novelty seeking, optimism, and pessimism, are moderately heritable and not greatly influenced by family environment. Beyond these dispositions are the more blatant disorders of emotions such as chronic anxiety or depression. Categorization of all these states is complex, and researchers disagree about some very fundamental issues:

• How many basic universal humans emotions are there?
• Should emotions be described as discrete entities, such as anger, fear, and disgust, or as points on a continuum, such as pleasant-unpleasant, aroused-unaroused, approach-avoid? Is there really a difference between the two descriptions?
• What is an unambiguous test of whether an emotion has occurred?

Emotions are hard to define not only behaviorally but also anatomically, because many different brain regions come into play in every emotion. Emotional circuits include the limbic system, which forms a ring around the brainstem and consists of cortex around the corpus callosum (mainly in the cingulate area) as well as cortex on the medial surface of the temporal lobe, including the hippocampus and amygdala (refer to Figures 3–3 and 3–4). These regions communicate between higher centers in the prefrontal and association cortexes and the hypothalamus. The hypothalamus contains centers whose stimulation can elicit stereotyped emotional performances. The location of these structures is shown in Figure 10–1. At the present time, we don't have a theory of the anatomical circuits of emotions, as we do for

Figure 10–1   Brain structures that are important in generating emotions. We are looking at the brain from the left side, as we have before in describing the surface features of the cortex, but now the entire left side of the brain has been removed so that we have a medial view of the inside surface of the exposed right hemisphere. Adapted from Figure 16.4 in Bear et al., *Neuroscience: Exploring the Brain.*

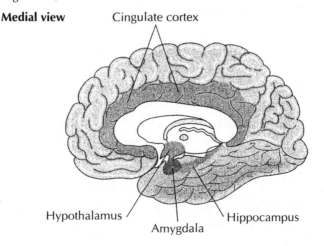

vision. The study of emotion, just like the study of visual or other kinds of cognition, requires a dissection of emotional processes into elementary operations. Such an effort is still in its early stages.

Emotions are evolutionary adaptations

The psychologist Nicholas Humphrey, whose ideas were mentioned in Chapter 2, suggests that we might trace the origins of affect back to such simple behaviors as the chemotaxis of *Escherichia coli* or the wriggles of acceptance or rejection displayed by amoebae. In more complex animals, specialized receptors evolved to report useful or noxious stimuli to the brain. Early in the evolution of the brain, sensory and emotional sensitivity was always linked to a corresponding bodily activity. A subsequent development was to make the responses a brain activity (attraction or repulsion) that was felt but not necessarily acted on (recall the itch that you can choose not to scratch.) The suggestion is that to "like" a stimulus might be to respond to it in such a way as to keep up or increase the stimulation (positive feedback), and to "dislike" it would be to respond in such a way as to keep down or reduce it (negative feedback). Affect might be linked with the way a stimulus is evaluated at a submodal level. For example, among visual stimuli, red light is typically exciting whereas blue is calming. Among the different kinds of tactile sensations, itches are irritating, gentle stroking pleasurable. Within the gustatory modality sweet tastes are pleasant, rotten tastes revolting.

Moving through vertebrate evolution toward humans, we can trace an increase in the complexity of autonomic nervous systems and emotional behaviors. One view is that the emotions are an evolutionary by-product of the neural regulation of the autonomic nervous system. Recall that a basic job of the sympathetic and parasympathetic divisions of the autonomic system is regulating the body during mobilization and energy expenditure, as well as during rest and recovery. During mobilization, the sympathetic system releases the neurotransmitter *norepinephrine* at many end organs—for example, on muscles to increase their speed and the effectiveness of their contractions. Parasympathetic activity is approximately the mirror image of this, a calming and return to emphasis on vegetative self-maintenance and restorative functions. It uses the neurotransmitter *acetylcholine* and is active during sleep. These systems are established in bony fishes and become more complex in amphibians and reptiles. In mammals a new complex of nerves appears, the *ventral vagal system*, which innervates the heart and other visceral organs, as

The origin of emotions might be traced back to responses, in simple animals, of "liking" or "not liking" some aspect of their environment. Emotional, or affective, behaviors probably evolved because they conferred some selective advantage on those who had them.

well as facial and vocal muscles involved in emotional expression. This is a system thought to permit emotional mobilization short of the full sympathetic arousal of the fight-or-flight response. It has components that inhibit sympathetic arousal to promote bonding and affiliative behavior. Emotional circuits appear to be much more malleable than hardwired reflexes such as pain withdrawal and the knee-jerk response. There can be large variations between individuals and between related groups of animals. Think of the difference between Staffordshire terriers (pit bulls) and St. Bernards, or between common and bonobo chimpanzees (described on page 78). These different variants of the same species have evolved very different emotional behaviors.

Emotions and the physical environment

We obtain some interesting clues about the possible origins of our emotions by examining common human phobias, which are resistant to change but can be extinguished by conditioning therapy. It is striking that there are only about two dozen common elicitors of phobic reactions, such as insects, snake shapes, heights, looming large objects, and growling noises, all of which would have been very relevant to the survival of our ancestors. We appear to have an innate predisposition to associate aversive stimuli with these objects. Psychological experiments have shown that most of us look at a picture of a boa constrictor without getting too rattled, but if that picture is paired with an electric shock just once, the next time we see the snake picture we become quite agitated. If we are shown a picture of a flower together with the shock, it takes a much longer series of pairings of picture and shock to induce the same level of aversion to the picture. More extensive experiments have been done in animals to demonstrate innate predispositions to certain kinds of conditioning. There can be single-trial learning of a response to selective stimuli even if there is a long delay between stimulus and result, and the learning is not easily extinguished. Laboratory rats become averse to bright light and noise if these are linked with pain but not if they are linked with nausea, whereas a particular taste can become aversive if linked with nausea but not if linked with bright light or noise.

Learning that is obviously relevant to survival, such as becoming averse to the taste of some food that once made you ill, is much easier and more rapid than learning to be repelled by a picture of a flower with which a shock is associated. Selective pressures over evolutionary time have favored formation of the brain circuits underlying such predispositions.

There is general consensus that our limbic system is the primary site of innate or preorganized primary emotions, containing circuitry that is especially responsive to features of the sort just listed. An unresolved issue is to what extent something like a "snake detector" might be hardwired by genetic instructions. We can sketch a plausible scenario for how genes might specify a detector for the "feature set" of a long, thin object that moves sinuously. However, it seems implausible that they might code the precise coloring or shape of the animal. Different parts of the world have snakes of different shapes and sizes. Similarly, the face detector cells mentioned in Chapter 8 and below might actually start as more generic icon detectors for certain sets of curves and lines, as in the "happy face" image. This image is made only of a circle containing an upwardly curved arc in its bottom half, positioned under one dot for the nose and two for the eyes. Newborn human children recognize this icon and distinguish it from others in which the elements have been scrambled.

Emotions and social exchange

Charles Darwin recognized the importance of emotions as signals that accurately inform one animal about the state of another. This is most clear in higher mammals like ourselves. All of us think that we can tell when a dog or cat is happy, playful, angry, fearful, curious, anxious, or in some other state in which an adjective ordinarily descriptive of human emotions seems appropriate. We know for ourselves, and usually assume it to be true for animals, that emotions are messages about our own internal state as well as direct, nonverbal signals to others. Here we might go with our common sense, as not inappropriately anthropomorphic, for some similar underlying mechanisms are clearly at work in both ourselves and other mammals.

Emotions can inform our intelligence what to think about, and in this sense we are, to use a phrase attributed to Richard Dawkins, "walking archives of ancestral wisdom." Practitioners of evolutionary psychology argue that common emotional states—fear of predators, guilt, sexual jealousy, rage, grief, and so on—are adaptations to repetitive features of the environment faced by the small groups of hunter-gatherers in Africa who are thought to be the ancestors of all modern humans. For example, discovering one's mate having sex with someone else signals a situation that threatens future reproduction and present "investment allocation." This cue should therefore activate sexual jealousy. The discussion of evolutionary psychology in Chapter 5 mentioned the importance of detecting cheating, and many aspects of anger, guilt, and shame revolve around this issue.

Basic emotional states common to humans of all cultures, such as enjoyment, sadness, anger, disgust, and fear, correlate with biologically significant events in the world, marking them as good or bad, as associated with life or death. These emotions, and their counterparts in other animals, are adaptations that have the purpose of informing or influencing the behavior of others.

The psychologist Steven Pinker suggests that our intellect is designed to relinquish control over our passions so that they serve as reliable guarantors of promises or threats that allay suspicions of double-crosses or bluffing. This would explain why we unconsciously advertise emotions on our faces—why our being "unable to control our emotions" is a guarantor of their authenticity. For the most part, it seems a good design to segregate voluntary cognitive systems from mainly involuntary housekeeping systems that regulate blood pressure, skin glands, and so on. But to prove an emotion's authenticity, perhaps selection has bound that emotion to a physiological control circuit (such as quavering, trembling, croaking, weeping, blushing, blanching, flushing, or sweating) over which we normally don't have much voluntary control. If we really want to know whether people are trying to fool us, or are displaying sham emotions, we insist on doing business with them in the flesh, so that we can see what makes them sweat. These arguments from evolutionary psychology, of course, contend that our emotions are behaviors that maximize not our fitness today but that of our ancestors in a now-vanished past. In this view, we humans are "adaptation executors" who respond to present circumstances in ways developed in our evolutionary past.

Subcortical systems underlying emotions

Emotions were identified with lower brain centers in the 19th century through experiments on dogs whose cerebral cortexes had been removed, leaving the diencephalon intact (including the thalamus and hypothalamus). These animals could still show rage and fear. In the 1930s, Papez proposed that the limbic system, acting through the hypothalamus, was the anatomical basis of emotions. During this period, brain lesion studies showed striking changes (such as loss of fear, indiscriminate eating, and increased sexual activity) in the emotional behavior of monkeys whose temporal lobes had been removed. Lesions in the frontal cortex, paralimbic cortex, or amygdala caused reduced and inappropriate social interaction. A similar syndrome (Kluver-Bucy syndrome) is found in humans with bilateral damage to the amygdala and inferior temporal cortex. The discovery that removing the frontal lobes of aggressive monkeys calmed them led to psychosurgery, an out-standing example being the frontal lobotomy of humans. This procedure not only calms the subjects but also severely impairs their social and affective behavior.

The autonomic background of emotions

Before focusing on the brain, however, let's start further downstairs, with the peripheral sympathetic and parasympathetic nervous systems that were introduced in Chapter 3 and mentioned above. These systems mediate our bodily experiences of emotions. Recall that our sympathetic nervous system is engaged during arousal and emergencies, expending energy, whereas the parasympathetic system regulates rest, recovery, and energy storage. The ratio of parasympathetic to sympathetic activation, set by the hypothalamus in the brain, is a central component of our affective life, correlating with whether we are relaxed, open, and engaging, versus avoiding, defensive, or aggressive.

SELF-EXPERIMENT

You can try a simple exercise to sense some of the global body correlates that go with activation of the peripheral sympathetic and parasympathetic nervous systems. The following exercise is probably best done by having someone read it out loud to you, but you can also read the instructions and try it on yourself. Close your eyes for a moment and imagine yourself on vacation, sitting on a rock by the ocean watching a beautiful sunset. Let time slow down so that all you are aware of is the colors in the sky and the gentle breeze from the sea. Be completely in the present moment. Let the pleasant feelings in your body take you back to an earlier time, perhaps when you were a child, when you felt secure and cared for. After you have spent at least a few minutes getting into this fantasy, just note how your body feels, note your breathing, and note what your shoulder and jaw muscles are doing. Now try a different fantasy, one less pleasant. Imagine yourself to be walking, late at night, down a deserted city street with only one or two streetlights. There are no other people around. You suddenly hear a scuffling noise, and four rough-looking men tumble from an alley 30 feet in front you. This surprises you and you stiffen a bit, as though you don't want them to notice you. But then, the moment they see you, they abruptly turn to face you, fan out, and start to approach you, slowly and deliberately, with very flat expressions on their faces. You look for a place to run, but it's too late. They break into a run towards you. Now scan your body again, and note how it feels. Even if you just read through these descriptions without really getting into them, you can probably sense differences in your body—in your breathing or in how tightly you are holding your muscles.

The self-experiment in this section has the goal of eliciting body changes that go with parasympathetic (relaxing) versus sympathetic (arousal) activation—changes that are intense enough for you to sense them clearly. Consider, now, that much of your daily attitude or temperament might be described as being somewhere between these two extremes. Indeed, the relative activation of these two systems sets a somatic background, or bias, that can influence your behaviors.

Strong sympathetic or parasympathetic activations can set a tone or mood that persists for some time. Think of the times, for example, when you have experienced a persistent sympathetic activation as you remained a bit jumpy for many minutes after being excited by suddenly having to avoid some danger, perhaps a speeding car. *Norepinephrine* released by your sympathetic nerves was causing increased attentiveness and excitation that decayed only slowly as the norepinephrine was taken back up into nerve cells.

Brainstem modulation of attention and appetite

Against this backdrop of overall sympathetic or parasympathetic activation, a whole host of mood-altering chemicals regulate our appetitive and attentional behaviors. These global modulators of our emotions are manufactured in restricted regions of our brainstem or basal forebrain and then sent via long axons to widespread regions of the cortex, where they are released. Central players are neurotransmitters such as the *biogenic amines* (dopamine, norepinephrine, and serotonin) and acetylcholine. These systems serve as brain "spritzers" regulating our states of alertness, anxiety, elation, depression, or aggression. They can speed up or slow down the rate at which our mental operations proceed.

Figure 10–2 shows the location of one of these systems, a small group of cells called the locus coeruleus. It is essentially an outpost of the sympathetic nervous system that can extend that system's arousal into the brain. Axons from these cells travel to multiple locations in the cerebral cortex and cerebellar cortex to release norepinephrine, which enhances our attention and memory processes. Another spritzing system releases the neurotransmitter serotonin in the brain. Reductions in the activity of circuits that use norepinephrine and serotonin apparently contribute to depression in many people. Serotonin levels appear to be inversely correlated with aggression. For example, mice that lack a certain postsynaptic receptor for serotonin are more aggressive in stressful situations. Lowering serotonin by drugs or genetic manipulation increases

Several different centers in the brainstem contain nerve cell bodies that send axons to many different areas of the cortex and cerebellum. Their activation can cause global changes in attention, alertness, appetite, and motivation.

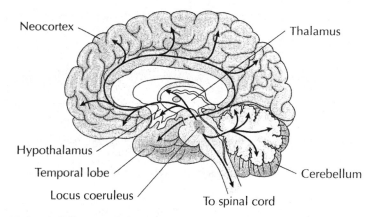

Figure 10–2 A diffuse modulatory circuit originates in the locus coeruleus. This brain nucleus, which occurs on both the left and the right sides of the pons regions of the brain, has only about 12,000 neurons. A single one of these neurons can make more than 250,000 connections, sending axon branches to both the cerebral cortex and the cerebellum. These release norepinephrine, which can enhance arousal, attention, and memory. Adapted from Figure 15.11 in Bear et al. *Neuroscience: Exploring the Brain.*

aggressiveness, and raising it has the opposite effect. Low levels of brain serotonin are associated with anxiety in humans and also in animal models for anxiety, and inhibitors of serotonin uptake into nerve cells—which raise the concentration of serotonin outside the cells—are used as antidepressants. The psychoactive drug LSD mimics the action of serotonin.

Dopamine, whose role in movement we mentioned briefly in Chapter 9, acts as a central activator. If nerve terminals secreting it are destroyed in rats, the animals lose desire, motivation, adaptability, and exploratory behavior. Dopamine levels are altered by cocaine and amphetamine, and they play a role in responses to heroin, alcohol, nicotine, and cannabis. Chemicals that modify dopamine receptors can alter drug-seeking behaviors. Some people who show stronger than average novelty-seeking behavior have a variant of one of the dopamine receptors.

Dopamine-containing cells in the midbrain are activated by novel appetitive stimuli, but not by aversive stimuli. This observation has suggested the simple model that when something interesting or good happens, these cells in our midbrain shower higher brain centers with dopamine, which causes an appetitive behavior. Cocaine and amphetamines mimic this effect by inhibiting the reuptake of dopamine into presynaptic terminals, thus maintaining activation of synapses longer than normal. Studies using mice initially showed that when the transporter that normally removes dopamine from synapses was deleted, the animals became hyperactive and also indifferent to cocaine and amphetamine. They presumably already had high dopamine levels and the "high" that the drugs usually cause. (These experiments are done by constructing "knockout" mutants in which the gene for the transporter has been deleted.) Alas, the clarity suggested by these initial knockout experiments did not persist, because repetition of this and similar experiments found that knockout mice in which either the dopamine or the serotonin uptake mechanisms were deleted were indeed sensitive to cocaine. Recent work has now suggested that brain circuits using the neurotransmitter glutamic acid are also involved in producing changes that lead to compulsive drug seeking.

Further experiments have suggested that the purpose of the dopamine system is not to produce feeling of pleasure but to draw attention to events that predict rewards, so that the animal learns, recognizes, and then repeats them. Dopamine surges are measured in an area called the nucleus accumbens during anticipation of food or sex. This could explain why many drugs that stimulate the dopamine system can drive continued use without producing pleasure, as when cocaine addicts continue to take hits long after the euphoric effects of the drug have worn off or when smokers still smoke after cigarettes become distasteful. These drugs have essentially hijacked a brain mechanism that evolved to signal rewards relevant to fitness and reproduction (such as food or sex) and instead enslave the organism to desires that have no adaptive value. Brain imaging using PET shows activation in the mesolimbic dopamine system as addicts describe feelings of intense craving for cocaine. (The mesolimbic dopamine system connects the orbitofrontal cortex, in the prefrontal area behind the forehead, with the amygdala and nucleus accumbens.) Different areas are preferentially activated during rush (the drug euphoria, or high) and during craving for the drug.

Other correlations of chemistry and emotional behavior

We can list several further correlations of chemistry and emotional behavior. Morphine and other opiates can block pain pathways in the brain, sometimes causing euphoria, by mimicking a different class of neurotransmitters made from peptides (small pieces of proteins). The brain contains complex families of these peptides, including a group referred to as the opioid peptides: the enkephalins, endorphins, and dynorphins. They also play a complex role in regulating social attachments and the distress caused by social isolation. Another peptide, *oxytocin*, appears to play a role in soothing and bonding behaviors, eliciting the parasympathetic opposite of the sympathetic fight-or-flight response. In some rodents (different species of prairie voles), monogamous versus polygamous social structure and behavior correlate with different expressions of the oxytocin and vasopressin systems. Some chemicals that influence arousal, anxiety, or aggression can come from sources outside the brain. Aggression (especially aggression between males) is influenced by testosterone, as we noted in Chapter 6. Castration of male mice reduces their aggressive behavior, and injections of testosterone can then reinstate it. Epinephrine and adrenocorticosteroid levels correlate with arousal and excitability; they typically are higher in emotive than in repressed individuals.

All of these systems certainly are regulated by our conscious cognitive response to objective aspects of our environment, especially whether it is nurturing or threatening. There are other internal explanations for why we feel this or that particular way. Many of the autonomic and brainstem systems discussed in the previous sections have cycles of their own, alternating periods of activity with intervals of rest and renewal of their neurotransmitter systems. This has been well documented in the cyclical activation of cholinergic versus adrenergic systems in sleep versus wakefulness, which is described in Chapter 12, and in changes in cognition and mood that accompany the monthly ovulation cycle in women. Perhaps we should consider that these cycles can generate feelings for which "there is no reason" in the usual sense, not withstanding our tendency always to invent a reason for the way we are feeling. Experiments with hypnotized, split-brain, or anosognosic patients have shown that we will cheerfully confabulate bogus reasons for a behavior if the real cause is not accessible to our consciousness. We should consider the possibility that during some feelings and emotions, the brainstem systems are calling the shots, and our fertile imaginations are merely supplying a cover-up story.

Thinking about the relationship between our brain chemistry and our emotional moods and thoughts presents us with the "Which came first, the chicken or the egg?" problem. Cognitive processes can direct the mood-altering chemistry that originates in the brainstem, and spontaneous changes in this chemistry can alter our thoughts. In the latter case, there may be no "reason" for our thoughts or feelings, in the way we commonly suppose.

Chemical imbalances in these systems can underlie affective disorders. We are learning that distinctive chemistries correlate with defense or arousal, with rest, with anticipation of novelty or appetitive behavior, with anxiety or depression, and so on. Legions of biotechnologists currently employed by pharmaceutical companies are trying to synthesize compounds that selectively enhance or depress these systems and provide more effective therapies for depression, anxiety, drug addiction, and *anhedonia* (the inability to experience pleasure).

Higher levels of emotional mind

Continuing to trace the components of our affective life further up into the brain, we encounter the limbic system that was mentioned in Chapter 3 (see the section "Layers of the Brain"). It is thought to mediate the basic survival-related programs of the brainstem (such as feeding, aggression, and sexuality) and also to regulate the social emotions of distress, bonding, and nurturing. The limbic structures shown in Figure 10–1 communicate between higher cortical centers and the hypothalamus (also mentioned in Chapter 3) as a central control center for coordinating our emotional responses. Electrical stimulation of nuclei of the lateral hypothalamus, in sequence from front to back, elicits appetitive behaviors related to temperature regulation, sex, drink, and food. Stimulation of medial structures in the hypothalamus seems to produce opposite, aversive behaviors. The hypothalamus directs the autonomic nervous system and integrates and coordinates the rapid behavioral expression of emotional states. Lesions or electrode stimulation can generate discrete, stereotyped expressions of fear, anger, pleasure, or contentment. Each of these emotions seems to possess the animal completely during its expression. You may have heard about a "pleasure center" in the brain. Actually, several such centers have been identified in rat and human brains.

Finally, the top element of the triune brain is the cerebral cortex overlaying the limbic system. Its frontal lobes are central to the regulation of emotions. Mood disorders have been correlated with abnormalities in the ventral prefrontal cortex. This region is consistently underactivated in familial depressive patients and is activated during periods of mania. Activity in our prefrontal lobes may be part of the answer to a fundamental question: How do we assemble the vast array of feelings we have in different situations, avoiding some and desiring others?

Emotional mind as a foundation of rational mind

The neuropsychologist Antonio Damasio has suggested that during our development we accumulate a large number of learned or acquired *secondary emotions* that necessitate activity of the prefrontal cortex; in this they differ from the more innate primary emotions associated with the limbic system. These secondary emotions are essentially feelings learned by associating primary emotions with different situations we encounter while growing up—situations that mark them as positive or negative, to be approached or avoided. A small positive or negative stamp is put on almost everything we encounter. We develop a set of rules, a morality, for what to do and what not to do. This training, the acquiring of secondary emotions, involves our visceral or autonomic nervous system. When we have aversive or positive reactions to something, our autonomic nervous system responds, usually outside of our normal consciousness, by changing such variables as the rate of moisture release by our skin, our heart rate, and our blood pressure. (Changes in skin conductance can be used as a convenient and crude assay of this autonomic nervous system arousal and have been found to correlate with changes in the activation of portions of the cingulate and motor cortex.) Subtle changes in muscle tension over the body may also accompany the pairings of feelings and autonomic activation. Damasio uses the term *somatic markers* to refer to these body correlates of feelings. These markers are discussed below, in the section "Emotional responses can be more rapid than reasoned ones."

SELF-EXPERIMENT

You can get a sense of the processes involved in acquiring secondary emotions if you pause for a moment, close your eyes, and recall a physical place—a house or room, perhaps—where you had either a very happy or a very unhappy experience, perhaps in your childhood. If, after a period of years, you recall this space, return to it, or perhaps enter a space that reminds you of it, what do you feel? Can you sense subtle, possibly flickering, changes in your body, perhaps small relaxings or tensings of muscles, that accompany the feelings?

The existence of learning processes by which we accumulate secondary emotions are revealed by their disruption in patients who have lesions or tumors in their frontal lobes, particularly the right ventromedial part. Their behavior is superficially normal most of the time—intellect and memory seem intact—but motivation, foresight, goal formation, and decision making are flawed. They are subject to bursts of immodest, impolite, or other inappropriate behaviors; they act almost as though their free will had been taken from them. Their emotions and feeling also are diminished.

Normal individuals, as well as those with brain damage located outside the frontal lobes, generate skin responses that indicate autonomic arousal when they are shown disturbing or erotically charged pictures. Patients with frontal lobe damage fail to generate these responses, in spite of realizing that the content of the pictures ought to be disturbing.

A typical response might be "I know I ought to react to that, but I can't. I just don't feel anything." It is fascinating that primary emotions (such as reacting fearfully to an angry face or an aggressive growl) can still be intact, but emotions based on experience, cognition, and learning are impaired. It is as though the link between frontal cortex and limbic system, the link to feeling in the body, has been severed. The frontal lobe patients appear no longer to be able to connect logic with good or bad. They do endless cost-benefit analyses of simple issues, such as when to schedule an appointment with the doctor, without being able to reach a decision. Their choices do not appear to be informed by their emotional histories. The use of their intelligence in the pursuit of a goal (deciding when to schedule that appointment) has been compromised. This observation suggests that emotions may be important in the selection of goals one at a time, so that they don't conflict.

A consequence of being unable to accumulate a feeling of the worth of different strategies during learning is a myopia for the future. In a clever gambling experiment in which cards are drawn from different decks for money or fines, normal patients begin to employ an advantageous strategy before they actually realize what strategy works best. They also generate an anticipatory skin conductance response if they ponder a choice that turns out to be risky, before they know explicitly that it is risky. Frontally damaged patients show no anticipatory responses to risky choices and continue to choose disadvantageously even after they know the correct strategy. Patients with large lesions elsewhere in the brain can learn to succeed in the gambling game just as normal subjects do, even if they are aphasic and indicate that they can make no sense of what is going on. Imaging experiments have now shown increased activity in several frontal cortical regions that correlates with learning reinforced by rewards. The implication of this finding is that reasons, at least some of them, require emotions.

Our thinking recruits our bodies. We don't plan for or anticipate futures unless we can link them with affect—with memories and hunches from similar situations accumulated over our personal histories.

Lateral organization of emotions

Reason and emotions are contrasted in our folk psychology, common-sense talk, and experience, and indeed they can correspond to activities in different parts of the brain. Damage to the right temporal area that is homologous to Wernicke's area in the left hemisphere leads to disturbance in comprehending the emotional content of language, whereas damage to the right frontal area homologous to Broca's area in the left leads to difficulty in expressing emotional aspects of language. Disorders of affective language, called *aprosodias*, can be classified as sensory, motor, and conduction aprosodias in the same way that the aphasias that compromise syntax and grammar are classified. Their anatomical organization mirrors the organization in the left hemisphere. Thus patients with aphasia can show not only cognitive defects in language but also defects in the affective components of language: intonation of speech (*prosody*) and emotional gesturing. PET scans show that when a subject is instructed to comprehend the meaning of words spoken in a foreign language, blood flow to the left hemisphere increases, whereas flow to the right hemisphere increases when the subject is asked to evaluate the emotional tone of the same spoken passage. These patterns of localization that form during development of a typical brain are not completely predetermined, because, as we noted in Chapter 6, young children in whom the left cerebral hemisphere is severely damaged or even removed early in life can develop an essentially normal range of language functions.

A number of experiments show that the left visual field (which projects to the left hemisphere) is superior at correctly identifying faces, whereas the right visual field (projecting to the right hemisphere) is better at perceiving facial expressions and emotions. The left ear (projecting to the right hemisphere) is better at detecting the emotional tones of voices, whereas the right is better at identifying their content. Lesions in the temporal lobe and temporal lobe epilepsy can cause a variety of emotional effects. Right temporal lobe lesions, as well as *epileptic foci*, not only can destroy ability to understand the affective content of language but also can trigger paranoia, anger, delusion, sexual feeling, *déjà vu*, and hallucinations.

During happy affect, the left hemisphere, particularly the frontal lobe, is more active than the right, and the opposite is true during unhappy affect. Brain lesions in the left frontal area are more likely to be associated with depression than similar lesions on the right. Work of the psychologist Richard Davidson has shown that strong positive feelings and approach behaviors correlate with left frontal lobe activation, whereas withdrawal and fear correlate with right frontal activation. Imaging studies are now showing in some detail the subareas within each hemisphere whose activities correlate with appetitive, pleasant, or pleasurable emotions. They can be distinguished from other areas whose activation correlates with aversive, negative, or unpleasant emotions. Activation of the left frontal lobe correlates with suppression of activity in the amygdala (discussed below), which is central to fear responses. Facial behaviors of happiness or disgust also correlate with the left/right frontal activation pattern. Emotional content of sensory stimuli influences even the primary sensory areas of the brain, for pictures with strong positive or negative affect cause significantly greater activation of the visual cortical areas discussed in Chapter 8.

Stable individual differences in the relative activation of the two hemispheres show a correlation with a person's basic temperament, sense of well-being, and vulnerability to depression and bad feelings. For each of us there may be a genetically determined set-point for temperament, analogous to brain regulation of our body metabolism to maintain a preset weight.

Do you think there are differences in the expression of emotions on each side of the body? Why is the smile of the Mona Lisa perceived as ambiguous? She is smiling with only the left side of her mouth, the part controlled by the right hemisphere, which is more active during negative affect. Which of the faces shown in Figure 10–3 do you perceive as happier or more pleasant? Most people say the face on the right looks happier. It has its right lip, controlled by the left hemisphere, curled upward. Facial expressions are not always symmetrical but rather tend to emphasize the left side of the face. This reflects the fact that the right hemisphere, controlling the left side of the face, has a more pronounced influence than the left in controlling emotional expression. This is true in humans as well as in other primates. Try to test lateralization of your own expressions by doing the accompanying self-experiment.

SELF-EXPERIMENT

You can experience lateralization of your emotions firsthand with a few simple facial expressions. Try curling up just the right side of your lips (controlled by the left hemisphere). Does this feel sort of like a smile? Now, curl up just the left side of your lips (controlled by the right hemisphere). Most people report that it doesn't feel nearly as friendly.

Emotional responses can be more rapid than reasoned ones

Why is it that we don't always do what we think we should do? Why do our emotions seem to have minds of their own? Recent findings have suggested an answer: Our emotions can use neural networks different from those used for conscious reasoned responses, and they can short-circuit those responses. This may help to explain why we have so little reflective insight into our emotional life.

Emotions are special-purpose organizers that can perform rapid positive-negative evaluations of events below our consciousness; they are rapid reaction systems especially useful for dealing with encounters with other people. A person who resembles someone who once caused us anxiety can trigger an immediate emotional response before

Figure 10–3 Mirror-image
faces. Which of these faces
looks happier to you?

rational thought cuts in. Repeated exposure can decondition the anxiety. For example, subway commuters who continually face strangers
start to like best those whom they have seen most frequently.
Emotional responses seem to be front-line reactions that spring quickly
into place before rational deliberation has had time to function. They
reflect the read-out of an emotional memory that is the basis of precon-
scious filters of the sort described in Chapter 8 for the visual system.
These filters can act on our perceptions to give a slight positive or negative affective bias even to stimuli that superficially appear neutral.
The building of our emotional history might be described as the development of a large number of somatic markers: correlated and rapid
reactions of the visceral, somatic muscular, and emotional brain pathways that have become linked to repetitive aspects of our environment,
both positive and negative. An example is the lasting influence of persons we admired or feared in our early childhood, causing us to react
unconsciously (with attraction or withdrawal) to people who have features reminiscent of those people we knew decades ago.

SELF-EXPERIMENT

Pause for a moment and repeat the word "lamujuva" to yourself several times. Now, do the same with the word "rakachaka." Does one
of these words seeming more pleasant than the other? (Most English-
speakers like the first and dislike the second.) This suggests that the brain
tags these percepts with a value, even though they carry no explicit cognitive meaning. Indeed, the brain may assign a value to virtually every perception.

Central role of the amygdala

The amygdala and hippocampus are key structures in forming our
emotional memories and in evaluating emotional stimuli. Although the
hippocampus has long been implicated in emotion, the current view is
that it is more involved with cognition and learning than with emotion.
The hippocampus would be involved in recognizing a face, perhaps

that of a cousin. The amygdala might add that you really don't like him. The amygdala appears to be required for the acquisition of conditioned autonomic responses to visual or auditory stimuli, but in the absence of the hippocampus, it is not sufficient for recalling the declarative knowledge relevant to those stimuli. The hippocampus, though required for the acquisition of such declarative knowledge, cannot support the autonomic conditioning in the absence of the amygdala.

The amygdala is a structure with an interesting evolutionary history. Its interactions with the thalamus play a major role in the mental life of fish, reptiles, and birds, whereas in mammals it is increasingly relegated to more specialized functions. Neurons of the amygdala show Pavlovian fear conditioning, and the whole structure plays a central role in triggering aversive and fear reactions. Such reactions can be triggered outside of our normal awareness if a fear-inducing picture is flashed for a brief instant before a masking stimulus that we actually perceive. We report nothing unusual, even though changes in skin conductance that are characteristic of a fearful response are recorded. Imaging studies show activation of the amygdala when human subjects encounter aversive stimuli, during aversive conditioning, and also in masking experiments. The storage of unpleasant memories associated with aversive stimuli is apparently facilitated by sympathetic arousal, for when human subjects are given propranolol (a drug that blocks the action of adrenaline) during exposure to an unpleasant story with pictures, they are less likely to remember the story than subjects who receive a placebo drug.

The amygdala enhances the storage and persistence of emotional memories in a process that is facilitated by the adrenaline released during stress.

The amygdala sends projections to all areas of the cortex, regulating an emotional bias of cognitive functions. In fact, there are many more nerve cells sending information from the amygdala to the cortex than from the cortex to the amygdala. This might be part of the reason why emotions can be so persistent and refractory to cognitive control. Its output is wired to parts of the brain needed to produce a panoply of fearful behaviors: shortness of breath, jumpiness, tension, and diarrhea. Different portions of the amygdala regulate different aspects of fear responses (such as autonomic nervous system arousal, emotional behaviors, and the hypothalamic-pituitary stress response). Each of these areas can be lesioned separately. (There are so many different structural and functional units within what is usually called the amygdala that some argue that it is misleading to refer to "the amygdala" as a structural and functional unit.) There appears to be a negative correlation between left prefrontal lobe activation and activation in the amygdala, such that the relative suppression of left frontal activity that correlates with withdrawal and depression goes with increased amygdala activity. Fearful situations that activate the amygdala can alter the intensity of conditioned responses. This appears to be what happens when, in a tense or threatening situation, our reaction to an unexpected noise is much greater than it would normally be.

SELF-EXPERIMENT

With a group of friends, you can conduct a simple demonstration of how activation of fear by amygdala-related mechanisms can influence our behavior. Start talking to the group about any old topic and then, without warning, startle your listeners by suddenly making a loud and unpleasant noise, such as slamming a book on a table. Then continue with your talking. After a while, begin to tell a story that becomes increasingly frightening. You might, for example, spin a tale of reading in the paper about a homicidal inmate escaping from a local prison and then later, while reading alone at night, hearing what sounded like someone trying to force an upstairs window open . . . etc. Now, again without warning, repeat the unpleasant noise you made previously and note whether the intensity of your friends' startle reaction has increased and whether they report this to have happened. (This exercise has to be done with some skill so that your friends don't figure out ahead of time what you are up to!)

We all seem to have a "negative-making" or "fear-making" system that can run semi-autonomously, the amygdala being a sort of "command central" that can program our overall emotional bias toward being apprehensive or anxious. We could view the arousal of this system, as happens during the period of heightened excitability that follows a sudden fright, essentially as "an amygdala attack." Its opponent would be a "positive-making system" that correlates with enhanced left frontal activity that can suppress the negative system and generate positive appetitive behavior. Test the idea of two such systems against your daily experience. Does the metaphor of "positive-making" or "negative-making" machines inside you, sometimes uncoupled from the input that may have initiated them but still biasing your reactions and decisions, make sense to you?

It is interesting that the amygdala of humans is more fully formed at birth than the hippocampus and develops more rapidly, such that fear behaviors are fully developed by 7–12 months. This may be why we remember essentially nothing from our first 2 years of life but apparently retain emotional experiences. It may also explain why these experiences, which psychoanalysts have long pointed to as a key to later emotional life, are so potent and so difficult to understand rationally. Behavioral and drug studies on monkeys have shown that corresponding fear behaviors appear at 9–12 weeks after birth, along with a peak of synapse formation in the prefrontal cortex and limbic system, including the amygdala.

Joseph LeDoux and his collaborators have done a series of fascinating experiments to demonstrate that the amygdala can trigger emotional reactions before the cortex has fully processed the triggering input. Previous experiments had shown that damaging part of the amygdala can abolish learned fear responses. In one set of studies, rats were trained to fear a flashing light by having the light paired with a shock. In normal rats, the fear response is extinguished if the light is displayed regularly without the shock. This process takes several weeks. If the visual cortex is removed, rats still learn to fear the lights, but when shown the lights without the shock for several weeks, they retain fearfulness, unlike rats with intact cortexes. The idea is that once it is established, an emotional aversion is permanent, but the cortex can learn to dilute that aversion by inhibiting the amygdala's response. The pathways suggested by LeDoux's experiment are summarized in Figure 10–4.

Figure 10–4 A schematic drawing of relationships among the thalamus, amygdala, and cortex. Sensory input via the thalamus to the amygdala permits crude identification of potentially significant features of the environment and rapid reaction to them. More careful identification of the stimulus uses slower cortical circuits. Adapted from LeDoux' *The Emotional Brain.*

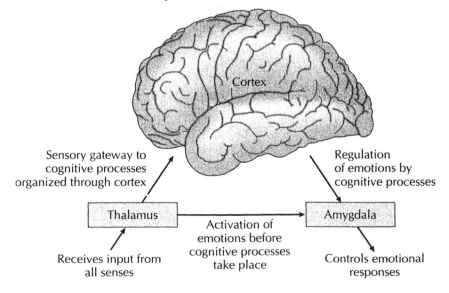

One possible explanation for post-traumatic stress disorder is that this cortical inhibition has been impaired. This model may explain how phobias are formed in humans and why they can be so tenacious. For a Vietnam veteran suffering from post-traumatic stress disorder, a clap of thunder may evoke the sweating and pounding heart he experienced during a battle. In people who have unlearned a phobia, a single scary experience can sometimes bring it back in full force. This suggests that the phobia has not been lost to emotional memory, even though the behavior has been extinguished under most conditions.

Experiments done on rat brains reveal a neural basis for reacting to something emotionally faster than we can think. Nerve pathways through the amygdala that short-cut or bypass slower cortical circuits follow the "better to be safe than sorry" principle and presumably, given that they exist in all unimpaired present-day members of our species, made the difference between life and death for our ancestors.

The amygdala is just one synapse away from the thalamus, whereas the hippocampus is several additional synapses away. That means it takes a sensory signal as much as 40 milliseconds longer to reach the hippocampus than to reach the amygdala. That time gap allows the amygdala to respond to an alarming situation before the hippocampus does. When out of the corner of your eye you see what looks like a snake, it is the amygdala that sends the signal of alarm that makes you jump. You react even before the hippocampus has had time to coordinate figuring out, in consultation with other parts of the cortex, whether what you saw was actually a snake or a piece of rope. The amygdala appears to be a central part of the rapidly acting pathway that tags many words and images with positive or negative affect before they reach awareness.

Perception of emotional and cognitive pathways

Because cognition and emotion emphasize different pathways, we might expect that their relative timing could be varied, with emotion occurring before or after thought. For example, we might recall a mental image of a snake and then, immediately afterward, the feelings that go with it, or we might notice a long, thin, sinuous object and have an aversive feeling before we note whether it is a snake or not. Try the accompanying self-experiment to examine the timing of your thoughts and emotions.

SELF-EXPERIMENT

This simple exercise might permit you to experience dissociation of feelings and cognition in yourself. It would be best to ask a friend to read these instructions to you, but again, you should be able to do the exercise by yourself: Sit comfortably, close your eyes, breathe gently, and attend to the breathing. Notice, but do not hold onto, thoughts that pass through your mind. Let thoughts enter your mind as easily as they go, but always gently return to being aware of your breathing. Next, notice the thoughts that arise and are accompanied by positive or negative feelings. When do you notice the thought, perhaps an image of a person or social situation, and when do you notice the feeling that goes with it? Do they arrive separately or together?

The purpose of the self-experiment is for you to experience associating spontaneous thoughts or images with affect on a time scale of 100–300 milliseconds. This is the time scale of the flickering of thoughts and the somatic markers that go with them. You may have noticed that when an image spontaneously occurs in your mind, your awareness of the cognitive content of the image (such as the identity or visualization of a face, or the relationships of a social context) occurs slightly before you experience the emotion usually associated with that image. This fact is used in cognitive therapy and disciplines such as Buddhist mindfulness meditation to permit dissociation of an image from the affect normally associated with the image. It is during the first milliseconds of connecting images and affect (particularly the negative affect of feeling threatened, afraid, or powerless), that self-awareness might intervene to present other options. After this window has closed, negative affect usually becomes harder to dislodge as it reinforces itself through other associations.

If we calm down and pay quiet attention to what is going on in our heads, we can experience many fascinating phenomena that reveal how the brain works over tenth-of-a-second intervals. Chapter 12 describes several experiments that demonstrate that the brain can rearrange time and space in the period of 50–400 milliseconds after an external or internal visual image is initiated. This is also the time frame of the exercises on initiating motor patterns that we tried in Chapter 9.

Up to this point, we have mentioned an array of balancing systems—sympathetic and parasympathetic, brainstem spritzers, right frontal and left frontal plus amygdala activation—that all contribute to the formation of our background emotions or predispositions. To these systems, we must add the systems that mark images and ideas from our emotional histories with limbic, visceral, and muscular correlates to form an array of somatic markers. These markers are elicited as recurring situations are encountered, and they can act as little filters or machines inside our head—autopilots that sometimes can take a neutral event and put a positive or negative spin on it. Such largely unconscious mechanisms can attach small quantities of emotional energy to ongoing events, determining, when someone cancels a lunch with us, whether we think "she doesn't like me," or "he must be very busy," or determining, when we confront a challenge, whether our immediate reaction is "I can't do it" or "I can do it."

We are also endowed with an amazing kind of cognition, exercised in the self-experiment, that can gain some awareness of these lower processes going on. This awareness of thinking, or thinking about thinking, is sometimes called *metacognition*. It is a limited ability to sense and review the vast number of rapidly acting autopilots that have assembled during our development. We couldn't live without these automatic routines. We don't reinvent the wheel each time we encounter a familiar situation; rather, we reserve our higher cortical resources for dealing with what seems novel. Still, when the underground routines are not working, our higher faculties can be used to sense, tinker with, and possibly alter them.

Modern cognitive therapies represent a very practical application of this ability. We have already made reference, in Chapter 3 (in the section "Imaging the activity of the brain"), to patients with obsessive-compulsive disorder (the behaviors exhibited may include excessive hand washing or ritualistic counting and checking).

The use of cognitive therapy techniques to reduce inappropriate emotional behaviors and actually change brain activation patterns provides an example of how consciousness can play a role in regulating brain physiology.

Some have learned to control their behavior by thinking, when they feel the initial emotional urge, "That isn't me. That is a part of my brain that is not working." Or "That feeling is just the result of a false message from my brain." As the aberrant behavior diminishes, the same decreases in frontal lobe activity that are observed during effective drug therapy occur. What is being developed here is the literal equivalent of a mental immune system. Just as we acquire an immune history—knowledge of pathogens that have invaded our system and that now can be quickly expunged if they appear again—so we can acquire a history of maladaptive emotional routines. The analog of the macrophage or T cell is a trained recognition mechanism that has become very sensitive to the onset of these states and can trigger cognitive procedures that essentially excise them, as soon as they are detected, by activating more functional routines.

Facial musculature and the communication of emotions

Having delved in some detail into the internal mechanisms that regulate our emotional life, let's draw back to consider some social aspects of emotions and the central role played by faces and facial expressions. The amygdala is a key player in the interpretation of expressions that communicate emotions. It receives information from various areas of the visual cortex, particularly the portion of the inferior temporal cortex that contains face-responsive neurons. It also sends information back to all these areas—a possible means by which affective states could modulate sensory processing. This could be part of the explanation for the biasing of perception by emotions that many psychological studies have revealed. Subjects with bilateral amygdala damage are much less discerning in their judgment of other faces. Recent studies have shown that the amygdala can be activated by the masked presentation of emotional facial expressions. When a subject is shown a fearful or angry face for about 30 milliseconds, followed by a neutral face for 170 milliseconds, only the neutral face is remembered or reported, but brain imaging reveals an increase in activation of the right amygdala that is not observed when the 30–millisecond exposure is to a happy or neutral face. Interestingly, conscious aversive conditioning to an angry face paired with a burst of unpleasant noise correlates with activation of the left amygdala.

These systems originate far back in our vertebrate lineage. We don't hesitate much in interpreting the facial expressions that dogs and cats use to communicate anger, fear, or pleasure. The same can be said, with a bit less clarity, of many higher mammals. Nonhuman primates have facial expressions and meanings that are less subtle than our own but that seem obviously similar. We observe a dramatic increase in the complexity of facial musculature and expressions when we move from monkeys to apes to humans. Increasingly, the face is turned into a kind of semaphore, signaling complex social interactions. As we noted in Chapter 5, the use of facial and vocal muscles in communication was a component of the development of the mimetic intelligence that is thought to have provided the foundation for the appearance of modern language and mythic intelligence.

During hominid evolution, the increasing number and complexity of facial muscles supported the development of an array of emotional expressions that are universal across modern cultures. The amygdala plays a central role in both interpreting and orchestrating the response to these expressions.

We all know from our daily lives that our emotions correlate with, and are communicated by, a complex set of facial muscle signals. These signals are only one of several parallel layers of the kinesic communication (body language) that is occurring as we talk with others. This is presumably why more brain area is devoted to facial musculature than to any other surface of the body. These areas direct stereotyped combinations of muscle contractions to denote surprise, fear, disgust, happiness, and grief. Darwin noted the universality of these patterns—how all people, from Oxford dons to Australian aborigines, express grief by contracting their facial muscles in the same way. Flirting signals too are the same across cultures: a lowering of the eyelids or the head, followed by direct eye contact.

The most telling experiments involve the presentation of photographs of Western faces showing basic emotions to New Guinea natives who have lived for millennia in isolation from all other humans except their immediate tribe. Studies conducted on three such isolated primitive cultures show photographs of Western faces to these Stone Age people, and vice versa, with the same results. The same stereotyped sets of muscle contractions are used by all. The psychologist Paul Ekman has cataloged 80 different facial muscles used in communication. These muscles can be trained separately to reconstruct emotional expressions, and each expression can be specified as a list of relevant muscle contractions or relaxations. Some of the named muscle sets for different emotions are cross-cultural, others culture-specific.

What about the changes we feel in our bodies as our faces are smiling and relaxed, or fearful and tense? Fear is sometimes correlated with mobilization of the sympathetic nervous system; happiness is more likely to be associated with parasympathetic activation. Are the parts of our cortex that drive facial muscles also directing the autonomic correlates of the facial expression? Or is some sort of feedback from the facial muscles responsible for autonomic changes? Davidson and Ekman, mentioned above, have addressed this issue in an interesting experiment on smiling. We all can recognize fake smiles, often used in deception, and we are fairly acute observers of the muscles involved. The difference is that a real smile that reflects happiness or joy involves not only the zygomatic major muscles which reach down from the cheekbones and attach to the corners of the lips, but also movement of the lateral part of the muscles (the orbicularis oculi) that encircle the eyes (making "crow's feet" at the corner of the eye). Electrical measurements show that when subjects are instructed to contract both of these muscles (but are not instructed to feel happy), the left frontal lobe becomes more active, just as in people who are experiencing positive emotions. This presumably accounts for the effectiveness of a form of therapy against depression: instructing the depressed person to move the muscles that make a smile. Doing so causes a lightening of underlying mood.

These are fundamentally important experiments, because they show that an emotional facial expression is not just a unidirectional command from the emotional centers of the brain to the face muscles, but rather that the facial expressions are part of a neural network in which activating one node (voluntarily activating the smiling muscles) can activate another node (the neural correlates of positive affect in the left frontal lobe). Recent experiments show that facial expressions of sadness, fear, and anger are similarly correlated with autonomic changes measured by skin conductance as well as with brain activation patterns measured by magnetic resonance imaging.

SELF-EXPERIMENT

You can do a simple exercise on yourself to appreciate the relationship between facial musculature and emotions. Pause in your reading right now, slow down, and pay attention to your breathing for 20–30 seconds. Now, recall an experience that made you very happy, perhaps with a friend or lover—something you really enjoyed, maybe it made you laugh or smile; take a moment to get into that and try to relive the emotion you felt. Now, don't smile; make your face absolutely flat. What does this do to the feeling? Is it harder to hold on to? Can you feel a whole muscle set that goes with the internal feeling of emotion? Is it possible to separate them? Let's try just one more. This time, think of something that made or makes you angry, maybe another person you are angry at. Imagine confronting the situation or person. Let yourself feel really angry, maybe wanting to strike out. Now, stop contracting and tensing your face; let it go flat. What happens to the angry feeling? Again, can you feel the correlation? Now, try to smile and feel angry at the same time.

Misapplication of ancestral emotions—the chronic stress response

What is the characteristic configuration of our autonomic nervous system and its correlated emotions?—for many of us living in modern industrial societies, it's not a very healthy one: chronic activation of a sympathetic nervous system designed for use only in episodic emergencies. This point deserves some elaboration. Each of us is blessed with an emotional repertoire controlling the four F's mentioned in Chapter 3 (fighting, fleeing, feeding, fornicating). These systems have evolved progressively through our vertebrate lineage up to our adaptations to the life of hunter-gatherers in the Paleolithic. The problem is that we frequently employ them in ways that are inappropriate in our contemporary surroundings. Many of us in complex high-tech and fast-paced societies chronically activate the stress response, rather than reserving it for genuine life-threatening emergencies. The endocrinologist Robert Sapolsky points out that we don't have the common sense of zebras, who don't get ulcers: They have a better handle on when to chill out (while grazing on grass) and when to go into high-gear stress (when the lion appears). Our physiological response mechanisms are superbly adapted for short-term emergencies, but our bodies are not built to sustain their long-term activation. The things that work for short-term emergencies, getting fuel rapidly from storage sites and inhibiting further energy storage, are debilitating in the long run. Suppressing immune function in the short term, for example, allows the energy required to be used elsewhere, but in the long run, it makes us more susceptible to infections and cancer.

Our stress response recruits a diverse array of hormones, but it can be described in a simple way as occurring in two waves (see Figure 10–5). Within seconds of our encountering a stressor, cells in the hypothalamus cause activation of the sympathetic nervous system, and catecholamines (epinephrine and norepinephrine) are released by both

Figure 10–5 Stages of the stress response. Within seconds of the onset of a stressful event, norepinephrine and epinephrine (also called noradrenaline and adrenaline) are released by sympathetic nerve endings and the interior portion of the adrenal gland (the adrenal medulla). These chemicals enhance the readiness and excitability of both nerve and muscle tissue. More slowly, ACTH is released into the blood stream by the pituitary gland and carried to the adrenal cortex, where it triggers the release of glucocorticoids that stimulate metabolism.

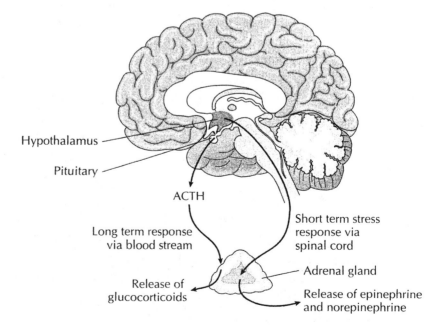

sympathetic nerves and the adrenal gland. These act to mobilize the viscera and muscle for quick action. These amines also activate the amygdala, which is central in orchestrating the behavioral reactions to a stressful event, but their prolonged release in prefrontal cortex can cause cognitive dysfunction. As a further reaction to a stressful thought or event, on the time scale of minutes, our hypothalamus releases *corticotropin-releasing factor*. This triggers ACTH (*corticotropin*) release from the pituitary, and ACTH moves through the blood stream to the adrenal gland, where it triggers release of glucocorticoids that stimulate glucose metabolism and suppress immune function. (It is worth mentioning that there can be another, opposite kind of reaction to stress and challenges: Parasympathetic rather than sympathetic overactivation can lead to a "freezing" sort of reaction that slows the heart, shutting down the body rather than mobilizing it. Such a slowing down may underlie a striking phenomenon observed in some Stone Age cultures: Individuals who have been cursed or ostracized by their group become increasingly immobile and eventually die.)

Chronic sympathetic activation and glucocorticoid release have a large number of deleterious effects. A partial list includes immune suppression, atherosclerosis, digestive disorders, and accelerated aging and death of nerve cells in the hippocampus and temporal lobes. Stress also is known to cause decreases in levels of the neurotransmitter acetylcholine in the cortex and hippocampus, impairing learning and memory.

The nervous, endocrine, and immune systems form a complex network that shares hormone and neurotransmitter molecules. Interactions within this network are the focus of the new field of *psychoneuroimmunology*. A class of peptides used as neurotransmitters is also used in signaling by cells of the immune system. Nerve cell endings in the skin can secrete chemicals that shut down the immune system nearby. This may partly explain why diseases such as psoriasis are exacerbated by stress. Prolonged exposure to stress hormones causes death of immune system cells and atrophy of neuronal connections in the hippocampus, leading to decay in memory and cognitive functions. The molecular mechanisms by which glucocorticoids can block immune system activation are being unraveled. Stress also decreases production of a trophic factor called *brain-derived neurotrophic factor* (BDNF), which neurons use to protect themselves from damage. A further array of exotic compounds, whose description is well beyond the scope of this book (cytokines, interleukins, tumor necrosis factor, and so on), come into play as internal mood and beliefs confront external disease vectors and social tensions. An increased ratio of the right/left frontal lobe activation mentioned above as being associated with withdrawal and depression also correlates with immune suppression.

Interactions among the nervous, endocrine, and immune systems are not just of a negative sort. There is clear evidence that people who have a positive outlook and are confident of overcoming stressful barriers have higher blood levels of the T cells and natural killer cells that correlate with robust immune function. Some quite remarkable cases of mood- or belief-caused remission of the symptoms of illnesses such as cancer, arthritis, asthma, and acute depression have been documented. In many of these cases, a sham treatment called a placebo (Latin for "I shall please") is administered; it is believed by the patient to be an effective drug or therapy. A brightly colored pill containing sugar, a doctor in a white coat with a stethoscope, a shaman wearing a feather head dress—all can apparently induce a patient's immune system to respond to a disease crisis. Several experiments have paired an actual therapy, such as an asthma medicine, with an arbitrary pleasant flavor such as vanilla. Subsequent administration of the flavor alone can cause a significant increase in lung function. All of these examples indicate that expectancy—what the brain is telling the body it expects to happen—has a powerful effect on the actual outcome. The mind-body connection reaches down to the intricate details of our immune system biochemistry.

Sapolsky has conducted some fascinating studies on social roles, stress, and corticosteroid levels in baboon tribes in the Serengeti. Like humans, these animals have to spend only a few hours a day gathering food and devote the rest of their time to driving each other crazy with elaborate social competitions. Measurements of physiological and hormonal changes relevant to stress show that virtually all of them are functions of rank. But it turns out on closer examination that rank is a less relevant variable than the baboon's "personality style." Those individuals who are best at telling the difference between threatening and neutral interactions, and who know clearly whether they won or lost, have the lowest glucocorticoid levels. It also helps, if you lose, to have somebody to take out your frustrations on. A second major factor in lowering corticoid levels is developing friendships. Does this sound familiar? Studies on humans yield the same results. And, as in humans, the animals who get agitated even when they see a rival at a safe distance are the ones that show hormonal correlates of stress.

SELF-EXPERIMENT

Try another simple exercise on yourself. Close your eyes, breathe, and relax for just a few moments. Now, imagine that you suddenly see a car about to hit you. You are terrified and want to get away fast! Freeze your body right there. What muscles are tense? Your neck? Your back? These are the muscles involved in the startle response. This response takes about half a second, starting in the upper trapezius and sternocleido-mastoid muscles and passing down the body. The curious thing is that the startle response is an extreme version of the slightly hunched-down "nor-mal" postures that most of us display. Consider the possibility that the cacophony of input that we humans must put up with in this culture leaves many of us partially frozen in a startle response, or low-level anxiety. This might cause the sympathetic nervous system to be chronically activated, rather than being reserved for emergencies. Back extensor muscles would be chronically overcontracted and front flexor muscles underused.

Our physiology clearly depends in part on our social context and can change with it. Social threats to our character have as a correlate threats to our integrated physiology. The effect of the social environment on stress extrapolates to susceptibility to, and recovery from, disease. An extensive literature documents correlations between resistance to disease and social class, stress, social support, and the belief system of the individual. Stress and isolation correlate with reduced life spans. Studies on communities of macaque monkeys and surveys on human communities show that close relationships buffer the immune system. Support systems that allow individuals to take life's ups and downs in stride enhance immune function and longevity. Depression, loss of status, or a sense of helplessness in an individual correlates with suppression of immune function. Our feelings of control versus helplessness exert a "top-down" control on our intimate biochemistry and neurophysiology. Comparison of subjects facing the same stressor shows that those who feel they have some control over the situation have lower cortisol levels than those who feel helpless. In short, there is a feedback loop between our social lives and our physiology. Our biological function is in a symbiotic relationship with our culture and society.

SUMMARY   This chapter has chronicled several different aspects of the ill-defined array of experiences that we refer to as our emotions. Their roots lie much deeper in our evolutionary past than such recent inventions as language, and their link to our autonomic physiology—heart rate, skin gland regulation, and the like—distinguishes them from our "higher" functions of abstract and analytic thought. These higher functions, however, can be decisively biased by chemical modulators of emotion, originating in lower regions of the brain, that are released diffusely across the cortex. It appears that the vast array of values, hunches, inclinations, and rules that guide our selection of current actions from an array of options is programmed during our development by an interaction between higher and lower centers, as the more primitive circuits are recruited to assign different feelings or values to contexts that have been repeatedly encountered. These assessments then can work more rapidly than our self-conscious cognitive processes to size up people or contexts that we encounter, when instantly (and, as it would seem, irrationally) we like or dislike someone we meet. They also can go to the extreme of becoming pathology, as in post-traumatic stress syndrome and obsessive-compulsive disorder. In both normal and abnormal circumstances, introspection techniques that enhance awareness of the distinction between emotional and self-conscious cognitive pathways in the brain can sometimes provide a useful tool for understanding or modifying one's behaviors. A maladaptive intrusion of our ancient emotional repertoire, causing damage that can include the immune system and brain, occurs if the stresses of daily modern life are permitted to activate chronically a nervous and endocrine stress system that evolved to deal with short-term life-and-death situations.

Our emotional minds, with their useful and their less useful elements, form another component of the mosaic of our modern minds, along with those outlined in previous chapters on plasticity, perception, and action. Now we are ready to tackle an issue distinctive to our human species: How is it that we are able to read and speak the words flowing past on this page? How do we acquire the faculty of language, the most important feature distinguishing us from the rest of the animal world?

1. Making a basic category of "the emotions" or coining terms such as "affective neuroscience" is a common-sense way of organizing descriptions of our experience, but it could be argued that these categories don't really correspond to fundamental entities—that emotions essentially are cognitions. Like a wide array of our sensory and motor behaviors, they reflect an analysis of some input to the organism that results in a behavior relevant to survival. Do you think emotions deserve description as a separate category? If so, why?

2. We could say that the main locus of linguistic cognition is our cerebral neocortex, the most recently evolved portion of our brain. How does this contrast with the location of the operations association with the emotions?

3. The psychologist Steven Pinker suggests that our lack of voluntary control over our emotions, and their link to basic physiological processes, is an evolutionary adaptation with a social purpose: to enhance the credibility of human social interchanges and make deception more difficult. Could such an idea be proved? Could there be other explanations?

4. Given the fact that many of our rapid and almost reflexive emotional behaviors can sometimes sabotage our effective performance in private and social contexts, do you think we would all be better off without these evolutionary vestiges of a former age—more like Mr. Spock of the television "Star Trek" series. If not, why not?

Suggestions for further general reading

Damasio, A.R. 1994. *Descartes' Error—Emotion, Reason, and the Human Brain.* New York: Putnam's. (A stimulating discussion of how rational mind is built on top of emotional mind. This chapter draws heavily on Damasio's ideas about the origins of rational mind in emotional mind, adopts his distinction of primary and secondary emotions, and makes use of his concept of "somatic markers.")

Goleman, D. 1995. *Emotional Intelligence.* New York: Bantam. (This best-selling book describes the mechanism and consequences of various kinds of "emotional hijacking." It also discusses the varieties and definitions of emotions.)

LeDoux, J. 1996. *The Emotional Brain.* New York: Simon & Schuster. (In this book, LeDoux, whose work is the basis of Figure 10–4, focuses on the neural mechanisms of fear.)

Pinker, S. 1997. *How the Mind Works.* New York: Norton. (In Chapter 6 of this book, Pinker discusses emotions from the perspective of evolutionary psychology and speculates that emotions are guarantors of the authenticity of our actions.)

Sapolsky, R.M. 1994. *Why Zebras Don't Get Ulcers: A Guide to Stress, Stress-Related Diseases, and Coping*. New York: W.H. Freeman. (This engaging book gives a fascinating summary of how body systems designed for episodically dealing with life-threatening stress can be chronically activated with debilitating results.)

Reading on more advanced or specialized topics

Bear, M., Connors, B., & Paradiso, M. 1996. *Neuroscience: Exploring the Brain*. Baltimore, MD: Williams & Wilkins. (Chapters 15 and 16 of this book describe the brain areas involved in modulating emotional behavior.)

Davidson, R.J., & Sutton, S.K. 1995. Affective neuroscience: the emergence of a discipline. *Current Opinion in Neurobiology* 5:217–224. (This is a more technical but very accessible review of brain mechanisms regulating emotions.)

Ekman, P., & Davidson, R.J. 1993. Voluntary smiling changes regional brain activity. *Psycholocial Science* 4:342–345. (An interesting experiment showing that brain activities for "fake" and "real" smiles are different, just as the facial muscle contractions are.)

Panksepp, J. 1998. *Affective Neuroscience. The Foundations of Human and Animal Emotions*. New York: Oxford University Press. (This is a textbook on the psychology and physiology of emotions.)

Pitkänen, A., Savander, V., & LeDoux, J.E. 1997. Organization of intra-amygdaloid circuitries in the rat: an emerging framework for understanding functions of the amygdala. *Trends in Neurosciences* 20:517–523.

Chapter 11

Linguistic Mind

We can trace a quite obvious continuity between the primate and human versions of the perceiving, acting, and emoting minds discussed in previous chapters. Mechanisms revealed in animal experiments are frequently found in our own brains, and vice versa. However, there is nothing in the language-like behavior of chimps or other animals that remotely approaches the language abilities of 3-year-old humans. Thus we have only ourselves to observe in trying to understand the development of our language competence and the underlying cortical mechanisms. Recall that we have touched on issues surrounding language several times. In Chapter 5 we looked at some speculations on how language might have arisen during hominid evolution from a precursor mimetic intelligence, and we also noted that the appearance of language made possible a mythic intelligence that accelerated the pace of evolution by transmitting culture and ideas between generations. And in Chapter 7 we briefly noted some stages in language development in human children.

Clearly, we have some genes and developmental routines lacking in chimps that ultimately facilitate the formation of a set of "language organs" universal in all modern humans. These organs effect a universal grammar or tree-like set of rules that can generate many possible languages. All these languages use the technique of metaphor to make varied descriptions of our world. What is not clear is how direct the linkage is between our genes and the operations of grammar and syntax. Is the wiring that underlies the distinction among subject, object, and verb categories instructed by the same sort of genetically pro-grammed molecular markers that direct cells in the lateral geniculate body to send axons to the visual cortex? Or does each developing human brain itself invent the wiring of subject, object, and verb opera-tions as a best solution to problems posed by the environment of other humans? We address this issue below, after offering evidence that humans do have an innate language capacity. The sections that follow then deal with brain mechanisms of language that are revealed by lesion and imaging studies, and the use of metaphors in constructing language.

The language instinct

One line of evidence for a universal and innate human language capac-ity comes from the observation that every known human culture has a language with complex grammar. None of these grammars is simple, and the complexity of a culture's language seems quite independent of the complexity of its social organization or technology. Different groups of humans, isolating themselves from each other, grow differ-ent languages. The inhabitants of the highlands of Papua New Guinea have been isolated from other humans for 40,000 years and speak about 700–800 different native languages within an area similar in size to Sweden. No single one of those languages is spoken by more than 3 percent of the population. One can move 20 miles across rain forest and cross the territories of three different xenophobic tribes who, fearing each other, have very little contact. Their languages have fundamen-tally different structures, rules of syntax, and grammar. The differences among these languages are much greater than the differences among modern European languages. A similar situation exists in West Africa, where more than 700 distinct languages are encountered. The lan-guages are most numerous in areas of greatest rainfall, where each group can produce its own food and doesn't need to communicate with outsiders to trade.

New languages can evolve within a generation or two from the rapid mixing of existing tongues. The new languages that arise because different groups need to communicate are called pidgins and are very crude. But whenever a group that contributes to a pidgin begins to adopt the pidgin itself as its native language, a creole develops, which has all the complex features of a normal language. The creole is invented by the children of the people who speak the pidgin. The fact that they aren't exposed to a complete language and yet make up one is a strong argument for a genetic blueprint for language-making ability. This blueprint gets carried out, however, only in the appropriate milieu of other humans. Language is absent in feral human children raised by wild animals, and in some severely abused children deprived of normal human contact.

When two adult populations who speak different languages mix together and must communicate, a crude form of a new language takes shape. Within a generation, children of these adult groups are able to invent a new, hybrid language, sometimes with unique features not shared by the parent languages.

Creoles, whether invented in South America, Africa, or the Pacific islands, are remarkably convergent. They place subject, verb, and object in that order; use singular and plural pronouns for the first, second, and third person; and employ relative clauses, anterior tense, and conditional mood. One of the best-documented examples of the evolution of a creole is a study of language in Hawaii after its annexation by the United States in 1898. Sugar planters had imported workers from China, the Philippines, Japan, Korea, Portugal, and Puerto Rico. The children of the original immigrants, who had maintained their normal language and a learned pidgin, had the problem of trying to speak with other children using this pidgin, which was an impoverished and inconsistent version of a human language. They spontaneously expanded the pidgin into a consistent and complex creole within a generation, by 1920. Researchers talking with adults of various ages obtained snapshots of the stages in the pidgin-to-creole transition, depending on the adults' birth year. Many features of Hawaiian creole grammar, whose vocabulary is largely English, differ from both English and the workers' native languages.

Universal language

Not only is having a language universal; so also is the fundamental design. Noam Chomsky is credited with uncovering universal properties of natural human languages, and some accord him a position in the history of ideas comparable to that of Darwin or Descartes. We have an inherited neural capacity for generating a system of rules into which words are plugged—a universal grammar underlying all languages. Every sentence, according to Chomsky, has a deep structure, a pattern in the mind, that is mapped onto surface structure, the actual spoken utterance, according to rules or "transformations." The details of the transformations vary from language to language, but all share certain abstract properties that constitute the universal grammar.

All languages use nouns and verbs, subjects and objects, cases and agreement, and vocabularies in the thousands or tens of thousands of words. Almost all languages have the same basic word order of subject and object. The 4000–6000 languages known today are sufficiently alike that an extraterrestrial observer might consider them all one language. A sentence in any spoken language can be diagrammed as an inverted modular tree containing noun phrases, verb phrases, and prepositional phrases that can be fitted inside each other. The technical jargon (N-bar, V-bar, X-bar) used to describe sentence structure is fully as intricate as the vocabulary used to describe visual pathways in the brain.

The case for language as an evolutionary adaptation

Both Chomsky and the evolutionary biologist Stephen Jay Gould deny that language is an evolutionary adaptation but suggest, rather, that it is an accidental consequence of having a complex cortex, or perhaps a by-product of some other faculty on which selection acted, as in Calvin's throwing model (see Chapter 9). The psychologist Steven Pinker and many other linguists argue, to the contrary, for the more plausible view that we have a language instinct that has appeared as a consequence of natural selection, just like our liver and our ears. In addition to the universality of language and its design, the stereotypic development of language in children of all cultures supports this view. In the uterus, human embryos react to the melody, stress, and timing of the mother's native speech, and immediately after birth they suck much harder when hearing their native language than when hearing a foreign one. Children begin to babble during their first year, and words appear after about 12 months. Inborn linguistic mechanisms (such as simple word combinations like "more candy") take off at about 18 months, are fully operating at about 3 years, and decline by puberty. Over a relatively narrow window of 6 months to around the age of 2, the entire grammar of a language appears.

The language instinct does not require conventional spoken language for its expression. The fact that congenitally deaf babies can babble in sign language and the fact that those who can neither hear nor speak communicate in a distinctly human way make a convincing case for the ability of humans to use abstract symbols independently of conventional language as a means of communicating with each other. Manual babbling occurs in deaf children who are exposed to signed languages from birth. The similarities between manual and vocal babbling suggest that babbling is a product of an amodal, brain-based language capacity. The speech modality is not critical. Rather, babbling is tied to the abstract

The appearance of language in infants follows a stereotyped time course that is similar across cultures. The ability to manipulate symbols, which underlies language competence, is amodal: It can be expressed by vocal or manual signs.

linguistic structure of language and to an expressive capacity capable of processing different types of signals (signed or spoken). One interesting report is of a deaf boy, the son of deaf parents who signed incorrectly (using American Sign Language learned after they were adults). The boy nevertheless appears to have learned correct grammar on his own, a remarkable result consistent with an innate ability to construct grammar. Even more dramatic is the invention of a complex sign language by a group of more than 500 deaf children in a Nicaraguan school. This is similar to the invention of creoles by children of parents who speak a more rudimentary, pidgin language.

The learning of language

Saying that language is an innate ability of humans, invented and expressed as human children grow up together, is not the same thing as saying that there is genetic control over formation of the detailed cortical modules, domains, or representations that make up linguistic competence. The alternative model is that our developing brains contain robust learning devices that permit each of us to invent, independently, very similar arrays of "language organs." This distinction brings us back to the nature-nurture debate discussed in Chapter 7, a debate that comes into sharpest focus as we try to understand the relationship between genes and language.

Genetic determinants of language ability

If it could be shown that a mutant gene influenced a detailed aspect of grammar, this might provide evidence that the gene in question was necessary for some fairly detailed brain wiring. It would not necessarily be a gene for grammar, but it presumably would be required for the relevant neuronal circuits to form. Showing that a gene mutation has an effect that is specific to language, sparing other abilities, would constitute powerful evidence for a segregated and genetically specified language faculty.

It appeared for a while that just such a mutation had been found, expressed in 16 of 30 individuals in a British family over three generations. Though they were able to memorize words and their meanings and to perform some grammar operations, these individuals frequently failed to perform past tense operations (such as generate → generated) and pluralization operations (cat → cats). A number of studies have now reported other families in which a form of developmental dysphasia (reflected by inability to distinguish singular from plural, and tenses of regular, but not irregular, verbs) is distributed in a way consistent with inheritance as a single autosomal-dominant mutation. However, subsequent studies of the British family members, as well as of other cases, have revealed that the deficits are not restricted to specific aspects of language. Rather, they cause low performance on a wide variety of language tests and are correlated with lower verbal and nonverbal IQ and poor control of oral-facial muscles.

Another candidate for genetic specification of grammar has been suggested by studies of abnormal development: the syndrome known as specific language impairment, or SLI. The syndrome, which has a clear genetic basis, delays language development and causes abnormal grammatical morphology, but nonlinguistic intelligence can be normal. It appears now that affected individuals are deficient in the processing of rapid temporal sequences of auditory, visual, and motor systems. These deficits are general, even though their most obvious effect is on language. Thus far, no inherited language deficits have been shown to be independent of more general brain developmental or processing mechanisms.

Rather than searching for genetic links to specific language deficits, another approach would be to seek out genetic defects that spare language as a "module of mind" but compromise other aspects of cognition. This would suggest the presence of genes that permit the development of a separate language competence even when other intelligences are compromised. One such case is found in Williams' syndrome, a genetic defect that occurs in about one of every 20,000 births. It involves deletion of a region of chromosome 7 that contains a gene for the protein elastin and a gene for an enzyme-modifying protein (a protein kinase) whose mutation has been shown to correlate with impaired visuospatial constructive cognition. Subjects have an elfin appearance, a narrowed aortic valve, and an IQ of around 50. They are unable to perform simple chores for themselves, have impoverished spatial abilities, and maintain the animism (belief that all moving objects are alive) that is left behind in normal development. Their language, however, is rich and fluent, and they are very sociable.

Those with Williams' syndrome are similar in general cognitive abilities to those with Down's syndrome, which is caused by another chromosomal abnormality (trisomy of chromosome 21). Autopsies and brain imaging show that the cerebral cortex has shrunk on both sides but that the frontal lobes, medial temporal lobes, and neocerebellum are closer to normal size. The neocerebellum is a thin layer of cells atop the older cerebellum brain region. It evolved more recently, along with the prefrontal cortex. Humans are the only animals with large versions of these two brain regions and the only animals with language. Moreover, brain imaging studies show that the neocerebellum is activated only when semantic reasoning is required. Perhaps this recently evolved circuit underlying language and sociability is spared in Williams' syndrome, and the gene deletion that marks the syndrome impairs an older set of instructions for brain development, while leaving the newer language circuit intact. In many autistic children who are antisocial and poor at language, but good at spatial tasks, these areas are small compared to their size in nondisabled children and those with Williams' syndrome.

Observations on some language idiot savants provide further support for a language faculty that can remain intact in a brain that has developed abnormally. There is the case of the 29-year-old subject with a nonverbal IQ of 65 who could not draw simple figures, add 2 and 2, or tie his shoes. He could speak 16 languages. His language abilities were independent of his cognitive ability; he never mulled over the meaning of passages and was not able to think about what he translated.

In spite of striking cases such as language idiot savants and children with Williams' syndrome, there is still no evidence that the language faculty is a wholly independent function. The current view is that it is more likely to consist of refinements of systems that coordinate nonlinguistic elements with each other. This suggestion is reinforced by the brain localization work described below.

Language development and brain structure

We have already mentioned several times, in Chapters 3 and 5, the two areas in the left frontal and temporal lobes (Broca's and Wernicke's areas) that are associated, respectively, with the production and comprehension of language. These are illustrated again in Figure 11–1. If these locations had the same constancy from individual to individual as do the primary sensory and motor cortices, this would provide an argument for their strong genetic specification. Quite to the contrary, however, children who have left focal lesions or who have undergone removal of the left hemisphere can develop language functions "within the normal range" using the right hemisphere, although deficits in syntactic and phonological tasks are frequently found. Deficits that the lesions cause in the development of spatial cognition do not show the same plasticity. Part of the explanation for this may lie in the fact that spatial cognition is an ancient system, having evolved throughout the

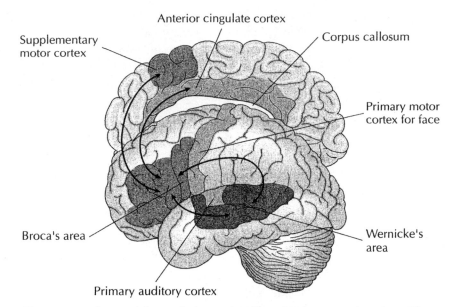

Figure 11–1 Some of the cortical areas implicated in language functions. The external view of the left hemisphere shows Broca's and Wernicke's areas, which are involved in the generation and comprehension of speech, respectively. The right hemisphere has been displaced in the drawing to show its inside surface with the anterior cingulate cortex, which is involved in arousal and attentional control in speech, and the supplementary motor cortex, which plays a role in speech initiation. Also shown is the location of the corpus callosum, which connects corresponding areas of the two hemispheres. Anatomical studies on other primate brains have shown rich reciprocal interconnections between these areas (arrows), but the corresponding anatomy in humans is not so well known.

vertebrate line, whereas the language system is much more recent. Although this language system is usually located in the left hemisphere, the underlying genetic equipment permits other placements.

Different languages can be put in different places. A stroke in one part of the brain can knock out a native language and leave intact languages learned later, or vice versa. Imaging of normal bilingual brains shows that two languages, such as French and English, can activate slightly different areas of cortex. The first language learned by a child is normally tightly organized in terms of nerve circuits in the left hemisphere, but later languages are more loosely organized. This is why it often takes longer to find words in them.

The normal placement of language in the left hemisphere usually involves both spoken and written language, but there is the fascinating case of a woman whose right hemisphere controlled writing. This was revealed because she underwent an operation for epilepsy that cut the bundle of fibers (corpus callosum) connecting the left and right hemispheres. Words that were presented to her right visual field (and thus to the left hemisphere) could be spoken out loud but could not be written. Words presented to her left visual field (right hemisphere) could not be spoken but could be written down with her left hand. Perhaps reading and writing, because they were invented much more recently than the evolved capacity for spoken language, can more easily be wired up in the brain wherever there are "spare areas."

A closer look at language development in children reveals that the developing language system is not the same as an immature version of the adult system. Massive reorganization occurs with experience. Brain imaging and electrical recordings demonstrate that word recognition tasks that at 13 months recruit both right and left cortexes condense by 20 months to activate mainly parietal and temporal regions of the left cortex. Left hemisphere injury that causes delays and deficits in the perception and production of fine-grained perceptual detail correlates with difficulties in expressive language, perceptions, and storage of the many sounds and meanings that are crucial for articulate speech. Right hemisphere injury that causes difficulties with integrating details into a coherent whole has a greater impact on word and sentence comprehension.

One theory is that children do not begin with innate representation for language but rather have innate left-right differences in the speed and style of processing, including a predisposition for extraction of perceptual detail on the left and for integration across inputs on the right. Under normal circumstances, the left temporal area recruits the left frontal cortex into an integrated system for the comprehension and generation of speech. Early focal brain injury can delay or redirect this process.

Language development as invention

One argument for innate specification of language mechanisms in the brain has been that the linguistic environment faced by a human baby is such a disordered cacophony that rules for extracting what is relevant must be preformed, not discovered. Against this argument, it has recently been found that 8-month-old human infants who are exposed for only 2 minutes to unbroken strings of nonsense syllables are able to detect the difference between three-syllable sequences that appeared as a unit and sequences that also appeared in their learning set but did so in random order. This means that infants are using simple statistical procedures to discover word boundaries in connected speech, at just the age when systematic evidence of word recognition starts to appear.

The ability to recognize words after only a few exposures and to retain this knowledge for a long time might be taken as evidence for a dedicated language-learning mechanism, but it turns out that this capacity is also seen in other domains than language learning, such as matching novel objects and sounds.

There appears to be an increasing consensus that genetic determination, or innateness, applies to the basic principles of brain organization, such as maturational schedules, input (sensory) and output (motor) pathways, processing, and representation. These are the basis of learning devices that generate higher cognitive functions, including language. Phonetic or grammatical structures may have evolved to exploit particular natural biases of the brain's perceptual and motor systems. This could make it appear that our brains were especially adapted to acquire natural language, but in fact it would be natural language that has had to change to fit the mechanisms of our brains.

Children are not just passively soaking up bits of language; they are actively constructing and inventing language as the brain develops. The modern cortex, including the areas on the left side that normally develop language functions, is multipotential in its early stages of development. Functional specificity derives from the specificity of sensory input and motor output, and linguistic knowledge and processing result from the rich connectivity that develops in between. The plausibility of these constructive models is enhanced by recent work on artificial neural networks simulated in computers, showing that they can detect patterns in input, extract phonetic and phonological structures from raw speech, and extract grammatical regularities. Models that grow by small and gradual changes show sudden vocabulary spurts of the sort that are observed in young children. Lesions in artificial networks can cause dissociations between, or differently influence, abilities to form regular and irregular verbs. Such dissociations are indeed observed in patients with brain lesions.

Brain mechanisms of language

Normally, the language faculty that each human child develops localizes the bulk of its operations in the left cortex. Sign language, like spoken language, also normally emanates from the left cerebral hemisphere, even though sign language relies on visuospatial signals that are usually processed in the right hemisphere. The lateralization of linguistic gesture (spoken or signed language) and nonlinguistic gesture (pantomime) has been compared in deaf and hearing individuals and in deaf signers with left hemisphere aphasia. The observations demonstrate a linguistic specialization of the left hemisphere that is distinct from motor or symbolic communication. A deaf signer with left hemisphere aphasia could spontaneously substitute pantomime for signs. This differential disruption of the linguistic gesture of signing and the symbolic gesture of pantomime emphasizes their functional separability and reinforces the idea that the mimetic intelligence discussed in Chapter 5 can be distinguished as an entity separable from language.

SELF-EXPERIMENT

You can demonstrate one consequence of the lateralization of language functions to one hemisphere with the following simple exercise. Ask a friend to start speaking, and then repeat what is said while he or she is saying it—that is, "shadow" your friend's speech. Now, at the same time, tap the third finger of your right hand in a regular rhythm. Then try the same thing tapping your left finger instead. Is tapping with the right finger a bit harder? For most people it is, because the right finger competes with language for the resources of the left hemisphere. The same thing happens for most deaf people when they shadow one-handed signs in American Sign Language while tapping their fingers.

Multiple language areas in the cortex

The brain location of specific language functions is being studied in increasingly fine detail by the analysis of discrete brain lesions that compromise some functions, and by the imaging of normal living human brains while they are performing those same functions. The results often are complementary. The number of "language areas" identified is multiplying on an almost daily basis as the temporal and spatial resolution of imaging techniques improve, just as is the case with other areas of perception and cognition. You might look back at the imaging experiment shown in Figure 3–8, which illustrates that speaking words activates motor areas of the left frontal lobe whose damage (as in Broca's aphasia) can interfere with speaking but not understanding. Recognition of spoken words engages the temporal-parietal areas whose damage (as in Wernicke's aphasia) can compromise understanding but not speaking. Visual presentation of words recruits the visual areas mentioned earlier.

Frontal and temporal areas become active when meaning must be attached to words, as in generating verbs to go with nouns or in grouping together related words or concepts, and the effect of practice can be monitored. An instruction to associate a verb with each noun projected on a screen initially activates frontal lobes. But after 15 minutes of practice, the activation has contracted mainly to those areas used in simply reading a word out loud. Not surprisingly, brain activation increases with the complexity of a task being faced; complex sentences cause more activation of Broca's and Wernicke's areas than simple sentences.

Different regions of the left temporal lobe, outside the classical language areas, are involved in retrieving words from our mental dictionary. Studies of patients with brain lesions and imaging studies on unimpaired patients suggest that knowledge of unique persons is associated with the anterior portion of the temporal lobe, knowledge of animals with activity in the middle part of the inferior temporal cortex, and knowledge of tools with the posterior part of the inferior temporal cortex (see Figure 11–2). Thus there appears to be a partial segregation of the systems required to bring these different classes of words or concepts into their spoken form.

Each of these systems, at its deepest level (the mental dictionary or concept level), associates an object (such as a dog) with its semantic features (furry, domestic, pet). The next level assigns proper syntax (grammatical features such as gender), and a final level matches the syntactic elements to the sounds required to make an utterance. It is at this final stage that the "tip-of-the-tongue" phenomenon can occur, when you can describe an object (furry, has four legs) but can't quite find the word.

Language relies on our current perceptions and actions as well as on our memories of objects and actions, and so it is not surprising that imaging experiments show that large areas of cortex that process sensory information and control motor output are involved not only in memory and learning but also in language. For example, speaking color words can selectively activate a region in the ventral temporal lobe just anterior to the area involved in the perception of color, and speaking action words activates an area just anterior to visual areas involved in motion perception, as well as parts of motor areas of the frontal cortex.

Figure 11–2   Regions of the temporal lobe that become active when information about persons, animals, or tools is being processed and verbally expressed.

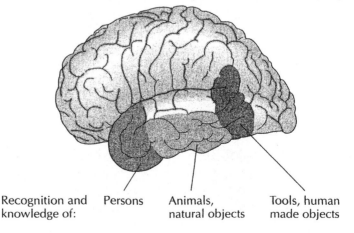

Recognition and   Persons   Animals,   Tools, human
knowledge of: natural objects   made objects

Language as accessory to other fundamental brain mechanisms

It seems reasonable to imagine that subject-verb-object ensembles (as in "I throw rock") were categories and actions that were chunked, localized, or given domains in the prelanguage brain. Language would then have been a useful adaptation that could "piggyback" on these fundamental operations by applying labels to what was already going on. Recall the evidence already cited that language is some sort of accessory module. Uniquely human capacities are found in the complete absence of language; in abnormal cases such as brain lesions and congenital lack of hearing and speech; and also in mime, tool making, and social intelligence (including the ability to comprehend complex events and remember roles, customs, and appropriate behavior). The conventional language system might be viewed as one kind of input and output domain, parallel to a mainstream of thought and awareness, possibly derivative of the basic perceiving, acting, and emotional intelligence we have discussed in the last several chapters.

The implication is that knowledge of objects that is accessible to language is stored in a distributed way, with attributes of objects stored close to the regions of cortex that perceive those attributes. At the level of word meaning, language systems have to be coordinated with non-linguistic brain areas that represent object and perceptual meanings. Brain lesion studies show that extensive systems in the left and right hemispheres process nonlanguage interactions between the body and its environment, categorizing representation (such as shape, color, sequence, and emotional state) and also more complicated, symbolic representations of objects, events, and relationships. There seems to be substantial overlap in the processing of the meanings of words and visual images. A word, with all the different kinds of information related to it, might be represented by a very far-flung net of neurons that code the thing it stands for, its sound, its syntax, its visual image, and its logic. Areas of the brain devoted to different aspects of language, grammatical rules, or storage of word meanings might be spread out in patterns, like the stripes or blobs of the visual cortex, but with finer resolution than can be revealed by brain lesions or current brain imaging techniques.

Studies on the classical aphasias we mentioned before (sensory, motor, and conduction aphasia) have been expanded to show just how discrete lesions can be, behaviorally and anatomically. The use of different aspects of language, such as proper nouns, common nouns, and irregular or regular verbs, can be specifically disrupted, which suggests that they are processed in different areas of the brain. These areas vary from person to person. The reading and/or writing of language can be disrupted by brain damage (alexia and agraphia) without damage to the hearing or speaking of language. The damage is usually in the parietal-temporal-occipital association cortex concerned with integration of visual, auditory, and tactile information.

An interesting point comes from studies of reading and writing disturbances among the Japanese. There are two distinct systems of writing Japanese. Kata kana is phonetic, with 71 graphemes in the system. Kanji is ideographic, based on the Chinese character system, with over 40,000 ideograms. Lesions of the angular gyrus of the parietal-temporal-occipital association cortex can disrupt reading of kana but leave comprehension of kanji intact.

The different functions and brain areas listed here do not send their signals to a common destination for integration, as though language appeared on a movie screen in the brain. There is no evidence for a central place where it all comes together to form the "I" that we subjectively experience when we listen and speak. Rather, language and other aspects of our cognition, such as vision, are governed by some yet-to-be-defined mechanisms that bind different brain areas together in time. How are our perception and generation of language unified? Some interesting clues on how we normally generate sentences come from normal slips of the tongue. In one rare form of aphasia, jargon aphasia, patients seem entirely normal and have normal intelligence, yet they utter sentences that are complete gibberish, like a "word salad." They do not perceive any problem as they emit complete but unrelated phrases and sentence fragments. It seems as though the underlying process that normally orders the fragments into longer, more meaningful sequences has gone awry. Speech errors such as Freudian slips (the unintended expression of a repressed sentiment) and spoonerisms (the transposition of parts of two or more words) point to how grammatical and lexical rules are working. They suggest that the act of speaking involves the generation of many possible options that vie with each other to be in a final utterance. Most of the options never reach awareness but can be revealed, for example, if we happen to say something like "barn door" when we mean "darn bore." The idea is that there is a competition among many sequences, or candidates, held in short-term unconscious memory, an interpretation not unlike the Darwin Machine model for choosing movement sequences that we described in the last section of Chapter 9. Most of these sequences are discarded after the winner—the actual utterance—has emerged.

Metaphor and the construction of language

We have said little thus far about the school of generative semanti-cists—heirs to Chomsky who place major emphasis on how context directs the shape and form of language. They claim that much of lan-guage is constructed by metaphoric operations (projections of a pattern from one domain of experience in order to structure another domain of a different kind) based on fundamental bodily functions. The idea is that the logic of muscle action in the world (up, down, sideways, in, out, containing, rotation) might be a foundation upon which logic operations of language are built. Recurring dynamic patterns of our perceptual interactions and motor programs give coherence and struc-ture to our experience. A verticality scheme, for instance, emerges from our tendency to employ an up-down orientation in picking out mean-ingful structures of our experience (trees, stairs, flagpoles, other humans). Our brains during development form themselves in an inter-action with vertical stimuli; some nerve cells are wired to specialize in them. Consider the simple and pervasive metaphorical understanding that "more is up." This derives from the verticality schema—we are understanding quantity in terms of verticality—as in "prices keep going up," and "his earnings fell." The metaphorical projection from up to more is natural, because it is related to common everyday experi-ences. When we add more liquid to a container, the level goes up. When we add more objects to a pile, the level goes up. There is, then, a physical basis for our abstract understanding of quantity. In this and many other cases, embodied human understanding is indispensable for meaning and rationality.

The in-out scheme gives rise to container metaphors based on the human body, our own in-out orientation. Examples include our speak-ing of moving into or out of a forest and our asking, "Are you in the race on Sunday?" (where the race is spoken of as a container). We use metaphors as a central tool in talking about our own mental states and the minds of others, usually without being aware of how this biases our inquiries at the outset. Most of us view our minds as containers and conceive of thoughts as being like physical objects inside them; we also take thoughts to be natural language utterances inside our heads. If you say "part of me doesn't believe he is telling the truth," you are using the convention of talking about mind parts as persons.

The hypothesis is that many of these operations are so fundamental to living in a human body that they lead to a class of perceptions, behaviors, and language conventions that are universal. They are part of the basis of the "universal mind" that we discussed in Chapter 5. The metaphorical operations used to build language, however, can be tied to specific cultural surroundings. For most of us, time not only has its basic meaning but also is treated as though it were money. ("You're wasting my time." "This gadget will save you hours." "He's living on borrowed time." "I've invested a lot of time in her.") Some cultures don't use this metaphor, just as they don't equate active with up and passive with down. In many cultures there is a metaphoric mapping of masculine and feminine onto many other dimensions, such as light-dark, public-private, science-arts, rational-intuitive, active-passive, and hard-soft. One counter-reaction to our immersion in metaphor is to argue that there is no "correct" way to perceive the world—that all the truths of our culture, including scientific dogma, are relative. Arguments against this position were outlined at the end of Chapter 7. Metaphors function as mind-tools, or as a scaffolding on which to arrange our complex physical and social reality, but they should not be taken as our only means of approaching and understanding it.

SUMMARY

The take-home message of this chapter is that the genetic endowment of all modern humans equips them to generate brain modules for processing language if they grow up in the company of other humans. The complex social organization that language makes possible is a quantum leap beyond that of our primate precursors. Studies of both human development and comparative anthropology show that isolated groups of humans can invent new languages with complex grammars and communicate them either by speaking or by making manual signs. Although we will never know exactly how and when the ability to deal with symbols in verbal or manual form first appeared, it is clear that the many specializations of our vocal apparatus that support spoken language are adaptations that have enhanced its usefulness. The same is probably true of the brain mechanisms that permit processing and analysis of rapid sound sequences. There are no obvious "language genes" whose appearance might have correlated with the evolution of language competence. It seems likely that this evolution entailed the refinement and expansion of many of the cognitive faculties already involved in sensing, acting, memory, and communication. Observations on brain lesions and imaging data both suggest that many areas of the cortex are recruited during language operations. The fact that the usual brain locations of language operations can be changed by genetic or developmental perturbations, as well as by injury, suggests that there is great plasticity in the mechanisms that put language components in place. These components appear to generate our language utterances by yet another "Darwin Machine" mechanism, in which an array of candidates for expression vie for predominance. The streams of information we emit then apply a variety of techniques, such as the use of extended metaphors, to stack meanings upon meanings to categorize our experience of the external world. It is this process that permits us to engage the topics of Part IV of this book—to share our thinking about how our self-consciousness and modern minds are integrated into a unitary whole.

Questions for Thought

1. A robust current debate centers on whether language is an evolutionary adaptation, or whether it is an accidental byproduct of humans having developed a very complex cerebral cortex. Can you offer some arguments relevant to one or the other side of this issue?

2. Several lines of evidence suggest that interacting children spontaneously invent the elements of language. Language development is not observed in the several known examples of feral children raised by animals in the wild. Can you develop the position that these observations are not relevant (or, alternatively, that they are relevant) to the question of whether stages in language development require the expression of "language enabling genes" unique to humans?

3. Brain lesions can cause specific language deficits, such as inabilities to understand, speak, write, or deal with specific categories of knowledge. Genetic mutations that influence human language ability do not cause such specific deficits. What does this suggest about how the more specific faculties are constructed?

4. Roughly normal language development can be observed in children who have had one brain hemisphere removed at an early age. Can you offer a suggestion for why, then, during normal language development, a number of language functions distribute between the two hemispheres?

Suggestions for further general reading

Crystal, D. 1987. *The Cambridge Encyclopedia of Language.* Cambridge, England: Cambridge University Press. (A presentation of the structures and varieties of languages.)

Diamond, J. 1992. *The Third Chimpanzee.* New York: Harper Collins. (Chapter 8 of this book describes anthropological studies that elucidate how different groups of humans grow different languages.)

Lakoff, G., & Johnson, M. 1980. *Metaphors We Live By.* Chicago: University of Chicago Press. (This book argues that many linguistic operations derive from basic physical operations of the human body and are further developed by the use of culturally specific metaphors.)

Pinker, S. 1994. *The Language Instinct.* New York: William Morrow. (If you are going to read only one popular book on language, this should probably be that book. It describes the construction of languages, argues that all humans have a similar evolved capacity to learn language, and discusses some of the brain mechanisms involved.)

Reading on more advanced or specialized topics

Elman, J.L., Bates, E.A., Johnson, M.H., Karmiloff-Smith, A., Parisi, D., & Plunkett, K. 1996. *Rethinking Innateness: A Connectionist Perspective on Development.* Cambridge, MA: M.I.T. Press. (This book opposes the argument of Pinker and others that many detailed aspects of language are genetically determined.)

Gazzaniga, M.S., Ivry, R.B., & Mangun, G.R. 1998. *Cognitive Neuroscience.* New York: Norton. (Chapter 8 of this book is devoted to language and the brain and is an up-to-date summary of what we have learned from lesion and imaging studies.)

Nobre, A.C., & Plunkett, K. 1997. The neural system of language: structure and development. *Current Opinions in Neurobiology* 7(2):262–268. (This is a summary of neuroimaging and brain lesion studies that suggest the neural system for language is widely distributed and shares organizational principles with other cognitive systems in the brain.)

Part IV

Modern Mind

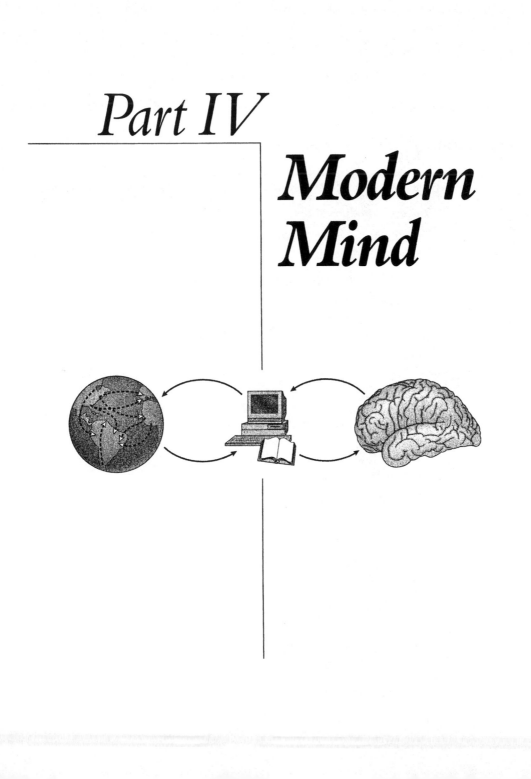

Chapter 12

Conscious Mind

The two final chapters of this book are included to paint a more comprehensive picture of our modern minds and how they exist in a sometimes uneasy alliance with bodies that were designed for conditions of the Paleolithic. The preceding chapters have elaborated on the theme that our brain is not a general-purpose problem solver, using one common process for all tasks, but rather a collection of semi-independent devices tailored to specific jobs. Large computational problems (such as seeing, hearing, moving, and talking) are split into many parts, all processed by specific brain regions. These regions and their tasks can be revealed when they are damaged by brain lesions or genetic mutations. They can sometimes be seen directly in living brains by using imaging techniques. The specialized modules interact extensively to perform their functions. Some of these modules (for example, the visual areas specializing in form, motion, or color) have been partially dissected not just logically but also literally, because their anatomical locations are fairly precise and well known. The anatomy and physiology—the where, what, and how—of other modules in the brain are generally less clear.

This chapter considers some ideas about how this all comes together to generate consciousness and our subjective experience. We begin by returning briefly to some issues we first raised in Chapter 1, to note some classical debates on the question of consciousness, whether "mindstuff" is in the same category as the rest of the physical reality we know and whether consciousness can ever be explained. Assuming a positive answer to this question, we then return to the arena of cognitive neuroscience to discuss our conscious awareness system more thoroughly, briefly outlining some of the neural underpinnings of the attention and working-memory systems of the frontal lobes. Then we review some experiments in cognitive psychology that show how the players or agents inside our heads, of which we are largely unconscious, render meaningless the "Where does it all come together?" question. The next section considers consciousness by examining its perturbations, as in sleep and other altered states. Finally, after reviewing current work on the neural correlates of consciousness, we outline several models and metaphors for consciousness, ideas of what our "operating system" is like, and how the "I" that you are experiencing right now might emerge from it. Our conscious awareness is a small fraction of the many operations going on in our brains, and the bottom line is that we must be disabused of any notion that "our" thoughts reflect, in any direct sense, the real operations of our minds.

The mind/body problem

René Descartes' famous formulation "I think, therefore I am" posited a clear dividing line between the mind and the brain. The accompanying self-experiment illustrates the depth to which this idea has permeated our culture and the way we construct ourselves. If you are a classical dualist, you might assign the "I" to the realm of the spirit and the brain to the realm of the physical body, thus taking issue with the materialism of modern science and the points outlined in Chapter 1, which argues that mind is the sum of the physical components of the brain— its ions, molecules, and cells and their activities. However, if the self or "I" is different from the stuff of the brain, what is it? Is it some special kind of mindstuff or essence distinct from the physical matter of which you are composed? Dualists have the problem of explaining how mind, as a nonphysical entity with no mass or energy, could interact with the physical stuff of the brain.

SELF-EXPERIMENT

Try the following exercise, which was suggested by the philosopher Daniel Dennett. Look away from this page while you repeat to yourself, "I have a brain." Now look away while you think or speak, "This brain has itself." The first statement probably feels comfortable to you, whereas the second feels a bit more alien, even though, as far as we know, both statements are saying the same thing. Thinking "I have a brain" corresponds to our daily experience of a narrative self, a little person or "I" inside our heads, distinct from our body, always seeing and commenting on what is taking place.

There is another way in which you might say that mind is different from brain without having to invent some sort of spiritual or nonmaterial essence. You could believe that mind is ultimately made up of atoms and molecules, like everything we know about, but distinguish what mind does—the functions it carries out—from the machinery that carries out those functions. Thus you take mind or consciousness to be more than just the electrical activities of cells in your brain in the same way a movie is different from a description of the moving parts of the movie projector and the path of the light through it, or the way writing is more than small pieces of graphite spread on a paper surface in a continuous line. You could argue that the input-analysis-output functions of our minds (taking in information, analyzing it, then acting on it) could be carried out by different kinds of hardware—perhaps by computers, Martians, or zombies. In this book, we have not been dealing with these more hypothetical options, but rather have focused on the biology of mind in humans and other animals as we know them. From this perspective, the analyses of what a mind does and what it is made of begin to converge as we learn more and more from experiments in basic neuroscience and cognitive psychology.

Thinking that you are just the physical stuff of your brain and that a "chemistry of consciousness" specifies your behavior may not feel quite right to you. But consider how profoundly your mood can be altered by just a bit of coffee or alcohol or by the brain chemistry underlying emotions that we discussed in Chapter 10. Consider the numerous cases in the psychiatric literature of people who, with no previous history of mental illness, became psychotic and were miraculously cured when a bacterial infection of their cerebrospinal fluid was diagnosed and antibiotics applied. Where does the body stop and the mind start in these cases? It makes more sense to think of them as a unit. Chemistry can alter our behavior, and our behavior can alter our chemistry. As an example of the latter, remember a time when you have moved quickly to avoid sudden danger—and then remained excited for a while as adrenaline continued to pump into your bloodstream.

Can the problem of consciousness be solved?

Some modern commentators despair of ever explaining consciousness. They just cannot grant that nerve signals are the kind of stuff that can make up the qualitative feel or content of consciousness. How can understanding nerve signals ever translate to what an apple tastes like? The philosopher Owen Flanagan describes these individuals as the new mysterians, the old mysterians being the Cartesian dualists described in the previous section. The new mysterians don't deny that mind and consciousness exist and operate in accordance with natural principles, but they argue that our very cognitive constitution prevents us from achieving a complete description of them. Asking ourselves to understand consciousness might be like asking a television set to report on its own inner workings. Just as we don't expect a dog's brain to understand quantum mechanics, we can't necessarily expect our own brains to understand everything. However, a useful approach is to act as though we *can* understand everything, because there is no way of knowing that we can't understand something until after we have tried.

It could be that, just as physicists and mathematicians have acknowledged the limits to our understanding that are imposed by Heisenberg's Uncertainty Principle and Godel's Incompleteness Theorem, we are closed off from knowing what sort of natural phenomenon consciousness is. It seems premature, however, to say that our brains can never understand themselves; after all, they can do any number of other unusual things. What we can do is pursue descriptions from cognitive psychology of how mental life works—descriptions given by neuroscience research—and also just listen carefully to what individuals have to say about how things seem. In some ways, we are similar to the subject of the familiar joke about the drunk looking for car keys he lost near some dark bushes. He is looking for them under a nearby street light "because the light is better here." We can mimic this drunk when we are looking for an explanation of our minds, and remain infatuated with our ideas of what a mind should be (by insisting, for example, that brains can be modeled on the architecture of modern computers) rather than trying to find out how the conscious human mind actually works. We can become so impressed by the richness of what we know that we lose sight of the much larger area of the unknown.

We are like the map makers of the 16th century who were very pleased with the sophistication of their efforts to depict the globe, especially when compared with Greek and Roman attempts. The large errors and unknowns that we now see in these old maps are revealed only in hindsight. We surely can expect our descendants to be acutely aware of the limitations of 20th-century efforts to understand the brain.

The machinery of awareness

Let's turn now from this brief discussion of what we might or might not be able to know to scientific studies on the nature of our awareness and attention. Our daily life is a constant checking of what is happening right now against what just happened a few moments ago. We hold information, anticipations, or goals in our short-term working memory for a time and then release them if they become irrelevant. Should we wish to retain knowledge of a face or a phone number, the mechanisms of episodic memory described in Chapter 6 are activated. If we later need to remember a name or number, we can fetch it from that long-term memory and place it back in our working memory.

The classical paradigm for engaging the interaction between current awareness and short-term memory is the *delayed-choice test*, in which a human volunteer or an animal subject is rewarded for recognizing a previously presented image or situation. Electrical recordings from animals and brain imaging experiments on human subjects show activation of the prefrontal cortex during such tests. This activation persists though a delayed-choice test even if distracting and irrelevant auditory and visual stimuli are presented. Prefrontal cortex is linked to all of the perceptual systems, and it apparently orchestrates an emphasis on cues that are relevant to current needs over irrelevant stimuli. This is why we are more likely to notice the smell of food when we are hungry than when we have just eaten.

It has been proposed that working memory has a central controller and a group of "slave systems," the two main slave systems being one for silent speech or verbal memory and the other for visuospatial information. Imaging studies, however, do not reveal an obvious activity corresponding to a central controller. Rather, different kinds of working memory (such as for spatial locations, object identification, facial memory, and verbal memory) may correlate with activation of different prefrontal regions. Moving from simple delayed-choice tests to more complicated tasks (such as articulating a random list of each number from 1 to 10 with no repetition, or saying which words in a list read aloud were vegetable names) causes activation to spread from a limited part of the right frontal cortex to higher dorsolateral areas of both right and left prefrontal cortex.

Phonological memory and subvocal rehearsal activate Broca's area of the left hemisphere as well as several other areas. Our visual working memory recruits areas of the frontal, parietal, and occipital lobes of the right hemisphere. PET scan studies demonstrate that while working memory is performing "what" tasks, different loci are active in our prefrontal cortex than when "where" tasks are being performed. Higher resolution magnetic resonance imaging shows sustained activation of different areas of frontal cortex for face memory and letter memory. Tasks that require working memory for locations activate mainly right brain regions, whereas letter-memory tasks activate primarily left brain areas. In both human and monkey brains, the ventral stream of "where" visual information mentioned in Chapter 8 moves into dorsolateral prefrontal cortex; the dorsal "what" stream enters mainly ventrolateral areas. This is shown in Figure 12–1. Interestingly,

The "what" and "where" streams of information sent forward from parietal and temporal lobes project into the working-memory areas of the frontal cortex.

there appears to have been a displacement of these areas in the human to make room for the expansion of prefrontal areas serving language and higher cognition. Recordings from individual cells in monkey prefrontal cortex show that they monitor expectancy and goal-directed behavior. Some cells fire while "what" information is being held, others fire while "where" information is being held, and still others register a combination of "what" and "where" activity. Working memory is impaired by lowered levels of the neurotransmitter dopamine (this happens in patients with Parkinson's disease) and is enhanced by increasing dopamine levels.

The contents of our awareness and working memory reflect only one of many parallel tracks that deal with perception and action. Many studies have documented this, such as experiments that have demonstrated and mapped brain regions that are responsive to novelty without awareness. Subjects were asked to press a keypad to indicate numbers (1, 2, or 3) appearing on a screen in what appeared to be random order but in fact followed a complex sequence. Improvement in performance indicated that subjects had learned the sequences even though they were unaware of the existence of any order. If the order of the sequence was then changed, changes in right prefrontal and other areas were noted, even though subjects remained unaware of the changes in number presentation.

Figure 12–1 Projection of spatial perception and object recognition into the frontal lobe working-memory areas of the brain.

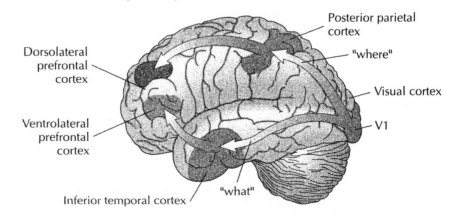

The brain's time and space: the disappearance of "I"

What we are holding in our working memory—our current awareness and recall of our immediate past—are central components of our experience of an "I." This "I" is the basis for our common-sense notion that our mind has some central point where sensations and perceptions ultimately are noticed, and where commands and actions ultimately begin. Naturally, this conviction leads us to look for an actual place in the brain where it all comes together. But then, who would be watching that central place? And wouldn't that watcher need yet another to watch it? It is one of the main messages of this book that there *is* no place where everything comes together and that looking for the place in the brain where the "I" is makes no more sense than looking for the place in a tornado where "the storm" is. The "I" is a construct—an idea that we employ to make sense of what many unconscious processes finally lead us to do—much as "the storm" is the sum of what the turbulent, spinning masses of air in a tornado do.

We have already noted that the distinction between perception and action grows very fuzzy as we work our way further into the brain and shift to the time interval of 50–500 milliseconds after a sensory stimulus or before a movement. This is because there is no single point in the brain through which all information funnels. The reason it seems natural to make the distinction is that most of our conscious experience of sensing or acting unfolds over a period of seconds rather than milliseconds, as when we see a ball tossed and look to where it will land, or when we perform the motions of peeling potatoes. But in the central brain processing that occurs in the interface between our acting and reacting, most of the action is very fast—so fast that auditory input, for example, can influence a visual search on the time scale of 100–300 milliseconds.

SELF-EXPERIMENT

To give you a feel for the lengths of time we are talking about, it takes about 1000 milliseconds to say "one Mississippi," we can start and stop a stopwatch in roughly 175 milliseconds, one frame of a movie film projects for about 40 milliseconds, most nerve cells work on a time scale of 1–10 milliseconds. If you can drum all the fingers of one of your hands on the desk five times while you are saying "one Mississippi" a finger is hitting the surface every 40 milliseconds.

Try the experiment of holding a 3×5 card just above a friend's thumb and forefinger and ask your friend to catch the card when you let it go. He or she can't do it if the card is immediately above the thumb and forefinger. The drop takes 100–150 milliseconds, faster than the nerve signal that it is dropping can go from eye to brain to fingers. If you hold the card 3 inches above the fingers, however, your friend can catch it; 300–400 milliseconds is enough time.

Plastic representations of time and space

Two well-known cognitive psychology experiments show that in these small time intervals, our brain is an assembly of agents with minds of their own (so to speak) that can play with even the most basic representations of time and space in ways to which we are normally oblivious. What happens during these intervals shows the impossibility of the "I" acting as boss or command central. These experiments emphasize perception, but a corresponding list could be drawn up of experiments dealing with the output of the brain, or action.

The first experiment involves a phenomenon that has been named the phi effect; it is depicted in Figure 12–2. Two stationary spots of light separated by as much as 4 degrees of visual angle are lit in succession. First one spot is on for 150 milliseconds, then both are dark for 50 milliseconds, and then the other spot is on for 150 milliseconds. They appear to be a single spot moving in a continuous line. If the first spot is red and the second is green, the moving spot appears to have changed its color from red to green abruptly in the middle of its passage, during the period of darkness. Why is it that our perception is that the color changed to green before the green light actually came on? There is virtually no difference in the response time if a subject is asked to press a button as soon as the red spot comes on, whether or not the green spot follows! It can be shown that button-pressing responses would have to have been initiated before the discrimination of the second stimulus, the green spot. Thus we did not hold up our conscious experience for at least 200 milliseconds and revise history. Rather, processing is continually going on. A revision occurs that leads us to think the spot changed color in mid-flight. At the level of basic brain operations, this could translate into something very straightforward. For example, the V5 region in the cortex (see Chapter 8) responds to motions and to apparent motion. Perhaps some activity in area V5 is the brain concluding that an intervening motion occurred.

Figure 12–2   The phi effect. If a red and a green spot of light are flashed on a screen, as shown, in rapid succession, they appear to be a single moving spot whose color changes in the middle of the motion.

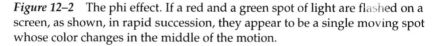

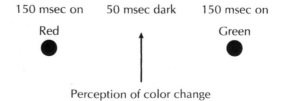

We must distinguish here between the representation and the represented: The brain's representation of time needn't use time-in-the-brain. The objective sequence of events occurring in the brain of an observer can be different from the subjective sequence of events reported. The mis-discrimination of red-turning-to-green occurred in the brain after the discrimination of the green spot (in objective time), but the subjective or narrative sequence is red spot, then red turning to green, then finally green spot. Another way of putting it is to say that a unit of subjective time can incorporate several units of physical time, as shown in Figure 12–3, and, if appropriate, rearrange them.

A similar situation occurs for the representation of space in the brain, which, as we saw in Chapter 8, does not always use space-in-the-brain to represent space. These discrepancies are no different in principle from shooting scenes in a movie in a different sequence from the one in which they finally appear, or reading "Bill arrived at the party after Sally, but Jane came earlier than both of them." You learn of Bill's arrival before you learn of Jane's earlier arrival. (In fact, the representation of time needn't be temporal at all. Think of the way in which different points of time are represented by a wall calendar.)

A second classical experiment involves what is called metacontrast. A display device that can flash a stimulus for very brief intervals, around 1–500 milliseconds, is used to show the two stimuli represented in Figure 12–4 for 30 milliseconds each, about as long as a single frame of television, the second stimuli immediately following the first. In the figure, the disc appears to the side of the ring, but in the experiment the ring is flashed right on top of the disc, and its inner diameter is exactly the same as the outer diameter of the disc.

Figure 12–3 Space and time in the brain. The brain can store events that occur during sequential units of physical time (indicated by the Roman numerals) in temporary holding spaces, or buffers (indicated by the Arabic numerals). These buffers can rearrange the events in a way that past experience indicates makes the most "sense" before a subjective report is generated. In the case of the phi effect, the brain appears to be following a rule that "two dots appearing in rapid succession near each other probably represent a single moving spot of light."

III..........IV...........V............VI..........VII........VIII.......

Physical time ⟶

234........345........456........567........678........789........

Subjective time ⟶

Figure 12–4 Metacontrast. If the first and second stimuli are flashed in rapid succession, only the second (the ring) is observed, even though the first (the disc) is observed if it is flashed by itself. (In the experiment, the disc to the left is actually flashed in the center of the ring.) Thus the brain takes a while to decide what is "really" there, and an initial stimulus can be overwritten by another that has features in common with the first.

Individuals report seeing only the second stimulus, the ring, although they can report the disc if it is shown separately. The brain, initially informed that something with a circular contour in a particular place happened, swiftly receives confirmation that there was indeed a ring, with an inner and outer contour. Without further supporting evidence that there was a disc, the brain arrives at the conservative conclusion that there was only a ring. The disc was briefly in a position—functional and spatial—to contribute to a later report, but this state lapsed. There is no reason to insist that the state was inside the charmed circle of consciousness until it got overwritten, or to insist that it never quite achieved this state. Preliminary versions that were composed at particular times and places in the brain were later withdrawn from circulation, replaced by more refined versions. Multiple preliminary versions might be withdrawn, but they also can influence a final version, even if they are not experienced. For example, a very brief presentation of a priming word can influence the judged meaning of a target word that follows within 100 milliseconds, even though the priming word is not experienced or reported.

Our intuition, what we think is happening, is that information gets moved around the brain with events occurring in sequence, like railroad cars on a track. The order in which the information passes some point, or station, will be the order in which it arrives in consciousness. But that isn't what we observe in the experiments described in this section, and there is a good reason. The brain's job is to use incoming information swiftly to "produce a future," staying one step ahead of disaster, and it has to do this efficiently. The processes that do this are spatially distributed across functional regions of a large brain, and communication between different regions is relatively slow. Why wait for everything to come together if appropriate action could be taken faster without that delay?

The futility of asking "where does it all come together?"

The philosopher Daniel Dennett uses an analogy to drive home the futility of the question "Exactly when do you become conscious of a stimulus?" Imagine your brain to be like the British Empire, and rephrase the question as follows: "Exactly when did the British Empire become aware of the truce in the War of 1812?" News of the truce, signed in Belgium on December 24, 1814, reached different parts of the British Empire (in America, India, Africa, and so on) at different times, and it did not reach the most far-flung outposts until mid-January 1815. There is no way to pin down a day and hour when "the Empire" knew. The battle of New Orleans was fought 15 days after the truce that made it moot. Even if we can give precise times for the various moments at which various officials of the Empire became informed, none of these moments can be singled out as the time the Empire itself was informed. This is entirely analogous to asking exactly when we become conscious of a stimulus. Because cognition and control, and hence consciousness, are distributed throughout the brain, no one moment can count as the precise moment at which each conscious event happens.

In Dennett's "multiple drafts" theory of consciousness, all varieties of perception—of thought or mental activity—are accomplished in the brain by parallel multitrack processes of interpretation and elaboration of sensory inputs. Information entering the nervous system is subject to continuous "editorial revision." The brain adjusting for movements of our head and eyes so that we experience a stable visual world is an example of such revision. Revision lets us watch a French film dubbed in English, not noticing the discrepancy between lip motions and sounds heard. All these editorial processes are occurring over large fractions of a second, during which time various additions, incorporations, emendations, and overwriting of contents can occur.

The "common-sense" idea has been that a where-it-all-comes-together hierarchy responds to a watcher and then instructs a director who commands output. This view has been decisively replaced by the idea of many competing parallel streams of input and output that are constantly being compared, sorted, and tested for appropriateness. The interpretations and actions that "work" or "are appropriate" rise to the surface to constitute our subjective experience.

Spatially and temporally distributed content fixations in the brain (such as visual, auditory, and locomotor) are precisely locatable in both space and time, but their onsets do not mark the onset of consciousness of their content. These content discriminations produce something rather like a narrative stream, or sequence, subject to continuous editing by many processes distributed around the brain. There are ongoing multiple drafts; there is never a final draft, just a current version. This applies not only to input and sensing but also to acting, moving, speaking, and responding to the question "What do I do next?"

The "extended present"—during which multiple drafts can be tested, expanded, contracted, and rearranged to make subjective time—is different from physical time. Different states of vigilance, or mind-altering drugs, appear to change the depth of the conscious present. In his description of being under the influence of mescaline, Aldous Huxley mentions greatly enhanced visual and auditory impressions, as though sensory activity were continuing to reverberate more strongly beyond its normal limits, perhaps changing the duration of the conscious present. Depressed people sometimes describe loss of visual intensity, colors appearing flat and washed out, as though sensory activity had been curtailed and the conscious present shrunk. The ultimate damping down might occur in sleep, when the conscious present effectively shrinks to nothing, and subjective time becomes the same as the stream of physical time.

Sleep and other altered states of consciousness

One route to getting a handle on the experience of consciousness is to contrast it with what might be going on when we either are not conscious or are in another state that feels very different. During a substantial fraction of all our lives, our brains are not computing an "I" but are doing something else: sleeping and dreaming. The two systems that alternate to control waking and sleeping roughly mirror the division of labor between the sympathetic (noradrenergic) and parasympathetic (cholinergic) branches of our autonomic nervous system. In the waking state, aminergic neurons in the brainstem that radiate to the cortex cause alertness by literally "spritzing" the brain with neuromodulators (see Figure 12–5) at the same time that the sympathetic (arousal) part of the peripheral autonomic nervous system is activated.

Waking and sleeping are controlled by two hierarchical systems spanning the brainstem to the cortex, systems so reliable that it is as rare for us to gain awareness that we are dreaming when we are dreaming as it is for us to hallucinate when we are awake.

Sleep occurs when this system is suppressed as a cholinergic spritzing system, also shown in Figure 12–5, which brings up parasympathetic (resting) nervous activity. Nerve cells in the rostral hypothalamus also play a central role in this sleep generation. During sleep, the brainstem is instructing your spinal cord that you can't feel and you can't move, and the cortex is disconnected from sensory input and motor output.

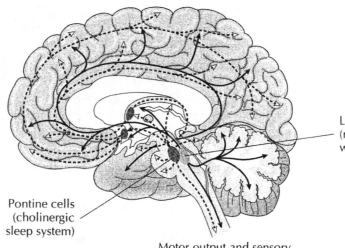

Locus coeruleus (noradrenergic waking system)

Pontine cells (cholinergic sleep system)

Motor output and sensory input blocked during sleep

Figure 12–5 During the waking state, a noradrenergic system is activated to maintain arousal of the cortex (solid lines). During sleep, this system is suppressed as a cholinergic system predominates and induces periods of REM sleep (dashed lines). Adapted from Figure 15.11 and 15.14 in Bear et al. *Neuroscience: Exploring the Brain.*

Stages of sleep and dreaming

A typical night of sleep proceeds in four or five cycles, each usually described as having four stages. A cycle starts with light dreaming (called *REM sleep,* for *rapid eye movement*), during which heart and respiration are active and vivid hallucinations and emotions are occurring. It then progresses through two intermediate stages to stage 4, wherein there is no dreaming, and body respiration and temperature are at their lowest point. This non-REM sleep is known to boost immune function. The cycle ends with a return to REM sleep. REM sleep appears to be essential for long-term maintenance of the brain; animal and human subjects deprived of it eventually die. Brain imaging experiments show that REM sleep correlates with the activation of several areas, particularly the amygdala.

Why do we dream? No one is sure, but one theory is that dreaming plays some role in the consolidation of memories, experiences, and emotions. One particularly fascinating study shows that in rats, hippocampal cells that show place-specific activity during waking are selectively activated in subsequent sleep, possibly participating in a memory consolidation process. During dreaming, the brain may be making up stories to make sense of emotions. (Human studies show that the emotions are twice as likely to be unpleasant than pleasant.) The sleep researcher Alan Hobson offers an "activation-synthesis hypothesis" that suggests that cholinergic and other activation rising from the brainstem stimulates the cortex relatively nonspecifically, causing it to confabulate the storylines of dreams, which are frequently bizarre and disconnected, to go with the underlying chemistry. Such a model is not unreasonable, given the examples of confabulation exhibited by split-brain and anosognosic patients mentioned in earlier chapters. The brain is essentially insane during dreams, exhibiting bizarre cognitive features such as discontinuity, incongruity, and hallucinations. Anyone who displayed the sort of mental activity during wakefulness that goes on during dreams would be judged psychotic.

What does all of this have to do with understanding consciousness? One interesting suggestion is that wakefulness and REM sleep may be very similar states, subserved by an internal thalamocortical loop that proceeds during both. The idea is that the thalamus and cortex are expending most of their effort talking back and forth with each other. At no time does sensory input constitute more than a fraction of what is going on. The major difference between wakefulness and sleep lies in the weight given to incoming sensory input. In this model, consciousness is essentially a closed loop, driven by intrinsically active cells. Thus we have the image of a central churning processor that can proceed in a manner either dependent on or independent of sensory input—an internal babbler that keeps on going in dreams. In this model, our brains would be continuously spinning a self, automatically generating a web of perceptions, words, and deeds. During waking, this spinning would be guided by the environment.

Mystical experience

The uncoupling of the brain from sensory input and motor output during sleep is reminiscent of another altered state: mystical experience. Mystical experiences involving a very different sense of "I" have been reported throughout history by individuals in different religious traditions. They frequently are accompanied by feelings of deep conviction, ineffability, and cosmic unity. The science journalist Timothy Ferris suggests possible correlations between these experiences and processes in the brain: The conviction is that something powerful has been learned beyond the world of the senses (an uncoupling of what the brain is doing from sensory input, as in sleep?). Ineffability is the experience of being beyond words (reflecting a core symbolic device lying at deeper levels than the modules of language that provide it with input and output?). The cosmic sense of unity is that everything contains the seed of everything else (is this the mechanism that makes a unified mind out of the disparate parts of the human brain?). Might enlightenment correspond to breaking through the barrier of language, to awareness of the mental modules responsible for representing the many functions of the brain as a whole? Or could meditation systematically reduce mental activity to the point of being devoid of content while still aware—a state independent of perceptions and actions?

We enter another sort of state in which we are not computing an "I" when we are made unconscious by anesthesia. Interestingly, human subjects show implicit memory of a random word list read while they are unconscious; thus, if presented with another random list, they are more likely to select the words that were read without knowing why. When the brain activity of unconscious and conscious subjects is imaged during reading of the first list, both show increased activity in verbal memory areas, but activity in the mediodorsal thalamic nucleus is much higher in conscious subjects. This suggests that distinctions between conscious and unconscious memory may depend on the presence or absence of correlated thalamic activity, and it reinforces the idea that thalamic activity is a necessary component of the conscious state.

Perhaps mystical phenomena have more to do with the internal architecture of the brain than with the phenomena of the outer world, corresponding to a mind detached from the thoughts that are its normal objects.

Humor and laughter

Does laughter give us a window on the mind? Ferris, whom we just mentioned, offers the interesting notion that laughter arises from the interaction of two programs in the brain: an Apollo program, which constructs plausible models of reality, and a Pan program, which challenges such models. The Apollo program is sober, responsible, and creative, but the models it creates always have flaws. The Pan program is irreverent, skeptical, and playful. Hence we have a god that builds models and a god that mocks and tears them down. A laugh is the energy released when the Pan program spots a potentially dangerous error in a model crafted by Apollo, but the error turns out to be harmless. The stress first aroused is then quickly dispelled through the physical manifestations of laughter. The idea is that we take pleasure in laughter both because we enjoy the release from anxiety that it provides and because the brain feels pleasure in discovering incongruities between perception and reality.

Possible locations for the Apollo and Pan programs are suggested by observations on anosognosic patients (see Chapter 7). Patients with right hemisphere damage who deny the possession of some parts of their body are much more likely to confabulate rationalizations of their situation. It is as though a right hemisphere locus of emotions involved in detecting and reacting to anomalies and discrepancies has been disabled. The left hemisphere, whose job is to make up plausible stories, is no longer edited or monitored by the right hemisphere. Another dissociation into component selves is observed in split-brain patients who confabulate with their linguistic left hemisphere the reason for a behavior that is initiated by an instruction directed to their nonverbal right hemisphere. Observations such as these remind us again that consciousness is far from being a unitary phenomenon.

Neural correlates and models of consciousness

Earlier we asked about the neuronal correlates of our visual experience (see Chapter 8); we would also like to know the explicit neuronal correlates of other aspects of our conscious experience. Are there specific neurons whose activity mediates consciousness, whose firing gives rise to the current content of our consciousness? We are looking for mechanisms that support the brain's awareness of a small fraction of all the information available to it—information that includes our experience, identity, sensations, perceptions, action, attention, memory, emotional states, and so on. Conscious awareness is just the tip of a large, unconscious iceberg. Its most common metaphor is that of a spotlight surrounded by a fringe, or halo, of lesser illumination.

You might suppose, given the increasing respectability of efforts to look for neural correlates of consciousness, that a well-defined problem was being pursued. This is far from the truth, because in most cases we lack a thorough or rigorous description of what it is we are trying to explain. Before we can make much headway regarding neural correlates of consciousness we need to specify what varieties of consciousness we're talking about. At a minimum we must distinguish, as outlined in Chapter 1, "consciousness" from "self-consciousness" from "reflexive self-consciousness." The latter consists of the internal simulation of self-reference—of thinking about thinking—that appears to be unique to humans. Humans have a variety of "meta" levels of cognition, of conscious states that think about each other (such as the ego states mentioned in Chapter 7) or about lower levels (such as the primary and secondary emotions described in Chapter 10). Furthermore, our consciousness is a constant mingling of our present experience with the past memories evoked by that experience. An underlying self-system appears to interpose itself as an editor of our perceptions, as noted in Chapter 8, a system that can alter or delete items that threaten it.

Determining what nerve-firing patterns correlate with even the simplest of these varieties of consciousness is a daunting task. Many so-called neuronal codes have yet to be cracked. At a fundamental level we have to know, for example, what the firing of action potentials by single nerve cells in our brain means. It has commonly been supposed that the information is contained just in the firing *rate*, the number of action potentials traveling down its axons in any given period. Recent work has suggested, however, that firing patterns may have clustered substructures, or temporal codes, that communicate several different meanings at once. It is also likely that the meaning of an action potential train is affected by whether it is in synchrony with the action potentials of other cells.

We have the technical problem that we can record the detailed activity of only one neuron or a small number of neurons at the same time. This is like trying to decipher a television video image one pixel at a time while the image is constantly changing. Remarkably enough, despite this, the activity of some cells in the visual cortex can be correlated with subjective visual perception. We also can use imaging techniques (such as EEG, PET, and MRI) that sample the activity of many nerve cells without giving much detail about each, but these do not yet provide the resolution required to define functional splotches, blobs, or columns of cells that have dimensions of less than 1 millimeter. What they can give us is gross neuronal correlates such as those showing activation of motion-processing regions of the visual cortex.

Brain structures required for conscious awareness

What, then, is it that binds together, and selects from the many assemblies of neurons, the awareness of the moment? Modern answers to this question of how brain cells might generate behavior or consciousness often start with a suggestion by the Canadian psychologist Donald Hebb: that nerve cells related to a particular function form a so-called cell assembly, a sort of "three-dimensional fishnet" that can be dispersed widely through the brain. As an analogy at the level of human culture, consider the residents of a large city who organize themselves into different interest groups: families, the Lutheran Church, a motorcycle gang, a university's alumni club, an environmental group, bridge foursomes, and so on. These social assemblies are interconnected by overlapping memberships. Any particular assembly reaches the threshold of being active as a group (in other words, it meets) only a small fraction of the time. And some of these groups may occasionally join together in larger associations to address common interests. Most individuals belong to many such groups.

What evidence is there for such nerve cell assemblies? The closest we come is in observations that neurons activated by the same object in the world discharge in synchrony. Recall that this correlated firing was proposed in Chapter 8 (in the section "A binding process underlies visual perception") as a solution to the binding problem of how different aspects of a visual stimulus are organized into a perception. Several observations suggest that the thalamus is needed to bring these bound assemblies to awareness. It sits at the center of the radial organization of the brain, much like the hub of a bicycle wheel, which connects to the rim of the wheel with a large number of spokes (see Figure 12–6). Large areas of cortex can be removed without abolishing awareness (as in patients who have lost most of their frontal, occipital, temporal, or parietal lobes yet remain aware), but bilateral lesions that occur in the relatively small intralaminar nuclei of the thalamus when its blood supply is interrupted do cause loss of conscious awareness. This area makes reciprocal connections with nearly all parts of the cortex.

Different cortical areas have different weights in contributing to consciousness and to subjective "what it feels like" experience. The temporal lobes, and in particular the amygdala, appear to be central. The most profound disturbances in consciousness are those that generate temporal lobe seizures. Nothing dramatic happens to consciousness if you damage the frontal lobes, or portions of higher sensory or motor areas. The temporal lobes could be viewed as being an interface between perception and action, where the significance or meaning of things to the organism is being determined.

How might the intralaminar nuclei interact with other cortical areas in generating consciousness? The neurophysiologist Rodolfo Llinas has suggested that the intralaminar nucleus is the seat of a scanning mechanism that operates every 12.5 milliseconds. This mechanism sends out a series of overlapping 40-cycle-per-second (hertz) signals (these are bursts of action potentials occurring every 25 milliseconds that sweep across the brain). These entrain synchronized cells in the cortex that are currently recording sensory information to their own rhythm (see Figure 12–6). The synchronized cells then fire a coherent wave of messages back to the thalamus. The phase of the 40-hertz signal can be reset by new input. Llinas likens the wave of nervous impulses, radiating out from around the intralaminar nucleus to overlying parts of the cortex, to the central arm of an old-fashioned radar screen, illuminating each object in its path as it moves. The responses received by the thalamus within one cycle of its scan are perceived as a single moment of consciousness. A succession of such moments are created so fast that they seem to be continuous. In this model, consciousness is the dialog

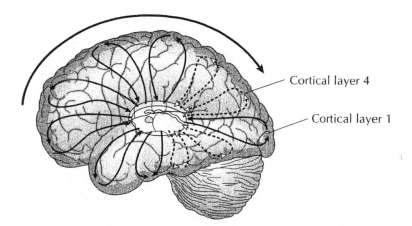

Cortical layer 4

Cortical layer 1

Figure 12–6 One model for how different aspects of a conscious experience may be bound together. Two systems linking thalamus and cortex are proposed. The first (dashed lines) is a series of closed oscillating loops between specific sensory or motor nuclei of the thalamus and the regions of cortex to which they report via layer 4 of the cortex. Within each modality (visual, auditory, somatosensory, and so on), the firing of cells reflecting the relevant percept are coordinated. Each of these is then bound or recruited into a larger unison by a second, more global assembly of loops between the thalamus and layer 1 of the cortex (solid lines). These sweep as waves of activity from the front to the back of the cortex, as indicated by the arrow at the top, starting every 12.5 milliseconds. Each of the waves has a frequency of about 40 hertz, corresponding to bursts of action potentials occurring every 25 milliseconds. Each of the sweeps that start every 12.5 milliseconds corresponds to one "quantum" of conscious experience.

between the thalamus and the cerebral cortex, as mediated by the senses. The thalamus playing the central role seems logical, because it is the structure through which all of the sensory information coming to the brain must pass.

It is interesting that coherent, 40-hertz electromagnetic activity is strong in people who are awake or in rapid eye movement (REM) dreaming sleep but is very reduced during deep sleep. It is reset by sensory stimuli in the waking state, but not during either REM or deep sleep. This is one basis for the suggestion that REM sleep might be a correlate of mental awareness, reflecting resonance between thalamo-cortical-specific and nonspecific loops. The specific loops may give the content of cognition, and a nonspecific loop the temporal binding required for the unity of cognitive experience. This system would be modulated by an arousal system, known since the 19th century, that originates in the brainstem reticular core and projects through relays in the thalamus to the cortex. Electrical stimulation of this core can enhance the 40-hertz signal as well as the synchronization of responses in the visual cortex. A word of caution is necessary here: We don't really have evidence yet that these 40-hertz signals are any more significant than the 60-hertz hum of the power transformer on your stereo sound system or personal computer. These signals may just be saying that the system is operational, not telling us much about its specific states.

Generating an apparent "I"

There is a growing consensus on what models for the mind would be appropriate; a view consensus shared by those working in psychology, neurobiology, artificial intelligence, anthropology, and philosophy. All see the mind as a "pandemonium"—a collection of specialized agents acting in parallel, communicating and competing with each other to generate perceptions and behaviors. The unifying idea is that the brain is essentially a Darwin Machine—an array of many modular processors working all at once, without any single center or processor (the "self") running the whole show—from which control and consciousness emerge. Previous chapters have already mentioned Darwin Machine models for skilled action and language generation.

What is being sought is a plausible model for how we generate an apparent "I." Many have remarked on the relatively slow, awkward pace of conscious mental activity, and on how little can be held in awareness at one time, compared with the vast amount of processing we know goes on. And some have long suspected that this might be because the brain was not really designed—hardwired—for such activity. Human narrative consciousness in particular might then be the activity of some sort of serial virtual machine implemented on the parallel hardware of the brain. This presumably would have been accomplished by the mythic mind that developed language and thus finally tamed the parallel pandemonium of the present-centered archaic *sapiens* brain so that very long sequences of verbal meaning could be developed and retained.

In this model, the contents of our awareness at each moment are the current winners from among a horde of competing specialists' reports. Most of these specialists were not designed for specifically human actions such as speaking but for the myriad components of perception, action, and emotions characteristic of higher vertebrates. Perhaps the most accessible metaphor is William Calvin's railroad marshaling yard, described in Chapter 9, in which parallel tracks all connect to one exit track. Each of the parallel tracks is a candidate sequence for perception or action, and a competition determines which one will make it to the exit. The brain produces a virtual center—the illusion of a central viewpoint—just as physicists find it useful to represent the earth's gravity as an attraction to the center of the earth, whereas in fact it is a function of interactions between individual atoms across the whole planet. Our consciousness is composed of many functional subcomponents, but nevertheless we have a unity of conscious experience and the virtual equivalent of a narrator.

The apparent unity and continuity of our experience may be generated like the emergent behavior of a mob, much as some flocks of birds maintain cohesion without having any single leader, or like the "hive mind" of bees, who become increasingly activated and then swarm when enough scouts have returned to the nest reporting a favorable destination. We could also invoke the image of a choir of individual voices coalescing into a synchronous chorus, having risen from the cacophony.

Introspection and the self system

At several intervals throughout this book, we have tried simple exercises on sensing, moving, thinking, and feeling that involve time scales of less than 1 second. They may have permitted you to notice some brain processes that you are normally unaware of. This chapter has reinforced the point that during this period, many normally unconscious agents can massage the self or "I" that emerges as our subjective experience. We are far from being human analogs of a camcorder, using rote neural hardware to link the onset of stimulation and the appearance of a conscious image. A variety of experiments have demonstrated that unconscious processes can bias our perceptions in the interval before they become conscious. After rote processing of elemental chunks of information, as described in Chapter 8 for visual input, we appear to interpose an additional strategic delay that allows for checking and editing the developing sketch or draft, so that elements that might threaten our underlying self system can be altered or deleted.

When incoming information is threatening to the self system, a dissociation can appear between our conscious report, which denies or ignores the potential threat, and behavioral indicators of unconscious processing (such as changes in skin resistance, indicating autonomic arousal). Denial reaches an extreme in anosognosic patients, who, in defense of their self system, might report that nothing is wrong with a paralyzed left arm.

Most of us, after the first 100–200 milliseconds of processing a new input or idea, permit an additional delay of 400–500 milliseconds for strategic editing and revision. This is the time window we were tuning in to during the self-experiments in Chapter 9 on movement and those in Chapter 10 on dissociating thoughts and feelings. By slowing down enough to notice quietly the flickerings in our thinking and body sensations during this period, we can engage in a sort of "attentional training" in which self operations during the strategic delay can be noted rather than ignored (see Figure 12–7). Such training is a central component of some meditation techniques. The reason why introspective techniques are a core of many cognitive therapies for modifying behaviors is that the observation of feelings associating with thoughts, or the coloring of perceptions by the self-system permits "editorial" modifications of these processes that are not possible if they remain unobserved. Like the Russian dolls that nest inside each other, we can ascend to the level of metacognition, a state of "thinking about thinking."

Human efforts to think about thinking have a long history, and it is interesting that what modern psychology and cognitive neuroscience say about how the mind works can be taken as a restatement, in modern form, of what Buddhist psychology has been saying about the nature of cognition for the past 1500 years. The labels and lists that are supplied by Buddhists and cognitive neuroscientists differ, but many of the underlying fundamentals appear to be similar. Buddhist texts carefully describe the "co-dependent arising" of observer and object, of sensing and acting, and emphasize the futility of trying to explain one apart from the other. Points about the relativity of knowledge that we have raised here are explicitly addressed. Meditation techniques best

Figure 12–7 A depiction of time frames of unconscious and conscious experience, suggesting that introspection techniques can expand conscious awareness into the time interval during which unconscious editing normally occurs, making it possible to observe such editing. The time frames shown are approximate.

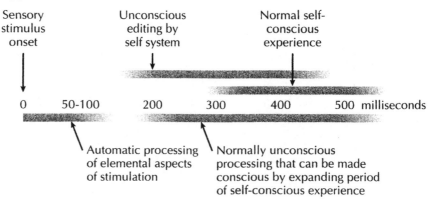

described as "mindfulness" or "awareness" are used to sense the transitory, shifting nature of all phenomena and the various guises of the ego self, "I," that we take to be who we are. An observer is established that is aware of the succession and variety of ego states that we have considered. The attitude of just observing is cultivated: observing the successive graspings or attachments to this or that goal or desire, observing the successions of radically different personalities that can inhabit our bodies from moment to moment. From this state of mindfulness or awareness, one grows to appreciate more and more the relativity of all things, which is called groundlessness or "sunyata" in the Buddhist tradition. This state of non-ego attachment is said to allow energy for compassion, empathy, and service to arise spontaneously.

This position, poise, or process is a logical stance for addressing and dealing with the sorts of questions raised in this book on how the mind works. In the absence of mindfulness we are likely to act from some sort of unconscious ego position as we study and evaluate phenomena. This can include having a set of unconscious starting assumptions or positions that bias how we look at things without our being aware of it (such as assuming the clean separateness of sensing and acting or of subject and object). We don't have to look far for examples of this. Even though many neuroscientists know Cartesian dualism to be discredited, they still are practicing dualists. Their research does not fully integrate an appreciation of the constructive interchange that is involved in cognition, the constant co-development and co-shaping of a nervous system and its environment. Being aware of the many selves, egos, or biases that we generate is a better basis for action in the world than being unconsciously wrapped up in one of those positions and unaware of the processes that generated it. Put more simply, it can be more useful to be conscious, than unconscious, of the relativity of the self that is driving you—the mind in place at any one time.

Computer metaphors

No discussion of models of the brain would be complete without mention of what has become a most pervasive model: the metaphor of the brain as a giant computer, with neurons being the hardware circuit elements. It has been postulated that the way computers carry out functions might be relevant to how the brain does similar things and that conversely, what brains do might serve as a model for designing more intelligent machines. A recent approach has been to ask how what we know about the workings of a brain and the organism it serves might inform the construction of computers or robots that have similar properties. In particular, because we know that the development and behavior of an organism are shaped through an evolutionary process of replicating what trial and error have shown to work, why not build computers that "try" to behave in a complicated way using these same Darwinian mechanisms?

The study of artificial neural nets modeled on computers is one example of this approach. An army of neuron-like elements are linked together in a parallel array with many interconnections. Such nets can be taught to recognize words, generate speech, distinguish male and female faces and their emotions, diagnose heart conditions from EKG data, or drive a truck down a freeway. During a training phase, intermediate results are fed back into the system to let it know how it is doing. Such neural nets have even been used to simulate the effect of brain damage on reading and to model the development of language capabilities. Because there is a lot of redundancy in the network, many of its elements can be removed with only a small effect on overall performance.

Another approach has been to play with the design of "creatures," small mobile robots attempting to mimic the behavior of a simple animal such as a cockroach. These are constructed from a number of activity-producing subsystems, each of which can individually connect sensation to action. The creatures are tested in the real world. (One example is a simulated cockroach with a neural net of 78 neurons and 156 connections). Learning rules are applied that select and reinforce the connections that work best in guiding the insect to wander, follow edges, and find and consume patches of food. This approach to trying to understand whole embodied agents interacting with a world, whether these agents are ourselves or simpler machines that we build, is an antidote to placing undue emphasis on the brain by itself. The generation of action and the problem solving done by the brain simply can't be separated from the environment it must continually exploit, interact with, and be transformed by. Mind includes the interactive loops an organism makes with its environment—a point raised in several previous chapters and developed further in the final chapter.

SUMMARY   We have taken several different trajectories in this chapter, trying to frame the central issue of explaining our self-consciousness. Even to engage the issue requires that we sidestep a number of arguments-in-principle that the problem of consciousness can never be solved and that we assert, instead, that it doesn't hurt to keep trying until a more convincing case for the impossibility of our quest has been stated. We can't help but feel that we are getting closer as we observe the activity of our prefrontal cortexes while they carry out tasks involving attention and working memory, or when we devise clever experiments that show how our brains can rearrange time and space. We can see, through studies of thalamus-cortical interactions during sleep and waking, as well as through brain lesion and brain imaging studies, some plausible candidates for neural correlates of consciousness.

Where does all this leave us, in trying to think about the "I" of our self-consciousness? It seems perfectly natural for us to think that our brains see and feel the world as "we" do—that they chunk concepts and perceptions according to the linguistic conventions "we" use. We encourage this inclination when we play with introspective exercises of the sort that have been sprinkled throughout this book. What we have to keep in mind is that such exercises may be dealing with only a very limited kind of access, for our brains basically are survival machines whose sophisticated perceptual and motor modules were shaped by evolution long before the recent add-on of linguistic abilities. The awareness we try to explain with these abilities is probably just that small fraction of our total brain/body activities that has proved useful for survival and reproduction. There would be no point in our consciously attending to the vast number of subterranean activities that massage and process our perception and action, for example, to directly sense knowledge of animals, persons, or tools being stored in different parts of our temporal lobes. What our brains display to our awareness is like the display panel on our car's dashboard: indicators that inform us and can make a difference in how we drive the car. Our linguistic habits for "chunking" reality bear no deep resemblance to the parallel and distributed brain mechanisms used in information storage and retrieval. Our main hope is that through new techniques such as more sophisticated monitoring of brain activity, we can gain better insight into the relationship among the local environment, brain activity, and the patchwork construction of our sense of self—between our "I" and the array of background processes going on. We have to accept, for the present, the jarring idea that the "I" inside our heads is a virtual "I" constructed anew in each moment from a cacophonous interaction among brain, body, and world.

At this point, you may feel you have been left with something like the proverbial Chinese meal that doesn't stick to your ribs. There is no clear "So that's how it works!" The chapters on perceiving, acting, emotional, linguistic, and now conscious minds have left us with bits and pieces waiting to be assembled into a whole. Many of us take it as an article of faith that it will someday be possible to do this; others think not. We do have some models for our consciousness that seem worth further pursuit and testing. More immediately, the information we have assembled thus far has consequences for how we view and comport ourselves in the modern world, and this is the subject of the next chapter.

Questions for Thought

1. Our prefrontal lobes play a central role in awareness, attention, and working memory. Are awareness and attention the same thing? If not, how would you distinguish between them? (Think about keeping your eyes directed at the middle of a clock face while you are being asked to describe one of the specific numbers for a time of day.)

2. Cite some of the evidence that supports the following contention: Our subjective experience of being a central observer in a constant world actually reflects the construction of a "best guess" of what that world is like from a series of fleeting "snapshots" (of visual, auditory, proprioceptive, and other sensory inputs)—snapshots that sample very narrow windows of time and are constantly renewed. What are some of the ways in which this process can be misled?

3. Consciousness can be abolished by lesions in a very small region of the thalamus. Does this mean that these regions are the seat or locus of consciousness?

4. This chapter outlines a "Darwin Machine" model for generating the apparent unity and continuity of our experience. In this model, our current thread of awareness is the winner that has emerged from a competition among many alternative options. Can you think of any other models—models that do not have the flaw of ultimately suggesting a little human, or homunculus, inside our heads that in turn has to be explained?

Suggestions for further general reading

Churchland, P.M. 1995. *The Engine of Reason, the Seat of the Soul: A Philosophical Journey into the Brain.* Cambridge, MA: M.I.T. Press. (This book presents the brain as a neurocomputational device and gives an accessible account of using artificial neural networks, simulated by computers, to model brain processes.)

Dennett, D.C. 1991. *Consciousness Explained.* Boston: Little, Brown. (This chapter's discussion of time and space in the brain (noting the phi and meta-contrast effects), and its account of the futility of asking "Where does it all come together?" was drawn largely from Chapters 5 and 6 of Dennett's book.)

Ferris, T. 1992. *The Mind's Sky—Human Intelligence in a Cosmic Context.* New York: Bantam. (This chapter notes some interesting speculations on altered states of consciousness that are offered in Part 2 of Ferris's book.)

Flanagan, O. 1992. *Consciousness Reconsidered.* Cambridge, MA: M.I.T. Press. (This book is a broad introduction to philosophy of mind and general models of brain mechanisms of consciousness. It discusses the idea of consciousness as arising from Darwin Machine–like mechanisms.)

Hobson, J.A. 1994. *The Chemistry of Conscious States: How the Brain Changes Its Mind.* Boston: Little, Brown. (This account of Hobson's sleep research also gives his more general views on how both "bottom-up" (from brainstem to cortex) and "top-down" (from cortex to brainstem) processes shape our cognition.)

Reading on more advanced or specialized topics

Gazzaniga, M.S., Ivry, R.B., & Mangun, G.R. 1998. *Cognitive Neuroscience.* New York: Norton. (Chapter 11 of this book deals with the role of the frontal lobes in awareness, executive functions, and complex behaviors.)

Llinas, R., & Ribary, U. 1993. Coherent 40–Hz oscillation characterizes dream state in humans. *Proceedings of the National Academy of Sciences* USA 90:2078–2081. (A proposal that an oscillation in cortical activity that occurs in the awake and rapid eye movement (REM) sleep states is a correlate of cognition.)

Newman, J. 1997. Putting the puzzle together. Towards a general theory of the neural correlates of consciousness. *Journal of Consciousness Studies* 4:47–66. (This article expands on a model that makes the thalamus a central part of an extended activating system that links cortex and lower brain centers to generate the conscious state.)

Ramachandran, V.S., & Hirstein, W. 1998. Three laws of Qualia: what neurology tells us about the biological functions of consciousness. *Journal of Consciousness Studies* 4:429–457. (This is a fascinating account of neurological syndromes in which consciousness seems to malfunction, suggesting regions of the brain that are central to maintaining a conscious state.)

Ungerleider, L.G., Courtney, S.M., & Haxby, J.V. 1998. A neural system for human visual working memory. *Proceedings of the National Academy of Sciences* USA 95:883–890. (A comparison of pathways in the monkey and human brains that regulate visual working memory, with different areas of prefrontal cortex serving spatial and object memory.)

Chapter 13

Theoretic Mind

We have now described many of the components that go into generating a human self, and in Chapter 12 we tried to draw together some ideas about what goes on in our narrative conscious minds. Given the fact that our modern brains are essentially those of hunter gatherers of 50,000–100,000 years ago, one could argue that any book on the biology of mind should stop at this point. We need to consider, however, the fact that modern conditions have generated new kinds of brains, even though their genetic instructions haven't changed much. Consider the well-documented and baffling fact that the IQ of the average citizen of advanced industrial countries has increased by 25 percent in this century. Has each generation of children, faced with an increasingly complex technological environment, grown increasingly sophisticated brains? Consider the fact that each of us constructs brain modules that specialize in handling such recent inventions as reading and writing. Understanding these more recent developments is as much a part of studying the biology of mind as knowing how a nerve cell works. The development of reading and writing represents another chapter in the story of humans increasingly becoming artifacts of their own artifacts (earlier installments include the inventions of fire, tools, oral language, and myth described in Chapters 5 and 11). The advent of writing has made what is in our heads even more symbiotic with external tools and information stores—devices that our culture uses to regulate our behaviors. Now we need to bring ourselves to the present, considering first the emergence of modern minds, then some conflicts that have emerged between our Paleolithic and our modern selves, and finally the issue of humankind's further evolution: our possible futures.

Emergence of the modern mind

In Chapters 4 and 5 we traced several possible stages in the development of ape and hominid minds, following an outline provided by the psychologist Merlin Donald, and this section draws further on his writings. These earlier stages included the episodic mind of chimpanzees, the mimetic intelligence of *Homo erectus,* and the linguistic mythic mind of archaic *Homo sapiens.* The transitions to mimetic and mythic minds occurred in biological hardware—adaptive changes in the muscular and nervous systems that were complete no later than 50,000 years ago. The last transition, to theoretic mind and culture, depends on equivalent changes in external technological hardware—specifically, external memory devices such as paintings on cave walls, scratches on clay tablets, and written texts. These external tools have made us their tools, and the development of our brains is shaped by them. The essential feature of this last transition is that it no longer depends solely on oral tradition, spoken language, and narrative styles of thought. Rather, cultural rules and procedures begin to be stored outside of individual minds, as graphical tools are used to inscribe symbolic memory representations on external storage devices.

The emergence of this theoretic culture, however, encompassed much more than the development of written language and the storage of written records in libraries. A substantial list of technological innovations came before writing: astronomical records, organized agriculture, ceramics and bricks made by heating, tailored clothing, simple maps, sailing vessels, and the like. Analog devices such as water clocks, calendars, and time sticks kept a record of time and astronomical events. These provided a foundation on which visual symbolic record keeping could develop. It seems likely that the first socially important theoretic development in human history was the science of astronomy. Many different cultures independently invented devices, such as the mounds of some Native American groups, for tracking the movement of constellations and monitoring seasons.

Graphic invention

The earliest artifacts with purposeful graphical markings are from 200,000-year-old upper Paleolithic sites. By 60,000 years ago, sophisticated animal drawings appear. The earliest writing dates to approximately 5–6 thousand years ago, when large city-states with records of trade emerged. Possession of spoken language does not automatically lead to graphical invention. Of the many thousands of languages spoken at different places and times by humans, fewer than one in ten has evolved an indigenous written form, and the number that has yielded a significant body of literature barely exceeds a hundred. Writing was not only a late development but also a rare one.

Three modes of visual symbolic invention can be distinguished: pictorial, ideographic, and phonological. Pictorial representation in Paleolithic cave art contained themes such as hunting and fertility. This is consonant with oral mythic traditions of many cultures that stress fertility rituals, animal power, and magical identifications. The next development was ideographic representation. Cuneiform lists appeared about 5000 years ago and persisted until the early Roman period. These are similar in principle to hieroglyphics (Egyptian) and ideographs (as in Chinese writing or Japanese kanji). An ideographic written language permitted China to develop an advanced bureaucratic, scientific, and literary culture in the absence of any phonetic writing system.

The phonetic alphabet that we are familiar with arose in the Middle East and the Mediterranean basin. Japanese kana is a similar but separate system that records syllables instead of phonemes, and the Korean alphabet is also distinct from ours. The alphabet, a simple set of phonological and letter representations invented in the first millennium B.C., represented an enormous increase in economy and speed. Written language enhanced tremendously the rise of external symbolic storage systems (such as written documents stored in libraries). Oral narrative could more easily be embedded in a larger external structure (such as a manuscript of the *Iliad* in the library). This period saw the development not only of language but also of other symbol storage systems, such as musical notation and scientific graphing.

Users of the phonetic Greek alphabet could become literate by familiarizing themselves with only about two dozen letters, instead of having to remember hundreds of hieroglyphics or cuneiform characters. Having to learn fewer visual symbols greatly reduced the memory load on the brain.

Early theoretic societies

Ancient Greece from around 700 B.C. is regarded as the birthplace of advanced theoretic civilization in the West. The appearance of mathematics, geometry, biology, geography, and philosophy was relatively sudden. (India and China were going through cultural explosions at about the same time.) These new disciplines were based on effective systems for numeration, geometrical graphing, and phonetic writing. Such tools permitted ideas to be entered into a public record so that they could be improved and refined. Central core ideas—the memes we discussed in Chapter 5—became more accurate and long-lived replicators. It is estimated that historical narratives can't last more than five hundred years in oral traditions before they are completely distorted. In contrast, today's libraries contain thousands of physical copies of the exact words of Herodotus's histories, and many more translations, summaries, commentaries, and so on, even though the original manuscripts turned to dust centuries ago. The core ideas, or memes, have been subjected to very different "selection pressures"—for logical coherence or explanatory power, for instance, instead of rhyme or integration with tribal rituals.

Ideas have always been replicative units, or memes, transmitted by gesture or speech from generation to generation, but with the advent of theoretic intelligence their vehicles changed. They began to be transmitted also by pictures, writing, and artifacts, instead of just by speech.

The transition from mimetic to mythic culture put great demands on biological memory. Theoretic culture reduced this load somewhat by shifting some storage tasks to the newly developed recording media. Now the short-term memory of the frontal lobes could work with externally stored information, and humans could engage in cognitive projects that were just too large and complicated for the oral-mythic mind. The brain may not have changed in its genetic makeup in going from mythic to theoretic culture, but this new link to an accumulating external memory unquestionably expanded its cognitive powers.

Merging of individual minds and external memory stores

Each human brain becomes part of a network when it operates in the context of an external symbolic storage system. Its memory structures are expanded, and the location of cognitive control shifts. Memory can reside at many locations in the network, as Figure 13–1 suggests. In early cultures, only the elite (such as scribes) were trained to deal with this system, while most of the population remained fundamentally oral-mythic, dominated by ritual and tradition. In modern society this has changed; even episodic event reporting is heavily dependent on electronic media (as when we watched the first moon landing live on television).

Because of the limitations of our consciousness, the connection between an individual's memory and external memory stores is always brief, but it can be repeated frequently, and any truly creative thought is an iterative process, where the thinker returns to the external database again and again—verbalizing, sketching ideas, thinking internally or aloud, referring to past outputs, revising, and cleaning up—until a

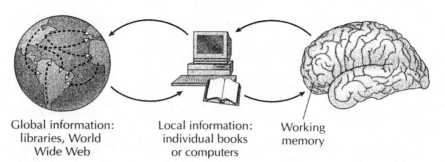

Global information: libraries, World Wide Web

Local information: individual books or computers

Working memory

Figure 13–1 Expansion of the power of the brain's working memory is made possible by exchanging information back and forth with local devices, such as personal computers and books, and also with more global information stores, such as libraries and worldwide computer networks. Memory and cognitive control comes to reside in the whole network.

satisfactory resolution is reached. This is very different from having the working-memory system of our frontal lobes be our only arena for performing complex mental tasks. This memory is distractible and transient, and it cannot sustain the cumulative building of the complex layers of knowledge needed to support theoretic society.

When we connect to our external memory networks—that is, when we read, write, draw, or calculate—we really *are* like computers plugged into a network, and our skills and powers are determined by both the network and our own biological inheritance. These networks can be assembled from many different kinds of hardware, some of which we barely recognize as technological: books, costumes, posters, traffic signs, vinyl audio recordings, punched paper tape, knotted strings, CD-ROM. When we deal with one of these objects or read a book, we enter a cognitive state in which our biological minds can be brought temporarily under the dominance of an external memory device: Our minds can literally be "played" by a book, moved into a state crafted by the author. The same thing happens when we succumb to the fascination of surfing the World Wide Web. (In this sense, cyberspace is a few thousand years old and doesn't so much replace literary culture as make it much more widely available.)

> *There is no difference in principle between a cuneiform scratch on a rock and information held in the many computers that constitute the Internet.*

Many ordering rules and search functions that used to be entirely internal to our biological memory now reside in external memory systems. Programs are designed to explore computer networks for us, asking our questions and retrieving relevant answers. One challenge facing cognitive scientists is to describe what happens to our individual minds as we tie them to electronic media—media that are themselves becoming global and active. Are the virtual selves that we can invent as personae in computer networks going to become more real to us than our biological selves?

Parallel expression of ancient and modern minds

The advent of our theoretic minds has given us a final mode of representational thought, encapsulating the episodic, mimetic, and mythic minds characteristic of earlier stages in our evolution (see Figure 13–2). Each of these has been a way of representing the world, a way that could support a certain level of culture, a survival strategy for the human race then present. Each style of representation that we acquired along the way has been retained, like the growth rings of a tree—only in us the older rings are still alive. The result is a system of parallel representational channels of mind that can process the world concurrently. As you look at a television program, you marshal mimesis, narrative, and logic in parallel to serve the common end of modeling ideas.

SELF-EXPERIMENT

Does the idea that previous stages in the development of our human intelligence persist in our modern minds make sense to you in terms of your own experience? Pause for a moment and think about distinguishing moments when your experience is mainly episodic (present-centered, limited mainly to feeling sensations), mimetic (nonverbal social exchange, body language), mythic (telling stories infused with meaning that define your place in the world, rich in metaphor and analogy), or theoretic (analysis, abstraction, dissection, generalizations that ignore mythic significance).

Conflict of Paleolithic and modern minds

This book has now sketched out two seemingly disparate threads. One is the evolutionary story that halts our genetic evolution in the Paleolithic, leaving us with many psychological mechanisms appropriate to

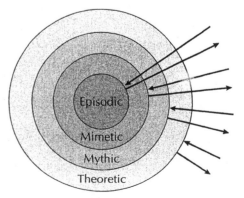

Figure 13–2 Different varieties of human intelligence, with later stages encapsulating earlier ones. The model is that the intelligences that evolved earlier are under the governance of later-appearing capabilities but that they also can have semi-independent exchanges with the environment on their own (arrows).

that time, not to the present. The other is the advent of our 21st-century mind that knows itself to contain no "I," that knows itself to be one of many possible generated selves—a mind that faces the prospect of merging with computer networks that leave our obsolete bodies behind. Can these two descriptions be integrated?

Paleolithic adaptations

We can start by noting some of the consequences of having theoretic minds in bodies whose psychology, physiology, and emotions are adapted to the Paleolithic, not the present. Our late-afternoon drop in blood sugar probably derives from rhythms of hunter-gatherers on the savannah 200,000 years ago, and our preferred temperature range, 60–85°F, reflects the climate then. We raise "gooseflesh" to erect fur that disappeared long ago, and we have emotional response systems that can be a complete mismatch for the modern world. Hormone cycles and mental alertness that used to be tuned to the natural light-dark cycle are now compromised by the use of electric lighting to shorten our periods of sleep. Our bodies are designed for a more stable social environment than exists in the modern world. We have to make do with a patched-together set of reactions to constant change.

Our modern minds still work best as detectors of abrupt changes, paying more attention to an isolated terrorist event than to the gradual thinning of the ozone layer. Culture changes even more slowly than the environment, and we haven't yet evolved institutions that force us to consider the long-term consequences of our actions. The adaptability that permitted our transition to modern culture may also contain the seeds of its destruction. Just as frogs sitting in a pan of water that is slowly heated will sit there, oblivious, until they die, we tolerate small, incremental degradations in our environment that may ultimately lead to our extinction. If the world's human population continues to double every 41 years, we will reach the biological limit to growth and will start fighting each other, in deadly earnest, for the decreasing slice of the pie. Over the geological time scale, there have been at least seven major extinctions that wiped out 90 percent of the species present. The rapidity of the current wave of extinction currently under way is unprecedented. Are we about to become number eight?

The Paleolithic mind did not need to react to changes that took place over years or decades, and it is through such slow changes that we are destroying our own environment.

Mythic components of modern intelligence

In many archaic systems, social order and coordination were modeled on the universe—the relationships among the planets and stars—and their mythology posits a natural harmony between humankind and the cosmos. Our modern secular world has lost this sense of unity, and many people turn to science as the only field through which the dimension of mythology can be again revealed. This may be one reason why science programs on public TV are so popular; perhaps scientists are the closest equivalent we have to a modern, global priesthood. Another reason, of course, is that science programs appeal to our sense of excitement and of the marvelous. In this sense we are taking scientists not as priests but as modern magicians. Our natural mind, if we have one, is closer to the animism, immersion, and symbiosis of mythic culture than to the kinds of intelligence required to survive in a highly technological world. And it is the emotional, mythic mind that determines so much of what happens in affairs of state, culture, and history.

Stories are the basis of our behavioral scripts, our unconscious self-images. This is why our behavior seems so resistant to "rational" analysis. It seems as though different kinds of brains are running in parallel. Our body physiology—its nervous and endocrine systems, its hardwired pathways for generating emotions—is tied to our archaic mythic mentality. Most of us probably feel robust only when these archaic functions can be expressed (as in life events or stories that purge the emotions). The overlap in our physiological, psychological, and social selves is brought home very forcefully by the emerging field of psychoneuroimmunology mentioned in Chapter 10, which describes how general health, immune status, neurotransmitter chemistry, and social interactions are interrelated.

The mythic self remains a core of our personality. Stories and myths came first and theoretic analysis appeared much later.

An evolutionary perspective that links physiological wholeness with self-image and storyline suggests why positive or negative personal scripts correlate so strongly with health. It suggests an explanation for our hunger for stories that give some sense of purpose to the modern world, from traditional religions, from science-as-religion, or from cosmic evolution theories based on modern physics or Eastern mystical traditions. We can see the consequences of the absence of a storyline or myth that supports morality and social order in the degraded environments that afflict many large cities. The developing nervous systems of young humans are subjected to sometimes violent and contradictory inputs that don't permit the pairing of somatic or emotional markers with experiences that can be designated as either good or bad. The tools needed to construct criteria for appropriate behavior are wanting.

We might regard our mimetic and mythic bodies as locked in a previous time, whereas our evolution is now proceeding at the level of symbolic manipulation. One requirement for preserving the richness of our lives might be to ensure that our symbolic evolution doesn't make our robust physiology wither away. Computer addicts who live on junk food, caffeine, and the Internet need to attend to their physical and emotional well-being if they are to avoid becoming analogs of the emaciated Hindu or Buddhist ascetics who have "transcended the body." We can allay fear of physical obsolescence if we realize that our bodies are a central component of the mythic personality that vitalizes our physiology. This mythic personality may underlie the interest the public shows in media accounts of our mythic origins: the overwhelming reception of the PBS series by Bill Moyers on the work of Joseph Campbell, interest in matriarchal societies, and fascination with man as hunter-warrior as described in Robert Bly's book *Iron John*. It may also explain the widespread formation of support groups of both men and women in an effort to develop their true archaic male or female selves. In our mythic selves, there may be an evolutionary ultimate cause of our individual need to have meaning—a story or script to fit into.

Addressing pluralism

We may reason much better than Paleolithic humans, but our emotions, especially our social bonds, seem to have changed very little since our mimetic and mythic brains were formed. The main driving force in the evolution of modern humans was probably competition with other groups of humans. The *xenophobia* (fear or hatred of anything strange or foreign) and genocidal behavior exhibited by groups of humans seems basic and constant, and it is similar to the behavior we observe in our nearest primate relatives, the chimpanzees. Is it possible that, just as a cat must still play at hunting when its belly is full, and scratch its declawed paws against the wall, so too the human brain's "threat" or "fear" agents must have their exercise, regardless of whether there is, in the external environment, an objective reason for this activity. Can we grasp this and override those primitive instructions? The fact that the identity, rituals, and perceived purpose of a human group must be enforced in order to maintain the social cohesion of that group, but also that the structures of different groups vary greatly, works against tolerance. To tolerate is to admit the relativity of at least some of the values of one's group, and such open-mindedness can threaten group cohesion. This is why different religious traditions can have a history of bitter opposition.

> *The myths with which we maintain our personal, tribal, and national stability can work both for and against us, because one of their functions is to maintain the integrity of the group by denying the validity of novel perceptions that clash with the world view and traditions of the group.*

The social units and their associated cohesion mechanisms that we discussed in the sections on mimetic and mythic mind in Chapter 5 are what have evolved to become tribes or nations in the modern world (as distinct from states, such as the United States, France, and so on). There are about 5000 such units in the world today united by language, culture, territorial base, political organization, or accepted history. Few of these were given a choice when they were made part of one of the 190 states of the world, the majority of which have been around only since World War II. Examples include Catholics in Ireland or ethnic Albanians in Serbia. Most of the shooting wars in the world today are being fought between nations and the states that claim to represent them, or between nations who come into conflict over their territory and identity.

Ancient and modern minds in an electronic age

The model we have been building is that we all have episodic, mimetic, mythic, and theoretic minds acting simultaneously and in parallel; that control rests sometimes, but not always, with the higher (that is, more recent) levels of encapsulation; and that our brains can spin a very large number of possible selves. Our individual minds then link to worldwide networks, most recently through electronic media. Such worldwide networks have the potential of acting to counter the tribal mentalities that ensure conflict between different groups as they scapegoat or demonize each other. These networks increasingly bring knowledge of the diversity of humanity to all, which may enhance tolerance for diversity. Certainly, they also offer economic benefits for participation. Greed isn't pretty, but it's usually better than hatred.

The World Wide Web now forms a very thin veneer, or epidermis, covering the immense variety of peoples and cultures, but it may eventually become part of the backbone of a common world culture that offers an antidote to the multiple territorial-kinesic (mimetic) or linguistic (mythic) systems that underlie tribal cohesion and also are at the base of the many wars between tribes currently in progress across the globe.

The on-line community is not, at present, really a community, because it is missing an essential ingredient of our traditional meeting and work spaces: chance encounters where a flicker of body language, a nod, or a glance communicates something very important. We want to see what other human animals look like when we talk with them. No one needs to look anyone else in the eye in cyberspace, and a sense of membership in larger communities can be lost. Insults are easier to hurl. Studies suggest that people who spend several hours a week on-line experience higher levels of depression and loneliness than others.

Isolated individuals can form isolated communities that don't have to rub elbows with others, facilitating the growth of hate groups. This can translate the xenophobia of traditional cultures to virtual reality. On the other hand, the Internet has strengthened social support for people who wish to share their personal stories of life, disease, and death in a way that is not possible in regular day-to-day social contacts. There is now an outpouring of books on the new cyber-reality, some warning of coming doom and some wildly optimistic about the human transformations it might facilitate. The history of society's reaction to the introduction of the telephone, radio, and television suggests that it takes at least 20 years for the effects of innovative technologies to sink in. Given that the World Wide Web is only about 3 years old at this writing, we can do little now but wait and see.

Future mind

In thinking about directions in which the human mind might develop in the future, we first ask whether we are justified in taking lessons from the past or extrapolating from the present. Unfortunately, the answer in both cases is no. A brief look at human history since the Paleolithic era dispels any underlying misconception that our present economic and social arrangements are in some way optimal or are even reliably heading in that direction. Evolution does not imply progress. In spite of evidence that evolution has generated human brains that are predisposed to develop a naive physics, an intuitive psychology, and language, there still is no "natural human" to return to, apart from the current cultural artifacts that we all appear to be. Notwithstanding the enthusiasm of New Age gurus and the deep ecology movement advocating a return to our authentic mythic roots, there never has been a golden age—only the clear propensity for humans at any time to think things must have been better in "the good old days." The Greeks, at the height of their civilization, described with nostalgia the golden age from which they had fallen.

The unfortunate reality is that since the Paleolithic era, human groups have engaged in genocide and environmental destruction. The only reason they weren't as good at it as we are is that their tools were more primitive. The documented decimation of the flora and fauna of New Zealand, Tasmania, small Pacific islands, and Madagascar by prehistoric human groups was confined to limited areas. Now our arena is the whole globe. We have a long list of examples of civilizations ruining their resource base. The Middle East, center of the ancient world, used to be a lush area of

Neither nostalgia for the past nor extrapolation from the present offers us much help in thinking about what human minds might be like in the future.

wooded hills and fertile valleys until thousands of years of deforesta-
tion, overgrazing, erosion, siltation, and salinization converted the area
to desert. The shift of the center of civilization to Greece and then to
Rome was accompanied by similar ecocide.

Apart from the global scope of modern human activity, another difference between us and the ancients is that they couldn't read about
ecological disasters of the past. We can, so our continuing to hunt
whales and clear tropical rain forests is based on willful blindness, not
ignorance. We could even wonder whether there might be a "biology of
illusion." Could the insistent denial of hard reality by human groups be
a universal trait that evolved because, during past human history, it
has proved to be adaptive to be unrealistic and avoid facing what you
don't want to know?

Our present industrial cultures, which reflect the conception of
humans as ascendant managers of a separate "nature," do not contain
the seeds of a sustainable future. Rather, they make it easy (if no less
chilling) to imagine our moving even further toward becoming a collection of disembodied minds in a virtual reality defined by the holding of knowledge in worldwide computer networks. The technocrats,
bio- and otherwise, might then rule with an arrogant pride that blocks
real appreciation of the symbiosis of humans and the rest of the biosphere. The 150th anniversary issue of *Scientific American,* September
1995, has a number of articles devoted to key technologies of the 21st
century. The unspoken assumption underlying the more than 30 contributions is that humans should manage and manipulate the geosphere
and biosphere to accommodate the ever-increasing numbers of us on
the planet.

A slightly more optimistic view is that we are moving toward a neo-
biological civilization in which technology adapts, learns, and evolves
in biological ways, and machines become more biological in character.
Organic life would continue to be the prime infrastructure of human
experience of the global scale, and technological networks might make
human culture even more ecologically sound and evolutionary.
Engineered biology and biotechnology would eclipse the importance
of mechanical technology. Our knowledge of the human genome and
mechanisms of brain development would allow us to begin to craft our
brains to the specification we desire. The old-fashioned kind of selection and adaptation that have shaped most of human history would be
tossed out the window.

Although more education and genetic tinkering would help us
address our maladaptive behaviors, any vision of being able to manage
our ecosystems has its detractors. A master plan for saving the planet

requires abstract purposes and central powers that cannot know—and thus might destroy—the integrity of local nature and local communities. The new movement of "ecopsychology" tries to soften the edges of the technocratic approach by emphasizing and arguing for restoration of the bond between species and the planet. This movement invokes a biophilia hypothesis: that humans have a deep genetically based emotional need to affiliate with the rest of the living world—a need perhaps as important as forming close personal relationships.

Teleological schemes

As we have seen, then, returning to the past or extrapolating from the present doesn't give us a very clear crystal ball. Another way of approaching possible futures has been to employ *teleology,* the attribution of some final purpose or goal to natural processes. Such schemes are offered by many of the world's religions and also in some scientific forms. The religious options avoid uncertainty, but in some cases they do so with a fundamentalism that can stifle, allowing little room to revise and refine one's positions. Outside the traditional religions, some writers try to claim the authority of science by spinning stories of the evolution of mind that parallel the evolution of the universe, with a beginning and an end. The end of the evolution of mind is usually described as a dropping away of the ego, so that everyone, not just a few of the wise, attains enlightenment, and in a brilliant flash the minds of many become one; union with "larger mind" is made. These writers sometimes suggest or make reference to an Anthropic Cosmological Principle: that the universe exists and evolves so that it can know itself. Other writers suggest the existence of long-range resonance or connection between physical entities. Their scientific trappings notwithstanding, these cosmic scenarios are essentially religious, and for some advocates of new-age enlightenment, they have replaced the storylines of conventional religions.

One version of the new-age creed professes that if we could only break the fetters of our false selves and see through our socially conditioned illusions, then a transcendent self would emerge in its final glorious form. This faith in some sort of innate, benign unfolding of wisdom or inner perfectibility to come is analogous to nostalgia about a golden age long gone. Unfortunately, our minds are as likely to harbor deceit, suspicion, paranoia, and aggression as parts of their intrinsic original nature as they are to evince curiosity, generosity, and love. Many of our less desirable features are a read-out of our Paleolithic minds; they enhanced our survival then, even if they are less adaptive now.

It seems unlikely that human egos have seen the last of the batterings they have undergone through history. Greek science through Copernicus made all matter subject to the same laws; the Darwinian revolution identified humans as derivative of animals; Freudian psychology and modern neuroscience put humans under the domination of fundamental drives; and now modern technology is increasingly subordinating humans to machines. There are signs in many contexts that the coupling of humans and machines in a virtual reality has begun to replace real life. Shopping malls contain computer games that completely enclose us in a computer visual world that we can manipulate with our head and hands, a very sophisticated version of arcade games. In Tokyo, sensorama machines invite the overstressed worker to crawl in and be transported into a soothing physical environment with massage, sound, music, and smell—perhaps giving the body physiology, at least for a moment, the Paleolithic social and endocrine environment it desires! The extreme of this trend would be for the social body to be rendered obsolete, as telecommunications replace physical contact and vastly diminish the sense of community among humans.

The increasing integration of humans and their machines can lead to the unsettling vision of completely merging our individual identities into the virtual reality of technology and computer networks.

The theme of encapsulation

The theme of encapsulation of lower by higher levels of organization that we have traced throughout this book, continuing up through the transitions of hominid evolution, can be carried on to the description of larger and larger group "minds." Each new level of integration reached by human culture has retained vestiges of its previous forms. We might consider an emerging stage to be a planetary consciousness, reflected by portable telephones that can be used anywhere on the earth's surface to reach any telephone number in the world. Each small component of this total ensemble thinks it has purpose and uses models of the past to structure its activities, even while it is really performing in a new order that has emerged. (Examples might include maintaining the form of nation-states, even though political and economic control has passed to a worldwide network of corporations, and maintaining the form of universities, even though an increasing fraction of new ideas and techniques are being developed elsewhere). The outcome of the whole is described only with statistics. This could be pictured as a return to symbiotic unity, a confluence of humans with the environment like that which prevailed at the beginning of human evolution— a cycling of human history. We fantasize that we are in control of our human institutions, corporations, and governments, just as Paleolithic humans thought their magic rituals appeased and regulated the behavior of the gods.

The evolution of evolution

Are there useful rules for change? Can we describe how a future human mind might be shaped, even if we can't specify the outcome of the process? This is equivalent to asking whether our picture of evolutionary processes is clear enough to be a real, operational model of them. The description of many of these processes has been one thread running through this book; to offer a brief summary is probably the best we can do to suggest not the form a future human mind and its environment will take, but rather how it may get there. Recall how, in the first chapter, we saw that to make predictions, we need not just general laws but also details about the circumstances under which those laws are acting. The one idea that seems to unite all complex adaptive systems, be they temperate forests, eyeballs, developing kangaroos, or tidal pools, is that of the Darwin Machine, which can be applied to all levels of physical, biological, and cultural organization. Stable entities that can reproduce themselves—whether macromolecules, organisms, or cultures—are modified as new variations are tested from generation to generation.

The study of complex adaptive systems has revealed that they share a number of features. Many are descriptions of how a Darwin Machine must work. Complex systems are distributed over a multitude of smaller units, and control rises from the bottom-up interaction of these units. Growth occurs by chunking, adding small new parts or changes and testing them. Some of these innovations originally arise as errors, and the small number that make the system work better are preserved. The survival and reproduction of complex structures requires that they serve many goals.

Perhaps the most heated debate in current thinking about evolution is over the relative importance of adaptation and Darwin Machines versus chance, accident, and the structural constraints inherent in complicated systems.

Changes that serve one goal superbly may compromise the achievement of another, so that the actual course taken is to satisfy a multitude of functions in a way that seldom optimizes any one but serves all "well enough." Too much constancy and too much change are both a bad thing. Systems that endure are stable enough to hold together but also are poised so close to the edge of instability that adaptive change can occur. Finally, the survival of a system such as an animal species clearly can depend on accident and luck. If our species had existed about 60 million years ago and had been confined to the Yucatan peninsula, the asteroid impact that contributed to the extinction of the dinosaurs would surely have taken us too.

The least-understood aspect of evolutionary theory, and the one perhaps most important to thinking about the future of human minds, is how change changes itself—how change can enhance the ability to adapt. We touched on this issue in Chapter 6, when we discussed the evolution of plasticity in the development of the nervous system. Animals that have more options in their design space are more likely to hit on adaptive tricks, so selection pressure favors genetic variation that permits even more flexibility. This is one way of changing the rules for changing entities over time. The speed of cultural evolution may have substantially reduced the importance of this mechanism, such that there probably is no longer significant natural selection for genetic differences in brain design. Are we, however, about to enter another realm of changing how change occurs—using our prowess in manipulating genes to direct the evolution of ourselves and other organisms in the biosphere? Or will evolution proceed mainly at the level of our complex symbolic artifacts, with computer networks and virtual realities evolving to change how they change themselves?

SUMMARY   *The Mind's Biology*

This brings us to the end of our attempt to trace some linkages among brain, body, and world and to see how our individual minds form through their confluence. We have now completed a trek through many topics germane to an understanding of the biology of mind. We started with the assertion that consciousness arises from the activity of neurons, and then we outlined evolutionary arguments that suggest we understand, in principle, how complicated brains may have evolved. After describing these plausible stages in the evolution of animal and human minds, we arrived at our own linguistic minds, whose plastic development and modular function we examined in several chapters. We now have a clearer picture of our conscious experience as a supra-individual biological phenomenon. This is because the construction of our brains during development draws not only on genetic instructions but also on programming from our physical and cultural environments. The fine details of the nerve circuits and muscles we use depend on many cultural factors, including the set of sounds emitted by our particular language and whether we are a musician, a scholar, a farmer, or an athlete. We all manage the amazing feat of growing brains and minds that can spin a story of the sort that has unfolded in this book, a story of different encapsulated minds that weave selves that strive for the certainty of a storyline or myth—a process aware of itself that is unique in the natural world we know.

We have to be impressed by the insatiable curiosity that our human species shows, by our desire to explain things. We seem hungry in particular for mechanical explanations, for "theories of everything" that protect us from having to admit the possibility that much of the way we are is due to the chance and accident of our particular history—that things might well have gone very differently. We strain to understand, and write books with titles like *Biology of Mind, Consciousness Explained*, and *How the Mind Works*, all of which promise more than they can deliver. The accounts offered by all these books will seem quaint and primitive in just a few years. In our rush to understand, we continually try to patch things together by skipping important steps. Just as evolutionary psychology criticized the sociobiology that preceded it for leapfrogging over evolved psychological mechanisms to explain culture, it can itself be faulted for assuming a detailed innate basis for evolved behavioral modules without considering fundamental information about the evolution of neurophysiological and neuroendocrine systems underlying face detection circuits, autonomic and emotional behaviors, pair bonding, social interactions, and so on.

Our evolutionary history has provided us with minds that quest for novelty and explanations, minds that invent myths, religions, and science to help us understand our world and placate our hyperactive imaginations. Our human purpose and conscious awareness are able to sample only a fraction of that world. The insights of modern neuroscience, as well as the mystical insights of the major religious traditions, point to an intelligence much greater than the narrative chatter in our heads. As powerful as our analytic mind has proved in probing the depths of our conscious experience, we don't want to slight the larger mind that generates poetry, music, art, fantasy, and an intuitive sense of wholeness. We are plunging, biotechnocratically, into a brave new world, and we must ask what this world is worth if we lose our sense of the whole of our human intelligence and compassion.

The best we can do as individuals is to strive for the sort of awareness that permits our minds to appreciate both the selves that they generate and the relativity of those selves, and to feel a resulting sympathy toward self and others. We can aspire to a poise, or process, that presents a logical stance for addressing the sorts of questions raised in this book on mind, as well as for dealing with larger social issues. It permits us to face the dissonance between a psychology that, having evolved under conditions that no longer prevail, can be xenophobic and genocidal and the modern society of minds that we now know ourselves to be. This dissonance mandates the evolution of new procedures for transcending our Paleolithic minds.

Let's end this book with a sentence from its preface: "Each of us is a society of minds that emerge from our evolutionary history and from the way our brains form as we grow up in a particular natural ecology and cultural setting." It is through understanding these details, and their relativity, that we have some prospect for guiding our future in an intelligent way.

Questions for Thought

1. A theme throughout this book has been that growing brains adapt to their particular physical and social environments, such that we might expect the brain of a preliterate Stone Age tribesman to be physically different from that of a biblical scholar. What functional areas would you expect to find in the latter that are not present in the former?

2. Human working memory is extremely limited in its capacity. How has its operation been influenced by the advent of external memory stores, libraries, and databases?

3. This chapter presents the model that there exists in each of us a series of semi-independent intelligences performing in parallel: episodic, mimetic, mythic, and theoretic, with more recent stages predominating most of the time, but not always. An alternative view is that later stages may have so thoroughly intruded on and patterned the earlier ones during development that such a model is not useful. This perspective would deny the validity of comparing our episodic intelligence, for example, to that of a chimpanzee. What is your view of this?

4. We have physiologies and emotional economies that are adaptations to conditions of the Paleolithic and that are sometimes inappropriately engaged or excited in modern contexts. What techniques, perspectives, or procedures would you suggest for dealing with this mismatch between our ancient and modern selves?

Suggestions for further reading

Diamond, J. 1992. *The Third Chimpanzee.* New York: HarperCollins. (This book gives an account of the ecological consequences of the rapid spread of humans across the planet in the past 50,000 years.)

Donald, M.D. 1991. *Origins of the Modern Mind.* Cambridge, MA: Harvard University Press. (The discussion in this chapter of the transition from mythic to theoretic intelligence follows Donald's outline. More detailed critiques of Donald's ideas are aired in Donald, M. 1993. *Behavioral Brain Science* 16:737–791.)

Wilson, E.O. 1998. *Consilience: The Unity of Knowledge*. New York: Knopf. (Wilson suggests that the integrative insights that have unified science, from physics through evolutionary biology, will be extended to include the humanities and social sciences.)

Kelly, K. 1994. *Out of Control: The Rise of Neo-Biological Civilization*. Reading, MA: Addison-Wesley. (This is a vision of the future in which the decentralized controls characteristic of living organisms and brain processes become models for post–Industrial Age global technologies.)

Lifton, R.J. 1993. *The Protean Self—Human Resilience in an Age of Fragmentation*. New York: Basic Books. (One of several recent books that discuss the mental poise and flexibility necessary to face the flux of modern life.)

Glossary

The chapter numbers that appear after each glossary entry denote the first significant use or thorough discussion of the term.

Acetylcholine: a neurotransmitter of the amine class that is excitatory at some synapses and inhibitory at others. [Ch. 6]

Achromatopsia: the inability to distinguish between colors while form perception remains unaffected; usually caused by a lesion in visual area V4. [Ch. 8]

Action potential: a rapid and transient decrease in membrane voltage that propagates down a nerve axon. [Ch. 2]

Adaptation: adjustment of a form, structure, or behavior in response to a particular environmental situation or stimulus. [Ch. 2]

Adrenaline: a hormone that activates energy metabolism and is produced by the adrenal medulla in response to stress; also called epinephrine. [Ch. 3]

Adrenocorticosteroids: steroid products of the adrenal cortex that play a role in the stress response. [Ch. 6]

Affect: feelings or emotions. [Ch. 2]

Affective neuroscience: the study of the neural correlates underlying emotions. [Ch. 10]

Agnosia: inability to recognize visual objects or combine visual stimuli into a complete pattern. [Ch. 3]

Agraphia: disruption in the ability to write, usually resulting from a lesion in the parietal-temporal-occipital association cortex. [Ch. 9]

Akinetopsia: inability to distinguish moving objects, while retaining some color and form perception; usually occurs as a result of a lesion to visual area V5. [Ch. 8]

Amygdala: temporal lobe structure that is central in regulating emotion and fear responses. [Ch. 3]

Amusia: inability to produce or appreciate music, usually resulting from damage to the right front and temporal lobes. [Ch. 7]

Analogous traits: similar physical characteristics, such as the wings of insects and birds, that have arisen from different structures in unrelated species through convergent evolution. [Ch. 2]

Anhedonia: loss of pleasurable emotional responsiveness. [Ch. 10]

Anosognosia: denial of, unawareness of, or failure to recognize one's own neurological defect or body part; often associated with damage to the right parietal lobe. [Ch. 3]

Anthropoid: the suborder of primates that includes monkeys, apes, and humans. [Ch. 4]

Anthropomorphism: ascribing human characteristics to nonhuman entities, such as animals, objects, or deities. [Ch. 4]

Aphasia: impairment, caused by brain dysfunction, of the ability to communicate through speech, writing, or signs. [Ch. 3]

Apraxia: difficulty in performing complex movement sequences requiring a series of muscle contractions or a planned strategy; usually caused by a lesion in the frontal association cortex or posterior parietal cortexes. [Ch. 9]

Aprosodia: a disturbance in the ability to perceive the affective (emotional) components of language or a dysfunction of the musical intonation evident in speech (prosody), usually resulting from damage to the right hemisphere. [Ch. 10]

Association cortex: areas of the cortex that coordinate and integrate activities arising in cortical regions dedicated to more primary motor and sensory processes. [Ch. 3]

Associative learning: learning process in which discrete ideas and percepts become linked to one another. [Ch. 4]

Australopithecus: genus name for an extinct African hominid displaying near-human dentition, a small brain, and bipedal posture. [Ch. 4]

Autonomic nervous system: the subdivision of the motor nervous system of vertebrates that regulates the internal environment of the body, controlling involuntary functions such as digestion and blood pressure. Its two major components, the sympathetic and parasympathetic systems, regulate these functions during arousal and rest. [Ch. 3]

Axon: thin process that extends from the body of a nerve cell and transmits nerve impulses away from the cell body toward target cells. [Ch. 2]

Basal ganglia: five large subcortical nuclei that participate in the planning of movement and also participate in some cognitive functions. [Ch. 9]

The binding problem: the question of how different aspects of the visual stimulus are organized into perception. The term is also used in a more general sense to refer to the question of how different brain regions collaborate to generate unitary conscious experience. [Ch. 8]

Biogenic amines: the group of neurotransmitters that includes dopamine, norepinephrine, and serotonin. [Ch. 10]

Blindsight: the accurate reporting of objects within blind spots in the visual field, even though there is no conscious awareness of seeing the objects, possibly through subcortical pathways bypassing damaged cortical areas that are required for visual awareness. [Ch. 8]

Brain-derived neurotrophic factor (BDNF): a trophic (maintenance) factor produced in the brain that acts to protect neurons from damage and prevents cell death. [Ch. 10]

Brainstem: region of the brain that includes the reticular formation, striate cortex, hypothalamus, midbrain, and hindbrain. [Ch. 3]

Broca's area: region of the left frontal cortex associated with speech production. [Ch. 3]

Central nervous system (CNS): in vertebrates, the division of the nervous system that consists of the brain and spinal cord. [Ch. 3]

Central sulcus: fissure in the cortex that separates the primary motor cortex of the frontal lobe from the primary somatic sensory cortex of the parietal lobe. [Ch. 3]

Cerebellum: a division of the hindbrain that regulates motor learning, coordination, and control and is also thought to be involved in some higher cognitive functions. [Ch. 3]

Cerebrospinal fluid: a fluid, rich in glucose, that circulates in the brain and spinal column to protect those structures from physical impact; often abbreviated as CSF. [Ch. 6]

Chemotaxis: the movement of a cell toward or away from a chemical that it detects in the environment. [Ch. 2]

Cingulate cortex: a portion of the limbic system that lies on the medial and ventral surface of the frontal lobe and is important in regulating motivation and emotional behavior. [Ch. 9]

Classical conditioning: the process by which an unconditioned stimulus (such as a bell or a light) is paired with a stimulus of behavioral significance (such as food). The unconditioned stimulus then becomes a conditioned stimulus, capable of inducing the behavioral response that has become associated with it. [Ch. 6]

Cognitive ethology: the study of animal thinking, consciousness, and mind. [Ch. 4]

Conduction aphasia: neurological dysfunction (resulting from a lesion in the circuit that connects Broca's area with Wernicke's area) that manifests itself in fluent speech with incorrect words or sounds. Patients have difficulty reading aloud, naming, and writing. [Ch. 3]

Cone photoreceptor cell: vertebrate photoreceptor used in color vision in bright light. [Ch. 2]

Confabulation: in this book, a spontaneously fabricated explanation that denies a perceptual or motor deficit caused by brain damage. It is observed in some split brain, anosognosic, and frontal lobe lesion patients. [Ch. 3]

Corpus callosum: thick band of transverse nerve fibers that carries information between the two cerebral hemispheres. [Ch. 3]

Cortex: a folded sheet of tissue consisting of layers of nerve cells that forms the most anterior portion of the forebrain and is associated with higher cognitive functions. [Ch. 3]

Corticotropin (ACTH): hormone released from the pituitary gland in response to stress. It passes through the bloodstream to the adrenal gland and stimulates the release of glucocorticoids that regulate the long-term stress response. [Ch. 10]

Corticotropin-releasing factor: hormone released from the hypothalamus that activates the release of corticotropin (ACTH) from the pituitary in response to a stressful situation. [Ch. 10]

Crenulation: infolding of the cortex. [Ch. 3]

Creole: a complex language that arises in the second generation of a group of people who had first constructed a pidgin language to permit communication between two separate languages. [Ch. 11]

Darwin Machine: a self-replicating entity that can evolve or change because small variations between its replicated forms are tested by selective forces. [Ch. 2]

Delayed-choice test: paradigm used to evaluate the ability of human or animal subjects to retrieve information from short-term memory. [Ch. 12]

Dendrite: branching process of a neuron that usually receives input from other nerve cells and conducts information toward the cell body. [Ch. 2]

Dentate nucleus: region of the cerebellum found exclusively in humans that appears to be associated with the development of language and cognition. [Ch. 4]

Developmental dysphasia: a heritable disorder that results in an inability to distinguish between singular and plural forms of words or recognize the tenses of regular (but not irregular) verbs. [Ch. 11]

Diencephalon: division of the forebrain that includes the thalamus and hypothalamus. [Ch. 3]

Down's syndrome: a heritable chromosomal disorder whose consequences are moderate to severe mental retardation, decreased life span, short hands, and distinctive facial features. [Ch. 11]

Dyscalculia: inability to carry out mathematical calculations; usually associated with damage to the inferior regions of the left parietal cortex. [Ch. 3]

Dysgraphia: a defect in writing ability (with no motor or sensory deficits in the upper extremities) that usually results from damage to the left parietal cortex. [Ch. 3]

Ectoderm: the outer layer of cells in a developing embryo from which skin and nervous tissue arise. [Ch. 6]

Effector cell: a cell, such as a muscle cell or gland cell, that carries out the body's response to a stimulus. [Ch. 2]

Electromagnetoencephalography (MEG): an imaging procedure that records small magnetic signals from the brain with detectors placed on the outside of the skull. [Ch. 3]

Emotional conditioning: the linking of perceptual stimuli with emotional responses; associated with the amygdala. [Ch. 6]

Endoderm: the inner layer of cells in a developing embryo from which tissue of the gut and internal cavities arise. [Ch. 6]

Ensemble coding: the representation of information by the coordinated firing of a large number of neurons. [Ch. 8]

Enteric nervous system: division of the autonomic nervous system that controls the smooth muscles of the gut. [Ch. 2]

Epileptic foci: the core or epicenter of epileptic activity observed in some forms of epilepsy; the region of the brain that constitutes the starting point of a seizure. [Ch. 10]

Episodic intelligence: a present-centered, environmentally driven intelligence of the sort observed in monkeys and apes, proposed by Merlin Donald to be an early stage in the cognitive evolution of hominids. [Ch. 4]

Episodic memory: long-term memory that requires the hippocampus for its formation and is used to store specific places, facts, numbers, or instances; often referred to as explicit memory. [Ch. 4, Ch. 6]

Ethology: the study of animal behavior. [Ch. 4]

Evolution: term used to refer to almost any process of formation, change, development, or growth. In this book, the term is used mainly with reference to the changes that have transformed life on earth from its simplest beginnings to its present diversity. [Ch. 2]

Evolutionary psychology: the study of psychological mechanisms as evolutionary adaptations. [Ch. 5]

Forebrain: the anterior portion of the brain, the telencephalon and diencephalon, including the thalamus, hypothalamus, and cortex. [Ch. 3]

Freudian slip: a slip of the tongue yielding unintended expression of a repressed sentiment. [Ch. 11]

Frontal lobe: neocortex anterior to the central sulcus; used in working memory (the immediate recall of facts), the planning of action, and the control of movement. [Ch. 3]

Ganglia: clusters of neurons found outside the brain and spinal cord; also used to refer to clusters of cells within the brain. [Ch. 2]

Ganglion cells: a layer of cells in the retina whose axons form the optic nerve and carry visual information to the brain. [Ch. 8]

Generic memory: recall that is formed in response to recurring episodes. [Ch. 6]

Genome: the complete set of a particular species' genes. [Ch. 2]

Genotype: the genetic profile that is inherited from an organism's parents and provides most of the initial instruction set for building the organism. [Ch. 2]

Gray matter: regions in the cerebral cortex containing many nerve cell bodies that appear gray because their myelin-sheathed axons are obscured. [Ch. 3]

Group selection: evolutionary selection for physical traits or behaviors that benefit a group or cultural unit made up of genetically unrelated individuals. [Ch. 5]

Gyrus: the crest of one of the infoldings of the cerebral cortex. [Ch. 3]

Hindbrain: the posterior portions of the vertebrate brain that evolved from an enlargement of the spinal cord, consisting of the medulla oblongata, pons, and cerebellum. [Ch. 3]

Hippocampus: a curved and folded ridge structure one cell layer thick that extends over the lateral ventricle of the brain; it is involved in memory consolidation and place recognition. [Ch. 3]

Homeostasis: the maintenance of a set of relatively stable internal conditions in an organism by various biological and behavioral control mechanisms. [Ch. 3]

Homeotic genes: genes that generate the segmental body plan of animals by controlling the development of groups of cells. [Ch. 2]

Hominids: primates that display bipedal posture, including all forms of humans. [Ch. 2]

Homo: the genus name for bipedal primates, including modern humans and all related hominids. [Ch. 4]

Homo erectus: early hominids, appearing 1.5 to 2.5 million years ago, credited with the domestication of fire, creation of shelters, fabrication of relatively elaborate tools, and extensive migration. [Ch. 4]

Homo habilis: the earliest of the *Homo* lineage, which was present 2 million years ago and had a larger brain than *australopithecus* and used crude tools. [Ch. 4]

Homo neanderthalensis: a tool-using hominid present 15,000—30,000 years ago in Western Eurasia. Neanderthals were heavyset and barrel-chested, with faces sloped out from underneath the cranium, pronounced brow ridges, and no evidence of a chin. [Ch. 5]

Homologous traits: structures, present in different species, that are similar because of a common ancestry. [Ch. 2]

Homo sapiens: "wise man," the genus and species to which modern humankind belongs. [Ch. 4]

Hormone: signal or control molecule that is secreted by one cell type and then transported to other cells where it regulates their activity. [Ch. 2]

Hypothalamus: region of the diencephalon that acts to regulate visceral functions such as sleep cycles, body temperature, and the activity of the pituitary gland. [Ch. 3]

Ideational apraxia: movement disorder characterized by the inability to carry out a particular series of movements when directed to do so (for example, the movements required to put on eyeglasses), even though the movements can be carried out under appropriate circumstances in the absence of instruction. [Ch. 9]

Ideomotor apraxia: movement disorder in which an individual is able to perform a sequence of movements but has difficulty executing the individual steps in the series. [Ch. 9]

Idiot savants: persons in whom developmental brain damage causing general mental retardation is accompanied by remarkable ability in a particular area, such as music, language, or math; a relatively rare condition. [Ch. 7, Ch. 11]

Intentionality: in the philosophy of mind, intentionality is typically understood as a cognitive state's being about something in the mind or in the external world. [Ch. 4]

Interneurons: nerve cells that intervene between sensory neurons and effector neurons to integrate and process information. [Ch. 2]

Jargon aphasia: a type of aphasia, or communication disorder, that results in the subject exhibiting normal intelligence but being unable to coordinate complex sentences, speaking only in fragments without logical order. [Ch. 11]

Kinesic communication: nonlinguistic body motions (such as gestures, facial expressions, and eye contact) that convey a meaning; also called body language. [Ch. 5]

Kinesthetic intelligence: mental operations underlying complex body movements, particularly as in dance, mime, or athletic performance. [Ch. 9]

Kinetic melodies: a term coined by Luria, the Russian psychologist, to refer to complex movement patterns that can be automatically performed and adjusted in order to execute a task. [Ch. 9]

Kin selection: selection for physical traits or behaviors that benefit a genetically related group. [Ch. 5]

Lateral geniculate nucleus: a nucleus of the thalamus that relays information from the retina to the primary visual cortex. [Ch. 6]

Limbic association cortex: association cortex, mainly on the inside surfaces of the cortex, that plays a central role in regulating emotion, memory, and motivation. [Ch. 3]

Limbic system: a group of interconnected structures that regulate affective behaviors; it includes the medial surfaces of the cingulate, frontal, and temporal lobes, and the hippocampus, amygdala, and hypothalamus. [Ch. 3]

Lipid molecules: substances such as fats, phospholipids, and steroids that are insoluble in water and are found in the membranes of cells and cellular organelles. [Ch. 1]

Magnetic resonance imaging (MRI): an imaging procedure that exploits the magnetic properties of atoms in the brain to construct a map of their distribution, which reveals brain structures. Functional MRI (fMRI) explicitly monitors the relative metabolic activities of different brain areas by measuring the ratio of oxygenated to deoxygenated hemoglobin. [Ch. 3]

Magnocellular pathway: a pathway of nerve cells in the visual system, beginning in the retina and continuing on through visual areas of the brain, that is sensitive to changes in light stimuli and specializes in analyzing motion, location, size, and spatial relationships. [Ch. 8]

Medulla: a hindbrain structure that contains centers regulating autonomic visceral functions such as breathing, heart and blood vessel activity, swallowing, vomiting, and digestion. [Ch. 3]

Meme: a bit of information stored in brains or books that is replicated by being passed between individuals and generations and that can be mutated, or changed, during the process; the cultural equivalent of the gene. [Ch. 5]

Mesoderm: the middle layer of cells in a developing embryo that gives rise to bone and muscle tissue. [Ch. 6]

Metacognition: awareness of mental ability, or thinking about thinking. [Ch. 10]

Midbrain: also called the mesencephalon, the central region of the brain that serves as a conduit for information passing to and from the spinal cord. Its dorsal surface forms the tectum, which is important in receiving and processing visual and auditory information, and its bottom portion has cell groups involved in control of voluntary movement. [Ch. 3]

Mimetic intelligence: a prelinguistic stage of cognitive evolution proposed by Merlin Donald that uses facial expression, gesture, vocalization, mime, and imitation to model and transmit social roles, crafts, and procedures. [Ch. 5]

Mind: in this book, the sum of the vast number of operations that proceed as the central and peripheral human nervous system interact with other body systems and the world to generate consciousness and cognition. [Ch. 1]

Mythic intelligence: the third stage of cognitive evolution proposed by Merlin Donald, based on the invention of symbols and language, which permits mimetic cultural elements to be integrated into verbal descriptions and stories. [Ch. 5]

Neocortex: cortical surface found only in mammals that has many cell layers, usually six, and overlies the hippocampus (one cell layer) and olfactory cortex (two cell layers). [Ch. 3]

Nerve net: used in two different contexts: (1) a network of nerve cells making multiple connections with one another, as in the nerve net that regulates the movement of food into and out of digestive cavities; (2) a computer-generated model representing a very simplified version of a real nervous system. [Ch. 2, Ch. 6].

Neural tube: tube from which the brain and spinal cord arise, formed from the fusion of embryonic neural tissue. [Ch. 6]

Neuron: a nerve cell, including cell body (soma), dendrites, and axons. [Ch. 2]

Neurotransmitter: any of several chemical substances, such as norepinephrine or acetylcholine, which are released from the synaptic terminal of a neuron at a chemical synapse, diffuse across the synaptic cleft, and bind to receptors on the postsynaptic cell, causing a variety of effects. [Ch. 2]

Norepinephrine: a neurotransmitter released by the sympathetic and central nervous systems that acts on various body organs and brain regions, usually to increase their readiness and excitability. [Ch. 10]

Nucleus: used in two different contexts: (1) organelle in eukaryotes that contains the cell's genetic material; (2) a clearly distinguishable group of nerve cells in the central nervous system. [Ch. 2, Ch. 3]

Occipital lobe: posterior lobe of the cerebral hemispheres that is shaped like a three-sided pyramid and contains the visual areas. [Ch. 3]

Olfactory cortex: region of the cerebral cortex that receives and processes smell information. [Ch. 3]

Optic ataxia: a deficit in employing visual guidance to manipulate an object, usually caused by brain damage. [Ch. 3]

Optic nerve: bundle of ganglion cell axons that carries visual information from the retina to the brain. [Ch. 6]

Oxytocin: a pituitary peptide hormone that is involved in parasympathetic responses and bonding behaviors; it also regulates uterine contractions and the secretion of milk. [Ch. 10]

Paraphasia: use of inappropriate words or word combinations, usually caused by lesions in language areas of the brain. [Ch. 3]

Parasympathetic nervous system: division of the autonomic nervous system that regulates blood circulation, respiration, metabolism, and digestive function during conservation and storage of energy. [Ch. 3]

Parietal lobe: the middle region of the neocortex, posterior to the central sulcus and lying beneath the parietal bone; involved in somatic sensation, body image, and analyzing spatial relationships. [Ch. 3]

Parietal-temporal-occipital association cortex: association cortex involved in integrating different sensory modalities and language functions. [Ch. 3]

Parkinson's disease: disease associated with the loss of dopaminergic cells in the basal ganglia, characterized by rhythmic muscle tremors, an increase in muscle tone, difficulty in movement initiation, and slowness in movement execution. [Ch. 9]

Parvocellular pathway: nerve pathways and cell types in the visual system that specialize in color and high-contrast processing to support object recognition. [Ch. 8]

Peripheral nervous system (PNS): the portion of the nervous system that lies outside the brain and spinal cord and contains many sensory and motor pathways as well as ganglia that regulate various organ systems. [Ch. 3]

Phenotype: the observable physical and physiological traits of an organism that result from expression of its genotype during development. [Ch. 2]

Pheromone: chemical released by one animal to influence the behavior or physiology of another member of the same species, as in attracting potential mating partners. [Ch. 2]

Photoreceptor cells: sensory cells specialized for the detection of light. (See also *cone photoreceptor cells* and *rod photoreceptor cells*.) [Ch. 2]

Pidgin: a crude language that develops to permit communication between two separate cultures with different languages. [Ch. 11]

Plasticity: in this book, plasticity refers to the ability of growing nerve cells to choose many alternative routes and wiring connections, as well the ability of mature nerve cells to revise or alter their connections when appropriate.

Pons: portion of the hindbrain ventral to the cerebellum and composed primarily of motor fibers extending to the cerebellum and the spinal cord; it is also involved in regulating several autonomic visceral functions, such as digestion and swallowing. [Ch. 3]

Positron emission tomography (PET): imaging technique that maps the location of radioactively labeled compounds that concentrate in different brain areas in proportion to their metabolic activity.

Postsynaptic receptor: protein molecule in the postsynaptic membrane that binds to neurotransmitter molecules that have crossed the synaptic cleft and then changes its shape to initiate excitation or inhibition of its postsynaptic cell. [Ch. 2]

Prefrontal association cortex: cortex that lies forward of the primary motor cortex and regulates motor planning and higher cognitive functions. [Ch. 3]

Premotor cortex: area of the frontal lobe that lies anterior to the primary motor cortex and is involved in planning movement. [Ch. 3]

Presynaptic terminal: swelling at the terminal end of an axon, from which neurotransmitter molecules are released. [Ch. 2]

Primary auditory cortex: area of the cortex responsible for processing auditory information that arrives from the ear; contains several distinct tonotopic maps of the frequency spectrum. [Ch. 3]

Primary motor cortex: area within the precentral gyrus, anterior to the central sulcus, that contains neurons that project directly into the spinal cord to mediate voluntary movements. [Ch. 3]

Primary somatic sensory cortex: portion of the postcentral gyrus of the cortex that receives primary somatosensory input and integrates information about sensation and action. [Ch. 3]

Primary visual cortex: region at the back of the neocortex, also called V1, that is the first relay station in processing visual information sent from the lateral geniculate body to the cortex. [Ch. 3]

Priming: a facilitation of the ability to perceive or act in a given context as a result of previous exposure to it; associated with cortical memory mechanisms. [Ch. 6]

Procedural memory: long-term memory of learned action patterns; associated with regions of the cortex, thalamus, and basal ganglia. [Ch. 6]

Prosody: the musical intonation of speech. [Ch. 10]

Prosopagnosia: inability to recognize faces; usually results from damage to the temporal cortex. [Ch. 8]

Psychoneuroimmunology: a relatively new discipline that focuses on studying interactions among the nervous, endocrine, and immune systems. [Ch. 10]

Rapid eye movement (REM) sleep: stage of sleep characterized by low-amplitude, high-frequency EEG waves, rapid eye movements, vivid dreams, and loss of body muscle tone. [Ch. 12]

Receptor: a protein molecule, frequently on the surface of a cell, that upon binding to specific sugars, hormones, or neurotransmitters alters some activity of the cell. [Ch. 2]

Receptor cell: nerve cell whose membrane contains receptor molecules, which are frequently located in a specialized region of the cell. [Ch. 2]

Receptor potential: change in the membrane voltage of a primary receptor cell that occurs when it is stimulated. [Ch. 2]

Reciprocal altruism: cooperation within a group of genetically unrelated members of the same species that serves to enhance the reproductive chances of all the members of the group. [Ch. 5]

Reflex: an involuntary and automatic response to a stimulus that can involve a relatively small number of nerve cells, as in the knee-jerk reflex of the spinal cord. [Ch. 2]

Reflex arc: the nerve pathway along which impulses move during a reflex action. [Ch. 2]

Representation: something in the mind that stands for, or reflects, something in the external world. [Ch. 2]

Retina: thin film of nerve tissue at the back of the eye on which the image produced by the lens is projected; it contains three main layers of nerve whose output is the optic nerve that connects the retina to the brain. [Ch. 6]

Rod photoreceptor cell: vertebrate photoreceptor cell used in vision in dim light. [Ch. 2]

Secondary emotions: term used by Damasio to denote emotions that are learned or acquired by associating primary emotions with life events; associated more with prefrontal cortex than with the limbic system. [Ch. 10]

Semantic memory: memory system used for the recall of specific facts, such as the location of cities or historical dates. [Ch. 6]

Serotonin: neurotransmitter that is involved in the expression of dominance and aggression and also plays a role in depression and anxiety. [Ch. 6, Ch. 10]

Sociobiology: study of the biological basis of social behavior. [Ch. 5]

Somatic markers: the array of somatic, or body, changes (such as changes in muscle tension or skin resistance) that accompany emotional experiences and mobilization of the autonomic nervous system. [Ch. 10]

Somatic nervous system: the branch of the vertebrate peripheral nervous system that carries voluntary motor commands to the skeletal muscles of the torso and limbs. [Ch. 3]

Speciation: the formation of new species through evolution. [Ch. 2]

Specific language impairment (SLI): a heritable impairment characterized by difficulty in language learning without evidence of other cognitive defects. [Ch. 11]

Spoonerism: transposing parts (usually the initial sounds) of two or more words to form a phrase that consists of valid words but has an entirely different meaning; an example is saying "sweeter hitch" when one means "heater switch." [Ch. 11]

Substantia nigra: one of five nuclei in the basal ganglia, it appears dark because of a concentration of a dopamine derivative in its neurons. The death of these cells is associated with the development of Parkinson's disease. [Ch. 9]

Sulcus: a small cleft or groove on the cortex created by infoldings of the cortical tissue; also called a fissure. [Ch. 3]

Supplementary motor areas: areas of the frontal lobe that function in programming complex sequences of movement such as opening and closing the hand. [Ch. 9]

Sympathetic nervous system: branch of the autonomic nervous system of vertebrates that increases energy use and mobilizes the body for action, typically increasing heart rate, decreasing digestive functions, increasing respiration, and secreting adrenaline into the bloodstream. [Ch. 3]

Synapse: the ensemble of presynaptic terminal, synaptic cleft, and postsynaptic membrane through which nerve signals are transmitted when a diffusible neurotransmitter is released by the presynaptic terminal and moves across the cleft to act upon the postsynaptic membrane. [Ch. 2]

Synaptic potential: change in potential or voltage of a postsynaptic cell membrane caused by the interaction of neurotransmitters from the presynaptic cell with postsynaptic receptor molecules. [Ch. 2]

Synaptic transmission: transmission of nerve impulses from one neuron to another neuron or muscle cell by the diffusion of a neurotransmitter across the synapse between them. [Ch. 2]

Synesthesia: comingling of the senses, as when a color stimulus also elicits the sensation of a sound; usually lost 4 months after birth as cortical sensory areas become more clearly separated. [Ch. 6]

Tectum: dorsal area of the midbrain that mediates the whole-body response to visual and auditory stimuli and regulates some basic bodily functions. [Ch. 3]

Telencephalon: the most anterior portion of the forebrain, from which the olfactory bulb, cerebral cortex, cortical white matter, and corpus callosum form. [Ch. 3]

Teleology: the attribution of goals or higher purposes to natural processes. [Ch. 13]

Temporal lobe: lateral lobe of the brain that is shaped like a forward-pointing horseshoe and deals with hearing, as well as aspects of object identification, learning, memory, and emotions. [Ch. 3]

Thalamus: a collection of nuclei that form the largest subdivision of the diencephalon, plays a primary role in relaying sensory information from lower centers to the cortex and is involved in many feedback loops with cortical and subcortical areas that regulate movement and other processes. [Ch. 3]

Theory of mind: the attribution of mental states such as thoughts and beliefs to other organisms. [Ch. 4]

Topographical map: in this book, a representation of the external world (visual, somatosensory, or auditory) that is plotted across an array of nerve cells, as with the projection of the pattern of visual stimulation of the retina onto the surface of the primary visual cortex. [Ch. 3]

Tourette's syndrome: a neurological disorder that is associated with abnormalities in the dopamine system of the caudate nucleus and causes movement tics and inappropriate social interactions. [Ch. 9]

Triune brain: model of the human brain that suggests three major functional components: the brainstem core (similar to the reptilian brain), the limbic system (a primitive mammalian brain), and the neocortex. [Ch. 3]

Vagus nerve: a complicated bundle of sensory and motor nerve fibers that connects the medulla to multiple sites in the vertebrate torso to regulate swallowing, blood circulation, and digestion. [Ch. 3]

Ventral vagal system: a complex of nerves observed in mammals that innervates the heart, visceral organs, and facial muscles involved in emotional expression; active in producing emotional responses more mild than the fight-or-flight response. [Ch. 10]

Ventricular system: a series of channels in the brain that carry the cerebrospinal fluid that protects various brain structures. [Ch. 6]

Vomeronasal system: a division of the olfactory system that responds to pheromones and projects to regions of the hypothalamus that are associated with sexual and affective behavior. [Ch. 6]

Wernicke's area: the posterior part of the temporal lobe associated with word perception and understanding. [Ch. 3]

White matter: collections of central nervous system axons that appear white because of their layer of fatty insulating myelin sheaths. [Ch. 3]

Williams' syndrome: a rare disorder caused by deletion of a region on chromosome 7; it results in mental retardation and difficulty with spatial cognition but leaves a remarkable degree of language fluency and sociability. [Ch. 11]

Working memory: memory that is associated with the frontal lobe of the cortex and is responsible for the immediate recall of facts, as in remembering a phone number just after you have looked it up. [Ch. 3]

Xenophobia: the fear and hatred of strangers or foreigners. [Ch. 13]

Detailed references can be found
on the author's web site:

http://mind.bocklabs.wisc.edu

Index

Deric Bownds is Chair of the Department of Zoology and Professor of Molecular Biology and Zoology at the University of Wisconsin, Madison. He received his undergraduate and doctoral degrees in biology from Harvard University, followed by post-doctoral research in neurobiology at Harvard Medical School. Over the past 30 years, he has taught the introductory neurobiology course and directed a research program on the molecular mechanisms of vision at the University of Wisconsin. Experiments from his laboratory have greatly expanded our understanding of how light is converted into a nerve signal in the eye. This book reflects the development of a parallel line of interest that has led to the introduction of an interdisciplinary course at the University of Wisconsin, "The Biology of Mind." He now has shifted all of his efforts to interdisciplinary scholarship with the goal of providing a continually updated, integrated, and critical summary of recent advances in mind/brain science.